Advance Praise

"If you have been considering buying a book about mobile development that [is] cross-vendor, you should stop right now and buy *Head First Mobile Web*. It's w[ritten by] people [who] have great experience on mobile and don't stop at one platfor[m...] Many developers spend days arguing [whether] they should go native or web. This book smoothly goes from introductory topics to advanced ones, giving you all the needed information to create exciting content for mobile."

> **— Andrea Trasatti, leader of the DeviceAtlas project and cocreator of the WURFL repository of wireless device capability information**

"A pragmatic introduction to the chaotic world of mobile web development as it is today, with a glimpse of how we can and should approach it for tomorrow. *Head First Mobile Web* successfully presents practical techniques all readers can use immediately, while giving plenty of foundation and resources for more experienced developers to build upon."

> **— Stephen Hay, web designer, developer, speaker, and cofounder of the Mobilism conference**

"Hands-on from the get-go, *Head First Mobile Web* provides an excellent introduction to the challenges and opportunities available when exploring the next chapter in web design."

> **— Bryan and Stephanie Rieger, founders of yiibu.com**

Praise for other *Head First* books

"*Head First Object-Oriented Analysis and Design* is a refreshing look at subject of OOAD. What sets this book apart is its focus on learning. The authors have made the content of OOAD accessible [and] usable for the practitioner."

— Ivar Jacobson, Ivar Jacobson Consulting

"I just finished reading HF OOA&D, and I loved it! The thing I liked most about this book was its focus on why we do OOA&D—to write great software!"

— Kyle Brown, Distinguished Engineer, IBM

"Hidden behind the funny pictures and crazy fonts is a serious, intelligent, extremely well-crafted presentation of OO analysis and design. As I read the book, I felt like I was looking over the shoulder of an expert designer who was explaining to me what issues were important at each step, and why."

— Edward Sciore, Associate Professor, Computer Science Department, Boston College

"All in all, *Head First Software Development* is a great resource for anyone wanting to formalize their programming skills in a way that constantly engages the reader on many different levels."

— Andy Hudson, Linux Format

"If you're a new software developer, *Head First Software Development* will get you started off on the right foot. And if you're an experienced (read: long-time) developer, don't be so quick to dismiss this...."

— Thomas Duff, Duffbert's Random Musings

"There's something in *Head First Java* for everyone. Visual learners, kinesthetic learners, everyone can learn from this book. Visual aids make things easier to remember, and the book is written in a very accessible style—very different from most Java manuals.... *Head First Java* is a valuable book. I can see the *Head First* books used in the classroom, whether in high schools or adult ed classes. And I will definitely be referring back to this book, and referring others to it as well."

— Warren Kelly, Blogcritics.org, March 2006

"Rather than textbook-style learning, *Head First iPhone and iPad Development* brings a humorous, engaging, and even enjoyable approach to learning iOS development. With coverage of key technologies including core data, and even crucial aspects such as interface design, the content is aptly chosen and top-notch. Where else could you witness a fireside chat between a UIWebView and UITextField!"

— Sean Murphy, iOS designer and developer

"Another nice thing about *Head First Java*, Second Edition, is that it whets the appetite for more. With later coverage of more advanced topics such as Swing and RMI, you just can't wait to dive into those APIs and code that flawless, 100,000-line program on java.net that will bring you fame and venture-capital fortune. There's also a great deal of material, and even some best practices, on networking and threads—my own weak spot. In this case, I couldn't help but crack up a little when the authors use a 1950s telephone operator—yeah, you got it, that lady with a beehive hairdo that manually hooks in patch lines—as an analogy for TCP/IP ports…you really should go to the bookstore and thumb through *Head First Java*, Second Edition. Even if you already know Java, you may pick up a thing or two. And if not, just thumbing through the pages is a great deal of fun."

> **— Robert Eckstein, Java.sun.com**

"Of course it's not the range of material that makes *Head First Java* stand out, it's the style and approach. This book is about as far removed from a computer science textbook or technical manual as you can get. The use of cartoons, quizzes, fridge magnets (yep, fridge magnets…). And, in place of the usual kind of reader exercises, you are asked to pretend to be the compiler and compile the code, or perhaps to piece some code together by filling in the blanks or…you get the picture.… The first edition of this book was one of our recommended titles for those new to Java and objects. This new edition doesn't disappoint and rightfully steps into the shoes of its predecessor. If you are one of those people who falls asleep with a traditional computer book, then this one is likely to keep you awake and learning."

> **— TechBookReport.com**

"*Head First Web Design* is your ticket to mastering all of these complex topics, and understanding what's really going on in the world of web design.… If you have not been baptized by fire in using something as involved as Dreamweaver, then this book will be a great way to learn good web design. "

> **— Robert Pritchett, MacCompanion**

"Is it possible to learn real web design from a book format? *Head First Web Design* is the key to designing user-friendly sites, from customer requirements to hand-drawn storyboards to online sites that work well. What sets this apart from other 'how to build a website' books is that it uses the latest research in cognitive science and learning to provide a visual learning experience rich in images and designed for how the brain works and learns best. The result is a powerful tribute to web design basics that any general-interest computer library will find an important key to success."

> **— Diane C. Donovan, California Bookwatch: The Computer Shelf**

"I definitely recommend *Head First Web Design* to all of my fellow programmers who want to get a grip on the more artistic side of the business. "

> **— Claron Twitchell, UJUG**

Other related books from O'Reilly

jQuery Cookbook

jQuery Pocket Reference

jQuery Mobile

JavaScript and jQuery: The Missing Manual

Other books in O'Reilly's *Head First* series

Head First C#

Head First Java

Head First Object-Oriented Analysis and Design (OOA&D)

Head First HTML with CSS and XHTML

Head First Design Patterns

Head First Servlets and JSP

Head First EJB

Head First SQL

Head First Software Development

Head First JavaScript

Head First Physics

Head First Statistics

Head First Ajax

Head First Rails

Head First Algebra

Head First PHP & MySQL

Head First PMP

Head First Web Design

Head First Networking

Head First iPhone and iPad Development

Head First jQuery

Head First HTML5 Programming

Head First Mobile Web

> Wouldn't it be dreamy if there were a book to help me learn how to build mobile websites that was more fun than going to the dentist? It's probably nothing but a fantasy...

Lyza Danger Gardner
Jason Grigsby

Beijing · Cambridge · Farnham · Köln · Sebastopol · Tokyo

Head First Mobile Web

by Lyza Danger Gardner and Jason Grigsby

Published by O'Reilly Media, Inc., 1005 Gravenstein Highway North, Sebastopol, CA 95472.

O'Reilly Media books may be purchased for educational, business, or sales promotional use. Online editions are also available for most titles (*http://my.safaribooksonline.com*). For more information, contact our corporate/institutional sales department: (800) 998-9938 or *corporate@oreilly.com*.

Series Creators:	Kathy Sierra, Bert Bates
Editor:	Courtney Nash
Design Editor:	Louise Barr
Cover Designer:	Karen Montgomery
Production Editor:	Kristen Borg
Production Services:	Rachel Monaghan
Indexer:	Ginny Munroe
Page Viewers:	Katie Byrd, Danny Boomer, the Future-Friendly Helmet, and Tephra

Printing History:

December 2011: First Edition.

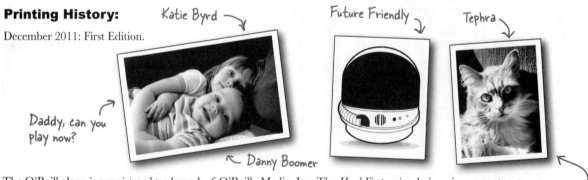

Katie Byrd

Future Friendly

Tephra

Daddy, can you play now?

Danny Boomer

aka /dev/cat

ISBN: 978-1-449-30266-5

To the phenomenal women in my family: my sister, Maggie; Momula, Fran; Aunt Catherine; stepmother, Christie; and above all, to the memory of my grandmother, Pearl, whose fierce and literate independence inspired generations.

—Lyza

To my parents for buying that Commodore 64 so many years ago; to my lovely wife, Dana, without whose support and understanding this book wouldn't have happened; and to Katie and Danny—yes, Daddy can play now.

—Jason

Lyza

Jason

Lyza Danger Gardner (*@lyzadanger*) is a dev. She has built, broken, and hacked web things since 1996. Curiously, Lyza was actually born and raised in Portland, Oregon, the town where everyone wants to be but no one seems to be *from*.

Lyza started college early and cobbled together a motley education: a BA in Arts and Letters from Portland State University, followed by a master's program in computer science at the University of Birmingham (UK).

Lyza has written a lot of web applications (server-side devs, represent!), defeated wily content management systems, optimized mobile websites, pounded on various APIs, and worried a lot about databases. Fascinated by the way mobile technology has changed things, she now spends a lot of time thinking about the future of the Web, mobile and otherwise.

Since cofounding Cloud Four, a Portland-based mobile web agency, in 2007, Lyza has voyaged further into the deep, untrammeled reaches of Device Land, exploring the foibles and chaos of mobile browsers and the mobile web. She has an odd set of anachronistic hobbies, and it has been said that she takes a fair number of photographs. She owns a four-letter *.com* domain. We'll bet you can guess what it is and go visit her there.

In 2000, **Jason Grigsby** got his first mobile phone. He became obsessed with how the world could be a better place if everyone had access to the world's information in their pockets. When his wife, Dana, met him, he had covered the walls of his apartment with crazy mobile dreams. To this day, he remains baffled that she married him.

Those mobile dreams hit the hard wall of reality— WAP was crap. So Jason went to work on the Web until 2007, when the iPhone made it clear the time was right. He joined forces with the three smartest people he knew and started Cloud Four.

Since cofounding Cloud Four, he has had the good fortune to work on many fantastic projects, including the Obama iPhone App. He is founder and president of Mobile Portland, a local nonprofit dedicated to promoting the mobile community in Portland, Oregon.

Jason is a sought-after speaker and consultant on mobile. If anything, he is more mobile obsessed now than he was in 2000 (sorry, sweetheart!).

You can find him blogging at *http://cloudfour.com*; on his personal site, *http://userfirstweb.com*; and on Twitter as *@grigs*. Please say hello!

Table of Contents (Summary)

Table of Contents (the real thing)

Intro

Your brain on mobile web. Here you are trying to learn something, while here your brain is, doing you a favor by making sure the learning doesn't stick. Your brain's thinking, "Better leave room for more important things, like which wild animals to avoid and whether setting this BlackBerry Bold on fire is going to activate the sprinkler system." So how do you trick your brain into thinking that your life depends on knowing mobile web?

1

getting started on the mobile web

Responsive Web Design

Hey there! Are you ready to jump into mobile?

Mobile web development is a wildly exciting way of life. There's glamour and excitement, and plenty of *Eureka!* moments. But there is also mystery and confusion. Mobile technology is evolving at bewildering speed, and there's so much to know! Hang tight. We'll start our journey by showing you a way of making websites called *Responsive Web Design* **(RWD)**. You'll be able to adapt websites to look great on a whole lot of mobile devices by building on the web skills you already have.

index.html

styles.css

responsible responsiveness

2 Mobile-first Responsive Web Design

That's a beautiful mobile site. But beauty is only skin deep.

Under the covers, it's a different thing entirely. It may look like a mobile site, but it's still a desktop site in mobile clothing. If we want this site to be greased lightning on mobile, we need to start with **mobile first**. We'll begin by dissecting the current site to find the desktop bones hiding in its mobile closet. We'll clean house and start fresh with **progressive enhancement**, building from the basic content all the way to a desktop view. When we're done, you'll have a page that is optimized regardless of the screen size.

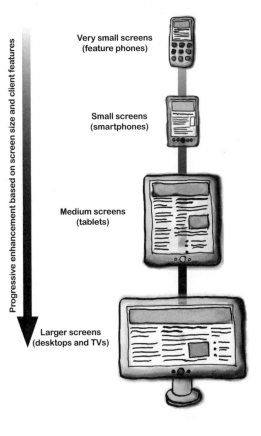

Progressive enhancement based on screen size and client features

**Very small screens
(feature phones)**

**Small screens
(smartphones)**

**Medium screens
(tablets)**

**Larger screens
(desktops and TVs)**

a separate mobile website

Facing less-than-awesome circumstances

The vision of a single, responsive Web is a beautiful one…

3

in which every site has one layout to rule them all, made lovingly with a mobile-first approach. Mmm…tasty. But what happens when a stinky dose of reality sets in? Like legacy systems, older devices, or customer budget constraints? What if, sometimes, instead of mixing desktop and mobile support into one lovely soup, you need to keep 'em separated? In this chapter, we look at the nitty-gritty bits of **detecting mobile users, supporting those crufty older phones, and building a separate mobile site**.

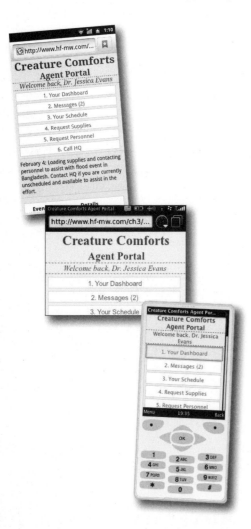

deciding whom to support

What devices should we support?

There aren't enough hours in the day to test on every device.

You have to draw the line somewhere on what you can support. **But how do you decide?** What about people using devices you can't test on—are they left out in the cold? Or is it possible to build your web pages in a way that will reach people on devices you've never heard of? In this chapter, we're going to mix a magic concoction of **project requirements** and **audience usage** to help us figure out **what devices we support** and **what to do about those we don't**.

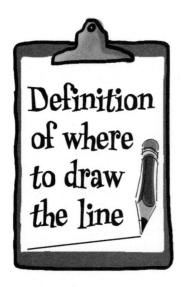

Definition of where to draw the line

device databases and classes

5 Get with the group

Setting the bar for the devices we support doesn't take care of a few nagging issues. How do we find out enough stuff about our users' mobile browsers to know if they measure up before we deliver content to them? How do we avoid only building (lame) content for the lowest common denominator? And how do we organize all of this stuff so that we don't lose our minds? In this chapter, we'll enter the realm of **device capabilities**, learn to access them with a **device database**, and, finally, discover how to group them into **device classes** so that we can keep our sanity.

I'm Freaking Out!

HELP

Pre-test late-night jitters? A math problem that just won't budge? Our expert on-call tutors are standing by to help you through tough moments.

build a mobile web app using a framework

The Tartanator

6

"We want an app!" Just a year or two ago, that hallmark cry generally meant one thing: native code development and deployment for each platform you wanted to support. But native isn't the only game in town. These days, web-based apps for mobile browsers have some street cred—especially now that hip cat **HTML5** and his sidekicks, **CSS3** and **JavaScript**, are in the house. Let's dip our toes into the mobile web app world by taking a **mobile framework**—code tools designed to help you get your job done quickly—for a spin!

Hmmm...it's...nice, but can you make it feel more...like a native app?

mobile web apps in the real world

Super mobile web apps

The mobile web feels like that gifted kid in the class.

7

You know, kind of fascinating, capable of amazing things, but also a mysterious, unpredictable troublemaker. We've tried to keep its hyperactive genius in check by being mindful of constraints and establishing boundaries, but now it's time to capitalize on some of the mobile web's natural talents. We can use **progressive enhancement** to spruce up the interface in more precocious browsers and transform erratic connectivity from a burden to a feature by crafting a thoughtful **offline mode**. And we can get at the essence of mobility by using **geolocation**. Let's go make this a super mobile web app!

build hybrid mobile apps with PhoneGap

8 Tartan Hunt: Going native

Sometimes you've got to go native. It might be because you need access to something not available in mobile browsers (yet). Or maybe your client simply *must* have an app in the App Store. We look forward to that shiny future when we have access to everything we want in the browser, and mobile web apps share that sparkly allure native apps enjoy. Until then, we have the option of **hybrid development**—we continue writing our **code using web standards**, and use a **library to bridge the gaps** between our code and the device's native capabilities. **Cross-platform native apps built from web technologies**? Not such a bad compromise, eh?

how to be future friendly

Make (some) sense of the chaos

9

Responsive Web Design. Device detection. Mobile web apps. PhoneGap. Wait…which one should we use?

There are an overwhelming number of ways to develop for the mobile web. Often, projects will involve **multiple techniques used in combination**. There is no single right answer. But don't worry. The key is to learn to go with the flow. **Embrace the uncertainty**. Adopt a **future-friendly mindset** and ride the wave, confident that you're flexible and ready to adapt to whatever the future holds.

leftovers

The top six things (we didn't cover)

Ever feel like something's missing? We know what you mean... Just when you thought you were done, there's more. We couldn't leave you without a few extra details, things we just couldn't fit into the rest of the book. At least, not if you want to be able to carry this book around without a metallic case and caster wheels on the bottom. So take a peek and see what you (still) might be missing out on.

set up your web server environment

Gotta start somewhere

You can't spell "mobile web" without the "web." There are no two ways about it. You're going to need a web server if you want to develop for the mobile web. That goes for more than just completing the exercises in this book. You need somewhere to put your web-hosted stuff, whether you use a third-party commercial web hosting service, an enterprise-class data center, or your own computer. In this appendix, we'll walk you through the steps of **setting up a local web server** on your computer and **getting PHP going** using free and open source software.

install WURFL

Sniffing out devices

The first step to solving device detection mysteries is a bit of legwork. Any decent gumshoe knows we've got to gather our clues and interrogate our witnesses. First, we need to seek out the brains of the operation: the **WURFL PHP API**. Then we'll go track down the brawn: capability information for thousands of devices in a single **XML data file**. But it'll take a bit of coaxing to get the two to spill the whole story, so we'll tweak a bit of **configuration** and take some careful notes.

install the Android SDK and tools

Take care of the environment

To be the master of testing native Android apps, you need to be environmentally aware. You'll need to turn your computer into a nice little ecosystem where you can herd Android apps to and from virtual (emulated) or real devices. To make you the shepherd of your Android sheep, we'll show you how to download the **Android software development kit (SDK)**, how to install some **platform tools**, how to **create some virtual devices,** and how to **install and uninstall apps**.

Index

how to use this book

Intro

In this section, we answer the burning question:
"So why <u>DID</u> they put that in a Mobile Web book?"

Who is this book for?

If you can answer "yes" to all of these:

(1) Do you have previous web design and development experience? ◄─── *It definitely helps if you've already got some scripting chops, too. We're not talking rocket science, but you shouldn't feel visceral panic if you see a JavaScript snippet.*

(2) Do you want to **learn**, **understand**, **remember**, and *apply* important mobile web concepts so that you can make your mobile web pages more interactive and exciting?

(3) Do you prefer **stimulating dinner-party conversation** to **dry, dull, academic lectures**?

this book is for you.

Who should probably back away from this book?

If you can answer "yes" to any of these:

(1) Are you **completely new** to web development?

(2) Are you already developing mobile web apps or sites and looking for a *reference* book on mobile web?

(3) Are you **afraid to try something different**? Would you rather have a root canal than endure the suggestion that there might be more than one true way to build for the Web? Do you believe that a technical book can't be serious if there's a walrus-themed pub and an app called the Tartanator in it?

this book is not for you.

[Note from marketing: this book is for anyone with a credit card. Or cash. Cash is nice, too. — Ed]

We know what you're thinking

"How can *this* be a serious mobile web development book?"

"What's with all the graphics?"

"Can I actually *learn* it this way?"

And we know what your *brain* is thinking

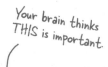

Your brain thinks THIS is important.

Your brain craves novelty. It's always searching, scanning, *waiting* for something unusual. It was built that way, and it helps you stay alive.

So what does your brain do with all the routine, ordinary, normal things you encounter? Everything it *can* to stop them from interfering with the brain's *real* job—recording things that *matter*. It doesn't bother saving the boring things; they never make it past the "this is obviously not important" filter.

How does your brain *know* what's important? Suppose you're out for a day hike and a tiger jumps in front of you. What happens inside your head and body?

Neurons fire. Emotions crank up. *Chemicals surge.*

And that's how your brain knows…

This must be important! Don't forget it!

But imagine you're at home, or in a library. It's a safe, warm, tiger-free zone. You're studying. Getting ready for an exam. Or trying to learn some tough technical topic your boss thinks will take a week, 10 days at the most.

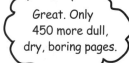

Your brain thinks THIS isn't worth saving.

Just one problem. Your brain's trying to do you a big favor. It's trying to make sure that this *obviously* nonimportant content doesn't clutter up scarce resources. Resources that are better spent storing the really *big* things. Like tigers. Like the danger of fire. Like how you should never again snowboard in shorts.

And there's no simple way to tell your brain, "Hey brain, thank you very much, but no matter how dull this book is, and how little I'm registering on the emotional Richter scale right now, I really *do* want you to keep this stuff around."

Great. Only 450 more dull, dry, boring pages.

We think of a "Head First" reader as a <u>learner</u>.

So what does it take to *learn* something? First, you have to *get* it, and then make sure you don't *forget* it. It's not about pushing facts into your head. Based on the latest research in cognitive science, neurobiology, and educational psychology, *learning* takes a lot more than text on a page. We know what turns your brain on.

Some of the Head First learning principles:

I need this web page, please.

client · request · web page · Sure, here you go. · CSS HTML images JS etc. · server

Make it visual. Images are far more memorable than words alone, and make learning much more effective (up to 89% improvement in recall and transfer studies). It also makes things more understandable.

Watch out, mobile web! Here we come!

Put the words within or near the graphics they relate to, rather than on the bottom or on another page, and learners will be up to *twice* as likely to solve problems related to the content.

Use a conversational and personalized style. In recent studies, students performed up to 40% better on post-learning tests if the content spoke directly to the reader, using a first-person, conversational style rather than taking a formal tone. Tell stories instead of lecturing. Use casual language. Don't take yourself too seriously. Which would *you* pay more attention to: a stimulating dinner-party companion, or a lecture?

Get the learner to think more deeply. In other words, unless you actively flex your neurons, nothing much happens in your head. A reader has to be motivated, engaged, curious, and inspired to solve problems, draw conclusions, and generate new knowledge. And for that, you need challenges, exercises, and thought-provoking questions, and activities that involve both sides of the brain and multiple senses.

Carrier 🔋 12:46 PM
ON TAP THIS MONTH:

BENSON'S BUBBLER · CHAPMAN'S TOWNSHIP

CRYSTAL SPRINGS RESERVE · HOYT

Get—and keep—the reader's attention. We've all had the "I really want to learn this, but I can't stay awake past page one" experience. Your brain pays attention to things that are out of the ordinary, interesting, strange, eye-catching, unexpected. Learning a new, tough, technical topic doesn't have to be boring. Your brain will learn much more quickly if it's not.

Touch their emotions. We now know that your ability to remember something is largely dependent on its emotional content. You remember what you care about. You remember when you *feel* something. No, we're not talking heart-wrenching stories about a boy and his dog. We're talking emotions like surprise, curiosity, fun, "what the...?", and the feeling of "I rule!" that comes when you solve a puzzle, learn something everybody else thinks is hard, or realize you know something that "I'm more technical than thou" Bob from Engineering *doesn't*.

Metacognition: thinking about thinking

If you really want to learn, and you want to learn more quickly and more deeply, pay attention to how you pay attention. Think about how you think. Learn how you learn.

Most of us did not take courses on metacognition or learning theory when we were growing up. We were *expected* to learn, but rarely *taught* to learn.

But we assume that if you're holding this book, you really want to learn about mobile web development. And you probably don't want to spend a lot of time. And since you're going to build more sites and apps in the future, you need to *remember* what you read. And for that, you've got to *understand* it. To get the most from this book, or *any* book or learning experience, take responsibility for your brain. Your brain on *this* content.

The trick is to get your brain to see the new material you're learning as Really Important. Crucial to your well-being. As important as a tiger. Otherwise, you're in for a constant battle, with your brain doing its best to keep the new content from sticking.

So just how *do* you get your brain to think that mobile web development is a hungry tiger?

There's the slow, tedious way, or the faster, more effective way. The slow way is about sheer repetition. You obviously know that you *are* able to learn and remember even the dullest of topics if you keep pounding the same thing into your brain. With enough repetition, your brain says, "This doesn't *feel* important to him, but he keeps looking at the same thing *over* and *over* and *over*, so I suppose it must be."

The faster way is to do **anything that increases brain activity,** especially different *types* of brain activity. The things on the previous page are a big part of the solution, and they're all things that have been proven to help your brain work in your favor. For example, studies show that putting words *within* the pictures they describe (as opposed to somewhere else in the page, like a caption or in the body text) causes your brain to try to makes sense of how the words and picture relate, and this causes more neurons to fire. More neurons firing = more chances for your brain to *get* that this is something worth paying attention to, and possibly recording.

A conversational style helps because people tend to pay more attention when they perceive that they're in a conversation, since they're expected to follow along and hold up their end. The amazing thing is, your brain doesn't necessarily *care* that the "conversation" is between you and a book! On the other hand, if the writing style is formal and dry, your brain perceives it the same way you experience being lectured to while sitting in a roomful of passive attendees. No need to stay awake.

But pictures and conversational style are just the beginning.

Here's what WE did:

We used **pictures**, because your brain is tuned for visuals, not text. As far as your brain's concerned, a picture really *is* worth a thousand words. And when text and pictures work together, we embedded the text *in* the pictures because your brain works more effectively when the text is *within* the thing the text refers to, as opposed to in a caption or buried in the text somewhere.

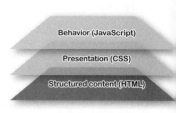

We used **redundancy**, saying the same thing in *different* ways and with different media types, and *multiple senses*, to increase the chance that the content gets coded into more than one area of your brain.

We used concepts and pictures in **unexpected** ways because your brain is tuned for novelty, and we used pictures and ideas with at least *some* **emotional** *content*, because your brain is tuned to pay attention to the biochemistry of emotions. That which causes you to *feel* something is more likely to be remembered, even if that feeling is nothing more than a little **humor**, **surprise**, or **interest.**

We used a personalized, **conversational style**, because your brain is tuned to pay more attention when it believes you're in a conversation than if it thinks you're passively listening to a presentation. Your brain does this even when you're *reading*.

We included loads of **activities**, because your brain is tuned to learn and remember more when you **do** things than when you *read* about things. And we made the exercises challenging-yet-doable, because that's what most people prefer.

We used **multiple learning styles**, because *you* might prefer step-by-step procedures, while someone else wants to understand the big picture first, and someone else just wants to see an example. But regardless of your own learning preference, *everyone* benefits from seeing the same content represented in multiple ways.

We include content for **both sides of your brain**, because the more of your brain you engage, the more likely you are to learn and remember, and the longer you can stay focused. Since working one side of the brain often means giving the other side a chance to rest, you can be more productive at learning for a longer period of time.

And we included **stories** and exercises that present **more than one point of view,** because your brain is tuned to learn more deeply when it's forced to make evaluations and judgments.

We included **challenges**, with exercises, and by asking **questions** that don't always have a straight answer, because your brain is tuned to learn and remember when it has to *work* at something. Think about it—you can't get your *body* in shape just by *watching* people at the gym. But we did our best to make sure that when you're working hard, it's on the *right* things. That **you're not spending one extra dendrite** processing a hard-to-understand example, or parsing difficult, jargon-laden, or overly terse text.

We used **people**. In stories, examples, pictures, etc., because, well, *you're* a person. And your brain pays more attention to *people* than it does to *things*.

Cut this out and stick it on your refrigerator.

Here's what YOU can do to bend your brain into submission

So, we did our part. The rest is up to you. These tips are a starting point; listen to your brain and figure out what works for you and what doesn't. Try new things.

- -

① Slow down. The more you understand, the less you have to memorize.

Don't just *read*. Stop and think. When the book asks you a question, don't just skip to the answer. Imagine that someone really *is* asking the question. The more deeply you force your brain to think, the better chance you have of learning and remembering.

② Do the exercises. Write your own notes.

We put them in, but if we did them for you, that would be like having someone else do your workouts for you. And don't just *look* at the exercises. **Use a pencil.** There's plenty of evidence that physical activity *while* learning can increase the learning.

③ Read "There Are No Dumb Questions."

That means all of them. They're not optional sidebars—*they're part of the core content!* Don't skip them.

④ Make this the last thing you read before bed. Or at least the last challenging thing.

Part of the learning (especially the transfer to long-term memory) happens *after* you put the book down. Your brain needs time on its own, to do more processing. If you put in something new during that processing time, some of what you just learned will be lost.

⑤ Drink water. Lots of it.

Your brain works best in a nice bath of fluid. Dehydration (which can happen before you ever feel thirsty) decreases cognitive function.

⑥ Talk about it. Out loud.

Speaking activates a different part of the brain. If you're trying to understand something, or increase your chance of remembering it later, say it out loud. Better still, try to explain it out loud to someone else. You'll learn more quickly, and you might uncover ideas you hadn't known were there when you were reading about it.

⑦ Listen to your brain.

Pay attention to whether your brain is getting overloaded. If you find yourself starting to skim the surface or forget what you just read, it's time for a break. Once you go past a certain point, you won't learn faster by trying to shove more in, and you might even hurt the process.

⑧ Feel something!

Your brain needs to know that this *matters*. Get involved with the stories. Make up your own captions for the photos. Groaning over a bad joke is *still* better than feeling nothing at all.

⑨ Create something!

Apply this to your daily work; use what you are learning to make decisions on your projects. Just do something to get some experience beyond the exercises and activities in this book. All you need is a pencil and a problem to solve…a problem that might benefit from using the tools and techniques you're studying for the exam.

Read me

This is a learning experience, not a reference book. We deliberately stripped out everything that might get in the way of learning whatever it is we're working on at that point in the book. And the first time through, you need to begin at the beginning, because the book makes assumptions about what you've already seen and learned.

We expect you to know HTML and CSS.

If you don't know HTML and CSS, pick up a copy of *Head First HTML with CSS & XHTML* before starting this book. We'll explain some of the more obscure CSS selectors or HTML elements, but don't expect to learn about that foundational stuff here.

We expect you to feel comfy around web scripting code.

We're not asking you to be a world-class JavaScript expert or to have done a graduate computer science project using PHP, but you'll see examples using both languages throughout the book. If the merest notion of a `for` loop makes you hyperventilate (or if you have no idea what we're talking about), you might consider tracking down a copy of *Head First PHP & MySQL* or *Head First JavaScript* and then heading on back here.

We expect you to know how to track things down.

We'll be blunt. The mobile web is an enormous topic, and mastering it involves expanding your *existing* web development skills. There are too many things to know about the Web for any one person to memorize, whether it's a detail of JavaScript syntax or the specifics of a browser's support for an HTML5 element attribute. Don't be too hard on yourself. Part of the toolset of a good web dev is keeping your Google chops sharp and knowing when and how to hit the Web to look up info about web topics. We bet you're good at that already.

We expect you to go beyond this book.

It's a big and beautiful mobile web world out there. We hope we can give you a shove to start you on your journey, but it's up to you to keep up your steam. Seek out the active mobile web community online, read blogs, join mailing lists that are up your alley, and attend related technical events in your area.

The activities are NOT optional.

The exercises and activities are not add-ons; they're part of the core content of the book. Some of them are to help with memory, some are for understanding, and some will help you apply what you've learned. ***Don't skip the exercises.*** They're good for giving your brain a chance to think about the ideas and terms you've been learning in a different context.

The redundancy is intentional and important.

One distinct difference in a Head First book is that we want you to *really* get it. And we want you to finish the book remembering what you've learned. Most reference books don't have retention and recall as a goal, but this book is about *learning*, so you'll see some of the same concepts come up more than once.

The Brain Power exercises don't have answers.

For some of them, there is no right answer, and for others, part of the learning experience of the exercise is for you to decide if and when your answers are right. In some of the Brain Power exercises, you will find hints to point you in the right direction.

Software requirements

As for developing any website, you need a text editor, a browser, a web server (it can be locally hosted on your personal computer), and the source code for the chapter examples.

The text editors we recommend for Windows are PSPad, TextPad, or EditPlus (but you can use Notepad if you have to). The text editors we recommend for Mac are TextWrangler (or its big brother, BBEdit) or TextMate. We also like Coda, a more web-focused tool.

If you're on a Linux system, you've got plenty of text editors built in, and we trust you don't need us to tell you about them.

If you are going to do web development, you need a web server. You'll need to go to Appendix ii, which details installing a web server with PHP. We recommend doing that now. No, seriously, head there now, follow the instructions, and come back to this page when you're done.

For Chapter 5, you'll need to install the WURFL (Wireless Universal Resource FiLe) API and data. And for Chapter 8, you'll need the Android SDK and some related tools. You guessed it: there are appendixes for those tasks, too.

You'll also need a browser—no, strike that—***as many browsers as possible*** for testing. And the more ***mobile devices with browsers*** you have on hand, the better (don't panic; there are many emulators you can use if you don't have hardware).

For developing and testing on the desktop, we highly recommend Google's Chrome browser, which has versions for Mac, Windows, and Linux. Learning how to use the JavaScript console in Google's Chrome Dev Tools is well worth the time. This is homework you need to do on your own.

Last of all, you'll need to get the code and resources for the examples in the chapters. It's all available at *http://hf-mw.com*.

The hf-mw.com site has the starting point of code for all the chapters. Head on over there and get downloading.

> The code and resources for the examples in the chapters are all available at http://hf-mw.com.

The technical review team

Brad Frost

Stephen Hay

Bryan Rieger

Andrea Trasatti

Trevor Farlow

Ethan Marcotte

Stephanie Rieger

Trevor Farlow is an amateur baker, recreational soccer player, and part-time animal shelter volunteer. When he's not walking dogs, scoring goals, or perfecting his New York–style cheesecake, he can be found learning the art of product ownership in a lean, mean, agile development team at Clearwater Analytics, LLC.

Brad Frost is a mobile web strategist and frontend developer at R/GA in New York City, where he works with large brands on mobile-related projects. He runs a resource site called Mobile Web Best Practices (*http://mobilewebbestpractices.com*) aimed at helping people create great mobile web experiences.

Stephen Hay has been building websites for more than 16 years. Aside from his client work, which focuses increasingly on multiplatform design and development, he speaks at industry events and has written for publications such as *A List Apart* and *.net Magazine*. He also co-organizes Mobilism, a highly respected mobile web design and development conference.

Ethan Marcotte is an independent designer/developer who is passionate about beautiful design, elegant code, and the intersection of the two. Over the years, his clientele has included *New York Magazine*, the Sundance Film Festival, the *Boston Globe*, and the W3C. Ethan coined the term *Responsive Web Design* to describe a new way of designing for the ever-changing Web and, if given the chance, will natter on excitedly about it—he even went so far as to write a book on the topic.

Bryan Rieger is a designer and reluctant developer with a background in theatre design and classical animation. Bryan has worked across various media including print, broadcast, web, and mobile; and with clients such as Apple, Microsoft, Nokia, and the Symbian Foundation. A passionate storyteller and incessant tinkerer, Bryan can be found crafting a diverse range of experiences at Yiibu—a wee design consultancy based in Edinburgh, Scotland.

Stephanie Rieger is a designer, writer, and closet anthropologist with a passion for the many ways people interact with technology. Stephanie has been designing for mobile since 2004 and now focuses primarily on web strategy, frontend design, and optimization for multiple screens and capabilities. A compulsive tester and researcher, Stephanie is always keen to discover and share insights on mobile usage, user behavior, and mobility trends from around the world.

Andrea Trasatti started creating WAP content in 1999 on the Nokia 7110, which in Europe was considered groundbreaking at the time. Andrea has led both WURFL and DeviceAtlas from their earliest days to success, and during those years built vast experience in device detection and content adaptation. You can find Andrea on Twitter as *@AndreaTrasatti*, regularly talking about mobile web and new trends in creating and managing content for mobile.

Acknowledgments

Our editor:

Thanks (and congratulations!) to **Courtney Nash**, who pushed us to create the best book we possibly could. She endured a huge raft of emails, questions, ramblings, and occasional crankiness. She stuck with us throughout this book and trusted us to trust our guts. And thanks to **Brian Sawyer** for stepping up at the end and taking us over the finish line.

Courtney Nash

The O'Reilly team:

Thanks to **Lou Barr** for her unfathomably speedy and masterful design and layout magic. We're seriously blown away here. Thank you. Our gratitude goes to **Karen Shaner** and **Rachel Monaghan** for all the help juggling drafts, reviewers, and details!

Thanks to the rest of the O'Reilly folks who made us feel so welcomed: **Mike Hendrickson**, for suggesting this crazy idea in the first place; **Brady Forrest**, for introducing and championing us; **Tim O'Reilly**, for being the genuine, smart, and nice guy that he is; and **Sara Winge**, for her graciousness and overall awesomeness.

Lou Barr

Our thanks:

Jason and Lyza work with the smartest people ever at Cloud Four. Our epic thanks to fellow cofounders **Aileen Jeffries** and **John Keith**, and the rest of the Cloud Four team: **Matt Gifford**, **Chris Higgins**, and **Megan Notarte**. This book is really a product of our collective mobile web obsession, and they, more than anyone, championed and endured this effort. Thanks a billion million zillion, you guys.

We'd also like to thank the mobile web community. In particular, we'd like to thank Josh Clark, Gail Rahn Frederick, Scott Jehl, Scott Jenson, Dave Johnson, Tim Kadlec, Jeremy Keith, Peter-Paul Koch, Brian LeRoux, James Pearce, Steve Souders, and Luke Wroblewski. We're proud and thankful to be part of this community.

Lyza's friends and family:

Thanks to **Bryan Christopher Fox** (Other Dev), without whose coding chops, insight, support, and all-around supergenius this book would not have been possible.

Huge shout-outs to my **friends** and **family**, who still seem to put up with me despite my long-term disappearance into Book Land. Thanks to Autumn and Amye, who showed stunning tenacity in the face of my constant unavailability. Thanks, Mike, always. And thanks to Dad, who always shows me how to find aesthetic and new adventure. Finally, thanks to Huw and Bethan of Plas-yn-Iâl, Llandegla, Wales, a fantastic, sheep-happy place where about a quarter of this book was written.

Jason's friends and family:

Thank you to my family for all of their support. Our parents, **Jan**, **Carol**, **Mark**, and **Doanne**, were a tremendous help in keeping our sanity as we juggled book writing, family, and moving.

Special thanks to my wife, **Dana Grigsby**, for making it possible for me to work on a book while we raised a baby and a preschooler and moved into a new house. I couldn't have done it without you.

Safari® Books Online

 Safari® Books Online is an on-demand digital library that lets you easily search over 7,500 technology and creative reference books and videos to find the answers you need quickly.

With a subscription, you can read any page and watch any video from our library online. Read books on your cell phone and mobile devices. Access new titles before they are available for print, and get exclusive access to manuscripts in development and post feedback for the authors. Copy and paste code samples, organize your favorites, download chapters, bookmark key sections, create notes, print out pages, and benefit from tons of other time-saving features.

O'Reilly Media has uploaded this book to the Safari Books Online service. To have full digital access to this book and others on similar topics from O'Reilly and other publishers, sign up for free at *http://my.safaribooksonline.com*.

Responsive Web Design

Dashing, exciting, fascinating, and oh-so-popular...but am I ready to take the plunge?

Hey there! Are you ready to jump into mobile?

Mobile web development is a wildly exciting way of life. There's glamour and excitement, and plenty of *Eureka!* moments. But there is also mystery and confusion. Mobile technology is evolving at bewildering speed, and there's so much to know! Hang tight. We'll start our journey by showing you a way of making websites called *Responsive Web Design (RWD)*. You'll be able to adapt websites to look great on a whole lot of mobile devices by building on the web skills you already have.

Get on the mobile bandwagon

There's a pretty good chance you own a mobile phone. We know that not simply because you bought this book (smart move, by the way!), but because it's hard to find someone who doesn't own a mobile phone.

It doesn't matter where you go in the world. Mobile phones are being used everywhere, from farmers in Nigeria using their mobiles to find which market has the best price for their crops, to half of Japan's top 10 best-selling novels being consumed and written—*yes, written*—on mobile phones.

At the beginning of 2011, there were 5.2 billion phones being used by the 6.9 billion people on Earth. **More people use mobile phones than have working toilets or toothbrushes.**

The time is now

So yeah, mobile is huge, but it's been big for years. Why should you get on the mobile bandwagon now?

Because **the iPhone changed everything**. It sounds clichéd, but it is true. There were app stores, touchscreens, and web browsers on phones before the iPhone, but Apple was the first to put them together in a way that made it easy for people to understand and use.

Are you ready to get on the mobile bandwagon?

Everyone has iPhones. And if they don't, are they really going to browse the Web?

The iPhone is fantastic, but people use a lot of different phones for a lot of different reasons. And the most popular phones are likely to change.

We have no way of knowing what the the leading phones will be when you read this book. Three years ago, Android was a mere blip on the radar. In 2011, it is a leading smartphone platform worldwide.

Mobile technology changes quickly, but there are a few things we feel confident about:

1 **Every new phone has a web browser in it.**
You can probably find a new phone that doesn't have a web browser in it, but you have to look pretty hard. Even the most basic phones now come with decent browsers. Everyone wants the Web on their phone.

2 **Mobile web usage will exceed desktop web usage.**
Soon the number of people accessing the Web via mobile phones will surpass those who use a computer. Already, many people say they use their phones more frequently than their PCs.

3 **The Web is the only true cross-platform technology.**
iPhone, Android, BlackBerry, Windows Phone, WebOS, Symbian, Bada—there are more phone platforms than we can keep track of. Each one has its own specific programming hooks, meaning that if you want to write software for each, you have to start from scratch each time.

Mobile web has its own challenges, but there is no other technology that allows you to create content and apps that reach every platform.

So you're in the right spot at the right time. Mobile web is taking off, and you're ready to ride the rocketship. Let's get started!

Something odd happened on the way to the pub

Mike is the proprietor of The Splendid Walrus, a pub with a clever name and a cult-like following of local beer enthusiasts. Mike always has unusual beers on tap and highlights several of them on his website.

Before he realized his lifelong dream of pub ownership, Mike was a web developer. So he had no trouble putting together a respectable website for The Splendid Walrus himself.

http://www.splendidwalrus.com

If mobile phone web browsers are so great...

Mike built the Splendid Walrus website several years ago, when mobile browsing was still rudimentary and uncommon. It was made for—and tested in—desktop browsers like Firefox, Internet Explorer, and Safari.

Lots of newer mobile browers have good reputations. They're increasingly sophisticated and powerful, and starting to feel like some of their desktop counterparts.

...shouldn't this just work?

Mike had a rude awakening when he looked at the Splendid Walrus site on his iPhone 4. It didn't look so hot on a friend's Android device, either.

Here's how the Splendid Walrus site looks on an iPhone 4...

...and here's how the site looks on a Motorola Backflip Android phone.

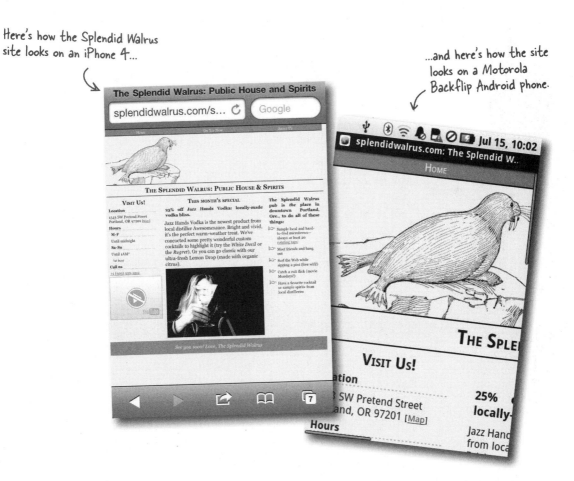

What's so different about the mobile web?

My iPhone has the Safari web browser on it. My site looks great in desktop Safari, so why does it look all messed up on my phone?

① There are 86 billion different mobile web browsers.
OK, not quite that many. But when you're developing for the mobile web, sometimes it feels this way. Unlike the handful of leading desktop browsers, there are hundreds of different mobile browsers. Yikes.

And just when you think you're on top of all of them, a new one will pop up in, like, Thailand.

② Support for web technologies varies wildly.
On older mobile browsers (or even recent ones on less powerful devices), you can pretty much forget about reliable CSS or JavaScript. Even the newest browsers lack support for some things, support them in bewilderingly different ways, or have weird bugs. It's the Wild West out here, folks!

③ Mobile devices are smaller and slower.
Yeah, we know. Newer mobile devices are state-of-the-art pocket computers. But they still pale in comparison to desktop (or laptop) computers in terms of processing power. Mobile networks can be flaky and downright poky, and data transfer is not necessarily free or unlimited. This means we'll need to think about putting our sweet but enormous, media-rich, complex sites on a performance-savvy diet.

④ Mobile interfaces require us to rethink our sites.
Just because a mobile browser can render a desktop website with few hiccups doesn't mean it necessarily *should*. Screens are smaller; interactions and expectations are different.

People with mobile devices use all sorts of input devices: fingers, stylus pens, the little nubbins they have on BlackBerry devices. Typing and filling out forms can be tedious at best. Squinting at type designed to fit a desktop browser window can give your users headaches and fury. You get the idea.

Exercise

Here's how Mike's iPhone 4 renders the Splendid Walrus website. It doesn't look so great. Can you spot the problem areas? Mark any problems you see.

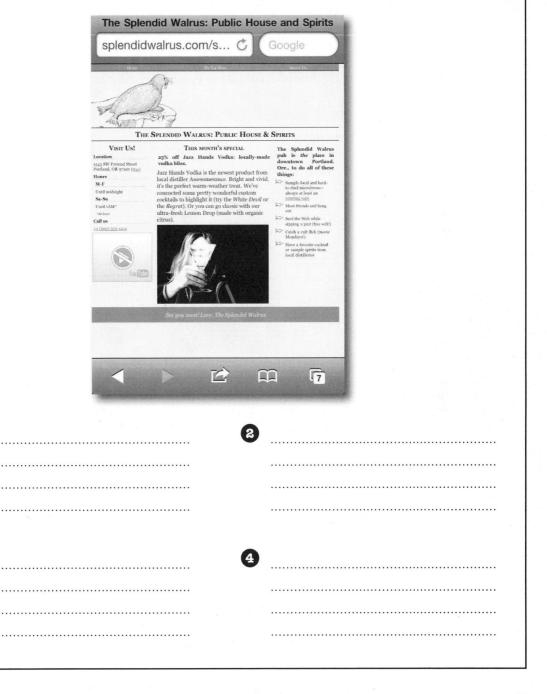

1 ....

2 ....

3 ....

4 ....

Exercise Solution

Did you spot some of these problem areas?

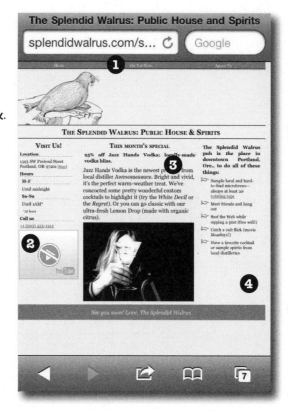

1 The navigation links are all tiny and too small to read or click.

2 The embedded YouTube video doesn't work.

3 The three-column layout feels tight on this screen resolution, and the text is hard to read.

4 There is a weird gap on the right edge of the screen.

This is confusing and embarrassing. I want my customers with mobile devices to see a nice site. I'm out of my depth here. Can you help?

Ugh! What a mess! We're totally going to have to start from scratch...

Jim

Frank

Frank: Hold on a minute. We know that Mike makes a big deal out of using clean, semantic HTML markup and uses CSS to control layout and styling as much as possible.

Jim: And? That's great and professional, but how does it help us make this better?

Frank: Well, let's think about this a bit. When I look at the CSS he's using for the Splendid Walrus site, I see a lot of widths and sizes defined to fit within a 960-pixel box. It looks like he's designed the site on a 960-pixel grid, with three main columns.

Jim: …and most mobile devices have resolutions considerably less than 960 pixels. Also, three columns seems like a lot for a smaller screen.

Frank: So…I have to wonder…*what if we could use different CSS for mobile devices?* Say, maybe, CSS designed to lay out in 320 pixels, which is the width of a lot of smartphone screens? And maybe reduce the number of columns?

Jim: Nice idea, Frank. But I don't see how we could do that without a lot of server-side programming. I mean, how do we get mobile devices to use completely different CSS?

Frank: You know how Jill just got back from the Awesome Cool Mobile Web Camp conference and is all excited about that thing called *Responsive Web Design*?

Jim: How could I forget? It's all she's been talking about.

Frank: Well, she says it's getting a lot of attention from web developers and it sounds like it involves, at least in part, applying different CSS for different situations, without having to do heavy-duty programming. Apparently it's especially useful for developing mobile websites. I can't really remember the details, but maybe we should check it out.

Responsive Web Design

Responsive Web Design (RWD) is a set of techniques championed by web designer Ethan Marcotte. Sites designed with this approach adapt their layouts according to the environment of the user's browser, in large part by doing some nifty things with CSS.

Read Ethan's original article for A List Apart about RWD at http://bit.ly/nRePnj.

Depending on the current value of certain browser conditions like window size, device orientation, or aspect ratio, we can apply different CSS in different circumstances. By rethinking the way we do page layouts, we can make formerly one-size-fits-all column and grid layouts flow more naturally across a continuum of browser window sizes.

RWD is one of the simplest and quickest ways to make a website work handsomely on a lot of devices—and you can use the web skills you already have.

The recipe for Responsive Web Design

There are three primary techniques for building a responsively designed website:

1 CSS3 media queries
Evaluating certain aspects of the current browser environment to determine which CSS to apply.

We can apply different CSS rules based on things like browser window width, aspect ratio, and orientation.

2 Fluid-grid layouts
Using relative CSS proportions instead of absolute sizes for page layout elements.

RWD uses percentages instead of pixels as units for columns and other layout elements.

3 Fluid images and media
Making our images and media scale to fit within the size constraints of their containers by using some CSS tricks.

Fluid images and media keep within the bounds of their parent elements, scaling proportionally with the rest of the layout.

An example of a responsively designed site

index.html

We deliver the same HTML and CSS to all devices and browsers.

styles.css

CSS media queries determine which of the CSS to apply to which environments.

A multicolumn, big, layout when there's plenty of room

Somewhat simpler layout as the window width decreases

Streamlined, single-column layout for narrower displays.

This is just one example of a responsive design approach.

Different CSS in different places

If you've been doing web development for some time (and are CSS-savvy), you might be friends with **CSS media types** already. **We can use @media rules to apply CSS selectively**.

CSS media type declarations inside of a CSS file look like this:

```
@media screen { /* CSS Rules for screens! */ }
```

"screen" is a media type.

The rules between the braces will only apply when the content is rendered on a screen.

Another way to use media types to apply CSS selectively is from within a `<link>` in your HTML document.

```
<link rel="stylesheet" type="text/css" href="print.css" media="print" />
```

The rules in this external stylesheet will only be applied if the content is rendered on a print device (that is, a printer).

"print" is another media type.

Referencing the `print` media type like this is a common approach to creating print stylesheets—that is, CSS styles that only get applied when the content is printed.

Media Types Up Close

Common (and useful) media types include `screen`, `print`, and `all`. There are other, less common media types like `aural`, `braille`, and `tv`.

Curious? If you're the kind of person who reads technical specs for fun or to satisfy curiosity, you can see all of the media types defined in CSS2 on the W3C's site at *www.w3.org/TR/CSS2/media.html*.

Media types, meet media features

You have certain features—your age, your height—and so do media types. And just like The Splendid Walrus might want to establish a rule that requires the minimum age of patrons to be 21 before they apply alcohol, we might want to define certain CSS that we only apply to browser window widths within a certain range.

We're in luck! `width`, along with `color` and `orientation`, is one of the **media features** defined in CSS3 for all common media types. So, again, media *types* have media *features*.

Media features on their own don't get us very far. We need a way to ask the browser about the states of the ones we care about and, well, do something about it. That's where ***CSS3 media queries*** come in.

screen → aspect-ratio, height, width, orientation

"screen" is a useful media type.

A few of the "screen" media type's media features.

P.S. There are more. But these are the most useful to us.

CSS media queries

"screen" media type, we meet again!

"width" is a media feature we want to evaluate on the "screen" media type.

These CSS rules will only get applied if the media query evaluates to TRUE.

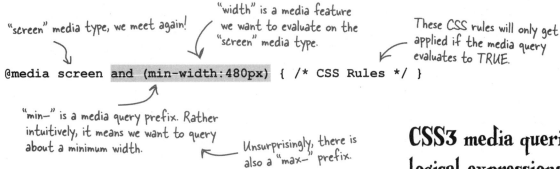

```
@media screen and (min-width:480px) { /* CSS Rules */ }
```

"min-" is a media query prefix. Rather intuitively, it means we want to query about a minimum width.

Unsurprisingly, there is also a "max-" prefix.

This means: **are we presently rendering content on a screen, *AND* is the window *currently* at least 480 pixels wide?** Yes? OK! Apply these CSS rules.

Another example:

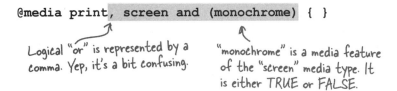

```
@media print, screen and (monochrome) { }
```

Logical "or" is represented by a comma. Yep, it's a bit confusing.

"monochrome" is a media feature of the "screen" media type. It is either TRUE or FALSE.

Is this being rendered on a printer *OR* is it being rendered on a screen that is monochrome (black and white)? Yes? Use these styles!

CSS3 media queries are logical expressions that evaluate the current values of media features in the user's browser. If the media query expression evaluates as TRUE, the contained CSS is applied.

Exercise

Translating CSS media queries: You try it! Match the media query and its meaning.

```
@media all and (orientation: landscape) {}
```

```
<link rel="stylesheet" type="text/css"
href="my.css" media="screen and (color)" />
```

```
@media print and (monochrome) {}
```

```
@media screen and (color) { }
```

Apply the rules in this external stylesheet to color screens.

Apply these styles to black-and-white printers.

Apply these rules to color screens.

Apply these styles to all media types when in landscape orientation.

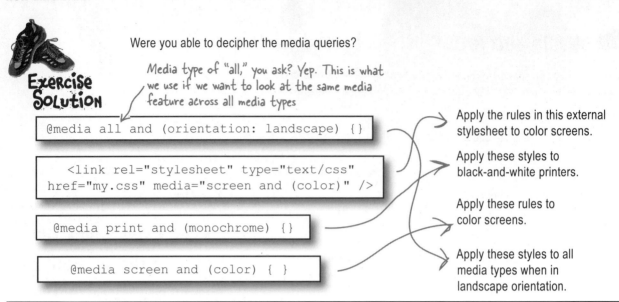

Exercise Solution

Were you able to decipher the media queries?

Media type of "all," you ask? Yep. This is what we use if we want to look at the same media feature across all media types

```
@media all and (orientation: landscape) {}
```

```
<link rel="stylesheet" type="text/css"
href="my.css" media="screen and (color)" />
```

```
@media print and (monochrome) {}
```

```
@media screen and (color) { }
```

Apply the rules in this external stylesheet to color screens.

Apply these styles to black-and-white printers.

Apply these rules to color screens.

Apply these styles to all media types when in landscape orientation.

OK. Now I can understand media queries and maybe even write my own. But what am I doing here? How do I write the CSS for mobile devices?

CSS: How different is different?

We have a tool that lets us apply different CSS to different situations. But now what?

Don't panic. We do need to write some mobile-friendly CSS, but we're not going to have to start from scratch. Nor are we going to have to have totally different CSS for our mobile devices—we can share a lot of what's already there.

To generate our mobile-friendly layout, we'll:

☐ Check out the current layout of splendidwalrus.com and analyze its structure.

☐ Identify layout pieces that need to change to work better on mobile browsers.

☐ Generate mobile-adapted CSS for those identified elements.

☐ Organize our CSS and selectively apply the mobile and desktop CSS using media queries.

We'll only write different CSS for those layout elements that need to be different for mobile.

The current structure of the Splendid Walrus site

Take a peek at the *index.html* file for the Splendid Walrus site in the *chapter1* directory. If you use your imagination and strip out the content, you can see a basic HTML page structure like this:

The three main content columns

```
<div class="navigation">...</div>
<div class="header">...</div>
<h1>...</h1>
<div id="visit" class="column">...</div>
<div id="points" class="column">...</div>
<div id="main" class="column">...</div>
<div class="footer">...</div>
```

Putting the righthand column before the center column in the markup is an old trick of the web design trade: it makes it easier to handle layouts using CSS floats.

The current, desktop-oriented CSS lays out the page like this:

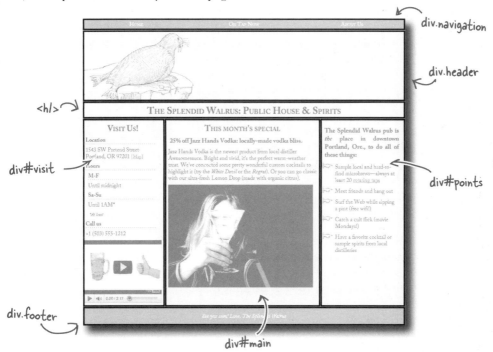

div.navigation

div.header

<h1>

div#visit

div#points

div.footer

div#main

Let's go look at the CSS that defines the layout and figure out what needs to change to adapt it to be mobile-sized.

Analyze the current CSS

Open the *styles.css* file for the Splendid Walrus site.

There's a bunch of CSS at the top of the file, but we don't have to worry about that. We can share the same colors, typography, and styling across both desktop and mobile variants.

What we care about is the **structural** CSS, near the bottom of the file.

> We're only interested in the structural part of the CSS file.

```css
/* Structure */
body, .header, .navigation, .footer {
    width: 960px;
}
.header, .navigation, .footer {
    clear: both;
}
.column {
    margin: 10px 10px 0 0;
}
.navigation {
    min-height: 25px;
}
.navigation ul li {
    width: 320px; /* 960/3 */
}
.header {
    background:url(images/w.png) no-repeat;
    height: 200px;
}
#visit {
    width: 240px;
    float: left;
}
#points {
    width: 240px;
    float: right;
}
#main {
    margin: 10px 260px 0 250px;
    width: 460px;
}
```

> The body is 960 pixels wide. The header, footer, and navigation elements span the full width.

> Because these elements span the full width, make sure nothing is floating next to them.

> clear:both just ensures that these elements start on a new "line"—that is, that nothing is next to them.

> Each column (visit, right, and points) has a 10px margin at top and a 10px margin at right (a.k.a. a "gutter").

> The navigation links are in a <ul>. Lay it out horizontally and make each <li> span 1/3 of the page width.

> Each <li> gets 1/3 of the page width because there are three links.

> The header has a background image, so it needs to be 200px high to show all of the image.

> The left and right columns are each 240 pixels wide and float.

> It seems like the main column should be 480 pixels wide (960 minus the two 240-pixel left and right columns). But it's 460 pixels wide to account for the two 10-pixel gutters between the columns.

> The main column uses margins to position itself—it doesn't float.

> Its left margin of 260px and right margin of 250px position it in the window.

What needs to change?

1 **Make the page and its structural elements fit within 320 pixels.**
As Frank mentioned on page 9, 320 pixels is a common screen resolution for mobile devices.

2 **Reduce three columns to a single column.**
In the original, desktop layout, three columns felt "crunched" on a mobile screen.

We're not going to have to rewrite all of the CSS.

We just need to adapt some of the structural layout elements. The rest—typography, colors, and whatnot—can stay basically unchanged.

For mobile, we need to go from this...

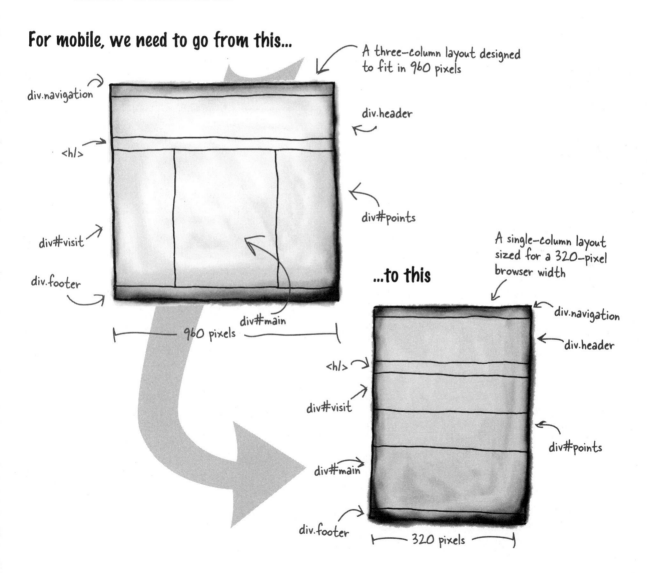

A three-column layout designed to fit in 960 pixels

div.navigation

<h1>

div.header

div#points

div#visit

div.footer

div#main

— 960 pixels —

...to this

A single-column layout sized for a 320-pixel browser width

div.navigation

div.header

<h1>

div#visit

div#points

div#main

div.footer

— 320 pixels —

Identify the CSS that needs to change

The highlighted code will need to be
adapted for our mobile version.

We need to change the width
of the page and the header,
navigation, and footer elements.

We don't <u>need</u> this rule in
our mobile version (but it
doesn't hurt anything).

Because nothing is floated
in our mobile layout, clears
aren't necessary.

This is actually fine: we
want the navigation links
to be at least this tall.

We need to adapt the
navigation link widths to
fit the smaller screen.

We need to remove the
floats and change the
width of the visit and
points columns.

The "columns" on the mobile
layout will lay out vertically, not
horizontally. Let's add some space
between columns (vertically) but
get rid of the gutter.

We'll use the same background
image for the header, so this
can stay the same.

It might seem like we would need
to adjust the 200px height here,
but we don't because we'll use the
same image.

We don't need the margins for
positioning anymore (#main
will span the full width), and
we need to change the width.

```css
/* Structure */
body, .header, .navigation, .footer {
    width: 960px;
}

.header, .navigation, .footer {
    clear: both;
}
.column {
    margin: 10px 10px 0 0;
}
.navigation {
    min-height: 25px;
}
.navigation ul li {
    width: 320px; /* 960/3 */
}
.header {
    background:url(images/w.png) no-repeat;
    height: 200px;
}
#visit {
    width: 240px;
    float: left;
}
#points {
    width: 240px;
    float: right;
}
#main {
    margin: 10px 260px 0 250px;
    width: 460px;
}
```

styles.css

Steps to creating the mobile-specific CSS

1 Change the width of the highlighted CSS rules.

2 Get rid of the CSS rules we don't need.

3 Factor out the common CSS rules. ⟵ We'll do this in just a minute.

Mobile CSS Magnets

Use the magnets to build the mobile-specific CSS.

```css
body, .header, .footer, .navigation {


}
.column {


  border-bottom: 1px dashed #7b96bc;
}
.navigation ul li {


}
#visit, #points, #main {


}
```

↖ This border is to add some visual separation to the columns (now vertical) as they lay out on the page.

```
width: 320px;
```

```
width: 106.6667px;
```

```
margin: 10px 0;
```

```
width:320px;
```

Mobile CSS Magnets Solution

```css
body, .header, .footer, .navigation {
    width: 320px;
}
.column {
    margin: 10px 0;
    border-bottom: 1px dashed #7b96bc;
}
.navigation ul li {
    width: 106.6667px;
}
#visit, #points, #main {
    width:320px;
}
```

Ta-da! Mobile-specific CSS

And we're done! These four CSS rules are all the mobile-specific layout we'll need. Now we need to be sure they'll get used by mobile devices.

And how will we do that? Our old friend Mr. Media Query to the rescue! We'll generate a media query shortly to apply this CSS to devices with a browser window of 480 pixels wide or narrower.

Why 480 pixels? That's the resolution for the "long side"(a.k.a. "landscape orientation") of many popular smartphones.

> Wait a minute. Some of the CSS rules disappeared. Where'd they go?

They didn't disappear...

...they just don't need to be contained inside our mobile-specific CSS. Why? Because the CSS rules in question are going to be the same for both layouts (desktop and mobile).

We'll put the shared CSS outside the media queries so that we don't have to have the same CSS rules in two places. Let's do that now.

The rest of our structural CSS

Shared structural CSS

See? Told you! None of the CSS actually disappeared. Here's the shared structural CSS that we identified on page 18, factored out and ready to go.

```
.header, .footer, .navigation {
   clear: both;
}
.header {
   background:url(images/w.png) no-repeat;
   height: 200px;
}
.navigation {
   min-height: 25px;
}
```

Our desktop structural CSS

We still need to have good CSS for desktop browsers!

After we remove the common structural CSS rules, here's what we end up with for the **desktop-specific CSS structure**.

We'll need to use a media query so that only viewports 481 pixels and wider apply this CSS.

```
body, .header, .footer, .navigation {
   width: 960px;
}
.column {
   margin: 10px 10px 0 0;
}
.navigation ul li {
   width: 320px; /* 960/3 */
}
#visit {
   width: 240px;
   float: left;
}
#points {
   width: 240px;
   float: right;
}
#main {
   margin: 10px 260px 0 250px;
}
```

What's next?

Let's check in on our to-do list for creating structural CSS that works for both desktop and mobile browsers:

- ☑ Check out the current layout of splendidwalrus.com and analyze its structure.
- ☑ Identify layout pieces that need to change to work better on mobile browsers.
- ☑ Generate mobile-adapted CSS for those identified elements.
- ☐ **Organize our CSS and selectively apply the mobile and desktop CSS using media queries.**

Put it together

Here's how we'll put together the updated version of *styles.css*.

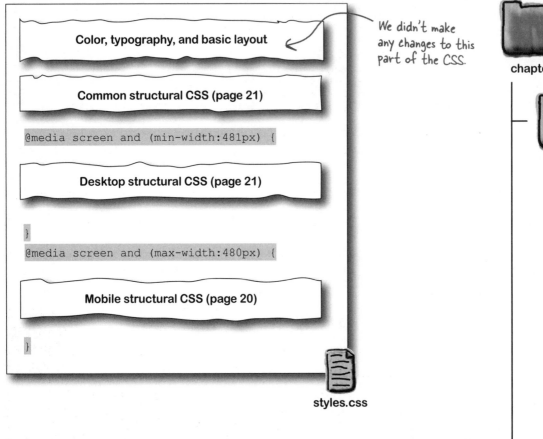

Color, typography, and basic layout

We didn't make any changes to this part of the CSS.

Common structural CSS (page 21)

```
@media screen and (min-width:481px) {
```

Desktop structural CSS (page 21)

```
}
@media screen and (max-width:480px) {
```

Mobile structural CSS (page 20)

```
}
```

styles.css

chapter1

images

point.png

sample.jpg

w.png

index.html

styles.css

One last thing...

You're going to need a **viewport** **<meta>** tag in the *index.html* file. These tags help tell the browser how "zoomed in" to render the content. We'll be taking a look at these guys a bit later on, but for now, just take our word for it: you'll want one of these.

```
<head>
<meta http-equiv="Content-Type" content="text/html; charset=utf-8" />
<meta name="viewport" content="width=device-width, initial-scale=1" />
<title>The Splendid Walrus: Public House and Spirits</title>
```

index.html

Do this! ⟶

① **Edit the index.html file.**
Drop in the `viewport` `<meta>` tag from page 22.

② **Open the styles.css file.**
You'll be replacing the structural CSS rules near the bottom of the file. Remove the existing rules for structural elements.

③ **Add the common rules.**
Add the shared structural CSS rules from page 21.

④ **Add the desktop- and mobile-specific CSS.**
Add the desktop rules (page 21) and mobile rules (page 20).

⑤ **Wrap the desktop- and mobile-specific CSS in media queries.**
Add the media queries (page 22).

Test Drive

Once you've made these changes, load the *index.html* file in your desktop browser and resize the window to less than 481 pixels wide to see the mobile-friendly layout.

> Watch out, mobile web! Here we come!

The page still looks the same in desktop browsers...

...until the browser window width is less than 481 pixels. Then you can see the mobile-optimized layout!

This is a good start, but there's a bit of a problem. If I scroll down on my iPhone, you'll see that the photo is too big for the page. It breaks the layout.

Frank

Jill

Frank: This is really frustrating. I thought the mobile CSS we created would fix this.

Jill: Your CSS makes the layout fit on a smaller screen, but it's still pretty rigid. I mean, look what happens if I put my iPhone in landscape orientation.

Frank: Ugh. The layout is still 320 pixels wide…but on a 480-pixel screen. Am I going to have to write different CSS for every single different possible viewport size?!

Jill: See, this is where **Responsive Web Design** practices could help us. Right now, you're delivering a rigidly sized structure to all browsers whose current window is 480 pixels wide or smaller, no matter what the actual specific browser window width is. That's not very flexible. I mean, not all mobile devices have a 320-pixel-wide browser window.

Responsive design helps us adapt our layout to different situations. Instead of dictating the exact size of elements—that is, using pixel-based measurements in our structural CSS like we are now—we can use a proportional layout, which adapts much better for different users.

Frank: Proportional? Is that like ems and percentages and stuff in CSS?

Jill: Yeah, sort of. We can use percentages instead of pixels when we code up our layout. That way, content stretches and shrinks to fill available space—kind of like water filling in gaps. That's why this kind of layout is often called a **fluid layout**. And, by the way, this will help us fix that wayward image as well.

Frank: So, all of that work with media queries was wasted time.

Jill: Not at all! Media queries are a big part of what makes responsive design work.

This photo is wider than 320 pixels, breaking out of the layout.

The next step to move toward a responsive design—one that will work more comfortably on more devices and browsers—is to convert our fixed, pixel-based layout to a proportional, fluid-grid layout.

The YouTube video is still broken on this iPhone.

Fireside Chats

Tonight's talk: **Fixed Grid meets Fluid Grid**

Fluid Grid:

Hey, Fixed Grid. I know you've been around a while and seen a lot of action. But, no offense, there are a few problems with your philosophy.

I mean…you're kind of a relic. Your rigidly defined dimensions make you seem brittle and inflexible. That is, you're not responsive.

You don't respond to changes in your user's environment. You stay the same, always.

At the cost of your users. Look at what happens when we look at you in different browser window sizes. Stuff is cut off, or there's a bunch of blank space.

Maybe that worked in your day, but these days there are simply too many kinds of browsers and devices. If you're willing to let go of pixel-perfect layouts—hey, they're a holdover from the old print days of yore, anyway—and let your content flow, like water, into the available space in the browser window, you can really adapt for different situations.

Fixed Grid:

What's that? What's a young upstart like you know about philosophy?

Responsive?

What's wrong with tradition? I'm staying true to what the designer intended! 960 pixels wide, with 240-pixel columns on the left and right.

If users don't like it, they should straighten up, get a haircut, and use a standard browser.

Well, pipsqueak, show me what you've got.

What's wrong with a fixed-width layout, anyway?

If the whole world were full of browsers whose windows were always the same size, it would be a safe, pretty world in which designers could have pixel-perfect control over what a website looked like.

Unfortunately, the Web has never been this controllable. Sometimes we try to design around "standard" window widths like 640, 960, or 1,024 pixels. But that is mostly an illusion: there is no standard browser window size. And that's before you even start thinking about mobile devices.

Sure, the fixed-grid layout for The Splendid Walrus looks fine at 960 pixels wide.

The site in a 960-pixel window

The layout doesn't adapt to other window sizes

But in a narrower window, look what happens. The column widths stay the same, which means content gets cut off and the user has to scroll horizontally. Ick.

The site viewed in a 700-pixel window

The right column isn't visible without scrolling.

Left and right columns are 240 pixels wide...always.

In a wider window, the entire layout is still only 960 pixels wide, leaving a blank gap of wasted space at the right side of the screen. Hmmm.

The entire width is constrained to 960 pixels.

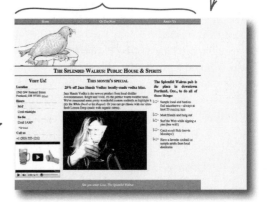

The site viewed in a 1,200-pixel window

How is fluid better?

Fluid-grid layouts use proportional units (percentages) instead of pixels for widths. We can stay true to the designer's vision of having the left and right columns span one-quarter of the page width by defining their widths as 25%, instead of 240 pixels.

A fluid version of the layout at 960 pixels. It doesn't look very different right now, does it?

The layout adapts as the window changes size

In different window widths, the content flows, like water, to fill the available spaces in the layout. The left and right columns always take up 25% of the window, and content is not clipped in narrower windows, nor is there any empty space in wider windows.

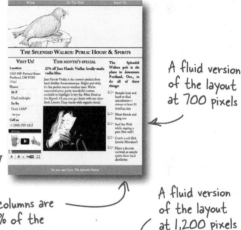

A fluid version of the layout at 700 pixels

Left and right columns are proportional: 25% of the window's width.

A fluid version of the layout at 1,200 pixels

BRAIN BARBELL

We're about to convert both the desktop and mobile CSS from fixed to fluid grids. Can you think of some ways this might help solve some of the problems Jill found with the site on mobile browsers?

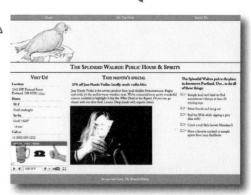

Go fluid

There are a number of things we'll need to do to address the problems Jill found and move toward a responsive design.

- ☐ Convert the pixel-based layout to a fluid one, using proportional widths instead of fixed.

- ☐ Make the default body font size 100% so our page's fonts can scale up and down proportionally.

  If we're going to make our layout fluid, we'll want to be sure our fonts are flexible, too.

- ☐ Fix the broken YouTube video.

- ☐ Fix the image that is too wide.

The fluid formula

To convert a pixel-based layout to a proportional, fluid one, use this formula:

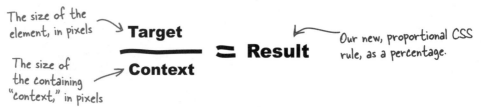

The size of the element, in pixels → **Target**

The size of the containing "context," in pixels → **Context**

$$\frac{\textbf{Target}}{\textbf{Context}} = \textbf{Result}$$

Our new, proportional CSS rule, as a percentage.

A closer look

Let's take a look at what this means, using the Splendid Walrus site's desktop layout.

We start with a **context** on which to base our proportions. In this case, our reference design is 960 pixels wide. We want our resulting, fluid layout to have the same proportions as the current design does. So we'll base our calculations on that 960-pixel baseline.

The navigation, header, and footer all span the full width of the page. That makes the fluid formula very easy to apply indeed!

$$\frac{\textbf{960 pixels}}{\textbf{960 pixels}} = \textbf{100\%}$$

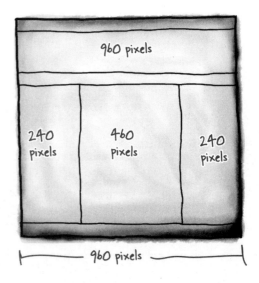

960 pixels

240 pixels   460 pixels   240 pixels

⊢————— 960 pixels —————⊣

Continue your fluid conversion

The left and right columns are both supposed to be 240 pixels wide, relative to the 960-pixel containing context. To get a proportional measurement, use the fluid formula again:

$$\frac{240 \text{ pixels}}{960 \text{ pixels}} \simeq 25\%$$

The columns span a quarter of the page width. So this feels pretty intuitive, right?

The main, center column is a bit different. It doesn't float. Instead, margins are used to position the element. But that's just fine. We can still use the fluid formula to convert the pixel-based margin sizes to percentages:

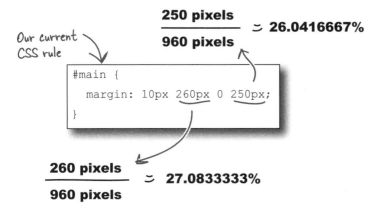

$$\frac{250 \text{ pixels}}{960 \text{ pixels}} \simeq 26.0416667\%$$

Our current CSS rule

```
#main {
    margin: 10px 260px 0 250px;
}
```

$$\frac{260 \text{ pixels}}{960 \text{ pixels}} \simeq 27.0833333\%$$

Our updated CSS rule

```
#main {
    margin: 10px 27.0833333% 0 26.0416667%;
}
```

Exercise

Finish converting the structural desktop CSS rules in *styles.css* to proportional widths. You'll want to edit each of the six CSS rules within the media query for window widths of 481 pixels or greater.

there are no Dumb Questions

Q: Why are there so many decimal places in these numbers? Do we really need all that?

A: We're demonstrating the purist fluid-grid approach here, which builds CSS units exactly as the numbers come off the calculator.

Realistically, browsers round these very long numbers. And—a bit concerningly—they round them in slightly different ways.

So, it's up to you. You might consider rounding the numbers down to one or two digits past the decimal point. Another approach is to leave some play in your layout—a percentage or two not accounted for at all. Your grid won't be as precise, but you avoid some of the pitfalls of rounding issues and make your arithmetic less rigorous.

Q: Wait. Why is the top margin on `.main` still 10px? Isn't that...wrong?

A: Vertical layout is a totally different beast than horizontal. We can't use the 960px context because the height of the design is never really a known quantity, and vertical layout using percentages is a tricky affair, supported in different (and sometimes poor) ways in different browsers. Using pixels like this for vertical margins is OK.

Let's take a look at that fluid desktop CSS.

Exercise Solution

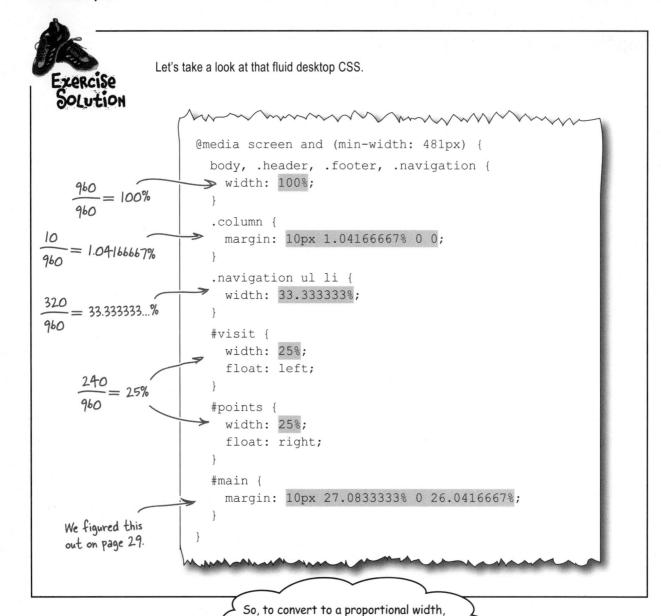

$$\frac{960}{960} = 100\%$$

$$\frac{10}{960} = 1.04166667\%$$

$$\frac{320}{960} = 33.333333...\%$$

$$\frac{240}{960} = 25\%$$

We figured this out on page 29.

```
@media screen and (min-width: 481px) {
  body, .header, .footer, .navigation {
    width: 100%;
  }
  .column {
    margin: 10px 1.04166667% 0 0;
  }
  .navigation ul li {
    width: 33.333333%;
  }
  #visit {
    width: 25%;
    float: left;
  }
  #points {
    width: 25%;
    float: right;
  }
  #main {
    margin: 10px 27.0833333% 0 26.0416667%;
  }
}
```

So, to convert to a proportional width, we divide the pixel width of an element by the overall layout width, right?

Not so fast!

Sometimes the "context" can change…

Context switching

Hey. I'm going to start offering some new beer specials, and I want to be able to feature those on the site—can you adjust the design?

Mike has a new monthly special that he wants to post on the Splendid Walrus site. Instead of text and a single image in the main column, as it is now, he wants to display the beer labels of two very special, limited-edition stouts—floated next to each other. In our pixel-based reference design, this looks like:

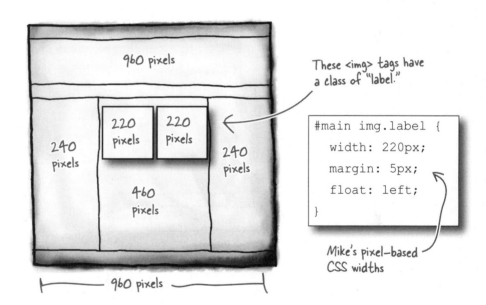

These <img> tags have a class of "label."

```
#main img.label {
    width: 220px;
    margin: 5px;
    float: left;
}
```

Mike's pixel-based CSS widths

It's tempting to think that the formula for converting these image widths to be fluid would be:

$$\frac{220 \text{ pixels}}{960 \text{ pixels}} \simeq 22.916667\%$$

Does this formula look right to you?

What's wrong with this picture?

The context changed!

If we set the images to span 22.9166667%, they will span 22.916667% all right—22.916667% *of their containing element.*

The containing element of these images isn't `body` (100% width, or 960 pixels in our reference design), it's `div#main`, which has a width of about 460 pixels (47.91667% of 960 pixels in proportional parlance). So we have just told the images to span a little less than 23% of 460 pixels—too small!

$$\frac{220 \text{ pixels}}{960 \text{ pixels}} = 22.916667\%$$

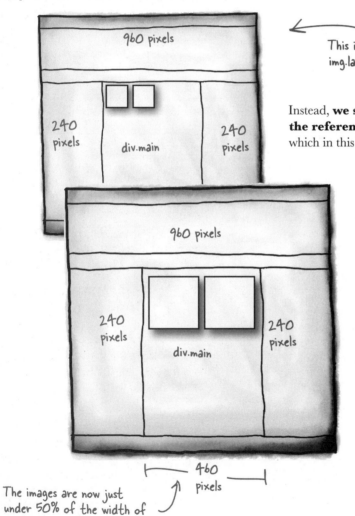

This is what you'll get if you set the width of img.label to be 22.916667%. Uh oh.

Instead, **we set the context in our formula to be the reference width of the containing element**, which in this case is 460 pixels.

Do this!

$$\frac{220 \text{ pixels}}{460 \text{ pixels}} = 47.826087\%$$

New context: width of div#main, the containing element.

The images are now just under 50% of the width of div#main—that's more like it.

Setting image widths as percentages? Turns out, this is on the right track to fixing one of our other problems with the mobile layout. Remember that photo that is too big and messes up the page width? We can use a variant of what we're doing here to fix that!

Fluid images ← And media!

There's a lot of power in this little gem of CSS:

```
img, object {
    max-width: 100%;
}
```

Ka-pow!

With this quick addition, we help to prevent any image or embedded media object from being wider than its containing element. Because they are limited to 100% width—100% of the width of their containing element—images and media obey their parents and don't try to break outside of the boundaries. Nice!

Fluid images and media, like fluid grids, scale proportionally within the layout.

A sad farewell...

Most great things don't come without a bit of sacrifice. To use the fluid technique on images and media, we have to forego our old friends: the width and height attributes.

The CSS rule above will override a width attribute but will not affect a height attribute. That means that, if we use height and width attributes, we could end up with an image that scales its width but not its height. End result: a sad-looking squished image in the wrong aspect ratio.

OK, there are some workarounds for this, and removing these attributes is not awesome. But we're going to jettison the height and width attributes for now.

Watch it!

Fluid images are not a get-out-of-jail-free technique.

Just because an image scales down on a narrower screen doesn't mean that it isn't still, at heart, a large image. An 800 KB JPEG is still an 800 KB JPEG, even if it's crammed down into a 120-pixel-wide column.

In Chapter 2, we'll talk about techniques to deliver different images to different devices and browsers, saving on otherwise wasted bandwidth and processor power (required to do the actual scaling).

Still, it's a powerful technique, and one definitely worth having in your arsenal.

Are we there yet?

We're making progress toward a responsive design that adapts to more devices. But we have a few things left to track down:

☐ Convert the pixel-based layout to a fluid one, using proportional widths instead of fixed.

We still need to convert the mobile CSS (we did the desktop CSS already).

☐ Make the default body font size 100% so our page's fonts can scale up and down proportionally.

☐ Fix the broken YouTube video.

☑ Fix the image that is too wide.

We did this using the fluid images technique.

Spiff up the mobile CSS

There are just a few mobile-specific CSS rules we need to convert to be fluid.

```css
@media screen and (max-width: 4
  body, .header, .footer, .navi
  {
    width: 320px;
  }
.column {
  margin: 1em 0;
  border-bottom: 1px dashed #
}
.navigation ul li {
  width: 106.6667px;
}
#visit, #points, #main {
  width: 320px;
}
```

current (fixed)

```css
@media screen and (max-width: 480px) {
  body, .header, .footer, .navigation {
    width: 100%;
  }
.column {
  margin: 1em 0;
  border-bottom: 1px dashed #7b96bc;
}
.navigation ul li {
  width: 33.333333%;
}
#visit, #points, #main {
  width: 100%;
}
```

Hey! Now that we're proportional here, these two rules are exactly the same as the desktop ones (see page 30). Might as well put them in the common structural CSS instead of having them in two places.

updated (fluid)

Details, details

Let's take care of a few remaining details to make our updated version of the Splendid Walrus site totally responsive.

Set up flexible fonts

So far, our layout is adaptive, but the fonts are stodgy and rigid. Just as percentages are the fluid ying to pixels' fixed-width yang, **ems** are proportional font-size units. Mike used ems in his original CSS, so we'll just add the following rule to the <body> element to be extra thorough:

```css
body {
  background: #f9f3e9;
  color: #594846;
  font: 100% "Adobe Caslon Pro",
  "Georgia", "Times New Roman", serif;
}
```

This baseline font-size reset is the CSS equivalent of dotting our *i*'s and crossing our *t*'s: it's setting an explicit reference against which the other font sizes in the CSS are defined. Not a big deal; just keeping things tidy!

Fix the YouTube video

Lots of mobile devices don't support Adobe Flash. The markup for the embedded YouTube is out of date: YouTube now provides an iframe-based embedding snippet that will work just fine on an iPhone (and other modern devices). We need to edit the *index.html* file and replace the current embed code.

```html
<object width="230" height="179"
type="application/x-shockwave-flash"
data="http://www.youtube.com/v/O-
jOEAufDQ4?fs=1&amp;hl=en_US&amp;rel=0"><embed
src=... /></object>
```

Instead of this
(Flash-only) version

Use this!

```html
<iframe src="http://www.youtube.com/embed/O-
jOEAufDQ4" style="max-width:100%"></iframe>
```

Font Sizes Up Close

With this edit to the CSS rule for the <body> element, we're setting the baseline font size for the page to be 100%. But what does 100% mean? Here's a quick-and-dirty (and *approximate*) rule of thumb:

1em = 100% ≈ 12pt ≈ 16px

But recall that we aim to adapt our content to the user's environment. If a user has changed the browser's font size, 100% is going to represent a different absolute size.

Also keep in mind that fonts on mobile devices are a complex thing, and that in some cases, 1em might equate to a (significantly) different point or pixel size.

This technique isn't limited to Flash! Other media can be made fluid this way, as well.

YouTube's newer embed code determines the appropriate video format to use depending on the browser. It can supply HTML5 video instead of Flash for devices—like Mike's iPhone—that support it. We simply grabbed this newer snippet from the "embed" section of this video's YouTube page.

Remember to be responsible

Just like fluid image resizing doesn't actually reduce the file size of images, neither does fluid media change the size of the actual media. It's up to you to determine whether using video (or other multimedia) on mobile devices is worth the file size and processor oomph required for playback.

Long Exercise

OK! Let's get all of these changes in place to give The Splendid Walrus a mobile-friendly site that uses Responsive Web Design techniques.

Edit the styles.css file

1 Edit the CSS rules within the media query for lower-resolution devices. Convert these widths to be proportional (page 34).

2 Identify the structural CSS rules that are common between both mobile and desktop variants now that they are proportional (page 34). Remove these rules from the media-query-specific sections and put them in the common structural section of the CSS file.

3 Add the CSS from page 33 to implement fluid images (and media).

4 Update the CSS rules for the `<body>` element to add a proportional font size baseline (page 35).

Edit the index.html file

5 Replace the Flash-only embedded YouTube with the smarter, `iframe` variant on page 35.

Try resizing your browser window and watching the content adapt.

Let 'er rip!

6 Save your changes and load the *index.html* page in any web browser.

Q: OK. I've seen ems as units in CSS, but I don't quite get it. What's the point?

A: 1em is—unspectacularly—a representation of the current font size, in the current context. That doesn't sound terribly exciting. But the magic comes when you define your font sizes in relation to this. So, if you set your `<h1>` element to display at 1.5em, it will be 150% of the baseline font size of its containing element.

You can actually use the same fluid formula to generate fluid, em-based font sizes from fixed font sizes. To create a fluid version of an 18-point font in a context where the baseline font is 16 points, you can do $18/16 = 1.125em$ (target/context = result).

Q: Wait. Why is it 1.125em instead of 112.5%?

A: Mostly tradition and clarity, but ems do tend to work a smidge better across platforms. It is common web practice to define block element widths in percentages and font sizes in ems. With some really teeny exceptions, percentages and ems are interchangeable for font sizes. About those teeny exceptions: we set the `<body>` element `font-size` to 100% to account for them.

Q: Is there any other use for CSS media queries beyond the mobile web?

A: Definitely. An example: just as mobile devices often represent the lower end of the screen resolution spectrum, some of the newer widescreen monitors and televisions have very high resolution. Sometimes it makes sense to adapt a layout—say, to add more columns—for these window widths.

Q: What actually caused the weird gap at the right side of the screen in the exercise way back on page 7?

A: This one's iPhone-specific. When displaying a web page "zoomed out" (i.e., when it's acting like a desktop browser), mobile Safari on the iPhone assumes a viewport width of 980 pixels. Before mobile optimization, the Splendid Walrus layout was 960 pixels wide, which leaves an awkward, 20-pixel gap on the right.

Q: What's the deal with the "3" in "CSS3 media queries"?

A: There are several versions of CSS. It's tempting to say that there are three, but the situation is a bit more cloudy. CSS2, which was published as a "recommendation" way back in 1998, is the flavor with which most web developers have had a longstanding familiarity. Media types were introduced with CSS2.

CSS3 is a different beast than earlier versions of CSS, in that it is modularized— there are something like 40 different modules, instead of a single big, complex spec. Fortunately, the Media Queries module is one of the more complete and stable.

Q: If CSS3 isn't all the way "done," do browsers support it?

A: Like we said, it's a jungle out there. Adoption for some of the more complete pieces of CSS3 is becoming widespread, but, as we'll see a bit later, is far from something that can be assumed in the mobile space.

Q: Why does the right column show up before the main column in the mobile layout?

A: The `div#points` content comes before the `div#main` content in the HTML markup. In the desktop layout, floats are used to position the `#points` content, such that it appears to the right of the `#main` content. The mobile layout doesn't use floats, and as such, the content is displayed in the order it occurs in the HTML.

Q: You skipped the @import syntax for media types. And can I use @import syntax with media queries?

A: @import syntax doesn't get a lot of love. So little, in fact, that we didn't even mention it. But, yes, it absolutely works for including stylesheets based on media types and for media queries, too.

Long Exercise Solution

Let's walk through the resulting CSS file and look at our changes.

```css
body {
    background: #f9f3e9;
    color: #594846;
    font: 100% "Adobe Caslon Pro", Georgia,
      "Times New Roman", serif;
}
```

This is right near the top of the CSS file.

To save space, we won't show these rules here.

...shared typography, colors, borders, etc. (shared, nonstructural CSS)...

Shared structural CSS

```css
.header, .footer {
    clear: both;
}
.header {
    background:url(images/w.png)
no-repeat;
    height: 200px;
}
.navigation {
    min-height: 25px;
}
img, object {
    max-width: 100%;
}
.navigation ul li {
    width: 33.333%;
}
.header, .footer, .navigation {
    width: 100%;
}
```

And now, the resolution-specific structural CSS.

Structural CSS for larger
browser windows (e.g., desktop)

```
@media screen and (min-width:481px) {
  .column {
    margin: 10px 1.04166667% 0 0;
  }
  #visit {
    width: 25%;
    float: left;
  }
  #points {
    width: 25%;
    float: right;
  }
  #main {
    margin: 10px 27.0833333% 0 26.0416667%;
  }
}
```

Structural CSS for smaller
browser windows (e.g.,
mobile devices)

```
@media screen and (max-width:480px) {
  .column {
    margin: 1em 0;
    border-bottom: 1px dashed
#7b96bc;
  }
  #visit, #points, #main {
    width: 100%;
  }
}
```

That's a responsive site!

You guys made big improvements, and hardly touched the HTML at all!

The photo fits correctly on this Android Nexus S phone, thanks to the fluid images technique.

Looking good on the Motorola Backflip (Android)

BRAIN POWER

We're using the same header background image in our mobile-optimized CSS, even though it's getting seriously cut off. Can you think of how to use RWD techniques to use a *different* image (to save on bandwidth and improve performance)?

Responsive design is also a state of mind

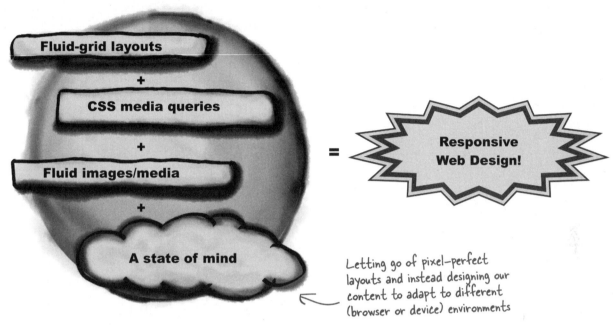

Fluid-grid layouts

+

CSS media queries

+

Fluid images/media

+

A state of mind

= Responsive Web Design!

Letting go of pixel-perfect layouts and instead designing our content to adapt to different (browser or device) environments

BULLET POINTS

- The mobile web is not unlike the Wild West—it's full of surprises and adventure. The mobile web browser landscape is diverse, and, sometimes, crazy-making.

- Just because we can use the same layout on a mobile device as in a "traditional" browser doesn't mean we necessarily should.

- **Responsive Web Design** (RWD) is a collection of approaches to make our web content adapt to the user, not the other way around (forcing the user to look at rigidly formatted pages).

- RWD is a combination of **CSS3 media queries**, **fluid-grid layouts**, and **fluid images**. It's also a way of thinking about layout and content.

- **CSS3 media queries** let us apply CSS selectively to different user environments based on the current value of relevant media features.

- **Media types** (e.g., `screen`, `print`, `projection`) have **media features** (`width`, `color`, `monochrome`, `orientation`). It's these media features we evaluate in our media queries.

- A **CSS media query** is a logical expression. When it evaluates to `TRUE`, the enclosed CSS rules are applied.

- A **fluid layout** is one that uses proportional widths instead of fixed widths such that the content of the page scales and flows naturally across a range of window widths.

- **Fluid images** are a CSS technique that keeps outsized images (or media) from "breaking out" of their parent elements when the parent element width is smaller than that of the image (or media). The images and media scale down as the parent element scales down.

- Using a simple **`font-size` reset** on the `<body>` element and defining font sizes in ems or percentages keeps our type fluid.

2 responsible responsiveness

Mobile-first Responsive Web Design

Darling, I don't care if you *are* cold. If you knew how much optimization it had taken to look this good, you'd wear a bikini on the beach in winter, too.

That's a beautiful mobile site. But beauty is only skin deep.

Under the covers, it's a different thing entirely. It may look like a mobile site, but it's still a desktop site in mobile clothing. If we want this site to be greased lightning on mobile, we need to start with **mobile first**. We'll begin by dissecting the current site to find the desktop bones hiding in its mobile closet. We'll clean house and start fresh with **progressive enhancement**, building from the basic content all the way to a desktop view. When we're done, you'll have a page that is optimized regardless of the screen size.

Just when you thought it was time to celebrate...

Mike called in a panic. As a reformed web developer, he normally resists the urge to tinker with his site, but he fell off the wagon and decided to make a few tweaks. He thinks he broke the Splendid Walrus site and needs help.

Mike added pictures for all of his new brews to the On Tap Now page. He didn't modify the code other than to add pictures, but now the page is loading very slowly on mobile phones. It's so slow that customers have started complaining.

> Sorry, guys. Not sure what I did, but the Splendid Walrus site is now dog slow.

Check out the On Tap Now page at http://hf-mw.com/ch2/chapter2/ontap.html.

Is there really a problem? How do we know?

Jim: Poor Mike. He knows just enough to get in trouble.

Frank: Exactly. But in this case, I'm not so sure he did anything wrong. Mobile phones have slower networks and processors. Of course the page loads slowly.

Jim: That makes sense, but it still seems slower than expected. Mike says that even on a WiFi network, it is unbearable. And he has a brand-new smartphone.

Joe: Hmm…it sounds like we should at least look into it to see if there is something obvious slowing it down.

Frank: How will we know what's going on? It could just be the network or any number of things between the phone and the server.

Joe: I've been using a plug-in for Firefox that gives you a grade on your page performance. We could use something like that.

Jim: That sounds awesome.

Frank: Can we install plug-ins on mobile browsers?

Joe: Ugh, you're right. There's no way to install plug-ins on my phone. Some of my favorite developer tools are browser plug-ins. Without them, how do we know what's really going on?

Jim: The other day, Kim was showing me how you can watch every request that is made on our WiFi network through the network router's log page. Could we look at something like that and watch what the phone does?

Frank: That's a great idea. But instead, let's use a *proxy server*. It is very similar to what Kim showed you, but it is designed for exactly this purpose. If we hook up the phone to a proxy server, we can see all of the web requests that the phone makes.

Joe   Frank   Jim

The YSlow plug-in gives you a grade for performance based on how a web page is constructed. Get YSlow at this URL: yhoo.it/yslow. Performance is something every web developer—especially mobile web developers—should care about.

Speaking of which, we're going to spend a little time looking at performance. Don't worry. We'll get to mobile-first Responsive Web Design soon, and we promise all of this performance stuff is related.

Waitress, will you take my order please?

A famous athlete is stricken with food poisoning the night before a big match against his archrival. The police suspect foul play and have assigned a detective. The detective quickly starts questioning the best witness: the waitress.

The waitress took the food order, wrote down the request, and handed it to the cook. After the food was ready, the waitress brought the food out. The waitress saw everything.

Most of the time when you're on the Web, you're talking directly to the cook. Nothing is between you and the web server for the page you're visiting.

But if we have a proxy server act like a waitress, it will record both what was ordered and delivered by the browser. Now we can be our own detectives and dig into what actually happened.

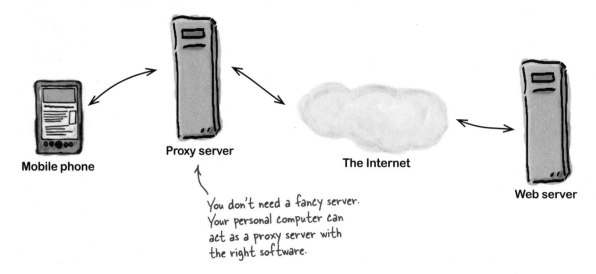

Mobile phone **Proxy server** **The Internet** **Web server**

You don't need a fancy server. Your personal computer can act as a proxy server with the right software.

Can I get a proxy to set up my proxy?

If you do a lot of mobile work, you may find it worth your while to learn how to set up a proxy server. It is the best way to see what's going on between the phone and server.

Unfortunately, setting up a proxy server can be a tad difficult. Thankfully, some kind souls at Blaze, a mobile performance company, have set up a free service that is the next best thing to installing your own tool.

What to do when things aren't blazing fast

Blaze provides Mobitest—a free mobile performance test using real iPhone and Android phones. Mobitest is located at *www.blaze.io/mobile*.

Blaze's Mobitest works like a proxy server. You tell it what web page URL you want to test and what device you want to test with. Mobitest then puts your test request in a queue for that device.

When the phone you requested is available, Blaze tracks all of the communication between its test phone and the web server so you can see what happened.

There is even a fun feature that records a video of the page loading so you can see what someone using that phone would see.

Test Drive

Ready for some detective work? It's time to figure out why the On Tap Now page is slow.

① Test the On Tap Now page at www.blaze.io/mobile.
The On Tap Now page is at *http://hf-mw.com/ch2/chapter2/ontap.html*.

② Look at the load time and page size.
The load time tells you how long the page took to load on this phone during this test. The page size is the total size of all resources associated with the page including HTML, CSS, JavaScript, images, fonts, etc.

③ Try two different phones and compare speeds.
Not only will the speed of networks vary, but the phones themselves may also vary in the speed at which they process and display pages.

Don't let its looks fool you, that's a BIG page

Yikes! The test says the page is approximately 3 megabytes in size. That would be a pretty big page for a desktop browser. It's a slow-moving elephant on a mobile phone.

In truth, it's too big for desktop too. Just because a screen is big doesn't mean the connection is fast. Performance matters everywhere.

No wonder Mike's customers complained about the page. It takes over 10 seconds to load on a test iPhone.

Blaze Mobitest results page using an iPhone

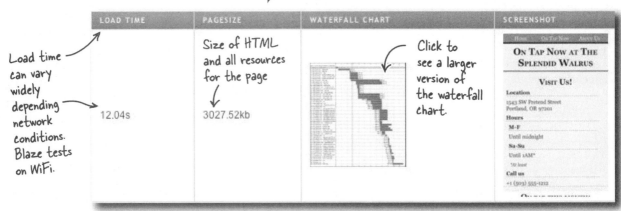

Load time can vary widely depending network conditions. Blaze tests on WiFi.

Size of HTML and all resources for the page

Click to see a larger version of the waterfall chart.

> What is a waterfall chart? I looked at it, and it doesn't tell me what's making the page so big. Is the chart even useful?

Waterfall charts are a common web performance report.

The chart shows the files that the browser requested from the server to build the web page. The bars represent the length of time spent downloading a resource. The resources are listed in the order in which the browser requested them from the server.

But don't go chasing the waterfall on the Blaze report page. It doesn't have the details we need for our detective work. We're going to show you how to find a waterfall that is more useful.

There's gold in 'em HAR hills

There is a nugget buried in the Blaze Mobitest results page behind the tiny **View HAR file** link.

Click that link, and you will go to a new site called the *HTTP Archive Viewer* and see a more detailed waterfall than the test results page.

This waterfall chart shows us every resource that the browser downloaded in much more detail than the picture of the waterfall on the Blaze report page.

Top part of the Blaze Mobitest results page.

You'll find the "View HAR file" link next to the Twitter and Facebook links.

The preview tab contains a waterfall chart for the page we tested. It was generated from a HAR file.

HTTP Archive (HAR) Viewer

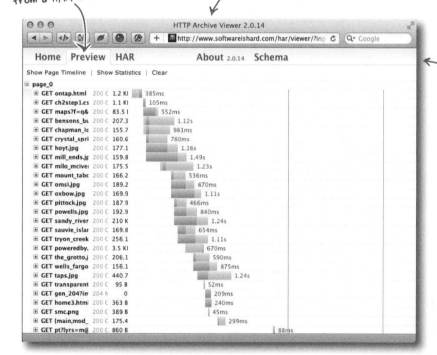

The HAR file can be used to make waterfall charts. Read more about HAR at httparchive.org.

HAR stands for HTTP Archive. It is a file specification that provides a standard way to record what happens when a browser requests a web page from a server.

Do you see any suspicious files being downloaded in the waterfall chart?

10,000-feet view: Show statistics

The HAR waterfall charts show you the files that were downloaded, how the server responded, and the time it took to download. But before we dig into the waterfall chart itself, let's take a look at the high-level statistics.

Click the Show Statistics link on the HAR Viewer page to see a series of four pie charts. The chart that matters most to us is the second one, which breaks down the page by type of file. Hover your mouse over each file type to see its total file size.

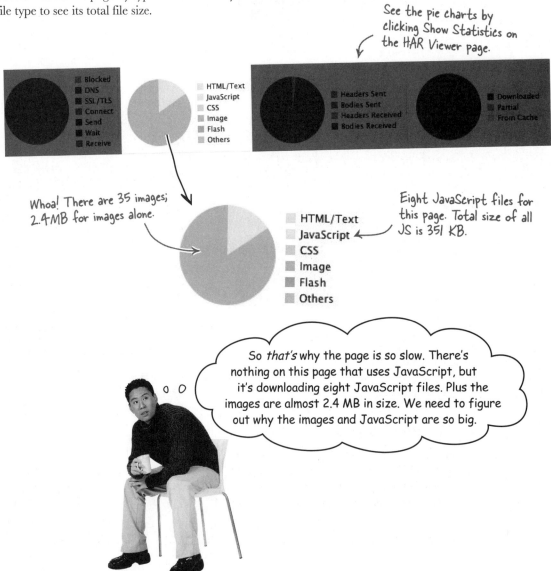

See the pie charts by clicking Show Statistics on the HAR Viewer page.

Whoa! There are 35 images; 2.4MB for images alone.

Eight JavaScript files for this page. Total size of all JS is 351 KB.

So *that's* why the page is so slow. There's nothing on this page that uses JavaScript, but it's downloading eight JavaScript files. Plus the images are almost 2.4 MB in size. We need to figure out why the images and JavaScript are so big.

Find the drags on page speed

Now it's time to dig into that waterfall chart to find where the big images and JavaScript are coming from. Here's a key to reading the chart.

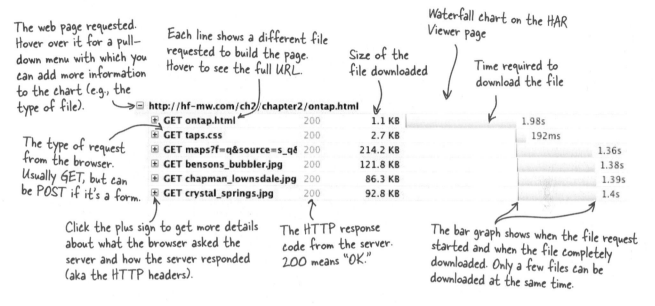

The web page requested. Hover over it for a pull-down menu with which you can add more information to the chart (e.g., the type of file).

Each line shows a different file requested to build the page. Hover to see the full URL.

Size of the file downloaded

Waterfall chart on the HAR Viewer page

Time required to download the file

The type of request from the browser. Usually GET, but can be POST if it's a form.

Click the plus sign to get more details about what the browser asked the server and how the server responded (aka the HTTP headers).

The HTTP response code from the server. 200 means "OK."

The bar graph shows when the file request started and when the file completely downloaded. Only a few files can be downloaded at the same time.

The amount of communication between the browser and the server can be overwhelming, but don't worry. You just need to look for two things: *which resources are the largest, and where is the JavaScript coming from?*

Exercise

Review the waterfall chart for the On Tap Now page. Find the five largest files and examine them. For each file, answer:

1 **What type of file is it?**

2 **What domain is the file coming from?**

3 **If the file is an image, what is its height and width?**
Hint: You may need to copy the image URL and open it in a new tab or download the image to find the dimensions.

What does this information tell you about what you might need to do to make the page faster?

Exercise Solution

Did you find the problems with the page? Let's review.

1 **What type of file is it?**
You can determine the type of file by hovering over the filename to see the full URL and extension. You can also add a column containing the file type so you can scan the list quickly.

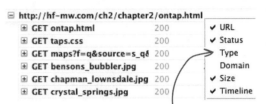

⊟ http://hf-mw.com/ch2/chapter2/ontap.html		
⊞ GET ontap.html	200	✔ URL
⊞ GET taps.css	200	✔ Status
⊞ GET maps?f=q&source=s_q&	200	→ Type
⊞ GET bensons_bubbler.jpg	200	Domain
⊞ GET chapman_lownsdale.jpg	200	✔ Size
⊞ GET crystal_springs.jpg	200	✔ Timeline

Hover over the page URL. Click on the down arrow next to the URL to add the file type column.

2 **What domain is the file coming from?**
Now we're getting somewhere. Check out where this big, 174.8 KB JavaScript file comes from.

The large file isn't the only suspicious file here. These files have strange names.

⊞ GET iVBORw0KGgoAA		?	328ms
⊞ GET {main,mod_util,m	200 text/jav 174.8 K		473ms
⊞ GET iVBORw0KGgoAA		?	152ms

Hover your mouse over the file name to see the full URL.

At 174.8 KB, this is the largest JavaScript file on the page.

⊞ GET iVBORw0KGgoAA	?	328ms
⊞ http://maps.gstatic.com/cat_js/intl/en_ALL/mapfiles/375b/maps2/{main,mod_util,mod_act,		
⊞ GET iVBORw0KGgoAA	?	152ms

Maps.gstatic.com is a domain for Google Maps. The browser is downloading JavaScript for a map that isn't displayed on the mobile view. Many of the mysterious files are related to Google Maps.

3 **If the file is an image, what is its height and width?**
Find the images with the largest file size. Copy the URL and open them in a new window. Without even looking at the height and width, you can tell that these images are far larger than the size they appear on a small screen.

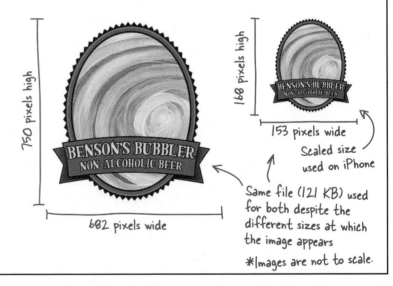

750 pixels high

682 pixels wide

168 pixels high

153 pixels wide

Scaled size used on iPhone

Same file (121 KB) used for both despite the different sizes at which the image appears

*Images are not to scale.

Where did that Google Maps JavaScript come from?

When you view the On Tap Now page on a mobile phone, the page doesn't contain a map. Why is that JavaScript downloaded? Let's open the page in our desktop browser and investigate.

Hey, there's the map. Mike must have set it up so that it only shows up on wider screens.

Hiding the map on the mobile makes some sense. It's a bit big for a small screen. Older phones may not be able to handle the map's complex JavaScript, and we've seen that the map has a lot of overhead.

So how did Mike hide the map?

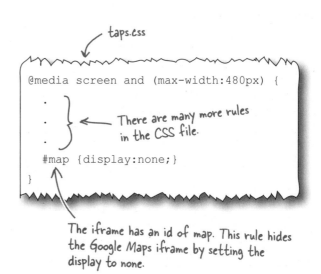

Hey, there's the elusive map!

One line to download them all

The map is included in the page via an `iframe`. The `iframe` loads all of the components necessary to make the map.

Look inside ontap.html to find this code.

```
<iframe id="map" width="300" height="300" frameborder="0" scrolling="no" marginheight="0" marginwidth="0" src="http://maps.google.com...""></iframe>
```

This single iframe causes 47 files to be downloaded!

Extremely long URL abbreviated

Mike hid the map with CSS

Mike figured out how we used media queries to modify the layout for mobile. He added in his own CSS rule inside our media query. The rule Mike added sets the display for the `iframe` to `none`.

Unfortunately, while setting the display to `none` will prevent the map from showing up, it doesn't prevent it from downloading.

taps.css

```
@media screen and (max-width:480px) {
  .
  .
  .
  #map {display:none;}
}
```

There are many more rules in the CSS file.

The iframe has an id of map. This rule hides the Google Maps iframe by setting the display to none.

What's with the big pictures?

The images on this page need to be put on a diet. Let's look at the waterfall to find the biggest images and see why they're so big.

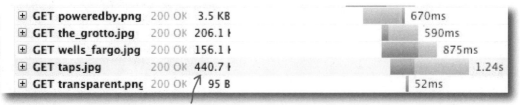

⊞ GET poweredby.png	200 OK 3.5 KB	670ms
⊞ GET the_grotto.jpg	200 OK 206.1	590ms
⊞ GET wells_fargo.jpg	200 OK 156.1	875ms
⊞ GET taps.jpg	200 OK 440.7	1.24s
⊞ GET transparent.png	200 OK 95 B	52ms

The taps.jpg file is 440.7 KB, making it the largest file on the page.

> But that huge file is the header image, and it isn't even displayed on mobile.

Right, but that doesn't mean it's not downloading.

The *taps.jpg* image has been hidden from the page in the same way as Google Maps—the display property has been set to none in the CSS. But, as we saw with the map, setting display:none doesn't stop the content from downloading.

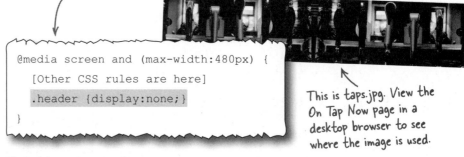

```
@media screen and (max-width:480px) {

    [Other CSS rules are here]

    .header {display:none; }

}
```

This is taps.jpg. View the On Tap Now page in a desktop browser to see where the image is used.

Fluid images are huge images

Another thing to notice from the waterfall is that the brew labels are all large files that range from 93 to 132 KB. They're desktop images scaled down to fit the screen using the fluid-image technique we learned in Chapter 1.

The total size of the 16 brew labels is nearly 2 MB. Finding a way to optimize these images is key to making the page faster.

So this isn't a new issue, but when we only had one or two images on the page, it wasn't noticeable. But when you put 16 brew labels on one page, suddenly the fluid images are an anchor slowing the page down.

It looks mobile friendly, but it isn't

Jim: Well, that's a bummer. I guess looks can be deceiving, eh?

Frank: At least we can tell Mike he didn't break the page.

Joe: Yeah, any of us could have made the same mistake. The problems are really bad on this particular page, but I think the same issues exist on every page on the site.

Frank: So what do we do? Build a whole separate site for the mobile version? Ditch Responsive Web Design?

Joe: Let's not get ahead of ourselves here. There's got to be a way to make it work. We're so close right now. Do the image and JavaScript problems have anything in common?

Jim: It seems like all of the problems stem from the fact that we're starting with desktop-appropriate content—images, maps, etc.—and then hiding that content.

Frank: Exactly. We've got big files going to the browser by default and then CSS is being used to try to cover them up. But it seems that, if we're not careful, the large files will still be downloaded by mobile devices. That's not the ideal fallback behavior if something goes wrong.

Joe: What if we flipped things around and sent the smallest files by default?

Jim: Oh, interesting. That might work. Start with the mobile templates first and then add on content for desktop.

Frank: What you're describing sounds a lot like *progressive enhancement.*

Joe: You're right. We've been using progressive enhancement for years. The only difference now is that we're starting from mobile and progressively enhancing the document to fit the desktop.

Jim: It seems like it should work. Let's try it out.

Progressive enhancement promotes building layered web pages. At minimum, everyone can see and use the content. Those with more capable browsers get additional layers of style and interactivity that enhance the experience.

Mobile-first Responsive Web Design

Mobile-first Responsive Web Design (RWD) is exactly what the name suggests: RWD techniques that start from a mobile template. Despite its simplicity, there is a lot of power that comes from this approach.

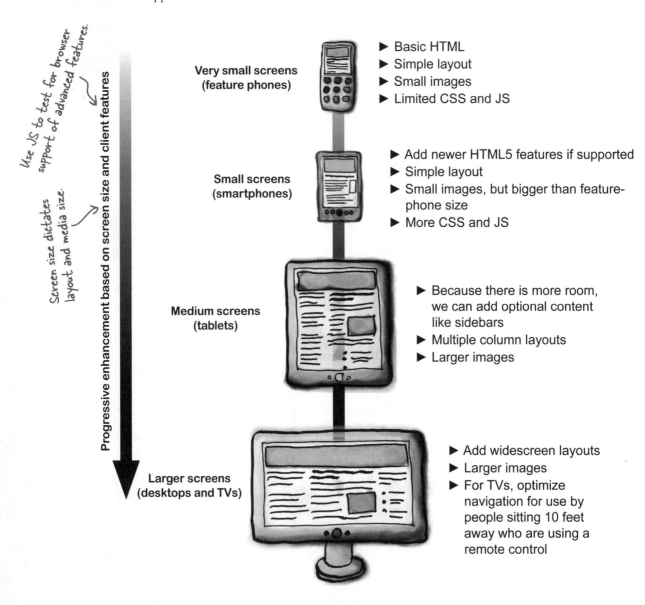

Use JS to test for browser support of advanced features.

Screen size dictates layout and media size.

Progressive enhancement based on screen size and client features

Very small screens (feature phones)
- ▶ Basic HTML
- ▶ Simple layout
- ▶ Small images
- ▶ Limited CSS and JS

Small screens (smartphones)
- ▶ Add newer HTML5 features if supported
- ▶ Simple layout
- ▶ Small images, but bigger than feature-phone size
- ▶ More CSS and JS

Medium screens (tablets)
- ▶ Because there is more room, we can add optional content like sidebars
- ▶ Multiple column layouts
- ▶ Larger images

Larger screens (desktops and TVs)
- ▶ Add widescreen layouts
- ▶ Larger images
- ▶ For TVs, optimize navigation for use by people sitting 10 feet away who are using a remote control

*These are just examples of enhancements. What you do depends on the project.

What is progressive enhancement?

Progressive enhancement views web design in a series of layers. The first layer is the content. Combine that with semantic markup to create structured content. If you stop right there, you have a document that nearly every browser in the world can read.

After you've got the basics out of the way, you add a presentation layer using CSS and a behavior layer using JavaScript. You never assume the browser supports those features, but if it does, visitors get a better experience.

For many years, web developers commonly built things that only worked on the most advanced browsers and tried to make sure the web page degraded gracefully on older browsers. Progressive enhancement flips this practice around.

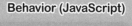

Progressive enhancement is like a layer cake. Mmm. Cake.

Benefits of mobile-first design

Mobile-first RWD isn't that different from progressive enhancement. Recognizing this fact, many call it *content-first design* instead because content is the first layer of progressive enhancement.

Regardless of what you call it, starting from the most basic document not only reaches the most people, it also has beneficial side effects.

Mobile first is like a small-plate diet. Simply by eating on a smaller plate, you're likely to eat less food.

The desktop home page is an all-you-can-eat buffet. All sorts of junk gets thrown on it.

Mobile is a small plate. You have to choose carefully and prioritize your content.

And once you've got a focused mobile site, you're better prepared to ask the tough questions like whether or not the things that didn't make the cut for mobile are really important enough to add back in for desktop.

Semantic Markup Up Close

Semantic markup means HTML tags and attributes that convey the meaning of the content.

For example, content surrounded by an `<h1>` tag is more important on the page than content marked up with an `<h2>` or a `<p>` tag.

`class` and `id` attributes can also add semantic meaning to documents if their values are things like `calendar` and not presentation values like `left` or `top`. Many web developers use classes in a standard way called *microformats* to provide more semantic meaning. Learn more at *www.microformats.org*.

Semantic markup doesn't mean you completely avoid tags like `<div>` and `<span>` that don't add meaning. Instead, you choose the right semantic tags and attributes for the content of a page whenever possible.

Let's turn this web page around

Because we're already using RWD, making our page mobile first won't take too long. Here is a short list of changes we're going to make.

☐ Make the HTML as simple as possible and swap the order of the CSS ← *We'll explain why in a bit.*
   so that the mobile version is first.

☐ Fix CSS background images so that only one file gets downloaded per image. Make sure `display:none` is being used appropriately.

☐ Supply different source files for `<img>` tags at different screen resolutions. Make sure the right size image is downloaded.

☐ Use JavaScript to add Google Maps to the page when the browser can support it and the document is wide enough to accommodate it.

The current structure of the On Tap Now page

Open up the *ontap.html* file for the Splendid Walrus site in the *chapter2* directory. The file looks very similar to the document we built in Chapter 1:

```
<div class="navigation">...</div>
<div class="header">...</div>
<h1>...</h1>
<div id="visit" class="column">...</div>
<div id="ontap" class="column">...</div>
<div class="footer">...</div>
```

Two columns instead of three →

Instead of a <div> called "main," Mike has created a new column with the id of "ontap." That <div> contains the list of current beers.

Because we did a good job of creating a template with semantic markup, the document is clean and simple already. It looks like our main task to make the content mobile first will be removing the Google map.

Because we're going to need to reference the code later, let's use HTML comments to prevent the iframe from being included in the page.

Comment out the Google Maps iframe by surrounding it with <!-- and -->.

Find the iframe in the #visit <div>.

```
<!--
  <iframe id="map" width="300" height="300" frameborder="0" scrolling="no"
marginheight="0" marginwidth="0" src="http://maps.google.com..."></iframe>
-->
```

Am I on a new page or not?

 The On Tap Now page looks so similar to the home page. How can visitors tell they're on a different page?

Good catch. We have a problem with the order of the content.

On the home page, it was fine if the first thing on the mobile view was the Visit Us information. But if the Visit Us content repeats on every page, visitors won't be able to tell that the page has changed without scrolling down.

We need to reorder the content so the On Tap Now info comes before the Visit Us content.

 **Do this!**

Copy everything in the `<div>` with the `visit id` and paste it below the `ontap <div>`.

```
<div class="navigation">...</div>
<div class="header">...</div>
<h1>...</h1>
<div id="ontap" class="column">...</div>
<div id="visit" class="column">...</div>
<div class="footer">...</div>
```

 ☢BRAIN POWER

Is the Visit Us content essential on this page? Would it be better to move it to a separate page and link to it? Or maybe leave it out of the mobile page and add it using JavaScript if the page is rendered on a larger screen?

Fix the content floats

The change we made to the order of the content broke the layout in a desktop browser. The Visit Us section is at the bottom of the page.

In Chapter 1, we mentioned how putting the right column before the main column was a trick to make it easier to handle floats for layouts. If you want a block to float next to something, you need to put it first in the source order.

Don't worry, though. There is a simple fix here. We've been floating the Visit Us content to the left of the On Tap Now content. Instead, we need to float the On Tap Now content to the right of the Visit Us content.

Open *taps.css* and make the following two changes.

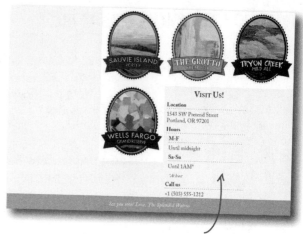

Visit Us is floating beneath the beer labels.

Before

```
@media screen and (min-width:481px) {
  .column {
    margin: 10px 1.04166667% 0 0;
  }
  #visit {
    width: 31.25%;
    float: left;
  }
  #points {
    width: 25%;
    float: right;
  }
  #main {
    margin: 10px 27.0833333% 0
26.0416667%;
  }
  #ontap {
    margin: 10px 0 0 32%;
  }
}
```

Change this... ...to this.

Change this... ...to this.

After

```
@media screen and (min-width:481px) {
  .column {
    margin: 10px 1.04166667% 0 0;
  }
  #visit {
    margin: 0 68.75% 0 0;
  }
  #points {
    width: 25%;
    float: right;
  }
  #main {
    margin: 10px 27.0833333% 0
26.0416667%;
  }
  #ontap {
    width: 67%;
    float: right;
    margin: 10px 0 0 0;
  }
}
```

Using 67% instead of 68.75% gives us a little wiggle room for the columns.

Mobile-first media queries

Now for a little housekeeping. In Chapter 1, we started with a desktop website and made it mobile. We're going to turn this around and start from the simplest content and build up to the desktop (and beyond).

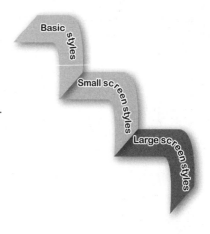

But first we have a confession. *Mobile first* is a little bit of a misnomer when it comes to the CSS. Before we apply any media queries for small screens, we're going to set all of the basic styles—for color, type, etc.—and then enhance them.

There is a good reason for doing this. Many mobile browsers don't understand media queries at all. So we need to make sure they at least get the basic style rules.

Put your CSS house in order

CSS files are often like the kitchen junk drawer. It may start out organized and logical, but over time chaos takes over. To put mobile-first media queries in place, you may need to untangle the basic style rules from the layout rules.

Fortunately, the CSS we built in Chapter 1 is already in good shape. Most of the basic style rules are already at the beginning of the file, with the media queries adding the layout and formatting later in the document. All we need to do is put the mobile media query before the desktop query.

CSS cascade follows the path from small screen to large screen.

Do this!

```
/* Wider viewports/higher resolutions (e.g. desktop)  */

@media screen and (min-width:481px) {

   [Desktop layout rules here]

}

/* Mobile/lower-resolution devices */

@media screen and (max-width:480px) {

   [Mobile layout rules here]

}
```

Move the mobile media query block above the desktop media query. By doing this, we're making sure the cascading effect of CSS is consistent with our mobile-first progressive enhancement approach.

Test Drive

We've made quite a few changes to the page:

- Removed Google Maps
- Reordered the markup
- Fixed the floats
- Reordered the media queries

We better check to make sure things still work. Load the page in a few desktop and mobile browsers to see how it looks. Be sure to check Internet Explorer.

Surprise! The page is broken in Internet Explorer

Don't tell us you didn't see this coming the moment we hinted you might want to test the page in Internet Explorer (IE). Battling IE is a rite of passage for web developers. You've probably been scarred enough from previous battles that you knew there was an IE-sized monkey wrench awaiting us.

So what's the catch? *IE doesn't support media queries.*

Now before you toss the book aside and curse us for teaching something that doesn't work in the world's most popular browser, take a deep breath and relax. There are ways to work around IE's (many) shortcomings.

We're being a little too harsh. IE9 and above do support media queries, so help is coming.

Because IE 8 and below don't support media queries, IE isn't getting the CSS rules that create columns.

Internet Explorer's escape hatch: conditional comments

Microsoft has provided a nice tool to help web developers target code specifically to Internet Explorer via conditional comments.

This tests to see if the browser is less than (lt) IE 9 and that it isn't IE Mobile (!IEMobile). We exclude IE Mobile because it should get the mobile layout. IE9 and above understand media queries, so they don't need the extra help.

See the full syntax for conditional comments at http://bit.ly/ie-comments.

Look carefully. The HTML comment opens on the first line, but doesn't close until "-->" is included on the final line. Other browsers will see this as a comment and ignore its content.

```
<!--[if (lt IE 9)&(!IEMobile)]>
<link rel="stylesheet" type="text/css" href="layout.css" media="all" />
<![endif]-->
```

If the conditions are met, IE will do whatever is in between the opening [if] statement and the closing [endif]. The example shows a link to a CSS file, but it could be anything you would find in an HTML document.

Use conditional comments with a media query

You probably noticed that the conditional comment points to *layout.css*. Time to create that file.

We're going to grab some of the rules from the current stylesheet. We've called the new file *layout.css* because it will only be used for browsers that have enough screen real estate that multicolumn layouts make sense.

① **Create a blank text file called layout.css and copy the desktop rules into it.**

Make sure you copy everything between the beginning and end of the media query, but not the `@media` rule itself.

taps.css

After you copy them, remove the rules and the surrounding media query from taps.css. We'll reapply the rules to the HTML document next.

```css
/* Wider viewports/higher resolutions
(e.g. desktop)  */
@media screen and (min-width:481px) {
  .column {
    margin: 10px 1.04166667% 0 0;
  }
  #visit {
    margin: 0 68.75% 0 0;
  }
  #points {
    width: 25%;
    float: right;
  }
  #main {
    margin: 10px 27.0833333% 0
26.0416667%;
  }
  #ontap {
    width: 67%;
    float: right;
    margin: 10px 0 0 0;
  }
}
```

Copy these rules to your new file. ←

layout.css

```css
  .column {
    margin: 10px 1.04166667% 0 0;
  }
  #visit {
    margin: 0 68.75% 0 0;
  }
  #points {
    width: 25%;
    float: right;
  }
  #main {
    margin: 10px 27.0833333% 0
26.0416667%;
  }
  #ontap {
    width: 67%;
    float: right;
    margin: 10px 0 0 0;
  }
```

2 Add a link to the new stylesheet.

For browsers that support media queries, we're going to add a link
to the new *layout.css* file if the screen size is wide enough.

```
<link rel="stylesheet" type="text/css" href="taps.css" />
<link rel="stylesheet" type="text/css" href="layout.css" media="all and
(min-width: 481px)" />
```

Add this link tag
to ontap.html.

The 481px value for min-width was
copied from the media query we
removed from taps.css.

This is the media query syntax
for link tags that you learned
in Chapter 1.

3 Add the IE conditional comment.

We've got it working for most desktop browsers. Now we just need
to add the conditional comment we created earlier to finish up.

```
<link rel="stylesheet" type="text/css" href="taps.css" />
<link rel="stylesheet" type="text/css" href="layout.css" media="all and
(min-width: 481px)">
<!--[if (lt IE 9)&(!IEMobile)]>
<link rel="stylesheet" type="text/css" href="layout.css" media="all" />
<![endif]-->
```

The conditional comment repeats the line above it,
ensuring that desktop IE sees our layout.css file.

4 Time to test again.

Check the page in a browser that supports media queries and
different versions of Internet Explorer. Looks good, huh?

Even our persnickety old
friend IE is showing the
layout properly now.

there are no Dumb Questions

Q: With super-fast 4G phones on the horizon, is performance really that big of a deal?

A: Absolutely. Even 4G phones end up on the EDGE network occasionally (EDGE is an older, slower network). Studies show that slow sites decrease usage and directly affect the bottom line.

Q: Why am I getting different results from the Blaze Mobitest?

A: There are many reasons why this can occur. Page download time will change with every test depending on network traffic. Google Maps code is different for each operating system and may change over time. The behavior of the phones will also change as new versions of the operating systems are released. For the book, we tested using Blaze's iOS 4.3, Android 2.2, and Android 2.3 test devices.

Don't worry too much about the variations in test results. What matters is the code and images being downloaded unnecessarily.

Q: By separating the stylesheet into two files, aren't you making the site load more slowly?

A: It is true that the number of HTTP requests makes a big difference in the download speed. So we shouldn't recklessly add requests. In this case, we thought it made more sense to separate them so IE could use the same file.

Q: You mentioned that setting up a proxy server might make sense. What do you recommend?

A: There are many proxy servers, including some fantastic open source ones. We happen to be fans of a commercial product called Charles Proxy.

Q: The lack of plug-ins seems like a big deal. How do you get anything done without Firebug and Web Inspector?

A: It isn't easy. First, a lot of your debugging work can be done in a desktop browser so long as you are careful to test on real devices at some point in the process.

There are also a lot of new tools that attempt to get around the plug-in limitations. The Mobile Perf Bookmarklet (*http://bit.ly/mw-perf*) includes many performance tools. weinre (*http://bit.ly/mweinre*) and Opera Dragonfly (*http://opera.com/dragonfly*) let you run Web Inspector on your desktop and examine what is going on in the phone browser.

Q: It doesn't seem like much changed when we switched to mobile-first media queries. Why bother?

A: For this page, there wasn't a big difference between a desktop-first CSS file and a mobile-first one. In our experience, however, this is the exception. With more complex styles, you often want the wider rules to override some, but not all, of the styles set for smaller screens. Reordering the media queries ensures that the CSS cascading behavior is consistent with the goal of progressively enhancing the page as the screen gets wider.

Q: It seems like the order of content may often be different between desktop and mobile. How do you handle this in more complex pages?

A: Ah, you caught that, huh? Yes, this is one of the common challenges for Responsive Web Design. In the long run, the Flexible Box Module (Flexbox) in CSS3 promises an easy way to reorder content in stylesheets. Combine Flexbox with media queries, and you can completely reorder pages as needed. Unfortunately, Flexbox is still young and isn't fully supported. So developers resort to JavaScript to reorder content or combine RWD with device detection (see Chapter 5). Frankly, content ordering and image handling remain two of the biggest challenges for RWD.

Q: Will the versions of IE that don't support media queries see the responsive design? Aren't media queries necessary?

A: Internet Explorer will display the desktop version. It will still have the fluid grids and flexible images. But it won't change based on any of the media query instructions. If media query support is critical, there is an open source library called Respond.js that fills in support for media queries for older IE versions. This is a fairly intensive script, so be sure to test extensively if you decide to implement it.

How are we doing?

We've got the basics in place and our CSS in order. What's next on our list?

☑ Make the HTML as simple as possible and swap the order of the CSS so that the mobile version is first.

☐ Fix CSS background images so that only one file gets downloaded per image. Make sure `display:none` is being used appropriately.

☐ Supply different source files for `<img>` tags at different screen resolutions. Make sure the right size image is downloaded.

☐ Use JavaScript to add Google Maps to the page when the browser can support it and the document is wide enough to accommodate it.

Play taps for the header image

Our waterfall chart showed us that we had one large CSS background image that was being hidden with `display:none`. Despite the fact that the image never shows up on the page, the browser still downloads the image.

So let's make sure the image is only downloaded when it is needed. How do we do that? By putting it in a media query so it only gets downloaded if the screen is wider than 480 pixels.

But instead of creating a whole new media query, put the CSS rules in *layout.css*, which is already being included in the page via a media query in the `<link>` tag.

Remember our friend, taps.jpg, which downloads on mobile but never shows up on the page?

Copy these lines from taps.css and add them to the end of layout.css.

```
.header {
    background:URL('images/taps.jpg') repeat-x;
    height: 300px;
}
```

Delete these lines from taps.css after you add them to layout.css.

TEST DRIVE

Check the On Tap Now page using the Blaze Mobitest to make sure *taps.jpg* is no longer being downloaded. Try both iPhone and Android devices. You can use *http://hf-mw.com/ch2/ex/3/ontap.html* if your copy of the page is not on a public server.

It works on iPhone, but the image is still downloading on Android.

GET sauvie_island.jpg	200 OK	102.5 KB
⊞ **GET tryon_creek.jpg**	200 OK	149.9 KB
⊞ **GET taps.jpg**	200 OK	440.7 KB
20 Requests		**2.1 MB**

Android appears to still be downloading taps.jpg.

Blaze's Mobitest says Android is still downloading the image, but it is a false report.

Blaze had to modify its phones to make them work for remote testing. This causes some occasional odd behavior.

When you use a stock Android phone, the *taps.jpg* image will not be downloaded.

Going old school with image optimization

Back in the early days of the Web, web developers spent a lot time worrying about image optimization. As bandwidth has increased, web developers stopped worrying about eking out every bit of performance from images. But mobile devices make image optimization paramount once again.

We'd argue that image optimization has always been paramount. Faster connections are never a given, even for desktop computers.

It looks like we can make the *taps.jpg* image smaller with some basic web image optimization. Changing the JPEG quality from 80 to 45 makes the image 78 KB instead of 440 KB, and you have to look very closely to see any difference in image quality.

For more on web image optimization, see Chapter 5 of Head First HTML with CSS & XHTML.

Images still not small enough? Smush them further at www.smushit.com.

Copy the optimized version of *taps.jpg* from the *extras* folder into the *images* folder to replace the original, large file with a smaller version.

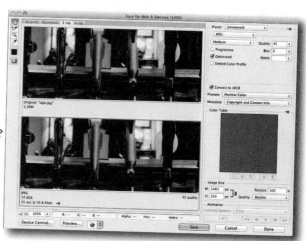

We're using Photoshop to optimize this photo for the Web, but you can use your favorite web image editor.

One src to rule them all

CSS images are just the beginning of our image woes. The <img>
tag presents problems for every responsive design because there can
only be one value for the src attribute regardless of screen size. So
how do we deliver the right size image?

There are 16 beer labels on the On
Tap Now page that use an <img> tag
like this one for Benson's Bubbler.

Despite the need for multiple versions of this image depending on the
screen size, HTML only allows <u>one value</u> for the src.

```
<img src="brews_images/bensons_bubbler.jpg" alt="Benson's Bubbler">
```

It's tempting to replace the value of the src attribute using JavaScript.
Unfortunately, most browsers look ahead at the HTML document and preload
images before the JavaScript has been fully evaluated. This often means
one size file downloads before the JavaScript changes the src, resulting in
duplicate downloads and causing the browser to reflow the page layout.

CSS can't be used to
override the value of the
src attribute, either.

A responsive image server to the rescue

If the browser can't ask the server for the right image, the server will just have
to figure it out for itself. That's what **Sencha.io Src** attempts to do.

The image resizing service
formerly known as TinySRC

We can use Sencha.io Src to deliver the best-sized image for every device.

Set the first part of the src to
http://src.sencha.io/.

Replace with your domain and
path to the images.

After the slash, add the full URL of
the image you want to have resized.

```
<img src="http://src.sencha.io/http://[DOMAIN]/[PATH]/brews_images/bensons_
bubbler.jpg" alt="Benson's Bubbler">
```

**Sencha.io Src
only *shrinks*
images.**

*It doesn't make
them bigger.
Enlarging images results in
poor quality. It is better to find
a higher-quality source image.*

Watch it!

Sencha.io Src will resize the image to fit the size
of the device screen. For example, if an iPhone
visits the site, the image will be constrained to its
screen size of 320 by 480 pixels.

Do this!

**Update all of the brew label images in the
ontap.html document to use Sencha.io Src.**

How Sencha.io Src works

Sencha.io Src works like magic. You request an image from an iPhone, it gives you an iPhone-sized image. Using a feature phone? No problem—Sencha.io Src will give you a tiny image. Sitting at your desktop? Here's the full image.

How does Sencha.io Src know what size image to deliver? It uses the browser's *user-agent string*—an identifier that every browser provides—to look up the device in a big database. The database contains information about thousands of devices. One of the things these device databases track is the size of the screen.

> ← What's a user-agent string? We'll take a closer look in the next chapter.

Once Sencha.io Src knows the screen size, it goes to work scaling the image to the maximum width of the device. It stores the image it created in a cache for 30 minutes so subsequent requests for the image at that size will be even faster.

> ← If you need Sencha.io Src to provide a specific image size, it can do that for you as well. See how at http://bit.ly/senchasrc.

No great solutions for <img> tags

Using Sencha.io Src has drawbacks. It relies on device detection, which can occasionally get things wrong (as we will discuss in more detail in Chapter 5). It also requires you to route all your images through a third party.

The reality is that there are currently no great solutions for how to handle different image sources for different screen sizes. But watch this space closely, because a lot of people are trying to find a better solution.

> ← Why is the <img> tag so difficult? Read more in this series on responsive images: http://bit.ly/rwdimgsl.

One final tweak: optimized beer label images

As with the *taps.jpg* image, we can reduce the file size of the beer label images by saving them at a slightly lower JPEG quality level. Don't worry, we've optimized them for you. Find them in the *extras/labels-optimized* directory.

Copy the optimized images into the *brew_images* folder, replacing any existing image files.

TEST DRIVE

We should have an efficient, fast, mobile-optimized web page now. Test it using *www.blaze.io/mobile* to see how we did. Select the option to have Blaze run three tests on the phone to get an average. Compare the total file size and download time of the new page to the original page.

If your pages are not publicly accessible, you can test using *http://hf-mw.com/ch2/ex/4/ontap.html*.

That's a blazing-fast mobile web page

Our diet plan worked! The On Tap Now page is 87% slimmer than it was before. iPhone download time has gone from almost 12 seconds to under 3 seconds.

Before

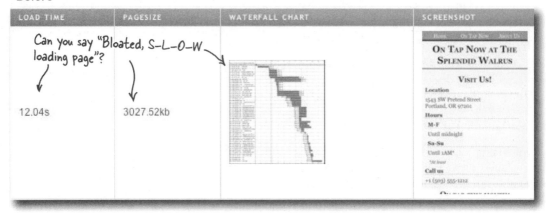

Can you say "Bloated, S-L-O-W loading page"?

12.04s

3027.52kb

After

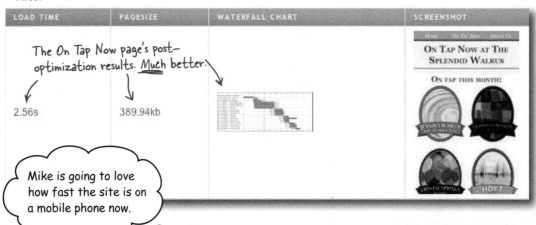

The On Tap Now page's post-optimization results. _Much better!_

2.56s

389.94kb

Mike is going to love how fast the site is on a mobile phone now.

BRAIN POWER

Web performance optimization is a growing field with many more ways to make pages faster. What other performance improvements could we make to this page?

<h1>there are no
Dumb Questions</h1>

Q: Why do browsers download CSS images that are never used?

A: The browser usually can't know for certain that an image isn't going to be used. It could be an image that shows up when some JavaScript or CSS activity triggers it. The browser downloads the images in advance so people don't have to wait if an activity suddenly triggers an image to be displayed.

Q: OK, so why don't they download images that are within media queries?

A: Originally, browsers downloaded them as well. Browser makers have seen how developers are using media queries and are adjusting browser behavior accordingly. All of this is fairly new, which is why some browsers still download resources inside a media query that doesn't apply.

Q: Is it safe to route our images through Sencha.io Src? It makes me nervous.

A: Being cautious is reasonable. Any time you integrate a third-party service into a critical part of your site, you're going to be impacted if that service goes down.

Sencha has said it is committed to providing this service and that it will remain free. At the same time, you can be sure that if a tremendously large site started using it, Sencha would need to be compensated or it wouldn't be able to run the service.

If you don't like Sencha.io Src, you could build a similar service using the device detection tools we teach in Chapter 5.

Q: Are there alternatives to Sencha.io Src? Are there solutions to the `<img>` tag problem that are client side only?

A: There are many different ways to handle `<img>` tags in responsive designs. A lot of work is currently underway to find a solution that doesn't require device detection. There are compromises with every solution, including the one we're using for this project. You can find an extensive review of the techniques at *http://bit.ly/rwdimgs2*.

Q: What about other media? Do video and audio suffer from the same problems?

A: In a word: yes. The HTML5 video and audio formats are a little better because they allow you to define fallback versions of the media in different file formats. If your browser doesn't support the first option provided, it will look at the second one.

But while better, this approach does nothing to address network speed or resolution. Someone using a mobile phone on a wireless network probably doesn't need an HD-quality movie. By contrast, Apple's QuickTime video offers a movie reference format that delivers movies based on Internet connection speed.

Q: Is it just me, or are there a lot of unknowns and problems related to Responsive Web Design?

A: There are definitely challenges. As with any new technique, people are still trying to figure out what works and what doesn't. RWD is bleeding edge. That's why we're covering a lot of techniques in this book. It's likely you'll need to combine techniques to deliver the best experience for your project.

Despite the challenges, the promise of RWD inspires many people to strive to build more complete solutions. Things are moving quickly when it comes to RWD.

Zoom, zoom, pow...

> Sorry, guys! I hate to spring a new requirement on you in the middle of your work, but one of my best customers has trouble seeing small text and is complaining that she can't zoom the page. Can you fix it?

Remember that `viewport <meta>` tag from Chapter 1? Time to look at it more closely.

The `viewport <meta>` tag tells the browser the intended dimensions and scaling (aka zoom level) for a page. It also contains controls that can prevent users from being able to change the size of the page.

Zoom in on the viewport <meta> tag

You'll find the `viewport <meta>` tag in the `<head>` of the *ontap.html* document. The syntax is pretty simple.

The content attribute contains a comma—separated list of instructions for the browser. See all of the options at http://bit.ly/metaviewport.

Width of the viewport. Can be set in pixels or can be set to "device—width," which tells the browser to match the viewport to the device resolution.

What type of <meta> tag is this?

```
<meta name="viewport" content="width=device-width, initial-scale=1, maximum-scale=1" />
```

Sets the initial scale (or zoom level) of the page. Setting it to 1 means that the document should be displayed at its normal scale.

Declares a limit on how much the page can be scaled up. There is also a similar minimum—scale setting.

The maximum—scale is what is preventing the users from zooming the page.

The right to zoom?

It seems like being able to zoom is important for accessibility. Why would anyone ever turn it off?

It can make a difference for accessibility. Some web developers have gone so far as to declare that zooming on mobile is a fundamental human right.

We wouldn't necessarily go that far, but zooming is important, and it should be considered carefully before it is disabled.

As for why designers disable scaling, there are a few reasons. If the page is using complex touch gestures, disabling zoom makes it easier for people to swipe successfully.

There is also a bug in iOS that causes the zoom level to change when the device is rotated into landscape mode. The bug zooms the page in, causing the right side of the page to get cut off.

When you rotate an iOS device, a bug causes the page to no longer fit in the viewport, cutting off the right side of the content.

Turn zooming back on

To turn zooming back on, we need to remove the `maximum-scale` setting from the viewport `<meta>` tag.

 Do this!

Edit the viewport `<meta>` tag and remove "maximum-scale=1."

```
<meta name="viewport" content="width=device-width, initial-scale=1" />
```

After you turn zooming back on, rotate an iPhone or iPod Touch to see the iOS zooming bug in action.

Make sure you remove the extra comma after "initial-scale=1."

Back to our regularly scheduled project

With our emergency viewport adventure out of the way, let's take a look at our progress. Our fast mobile page puts us very close to a mobile-first RWD. All that's left to do is add the map back in if the screen is big enough.

☑ Make the HTML as simple as possible and swap the order of the CSS so that the mobile version is first.

☑ Fix CSS background images so that only one file gets downloaded per image. Make sure `display:none` is being used appropriately.

☑ Supply different source files for `<img>` tags at different screen resolutions. Make sure the right size image is downloaded.

☐ Use JavaScript to add Google Maps to the page when the browser can support it and the document is wide enough to accommodate it.

Add the map back using JavaScript

The only remaining item is to add the map back if the browser window is wide enough. We've already seen that, if we hide and show the map using CSS, the resources for the map will still get downloaded.

So we're going to need to use JavaScript to add the map when appropriate. Think of it as a JavaScript version of the media queries we know and love.

Grab that Google Maps iframe code that we set aside earlier. We're going to need to put that back into the page in order to show the map. Let's take a closer look at the iframe code.

Remember this iframe snippet that we commented out? We're going to use JavaScript to insert it into the page.

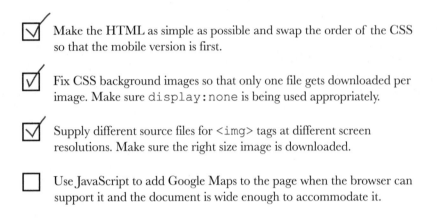

```html
<!--
  <iframe id="map" width="300" height="300" frameborder="0" scrolling="no"
marginheight="0" marginwidth="0" src="http://maps.google.com..."></iframe>
  -->
```

On second thought, a map would be useful

Location. Location. Location.

The old saying takes on new meaning when it comes to mobile phones. Because many phones can tell where you are via GPS and other forms of triangulation, using location to provide more relevant content is common.

Mike hid the map on mobile because it was too big. Now that we've seen how many files it downloads, it makes sense to keep the map hidden.

But that doesn't mean a map wouldn't be nice. So instead of embedding a map on narrow screens, let's link to the map.

Add a link to the map

To link to the map, we'll need a `<div>` that our JavaScript can reference. The `<div>` will contain a `<p>` tag with a link to the map. Why do you think we need to order it that way?

Do this!

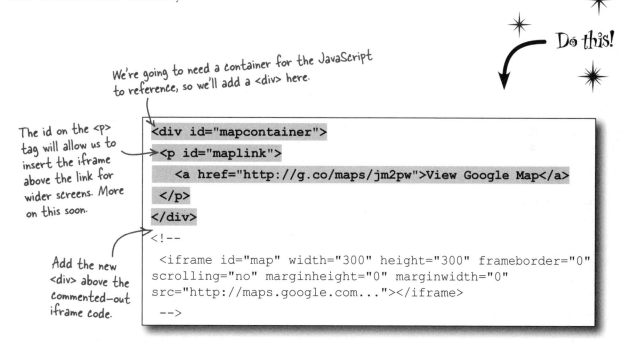

We're going to need a container for the JavaScript to reference, so we'll add a `<div>` here.

The id on the `<p>` tag will allow us to insert the iframe above the link for wider screens. More on this soon.

Add the new `<div>` above the commented-out iframe code.

```html
<div id="mapcontainer">
<p id="maplink">
    <a href="http://g.co/maps/jm2pw">View Google Map</a>
</p>
</div>
<!--
  <iframe id="map" width="300" height="300" frameborder="0"
scrolling="no" marginheight="0" marginwidth="0"
src="http://maps.google.com..."></iframe>
  -->
```

Build a pseudo-media query in JavaScript

Let's take a look at the JavaScript code we're going to use to insert the iframe into the page. The code acts like a very simple media query.

This variable is for the id of the element we want to add the map to. We're using a variable to make the <div> easier to change in the future.

Sets the breakpoint variable to 481 pixels. The breakpoint is the width at which the map will be added to the page.

Checks to see if the window viewport is larger than the breakpoint

These lines add all of the attributes to our new iframe element. The attributes and their values were copied from the Google Maps iframe snippet.

This final step adds the iframe (mapElement) into the mapcontainer <div> (id) before the paragraph containing the link (maplink).

Adds a new iframe element and assigns it to the mapElement variable

The URL Google Maps provides is ugly. You probably don't want to retype it. Find a copy of this code in extras/map.js.

```
<script type="text/javascript">
var breakpoint = 481,
    id = 'mapcontainer',
    viewportWidth = window.innerWidth;
if (viewportWidth > breakpoint) {
    var mapElement = document.createElement('iframe');
    mapElement.id = 'map';
    mapElement.width = '300';
    mapElement.height = '300';
    mapElement.frameborder = '0';
    mapElement.scrolling = 'no';
    mapElement.marginheight = '0';
    mapElement.marginwidth = '0';
    mapElement.src = 'http://maps.google.com/maps?f=q&so
urce=s_q&hl=en&geocode=&q=334+NW+11th+Ave,+Portland,+O
R+97209&aq=&sll=37.0625,-95.677068&sspn=58.164117,80.3
32031&vpsrc=0&ie=UTF8&hq=&hnear=334+NW+11th+Ave,+Portl
and,+Oregon+97209&t=m&ll=45.525472,-122.68218&spn=0.01
804,0.025749&z=14&output=embed';
    document.getElementById(id).insertBefore(mapElement,
    maplink);
}
</script>
```

Remove the commented-out iframe code

We no longer need the original `iframe` code, so delete it from the HTML document.

```
<!--    Delete these lines!
<iframe id="map" width="300" height="300" frameborder="0" scrolling="no"
marginheight="0" marginwidth="0" src="http://maps.google.com..."></iframe>
-->
```

Add the JavaScript to the On Tap Now page

Now we need to add the JavaScript to the page. Because the map is a nice-to-have feature and not essential, we're going to make it one of the last things the browser adds to the page.

Open ontap.html and find the bottom of the HTML document.

We're going to add our JavaScript as the very last thing on the page before the closing </body> tag.

```
<div class="footer">
    <p>See you soon! Love, The Splendid Walrus</p>
</div>
[INSERT SCRIPT HERE]
</body>
</html>
```

Putting nonessential JavaScript at the bottom of the page is a great way to make a page load faster. The browser will parse all of the HTML and CSS before it gets to the JavaScript. Our visitors will have a usable page more quickly and won't be stuck waiting for the map code to load.

Exercise

Time to put our work to the test. Grab *ontap.html* and answer the following:

1 **Does the JavaScript get downloaded on mobile phones?**
Load the page on iPhone and Android using *www.blaze.io/mobile/*. Check the waterfall chart to see if the Google Maps code is downloading. If your web page isn't on a public network, you can use *http://hf-mw.com/ch2/ex/5/ontap.html* to test.

2 **Does the map show up on larger screens?**
Open the On Tap Now page in your favorite desktop browser. Does the map show up when the window is wider than 480 pixels?

3 **How does the map fit into the responsive design?**
Try adjusting the size of your browser window. Does the map scale like the rest of the design? Are there any problems with the map?

Exercise Solution

How's it looking? Any problems?

⊞ GET ontap.html	200	1.4 KB
⊞ GET style.css	200	975 B
⊞ GET layout.css	200	279 B
⊞ GET bensons_bubbler.jpg	200	26.8 KB
⊞ GET chapman_lownsdale.jpg	200	18.6 KB
⊞ GET crystal_springs.jpg	200	21.4 KB
⊞ GET hoyt.jpg	200	22.8 KB
⊞ GET mill_ends.jpg	200	22.7 KB
⊞ GET milo_mciver.jpg	200	24.3 KB
⊞ GET mount_tabor.jpg	200	21.3 KB
⊞ GET omsi.jpg	200	27.1 KB
⊞ GET oxbow.jpg	200	23.8 KB
⊞ GET pittock.jpg	200	23.9 KB
⊞ GET powells.jpg	200	22.2 KB
⊞ GET sandy_river.jpg	200	29 KB
⊞ GET sauvie_island.jpg	200	21.1 KB
⊞ GET the_grotto.jpg	200	25.9 KB
⊞ GET tryon_creek.jpg	200	28.6 KB
⊞ GET wells_fargo.jpg	200	22.7 KB
19 Requests		**384.8 KB**

Look Ma, no Google Maps downloads.

1 Does the JavaScript get downloaded on mobile phones?

Check the page using an iPhone on the Blaze Mobitest service. Make your way to the detailed waterfall chart by clicking the HAR file link on the results page to see all of the files downloaded.

The map files are not getting downloaded. Perfect.

Now what about Android? Blaze says the JavaScript still downloads, but it is another false report.

We mentioned that Blaze had to modify its phones to make them work for remote testing. One odd by-product of this modification is that JavaScript running on its test phones reports the screen width as much wider (800 pixels!) than what unmodified phones do.

You'll have to take our word for it that the JavaScript works and the map code isn't downloading on Android, either.

2 Does the map show up on larger screens?

Yep. The map looks great in our desktop browser.

The map shows up in Chrome, which means our JavaScript is working.

3 How does the map fit into the responsive design?

Uh oh. We've got some problems here. The map doesn't scale like the rest of the responsive design. Not only that, but there are some screen widths where the map overlaps the beer labels.

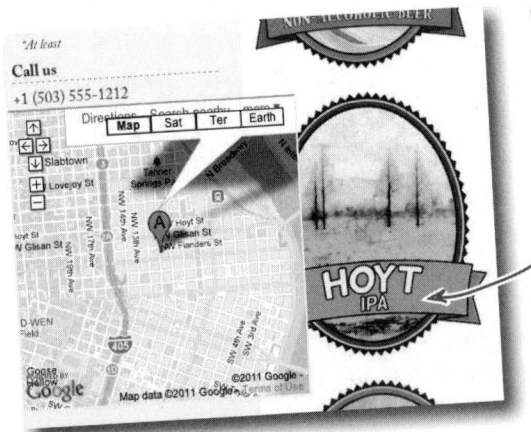

Yikes. When the browser window narrows, the map overlaps the beer labels.

Why isn't the map scaling like the images on the page?

These widgets aren't responsive

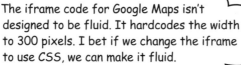

The iframe code for Google Maps isn't designed to be fluid. It hardcodes the width to 300 pixels. I bet if we change the iframe to use CSS, we can make it fluid.

Responsive Web Design is so new that widgets like Google Maps are unlikely to be fluid by default.

When companies provide widgets to embed in other web pages, they do everything they can to make sure the widget will work regardless of the page layout. That often means hardcoding things like `height` and `width` in the HTML itself.

Dealing with poorly built third-party widgets is a problem for nearly every mobile site. Responsive designs have an additional requirement that widgets be fluid.

Width and height are fixed, which prevents the map from scaling.

```
<iframe id="map" width="300" height="300" frameborder="0" scrolling="no"
marginheight="0" marginwidth="0" src="http://maps.google.com..."></iframe>
```

Many of the attributes on this iframe could be moved to CSS.

Ideally, our HTML would only contain the content and markup. It wouldn't contain any presentation information.

BRAIN POWER

Which CSS properties map to the attributes used in the iframe?

Move iframe attributes to CSS equivalents

Let's move as many of the `iframe`'s attributes to CSS as possible and make them fluid while we're at it.

First, we need to create a list of attributes we want to move to CSS by identifying which attributes are for presentation and which are content or metadata.

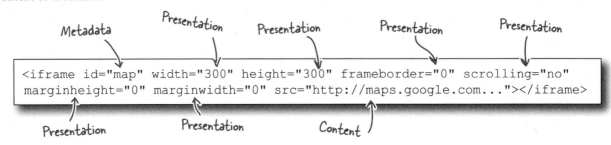

All those presentation attributes belong in the CSS.

Match styles to attributes

Some of the attributes share the same name with their CSS comrades. We don't have to look hard to find the CSS version of `width` and `height`. Others, like `frameborder`, are obscure attributes. Fortunately, the CSS counterparts are still fairly straightforward.

Do this!

Add these rules to *layout.css*.

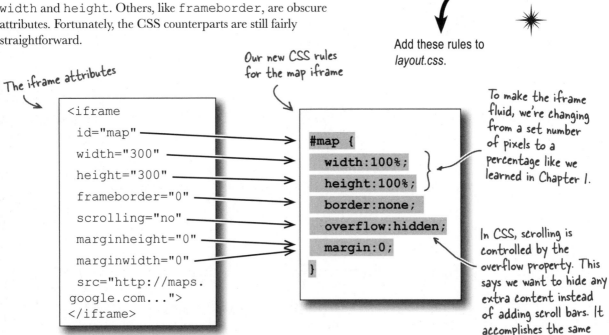

The iframe attributes

```
<iframe
  id="map"
  width="300"
  height="300"
  frameborder="0"
  scrolling="no"
  marginheight="0"
  marginwidth="0"
  src="http://maps.
  google.com...">
</iframe>
```

Our new CSS rules for the map iframe

```
#map {
  width:100%;
  height:100%;
  border:none;
  overflow:hidden;
  margin:0;
}
```

To make the iframe fluid, we're changing from a set number of pixels to a percentage like we learned in Chapter 1.

In CSS, scrolling is controlled by the overflow property. This says we want to hide any extra content instead of adding scroll bars. It accomplishes the same thing as scrolling = "no".

Remove attributes from the JavaScript

Now that we've got CSS doing the heavy lifting, let's modify our JavaScript so the presentation attributes aren't set. Remove the lines that add the presentation attributes that we identified.

Find the JavaScript at the bottom of ontap.html.

Delete these lines from the JavaScript.

```
<script type="text/JavaScript">
var breakpoint = 481,
  id = 'mapcontainer',
  viewportWidth = window.innerWidth;
if (viewportWidth > breakpoint) {
  var mapElement = document.createElement('iframe');
  mapElement.id = 'map';
  mapElement.width = '300';
  mapElement.height = '300';
  mapElement.frameborder = '0';
  mapElement.scrolling = 'no';
  mapElement.marginheight = '0';
  mapElement.marginwidth = '0';
  mapElement.src = 'http://maps.google.com/maps?f=q&so
urce=s_q&hl=en&geocode=&q=334+NW+11th+Ave,+Portland,+O
R+97209&aq=&sll=37.0625,-95.677068&sspn=58.164117,80.3
32031&vpsrc=0&ie=UTF8&hq=&hnear=334+NW+11th+Ave,+Portl
and,+Oregon+97209&t=m&ll=45.525472,-122.68218&spn=0.01
804,0.025749&z=14&output=embed';

  document.getElementById(id).insertBefore(mapElement,
maplink);
}
</script>
```

TEST DRIVE

Save *layout.css* and *ontap.html*. Load the On Tap Now page in Safari. You can use *http://hf-mw.com/ch2/ex/6/ontap.html* if it's more convenient. How does the map look?

No one should have trouble finding the pub now

The map got a little full of itself, didn't it? It nearly took over the whole left column. Soon it will start singing, "*I'm the map, I'm the map*" to get our attention—unless we tame it.

If you make the window narrow, you can begin to see why the map might be trying to get our attention. The map gets squeezed until it turns into a thin, tall strip that is completely unusable.

We still want the map to scale, but we need to set some boundaries on how far it scales in each direction.

These screenshots are from Safari. Other browsers behave differently. The map isn't doing what we want in any of them.

1 **The height of the map is too big.**
Setting the height to 100% makes the map longer than the tallest image on the page. Let's keep the map a little more under control by setting the height to 400px.

Add this line to the #map CSS rule.

```
height: 400px;
```

2 **Hey look, the map is wearing skinny jeans.**
When the window gets narrow, the map gets so thin that most of the information cannot be seen. We need to set a minimum width so that the map doesn't go beanpole on us.

After adding the two new lines, your #map rule in layout.css should look like this.

```
#map {
    width:100%;
    height:400px;
    border:none;
    overflow:hidden;
    margin:0;
    min-width: 200px;
}
```

The map overlap is back

> I thought the whole reason for making the iframe fluid was to get rid of the overlap. We've got everything in CSS now, but the map is still covering up the beer labels when you make the browser window narrow.

Moving the `iframe` presentation attributes into CSS was the first step. Now we need to take a fresh look at our media queries.

In Chapter 1, we used media queries to switch the layout at 480 pixels. We determined that width based on the width of popular smartphones.

What we're seeing with the map is that we need to look at the content of the page when we make decisions about where to apply media queries.

The map is covering up the beer labels again when the window is narrow.

Let the content be your guide

There's a problem with using 480 pixels as our breakpoint for the media query. Not every phone has the same width. And even if a majority of them do today, who's to say that 540 pixels won't be the most common size in the future?

A better approach is to let your content be the guide on when to make changes to the layout.

We're not asking you to commune with your content until it starts to speak to you. But if you adjust the size of your browser window until things don't look right, the content will tell you a lot.

Maybe images are getting too small. Maybe the columns are too narrow.

When those things happen, that's where you need a breakpoint. Then you can craft a media query to change the presentation at that breakpoint.

We shouldn't pay so much attention to typical mobile and desktop screen sizes. When the content breaks the layout, it is telling us to adjust our media queries and JavaScript.

Time to bend and stretch that browser

We need to put our content through its paces by making the page as big and as small as we can while watching for when the layout breaks.

But before we do that, we need some way of knowing how big the screen is when something looks wrong on the page. The easiest way to do this is to install a *bookmarklet* that will show you the window size.

A bookmarklet is a little bit of JavaScript stored in a browser bookmark.

Install the bookmarklet in your browser

Go to *http://bit.ly/window-resize* and drag the link labeled Window Size into your bookmarks toolbar to create the bookmarklet. Click the bookmarklet to activate it. Resize your browser and watch the numbers change in the upper-left corner of the browser window.

The Window Size bookmark in Safari's bookmark bar.

When you click the Window Size bookmarklet, it adds the size of the window in the upper-left corner.

Optional: Install an extension

There is an extension for Google Chrome that not only will show the window size, but will also resize your window to match common screen resolutions. You can get it at *http://bit.ly/chrome-resizer*.

The Web Developer Toolkit (*http://bit.ly/webdevtoolkit*) will display page size in the title bar along with a bunch of other useful tools. It works in Firefox and Chrome.

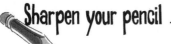 **Sharpen your pencil**

Load the On Tap Now page in the browser with the Window Size bookmarklet (or a browser extension). Activate the bookmarklet. Resize the browser.

Write down the width of the browser when the layout breaks or the content looks odd.

Sharpen your pencil
Solution

Let's review some of the trouble spots that show up when you resize the browser.

610 pixels: Beer labels touch the map.

At around 610 pixels, the labels touch the map. If we're going to create a new breakpoint to address this problem, we'll need to do it before they touch. This means instead of using 610, we'll use 640 pixels as the breakpoint.

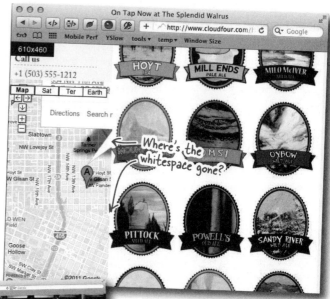

1,200 pixels: Huge beer labels.

As the browser gets wider, the beer labels become ridiculously big. *Where* they become too big is an aesthetic judgment. For our tastes, they start getting too big when the browser is 1,200 pixels wide.

⚛ BRAIN POWER

Did you see other problems as you resized the browser? How significant do you think a problem needs to be before it makes sense to address it with an additional media query?

Breakpoints to the rescue

All in all, not too bad. Just a couple of small tweaks to the CSS should do it.

Shrink the humongous beer labels

There are currently three beer labels in each row. When the page gets wider, there is room for four beer labels per row.

Create a media query for windows wider than 1,200 pixels that changes the beer labels to four across the page.

This change only happens if the window is bigger than 1,200 pixels.

Setting the width of the list item (li) containing the beer labels to 25% will put four labels on each row.

```
@media screen and (min-width:1201px) {
  .taplist li {
    width: 25%;
  }
}
```

Add these rules to layout.css

It's common to make images smaller proportionally as screens get wider.

Going to one column sooner

Even if the beer labels didn't overlap with the map, the layout is getting very crowded at 640 pixels. Instead of adding a new breakpoint to address the overlap, we can move our existing media query from 480 pixels to 640 pixels.

Our HTML, JavaScript, and CSS all reference 480 pixels, so we'll need to update all three.

Making this change will convert the layout to a single column and hide the map. This has the added benefit of applying the single-column layout to phones bigger than 480 pixels.

ontap.html

```
<link rel="stylesheet" type="text/css" href="layout.css"
media="all and min-width: 641px)">
```

Set min-width to 641px.

```
<script type="text/
javascript">
var breakpoint = 641,
   ...
</script>
```

Set breakpoint in JavaScript to 641px.

taps.css

```
/* Mobile/lower-resolution devices
*/
@media screen and (max-width:640px)
{
```

Set max-width to 640px.

Widescreen view with four beer labels per row

You guys rock! The page is fast and looks great. Drinks are on the house.

Narrower views go to one column and hide the map.

Lightweight and fast on mobile

You can use http://hf-mw.com/ch2/ex/8/ontap.html to run your own speed tests.

Our mobile-first responsive design is complete

☑ Make the HTML as simple as possible and swap the order of the CSS so that the mobile version is first.

☑ Fix CSS background images so that only one file gets downloaded per image. Make sure `display:none` is being used appropriately.

☑ Supply different source files for `<img>` tags at different screen resolutions. Make sure the right size image is downloaded.

☑ Use JavaScript to add Google Maps to the page when the browser can support it and the document is wide enough to accommodate it.

there are no
Dumb Questions

Q: What exactly is a viewport?

A: Imagine taking a sheet of cardboard and cutting out a rectangle in the middle of it. Lay that rectangle over your monitor so you can only see the portion of the web page that shows through the rectangle. That's what a viewport does for web pages.

Q: So the `viewport <meta>` tag tells the browser what size to make the viewport?

A: Exactly. By default, iOS sets the viewport to 980 pixels. If you've optimized your page for smaller screens, setting the `<meta-viewport>` tag lets the browser know to set the viewport accordingly.

Q: What are breakpoints?

A: Breakpoints are just a fancy way of describing the resolution at which a designer decides to change the layout of a page. This is usually done via media queries checking to see if a page is narrower or wider than a certain number of pixels.

A complex responsive design may have multiple breakpoints, including some that make wholesale changes to the layout as well as some minor breakpoints that only make a few targeted tweaks to fix minor layout issues.

Q: I don't want to prevent people from zooming, but that iOS bug is pretty heinous. Is there any way to enable zooming and not have a broken page?

A: You can find a JavaScript workaround at *https://gist.github.com/901295*.

Q: Why does the overlap with the map occur in the first place?

A: Because the map is an element that doesn't scale with the browser window. When the window is small, the browser can't scale the map any smaller, so the left column ends up overlapping the right column.

Q: Doesn't adding a `min-width` to the map break the responsive design by creating an element that doesn't scale with the browser window?

A: Technically, yes. It seems like a decent solution here because we've modified the media queries to address overlapping content. Another option would have been to use media queries to adjust the dimensions of the map and proportions of the columns.

BULLET POINTS

- Adding media queries to an existing desktop site may make it look good on mobile, but doesn't mean that it is **mobile optimized**.

- Because **most mobile browsers don't support plug-ins**, there are fewer tools to assist mobile web developers.

- Using a **proxy server** or a testing solution like Blaze Mobitest can help you see what is **actually getting downloaded by a mobile browser**.

- **HTTP archive files and waterfall charts** are essential performance tools.

- **Mobile-first Responsive Web Design** helps optimize web pages by making sure that **smaller resources are downloaded by default**.

- Mobile-first RWD is another form of **progressive enhancement** that uses screen size to determine how to enhance web pages.

- Designing for mobile first forces you to **focus on what really matters**, thus helping you remove cruft from pages.

- Internet Explorer 8 and below do not support media queries. **Conditional comments** are a workaround.

- **JavaScript can augment media queries** by testing for screen size and adding content when appropriate.

- Instead of designing breakpoints based on the typical screen resolutions, **let the content dictate the resolutions** at which you need to modify the layout.

3 a separate mobile website

Facing less-than-awesome circumstances

Beautiful, harmonious, responsively designed websites that work for all browsers and devices known to man...was it all but a wonderful dream?

The vision of a single, responsive Web is a beautiful one...

in which every site has one layout to rule them all, made lovingly with a mobile-first approach. Mmm...tasty. But what happens when a stinky dose of reality sets in? Like legacy systems, older devices, or customer budget constraints? What if, sometimes, instead of mixing desktop and mobile support into one lovely soup, you need to keep 'em separated? In this chapter, we look at the nitty-gritty bits of **detecting mobile users, supporting those crufty older phones, and building a separate mobile site**.

Creature Comforts has agents in the field

Creature Comforts International is a worldwide, nonprofit agency that helps treat sick or injured livestock in areas hit by natural disasters and provides support to affected farmers and ranchers. Until recently, the organization relied on voice communications or the occasional ruggedized laptop for their agents to coordinate personnel and supplies.

Creature Comforts serves a lot of areas where the health and safety of livestock is tantamount to the citizens' financial well-being and recovery after a disaster.

But being able to access and exchange information—quickly—about people and supplies in our system is getting harder as we grow.

Creature Comforts' VP of Communication

How can agents get and share the info they need?

Creature Comforts is not a new organization; its roots go back over two decades. It already has a lot of internal infrastructure, including a significant "traditional" web presence built on a proprietary content management system (CMS).

> We've got people worldwide who need to stay in touch and get information while in the field. We have web tools for that already...

> ...but our current website doesn't look good or work well on mobile phones.

An increasing need for mobile web

Increasingly, the Creature Comforts staff is finding that the most reliable—and often only—connectivity in the field is via the local cellular network. Land-based Internet connections are hard to find, require more equipment, and restrict mobility.

Creature Comforts needs a mobile website: one that can support a wide array of devices on a wide array of connections.

This sounds like a great project. Can't wait to get in and make the agency's CMS deliver more mobile-friendly content and use some responsive design goodness.

Frank: I've got a bit of bad news. Creature Comforts doesn't have a very big budget. There are some internal politics involved. And it would take a huge effort to extract the group's administrative and content-publishing processes from its older, proprietary CMS. We can't touch the desktop site, at least for now.

Jim: Doesn't that make our job impossible?

Frank: No, but it might require a bit of compromise. Creature Comforts' website is big and complicated, but the only part the group feels it is vital to make mobile-optimized is its so-called Comforts Logistics Portal. This web application lets agents give and receive updates and coordinate scheduling and supply drops. This part of the desktop website is relatively contained and has APIs that we can use.

Jim: I don't get it. How do we selectively change only part of the site?

Frank: In this case, I think we're going to need to develop a separate site for mobile users.

Jim: That sounds messy.

Frank: The mobile web can be a messy job. You know that. We need to make this work, and work reliably, for a lot of people scattered around the globe. This is not the spanking-new-smartphone crowd, either. A lot of the staff members' devices are donated, older phones, and the mobile connections in some of the areas they serve are spotty at best. We need a lean, simple, and functional mobile website that helps these folks get their jobs done. We simply can't wrangle their existing desktop stuff into what we need.

Frank

Jim

Sometimes it makes sense to create a separate, standalone site for mobile devices.

Scared of programming? Don't sweat it too much.

There is some talk of APIs and web applications whirling around, but we won't make you do any of the heavy lifting. Leave the programming up to us—your job is to help us make it look good and work well on the mobile web.

there are no
Dumb Questions

Q: What does a content management system (CMS) do?

A: A web CMS is a combination of editing, publishing, and rights management tools for creating and managing web content. Some CMSes are quite full-featured and provide an environment for developing web applications quickly (sometimes these are called *content management frameworks*, or CMFs).

CMSes let administrative users, who might not be familiar with HTML markup or web design, create and manage content.

There are CMSes in both the open source and commercial spaces, written in every programming language you can think of. Examples include WordPress, Drupal, DotNetNuke, Joomla!, and SharePoint. Larger or specialized organizations sometimes create their own CMS software.

Most CMSes also handle the publishing of content, using templating systems or other mechanisms. This can make the transition to support mobile devices tricky, as, in many cases, the content is tangled up with presentation layers.

This is the situation with Creature Comforts. Its CMS, designed several years ago, has only one set of templates. Retooling the system from the ground up would be too expensive for the organization right now.

Q: Is adapting for mobile devices a problem with every web CMS?

A: The number of CMSes out there is bewildering. Some are more easily adapted for mobile devices than others. The problem of mixing content, logic, and presentation is certainly one suffered by many popular CMSes.

The development communities and companies behind many CMSes are actively working on subsequent releases that are optimized for delivering content to different types of clients. And forward-thinking folks in the mobile web world are reimagining ways of structuring content—treating content more systematically, like application data, to makes its reuse across multiple platforms more straightforward.

APIs Up Close

APIs (application programming interfaces) are systematized, clearly defined interfaces created so that different software systems can talk to one another. An example of a popular API on the Web is the Twitter API. The Twitter API defines a set of methods that web programmers can use to retrieve and alter data in the Twitter system.

The Creature Comforts web application team coded the part of the website that allows agents and admins to manage people and supplies among the far-flung teams. As part of this development, the team created an API that can be used to get and update information for team members and materials.

The API returns structured data that our mobile web dev team can use to build a mobile web version of the Creature Comforts site.

Unlike its CMS, Creature Comforts' API doesn't conflate logic and presentation. So it will make our mobile optimization a lot easier.

Send mobile users to a mobile-optimized website

Sometimes it's necessary to have a separate website for mobile devices and desktop browsers. Often, you'll want your users to be able to go to a single domain—e.g., *www.example.com*—and automatically get routed to the appropriate site based on their devices.

Different kinds of devices and browsers request the website (e.g., www.example.com).

A script on the web server examines the incoming request and attempts to determine whether the client is mobile.

www.example.com

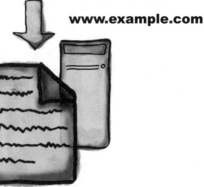

Mobile clients are redirected to the mobile site.

Desktop clients stay on the desktop-oriented site.

m.example.com

www.example.com

Sniff out mobile users

To make this setup work—rerouting mobile devices to the mobile-optimized site—the web server needs to know if an incoming request comes from a mobile device or not.

How can you "know" which browsers are mobile?

We're going to make a stab at determining whether a user is on a mobile device or not by looking at the `User-Agent` **HTTP header sent by the browser.**

There are other techniques, but user-agent detection is a very common server-side approach for device detection.

This technique is commonly called "user-agent sniffing."

A <u>**user-agent**</u> string is a piece of text that serves as a sort of ID card for a client application (in our case, web browsers). Each unique browser is a unique user agent.

"User agent" is often abbreviated to "UA."

Getting to know user agents

Web browsers—and, yes, that includes mobile browsers—send a **User-Agent header** as part of the **HTTP request** whenever the browser sends a request for a web page or resource.

User-agent strings have long been used (and misused) by webmasters to identify (and misidentify) browsers. Way back in the misty history of the 1990s, so-called *user-agent sniffing* was the bane of millions of users faced with ubiquitous "This site better viewed in Internet Explorer" (or Mozilla or Netscape or whatever the preferred browser flavor was at the time).

```
GET /pretty.png HTTP/1.1

Host: www.example.com
Accept: text/html,application/xhtml+xml,application/xml
Accept-Encoding: gzip,deflate,sdch
Referer: http://www.example.com/foo
User-Agent: Opera/9.64(Windows NT 5.1; U; en) Presto/2.1.1
```

Request line

Request headers

Request body (if any)

Simplified structure of an HTTP request

User-agent archaeology

The structure of user-agent strings today is a curious and sometimes confounding patchwork of convention, confusion, and trickery. Full order has never successfully been imposed over how they are written. So you can end up with things like:

```
Mozilla/5.0 (Windows NT 6.0) AppleWebKit/535.1 (KHTML, like
Gecko) Chrome/14.0.792.0 Safari/535.1
```

Chrome 14 running on Windows Vista...of course!

Why would the user agent for Chrome on Windows mention Safari? What's KHTML, and how is it "like" Gecko? Like your appendix or the stumpy leg remnants in whales, some of this is evolutionary cruft.

The vestigial "Mozilla compatibility flag" (Mozilla/5.0 in the example above) is practically omnipresent to this day, though it doesn't mean much anymore. Mentions of Mozilla, KHTML, Gecko, or WebKit are UAs' way of claiming that their layout engines are comparable to or "better" than those. At the time of this writing, all WebKit-based browsers on mobile devices except for Android mention "Safari" in their user-agent string (Apple originally developed WebKit, basing it on KHTML).

User Agents Way Up Close

Let's take a deeper look at the pieces of some real-life user-agent strings.

Chrome 14 running on Windows Vista (we met this on page 98).

```
Mozilla/5.0 (Windows NT 6.0) AppleWebKit/535.1 (KHTML,
like Gecko) Chrome/14.0.792.0 Safari/535.1
```

```
Mozilla/4.0 (compatible; MSIE 7.0; Windows Phone OS 7.0;
Trident/3.1; IEMobile/7.0; SAMSUNG; SGH-i917)
```

A Samsung phone running Windows Phone 7

A BlackBerry 9700 (Bold)

```
BlackBerry9700/5.0.0.442 Profile/MIDP-2.1 Configuration/CLDC-1.1
VendorID/612
```

Analyze some of the pieces

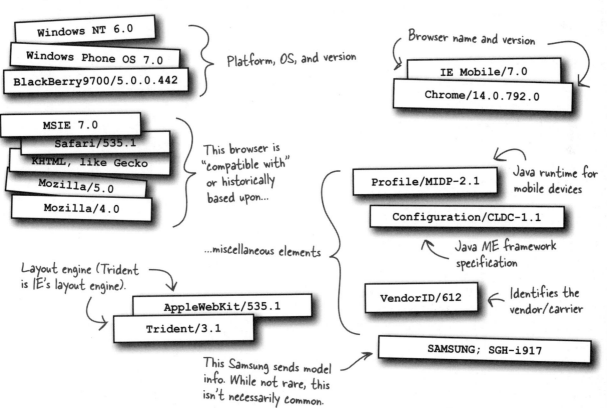

Windows NT 6.0

Windows Phone OS 7.0

BlackBerry9700/5.0.0.442

Platform, OS, and version

Browser name and version

IE Mobile/7.0

Chrome/14.0.792.0

MSIE 7.0

Safari/535.1

KHTML, like Gecko

Mozilla/5.0

Mozilla/4.0

This browser is "compatible with" or historically based upon...

Profile/MIDP-2.1

Java runtime for mobile devices

Configuration/CLDC-1.1

Java ME framework specification

...miscellaneous elements

Layout engine (Trident is IE's layout engine).

AppleWebKit/535.1

Trident/3.1

VendorID/612

Identifies the vendor/carrier

SAMSUNG; SGH-i917

This Samsung sends model info. While not rare, this isn't necessarily common.

WHAT'S MY PURPOSE?

1
```
Mozilla/5.0 (Linux; U; Android 2.1; en-us; ADR6200 Build/ERD79)
AppleWebKit/530.17 (KHTML, like Gecko) Version/4.0 Mobile Safari/530.17
```

2
```
Opera/9.64(Windows NT 5.1; U; en) Presto/2.1.1
```

3
```
Mozilla/5.0 (BlackBerry; U; BlackBerry 9800; en-US) AppleWebKit/534.1+
(KHTML, like Gecko) Version/6.0.0.246 Mobile Safari/534.1+
```

You've seen a few user-agent strings dissected. Now you try it. Match each snippet, extracted from the user-agent strings above, to its purpose.

Presto/2.1.1	OS, platform, and version
Apple WebKit/534.1+	Historical/compatible flag
Windows NT 5.1	Browser name and version
Mozilla/5.0	Layout engine
Version/6.0.0.246	Historical/compatible flag
KHTML, like Gecko	Layout engine
Opera/9.64	Browser version

Answers on page 102.

User agents: spawn of Satan?

So, if we use user-agent sniffing to figure out which devices are mobile, isn't that just enforcing the same old bad behavior that created the user-agent mess in the first place?

Well, sort of.

Utter the term "user-agent sniffing" loudly in a room full of web developers, and you'll invariably get some stern looks of disapproval and a couple of urgent, strangled sounds.

User-agent sniffing rubs a lot of developers the wrong way. We've already seen how complex user-agent strings can be. In addition, user-agent **spoofing**, in which a user (purposely or not) configures his or her browser to send a different UA header, is common. And there are thousands upon thousands of unique UAs, with more entering the market every single day.

Detecting mobile browsers by sniffing user agents on the server can definitely seem like an inelegant and inaccurate hack. But sometimes it's the best (if crude) tool for the job.

BRAIN BARBELL

Can you think of some reasons why user-agent sniffing might be a necessary evil?

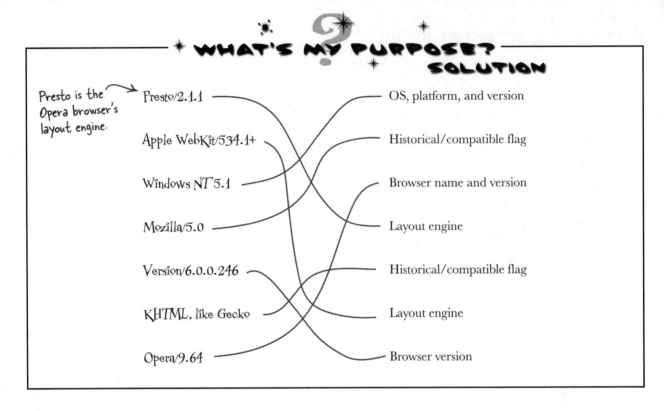

WHAT'S MY PURPOSE? SOLUTION

Presto is the Opera browser's layout engine.

Presto/2.1.1 — OS, platform, and version

Apple WebKit/534.1+ — Historical/compatible flag

Windows NT 5.1 — Browser name and version

Mozilla/5.0 — Layout engine

Version/6.0.0.246 — Historical/compatible flag

KHTML, like Gecko — Layout engine

Opera/9.64 — Browser version

What browsers are these?

Curious about the example user-agent strings used for this exercise (on page 100)? Here are the clients they came from, unmasked for you:

1 A Droid Eris (aka HTC Desire) Android phone running the Android 2.1 browser

2 Opera 9 running on Windows XP

3 BlackBerry 9800 (Torch) running the BlackBerry OS 6 browser

Compare the BlackBerry Torch (OS 6) UA on page 100 against the BlackBerry Bold (OS 5) UA on page 99. Different, huh? As of OS 6, BlackBerry browsers use the WebKit layout engine, and their UA strings look a lot more like other WebKit browsers.

Watch it!

Not all user-agent strings follow consistent patterns.

Some user-agent strings make a lot more sense than others. User agents don't all use the same constituent parts, and some are outright peculiar. There are some basic patterns that most follow, but don't rely on that too much. Don't worry! We have some good tools to account for (most of) this.

Q: What about the other parts of user-agent strings on page 99 that you didn't explain? What does `en-us` mean? What does U mean?

A: The "en-us" is language information, and means that the browser and its interface elements are localized for English, US-style. The "U" indicates that the browser has "strong" security (as opposed to "I" for "weak" security, or "N" for no security at all). To analyze other various bits of user-agent strings like this, make a trip to the ever-so-useful *www.useragentstring.com*.

Q: Is there seriously a different user agent for every build, release, version, platform, device, whim, and vendor out there?

A: Pretty much.

Q: Does anything else send `User-Agent` headers besides browsers?

A: Several other kinds of applications that make requests to web servers also send `User-Agent` headers. These include, but aren't limited to, search engines, crawlers, and various Internet bots (both benign and nefarious). Sometimes web server logs capture user-agent information about unusual things that are accessing our sites, like a web viewer built into, say, a note-taking desktop application, or a web bookmarking tool, or a monitoring service that pings a site to make sure it is operational.

Q: Why would people "spoof" their browser's user agent?

A: Why would anyone purposely ask their browser to "lie" for them, you ask?

A few reasons. Two common motivations are privacy and the desire for a specific experience. Some users don't want to share information about what browsers they are using. In other cases, a user might want to try to see web content in a particular way. A popular example is the "desktop mode" available in several mobile browsers. By turning this on, users are often (and sometimes unknowingly) causing the browser to send a different `User-Agent` header, one that looks more like a desktop browser. Sometimes this is done sanely, and is just fine—Windows Phone 7 desktop mode user agents are relatively easy to spot. But not always. Take a look at the user-agent string that one of the Android versions of the mobile browser Skyfire sends when in desktop mode:

```
Mozilla/5.0 (Macintosh;
U; Intel Mac OS X 10_5_7;
en-us) AppleWebKit/530.17
(KHTML, like Gecko)
Version/4.0 Safari/530.17
```

If that looks an awful lot like desktop OS X Safari, that's because that user agent *is* completely identical to one of the user agents for desktop Safari.

Q: But if someone has gone to the trouble of disguising his mobile browser as a desktop one, shouldn't we respect his wishes and give him a desktop experience?

A: Though this is a delicate question of philosophy, we tend to lean toward "yes," and fill in the gaps with responsive design (which will adapt to the environment no matter who or what the browser claims to be, assuming the browser is modern enough to support media queries and the like). There's a bit of a gray area in terms of whether users know what they're doing or not, but, hey, as far as we're concerned, you should get what

you ask for. Disagreement abounds between developers on this point. There be dragons. Tread lightly.

Q: Hey, you totally neglected to mention UAProf.

A: Many mobile devices send UAProf (User-Agent Profile) headers when making requests, often (but not always) as the `x-wap-profile` request header. The UAProf specification gives mobile handset manufacturers a way to provide information about the device. Usually, a link to the location of the UAProf is provided in the request header.

This sounds pretty good, but unfortunately, not all devices and browsers send UAProf headers. Additionally, a rather unpleasant percentage of the links to UAProfs are not valid. And there is inconsistency in the amount and quality of the data in the UAProf files themselves.

Q: OK, so, there are a million billion user agents and UAProfs aren't all that reliable, yet you claim that there is a sane and reasonable way to do user-agent-based detection?

A: In Chapter 5, we'll be meeting some organizations and projects whose entire existence is concerned with tracking user agents and building databases of metadata about them and other data sources like UAProfs. Until then, we'll keep it simple and use a basic server-side script to look for user-agent strings that bear the primary hallmarks of mobile browser user agents.

Straight talk: Most major sites have a separate mobile website

The majority of the world's biggest websites have a separate mobile site, and a majority of those use some form of user-agent sniffing to route traffic. If user-agent sniffing is so derided, why is this the case? There must be *some* goodness in the user-agent approach.

Some things seem more natural on the server side...

Redirecting incoming traffic to a mobile site is something that fits naturally on the server side. If we're sending mobile requests off to a separate site—something that we'll need to do for Creature Comforts—**decisions are best made before content is sent to the client**.

...and the User-Agent header is our best clue

The `User-Agent` header, while imperfect, is the **most straightforward and reliable clue the server has about the requesting browser**. There are a few other HTTP request headers that provide hints to a client's "mobileness," but none so ubiquitous as that maddening `User-Agent` header. It's the best option in a pile of not-so-great alternatives. And, while we've gone to certain lengths to point out where user-agent sniffing can go wrong (hey, devil's advocate!), most of the time it can be used accurately, especially when wielded responsibly.

OK. Say we *do* build a separate mobile site. How exactly are we going to see the user agents of requesting browsers...and how are we going to get the mobile traffic to the new, mobile version of Creature Comforts?

We can use a simple, freely available script to perform basic mobile device detection.

When what you really want to do is (re-)direct

Wouldn't such a script need to go on *Creature Comforts'* existing (desktop) web server so it can detect mobile browsers and redirect them to our mobile site? I thought we couldn't make any changes to the existing site.

Good catch. Fortunately, Frank and Jim have been able to work with Creature Comforts' IT department.

We'll be able to put a simple redirect script on the agency's existing web server. The web team at Creature Comforts will include the mobile detection script at the top of each page, so that mobile traffic can be redirected.

Get ye to the script

Time to make a quick trip to *www.detectmobilebrowsers.com*. There you'll find a free, simple mobile detection script. We want to be sure you have the latest version, so go get it now! Make sure to download the PHP version.

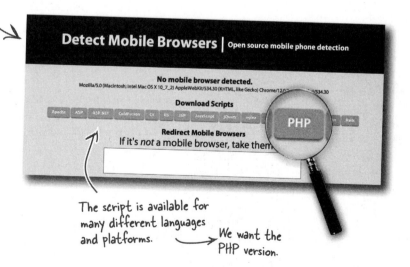

The script is available for many different languages and platforms.

We want the PHP version.

Take a peek at the script

```php
<?php
$useragent=$_SERVER['HTTP_USER_AGENT'];
if(preg_match('/android|avantgo|blackberry|blazer|compal|elaine|fennec|hiptop|iem
obile|ip(hone|od)|iris|kindle|lge |maemo|midp|mmp|opera m(ob|in)i|palm( os)?|phon
e|p(ixi|re)\/|plucker|pocket|psp|symbian|treo|up\.(browser|link)|vodafone|wap|wi
ndows (ce|phone)|xda|xiino/i',$useragent)|| preg_match('/1207|6310|6590|3gso|4thp
|50[1-6]i|770s|802s|a wa|abac|ac(er|oo|s\-)|ai(ko|rn)|al(av|ca|co)|amoi|an(ex|ny
|yw)|aptu|ar(ch|go)|as(te|us)|attw|au(di|\-m|r |s )|avan|be(ck|ll|nq)|bi(lb|rd)|
bl(ac|az)|br(e|v)w|bumb|bw\-(n|u)|c55\/|capi|ccwa|cdm\-|cell|chtm|cldc|cmd\-|co(
mp|nd)|craw|da(it|ll|ng)|dbte|dc\-s|devi|dica|dmob|do(c|p)o|ds(12|\-d)|el(49|ai)
|em(l2|ul)|er(ic|k0)|esl8|ez([4-7]0|os|wa|ze)|fetc|fly(\-|_)|g1 u|g560|gene|gf\-
5|g\-mo|go(\.w|od)|gr(ad|un)|haie|hcit|hd\-(m|p|t)|hei\-|hi(pt|ta)|hp( i|ip)|hs\-
c|ht(c(\-| |_|a|g|p|s|t)|tp)|hu(aw|tc)|i\-(20|go|ma)|i230|iac( |\-|\/)|ibro|idea|
ig01|ikom|im1k|inno|ipaq|iris|ja(t|v)a|jbro|jemu|jigs|kddi|keji|kgt( |\/)|klon|kpt
|kwc\-|kyo(c|k)|le(no|xi)|lg( g|\/(k|l|u)|50|54|e\-|e\/|\-[a-w])|libw|lynx|m1\-
w|m3ga|m50\/|ma(te|ui|xo)|mc(01|21|ca)|m\-cr|me(di|rc|ri)|mi(o8|oa|ts)|mmef|mo(
01|02|bi|de|do|t(\-| |o|v)|zz)|mt(50|p1|v )|mwbp|mywa|n10[0-2]|n20[2-3]|n30(0|2
)|n50(0|2|5)|n7(0(0|1)|10)|ne((c|m)\-|on|tf|wf|wg|wt)|nok(6|i)|nzph|o2im|op(ti
|wv)|oran|owg1|p800|pan(a|d|t)|pdxg|pg(13|\-([1-8]|c))|phil|pire|pl(ay|uc)|pn\-
2|po(ck|rt|se)|prox|psio|pt\-g|qa\-a|qc(07|12|21|32|60|\-[2-7]|i\-)|qtek|r380|r60
0|raks|rim9|ro(ve|zo)|s55\/|sa(ge|ma|mm|ms|ny|va)|sc(01|h\-|oo|p\-)|sdk\/|se(c(\-
|0|1)|47|mc|nd|ri)|sgh\-|shar|sie(\-|m)|sk\-0|sl(45|id)|sm(al|ar|b3|it|t5)|so(f
t|ny)|sp(01|h\-|v\-|v )|sy(01|mb)|t2(18|50)|t6(00|10|18)|ta(gt|lk)|tcl\-|tdg\-
|tel(i|m)|tim\-|t\-mo|to(pl|sh)|ts(70|m\-|m3|m5)|tx\-9|up(\.b|g1|si)|utst|v40
0|v750|veri|vi(rg|te)|vk(40|5[0-3]|\-v)|vm40|voda|vulc|vx(52|53|60|61|70|80|8
1|83|85|98)|w3c(\-| )|webc|whit|wi(g |nc|nw)|wmlb|wonu|x700|xda(\-|2|g)|yas\-
|your|zeto|zte\-/i',substr($useragent,0,4)))
header('Location: http://detectmobilebrowser.com/mobile');
?>
```

detectmobilebrowser.php.txt

This is the script! The one you download might not look <u>exactly</u> the same (it might be a newer version), but it should be similar.

The script might look a bit beastly right now, but we don't have to do much to tame it.

When you first open up *detectmobilebrowser.php* in your preferred text editor, you might find it a bit…brutal-looking. But fear not. We're going to walk you through the basics of how it works, but, really, all you have to do to get it to work is make a couple of small changes—and we'll show you how.

Do this!

Rename this file **redirect.php** and save it inside the *chapter3* folder.

How does the script work?

The script examines the user-agent string and determines whether it seems mobile—and if so, it redirects. It does this in three steps:

① **It grabs the requesting browser's user-agent string.**
In PHP, this is accessible in the global `$_SERVER['HTTP_USER_AGENT']` variable.

② **It uses some carefully crafted regular expressions.** ←
There are two regular expressions here. Both look at the user-agent string and see if it matches known mobile values. You can probably spot some obvious snippets like "hiptop" or "symbian." But there are some more obscure things in here as well—these regular expressions were developed by people who really know the mobile landscape!

A regular expression, a.k.a. "regex" or "regexp," is a formal means of matching patterns in strings.

③ **It redirects browsers whose user-agent string matches either of the regular expressions.**
If the browser's user-agent string matches either of the regular expressions, the script sets a Location header with the designated place to redirect mobile traffic. ↖

By default, mobile traffic is redirected to www.detectmobilebrowser.com/mobile — we'll need to change this.

Make sure your working environment is seaworthy

A few safety checks before we continue! The next sections—and many more in the book—require you to have a working web server that allows you to use PHP. This can be your own computer, or you can use a hosting provider; we're not picky. But if you haven't done so yet, go now to Appendix ii and find information about how to get yourself squared away.

Make a mobile mockup

Jim: Hey, Frank, how are you going with getting started on Creature Comforts' mobile site?

Frank: I thought it might be a bit much to try to handle writing code to work with the agency's APIs and do the mobile design at the same time, so I've whipped up some quick mockups for us to start with. One thing at a time, right?

Jim: Sounds good. Did you use responsive stuff?

Frank: Well, yes and no. I used proportional widths, but figured we're working with older phones that might not understand media queries and other things that make responsive designs work so well. I took the desktop HTML templates for the current Agent Portal landing page dashboard thingy, simplified the heck out of them, and refactored the CSS to be mobile-friendly. I used some sample data so we don't have to worry about functionality or APIs or anything for now.

Jim: What about the mobile device detection and redirect script? How are we going to test that?

Frank: Well, you heard that we'll ultimately put it on Creature Comforts' server and those folks will call it from every page they serve. But for now, we'll want to test it locally to check out how the redirect will behave.

A few tweaks to the mobile redirect script

We'll need to make a few customizations to the redirect script so that we can see it in action. We'll want to **add a new line** to define where the script should redirect if it sees a mobile user. The PHP `$_SERVER['HTTP_HOST']` variable is the name of the web host that the script is running on.

> The name of the web host (e.g., "www.example.com," "localhost," or "10.0.0.2" or somesuch if you're doing your work on your own computer)

We'll also want to **edit the line that sends the Location** response header—we want to redirect mobile traffic to our mobile mockup, not the *www.detectmobilebrowser.com* site.

> Just as there are request headers (like User-Agent), HTTP responses (sent back by the server) also have headers.

```php
<?php
$useragent = $_SERVER['HTTP_USER_AGENT'];
$mobile_location = 'http://' . $_SERVER['HTTP_HOST'] . '/index_mobile.html';
if(preg_match(...))
    header('Location: ' . $mobile_location);
?>
```

redirect.php

TEST DRIVE

Copy the <u>contents</u> of the chapter3 folder to your web server's document root.

chapter3

CSS background image

cows.jpg

Stuff for later; ignore for now.

extras

index.php

There's no need for PHP processing in this file, so we'll just make it .html.

index_mobile. html

redirect.php — This is the redirect script you downloaded and edited.

styles.css

❶ Put the <u>contents</u> of the chapter3 folder at the root of your web server.

If you don't want to put the files at the document root, no biggie. Just be sure to update the path in the line that defines `$mobile_location`.

❷ Make the edits from page 108 in the redirect script.

Open the redirect script again in your text editor (if it's not open already). Make the edits in the script and **save it.**

❸ Edit index.php.

Add the following line to the very top of the *index.php* file:

```php
<?php require_once('redirect.php'); ?>
```

Save the file.

❹ View the mockup in a mobile browser (emulator or real life).

The mockup viewed on an iPhone 4—simple, but it works.

These are just mockups.

The mobile mockups we'll be using throughout this chapter are just that— mockups. They use sample data to represent what the site will look like when "plugged into" real data APIs. The data represented is imaginary, and many links aren't functional. Don't worry about it!

Special delivery...of complicating factors

Hey, Frank. I checked with the team that handles distributing phones to our staff, and it says that a lot of the phones are running a browser called Opera Mini.

I also overnighted you a package of some of the common phones we're using so you can test them out.

Opera Mini, huh?

Hotshot browsers like BlackBerry's WebKit browser and iOS's Safari get a lot of glory, but don't discount Opera Mini! The sister browsers **Opera Mini and Opera Mobile are the most popular mobile web browsers in the world.**

In the middle of 2011, for example, Opera reported over 110 million users. That accounted for more than half of mobile web traffic in India, and over 90% of mobile web traffic in Nigeria.

Opera Mini is especially popular in places where connectivity is slow, or data is expensive or limited.

Opera Mini is actually a **mobile transcoder**. This means that when a user goes to a web page in Opera Mini, the request is routed through Opera's servers, where web pages and resources are compressed and optimized for mobile devices. This optimization means fewer bytes are ultimately delivered to the device—resulting in a faster (and often cheaper) experience.

Because it's made to support a wide range of (often lower-end) phones, Opera Mini acts a bit differently than full-featured smartphone browsers.

Opera Mini isn't just a developing-world concern. It's also quite popular on feature phones in the US and Europe.

Cool. It'll be handy to have these phones on hand for testing. On the other hand, wow. Some of these phones are pretty old and obscure...and I wonder how the mockup will look on Opera Mini.

Do this!

We're going to be looking at the mobile mockup in Opera Mini 4.2. Fortunately, Opera has a convenient, web-based simulator (it's a Java Applet) that you can use. Point your web browser at:

http://www.opera.com/mobile/demo/?ver=4

Sharpen your pencil

Let's see how the mobile mockup looks in the Opera Mini 4.2 simulator. Use the web-embedded Opera Mini simulator to view the mockup at *http://hf-mw.com/ch3/ex/1/*.

Make some notes about what looks different (or, alas!, broken). Can you find at least four differences between the way the mockup looks in the Opera Mini simulator versus the iPhone or Android simulator (page 109)?

1 ....

....

....

....

2 ....

....

....

3 ....

....

....

....

4 ....

....

....

....

Sharpen your pencil
Solution

The mockup looks pretty different in Opera Mini 4.2, huh? Let's look at some of the places where it differs or is weird. We found five trouble spots.

① The <h1> and <h2> tags are not styled and are quite small. Because of this, the background image in the header seems kind of silly.

We can't really style any of the heading elements in Opera Mini.

② The entire page is too wide and disappears off the right side of the screen.

This one's a doozy.

③ Text formatting is not getting applied very well. Italic text is not italic, and bold text is not bold.

④ Instead of rounded corners, we get square ones.

⑤ The status message uses overflow: scroll, which is an absolute no-no on all mobile devices. Content is cut off, and scrolling is not working.

Bonus points if you noticed this on the iPhone or Android already!

there are no
Dumb Questions

Q: Why do I have to view this example on *http://hf-mw.com*? Why can't I use my own copy?

A: Opera Mini is a *proxy browser*. That means that all web traffic goes through an Opera server. So, the example mockup and other code bits have to be hosted somewhere that Opera's servers can reach.

If you are doing your work on your own computer, you may well have an IP address that is not visible to the entire Internet (a so-called internal IP address only visible to the network you are connected to).

If you are doing work on a hosting provider or otherwise have the web pages for Creature Comforts on an externally accessible web server, you can certainly use your own copy.

Not all phones are smartphones...not by a sight

In many of the countries that Creature Comforts works in, seeing a smartphone is a rarity. In India, smartphones sales are projected to be less than 6% of the total phones sold during 2011. No big deal...right?

How many phones does India have, anyway?

As of August 2011, India had over **850 million** mobile phone subscribers. This makes India second only to China in total number of mobile phones.

While smartphones are a rarity in India, mobile phones are more common than toilets!

This is no joking matter. The UN issued a report comparing the easy access to mobile phones to poor sanitation infrastructure.

What if my users aren't in India? In the US, everyone uses smartphones. I shouldn't have to worry about those feature phones.

Emerging markets aren't the only places where feature phones outnumber smartphones.

Only recently did the sales of smartphones exceed feature phones in the United States. Sometime in 2012, smartphones will finally represent the majority of phones in America. The same is true of most European countries.

When you see reports about the explosive growth of smartphones, keep in mind that even with that growth, it will take quite some time before all of those old phones have been replaced.

And, hey, feature phones aren't all that bad

Sure, they cause us heartache with their older, quirkier browsers and often poor connections, but feature phones have made a huge difference in the lives of many people around the world.

If you want to see some serious innovation, travel to a country with an emerging market and watch how they use mobile phones for everything from farming to banking.

For many, a phone isn't a cute, pocket-size, lesser version of a modern computer. It is their primary connection to the world.

Let's keep it basic: Meet XHTML-MP

If you look again at `index_mobile.html`, you'll see that the mockup currently uses this DOCTYPE declaration:

```
<!DOCTYPE html>
```

That's the DOCTYPE for HTML5, an excellent and exciting choice for robust websites and web apps in this modern world, but not necessarily right if we want to reach and support the kinds of mobile devices that the Creature Comforts staff members use. It's time to introduce you to our newest friend, **XHTML Mobile Profile (XHTML-MP)**.

XHTML-MP is a flavor of XHTML developed specifically to support mid-level and feature phones with fair to middling web browsers. It's a few years old now—and increasingly overlooked in favor of its sexier, younger cousin, HTML5—but it's still useful for projects like the Creature Comforts mobile site.

XHTML Mobile Profile is a subset of the desktop (X)HTML you know and love. It's a streamlined version of HTML, designed to perform well on a lot of different mobile browsers. And a lot of mobile browsers are designed to support it.

Ready Bake DOCTYPE

Let's convert the mockup page to be an XHTML-MP document. **Edit the index_mobile.html file** and replace the HTML5 DOCTYPE (top line of the file) with the following two lines:

```
<?xml version="1.0" encoding="UTF-8" ?>
<!DOCTYPE html PUBLIC "-//WAPFORUM//DTD XHTML Mobile 1.2//EN"
"http://www.openmobilealliance.org/tech/DTD/xhtml-mobile12.dtd">
```

XHTML-MP is a kind of XML, so we need this XML declaration, too.

This is the DOCTYPE for XHTML-MP version 1.2. That's the most recent version.

And yes, we know we said "two lines," but it doesn't all fit onto the page.

index_mobile.html

Why would we want to use that old thing?

All we did was change the DOCTYPE declaration. That seems totally pointless. Why can't I just use HTML5?

We admit it. On the surface, using XHTML-MP doesn't seem very thrilling...

It doesn't support some of the things we like to use in our HTML, and modern phones are increasingly supportive (or at least tolerant) of HTML5 markup.

...but something actually did happen as a result of our DOCTYPE change.

If you load *http://hf-mw.com/ch3/ex/2* in the Opera Mini 4.2 simulator, you'll see a striking change. **Explicitly using XHTML-MP as our DOCTYPE changed the way the browser behaves!**

No longer do we have the content escaping the bounds of the page. Instead, the buttons and floats all fit within the page width.

Turns out, Opera Mini takes the HTML5 DOCTYPE as a "hint" that it is supposed to behave a bit more like a desktop browser. That means layout that has percentage-based widths—responsive layouts, for example—might not work exactly as we expect.

Hey, look at that! The content fits on the screen now.

Watch it!

Our job is not done here: we can't just change the DOCTYPE and call it a day.

We've changed the DOCTYPE *to XHTML-MP, but that doesn't mean that the markup is valid XHTML-MP markup. We also need to make some changes to our code to make it **actually** XHTML-MP.*

Keep your nose clean with XHTML-MP

It's not always a thrill a minute, but using a mobile-specific DOCTYPE helps us because:

1 **It ensures support on many older mobile browsers.**
Though most mobile browsers won't choke and die when they encounter an HTML5 document, they might. And some of the features supported in HTML5 just plain won't work on a lot of older phones.

2 **It reminds us of potential mobile pitfalls and keeps us honest.**
If a feature isn't supported in XHTML-MP, there is quite likely a reason. Using XHTML-MP and staying within its bounds keeps us from wandering off into dangerous territory. Just like mobile-first RWD keeps us focused on constraints, cleanliness, and the tasks at hand, so too does XHTML-MP provide a framework within which to create a widely supported mobile website.

—————————— there are no
Dumb Questions ——————————

Q: Apparently I missed the memo. What's a DOCTYPE?

A: A DOCTYPE (more formally, a *document type declaration*) is a short piece of text at the top of SGML and XML documents that informs the client (i.e., browser) which DTD to evaluate the document against.

Q: Too many acronyms. SGML and XML documents? DTD?

A: HTML is descended from SGML (Standard Generalized Markup Language), while XHTML is a kind of XML (and thus is more rigidly structured than its "X"-less kin), so both warrant DOCTYPEs.

Document type declarations (DTDs) are formalized definitions of what elements (tags, attributes, etc.) are allowed, and where, in the type of document they describe. Each specification of HTML and XHTML has its own DTD.

Nominally, associating a document with its intended DTD would allow the rendering client to go validate the document against that DTD. In real-life web browsers, this doesn't happen—web browsers never actually go out and validate against DTDs.

Q: So what's the point of a DOCTYPE, and why do browsers insist on them?

A: Browsers perform a kind of "sniffing" (not too different from our own user-agent sniffing earlier) on DOCTYPEs. While they don't formally validate documents, they use the DOCTYPE as a hint about what "mode" to assume and how to render the content.

Remember the Opera Mini situation, wherein changing the DOCTYPE from HTML5 to XHTML-MP (or XHTML-Basic) caused the layout mode to change? That's a good example of this at work.

Other browsers use the DOCTYPE to determine whether to render the content in "standards" mode or in "quirks" mode, a backward-compatible, more tolerant mode.

As of HTML5, all pretense of the browser going out and actually looking at a DTD has been dismissed, which is why one ends up with the short and simple `<!DOCTYPE html>` (no URL to a DTD).

XHTML-MP Exposed

**This week's interview:
Why bother with XHTML-MP?**

Grumpy Mobile Web Developer: You're looking a bit long in the tooth there, XHTML-MP. How long until you buy the proverbial farm, or sell it to HTML5?

XHTML-MP 1.2: I'm not dead yet! Some people think I've been put out to pasture, but I'm a useful old coot. I keep those older mobile browsers in line. You can depend on me. I can help keep you out of trouble.

GMWD: What kinds of trouble can you keep me out of?

XHTML-MP 1.2: You want examples? OK. What's the point of having an anchor (`<a>`) tag with a `target` of `_new` or `_blank` if you're on a mobile device? Many mobile browsers won't let you open a new window from a link. So, I don't support targets. Oh, and, frames—those are dangerous mojo. I don't support any frames, not even those fancy-pants `iframes`.

GMWD: No `iframes`? Bah.

XHTML-MP 1.2: Don't forget that my XHTML-MP family—ever since my granddad XHTML-MP 1.0 was a boy—brings you access keys.

GMWD: Access keys?

XHTML-MP 1.2: The entire XHTML-MP lineage gives you the `accesskey` attribute on anchor (`<a>`) tags. That lets you assign digits 0–9 as shortcut keys for those anchors. This can be very nice on phones that have numeric keypads. It can also help cut down on tedious scrolling.

GMWD: So…XHTML-MP invented access keys?

XHTML-MP 1.2: Well, technically that was passed down through generations, from WML through C-HTML to us. It's quite an heirloom.

GMWD: WML? C-HTML?

XHTML-MP 1.2: I'm not dead yet, but those guys sure are. Wireless Markup Language (WML) is gradually being phased out entirely. It's quite different than HTML, and my family replaced it as the preferred mobile markup variant.

C-HTML (Compact HTML) was used a lot in Japan in days of yore by DoCoMo. Some people call it iMode. You want emoticons? C-HTML has emoji in spades. But what it doesn't have fills volumes: no tables, no CSS, no images. Oh, and no color. Ah, yes, the good old days.

Watch it!

We need to keep our markup tidy.

We're pretty serious about that "choke and die" thing. Mobile browsers (especially older ones) are less fault-tolerant of poorly formed markup than their desktop counterparts. You need to be diligent about validating your markup—bad markup can cause mobile browsers to crash, or, even worse, wretched things like making the phone reboot entirely. Ick.

Jim: So, Frank, you think we should use XHTML-MP?

Frank: It sounds like the safest bet. It looks like we need to keep it clean and simple for these older browsers.

Jim: Is that going to require us to make other changes?

Frank: It's cool that the XHTML-MP DOCTYPE fixed the floated `<div>`s in Opera Mini, but I'm starting to feel really paranoid about floats on those older browsers. **I know it's a bit old-school, but I was thinking of using tables to lay out the dashboard information.**

Jim: I thought HTML tables were relics of the '90s, man.

Frank: Usually I avoid them like the plague, but they're not, like, invalid. And this dashboard stuff does feel like tabular data. I'm just not convinced that floated, `<div>`-based columns are going to work reliably in all of the mobile browsers we need to support.

Jim: Yeah, tables are kind of uncool, but I guess we know that they'll work. Also…what about all that CSS we already wrote for the mockup?

Frank: I'm feeling a bit overwhelmed by which HTML tags are supported and what kind of CSS support we can depend on.

I think I'd like to take this one thing at a time. I want to figure out which HTML elements are valid and supported on these phones, first. So, **I'm going to strip out all the CSS for now and add it back later.**

Hey, guys. One last thing before you do another round of mockups. Some of the feedback from *Creature Comforts* is that it feels like users on phones with small screens have to scroll through a lot of links to get to their dashboard section… Any ideas?

We can assign access key attributes to the links in the #tools `<div>` to give quicker access to the dashboard and the other links.

Without having to do so much scrolling

By the way, scrolling sucks

Not everyone has the luxury of a touchscreen. On many phones, the way to navigate through web pages is to use a key or a cursor to scroll through the content. In many interfaces, each clickable item is highlighted as the users scroll down the page, giving them an opportunity to follow the links. The more links and content, the more scrolling.

...thank goodness for access keys

The `accesskey` attribute on the anchor (`<a>`) tag lets us assign a numeric shortcut key to any anchor, reducing the amount of potential scrolling for our users. This lets users use the number keys on their phones to access links quickly. Access key syntax looks like this:

```
<a href="#dashboard" accesskey="1">Your Dashboard</a>
```

Access keys let users use their numeric keys as shortcuts!

The access key number assigned to a link doesn't show up automatically, so it's often handy to use ordered lists (`<ol>`) instead of unordered lists (`<ul>`) for lists of links (assuming the first item in the list uses `accesskey 1`).

One last curveball

OK, there's something we neglected to tell you. If this makes you want to throw up your hands and make very irritated noises, we understand.

XHTML-MP 1.2 was superseded by XHTML-Basic in 2008. Sorry.

XHTML-Basic 1.1 gives you everything that XHTML-MP 1.2 did, with a few bonuses. You get the `target` attribute on anchor tags back (not that we're suggesting that you use that, necessarily). You also get a few treats like `<sup>` and `<sub>`. Bottom line: you don't lose anything you already had in XHTML-MP 1.2.

*Also, XHTML-MP 1.2 **does** still work—just fine—in mobile browsers.*

 *Relax*

There are a whole lot of confusing markup options for mobile devices, but we'll stick to XHTML-Basic for the rest of this chapter.

Sorry we made you go through that, but it was for your own good. The mobile web markup landscape is complicated, and you should have a sense of what's out there. Now we'll stop flailing around and stick with XHTML-Basic. It's not too hard: we'll just need to identify what tags aren't supported, and avoid them. And we won't even worry about CSS styling or layout right now.

Test Drive

① **Convert the document to XHTML-Basic.**

Replace the current `DOCTYPE` tag with the following:

```
<!DOCTYPE html PUBLIC "-//W3C//DTD XHTML Basic 1.1//EN"
"http://www.w3.org/TR/xhtml-basic/xhtml-basic11.dtd">
```

② **Remove the CSS for now.**

Delete the CSS `<link>` tag; we'll deal with CSS later.

③ **Convert the `<ul>` in the #tools `<div>` to an `<ol>`.**

This will make numbers show up next to the links and helps with the next step.

④ **Add accesskey attributes to the `<a>` tags in the #tools `<div>`.**

See page 119 for syntax hints.

⑤ **Convert the floating, `<div>`-based #dashboard `<div>` to a table.**

Replace the content inside the **#dashboard `<div>`** with a `table`. This is a bit tedious, so you can use the ready-bake markup on page 121 (or find this code in the *extras* directory in the *chapter3* folder—it's in a file called *table.txt*).

⑥ **Save your changed file as index.html.**

Save the file as *index.html*—we're done testing the mobile redirect now, so it's easier to just use *index.html*.

> http://www.hf-mw.com...
>
> ## Creature Comforts
>
> **Agent Portal**
>
> **Welcome back, Dr. Jessica Evans**
>
> 1. Your Dashboard
> 2. Messages (2)
> 3. Your Schedule
> 4. Request Supplies
> 5. Request Personnel
> 6. Call HQ
>
> February 4: Loading supplies and contacting personnel to assist with flood event in Bangladesh. Contact HQ if you are currently unscheduled and available to assist in the effort.
>
> **Type**   **Details**

Our plain, but functional, mockup on an Android device.

Make sure to keep the #dashboard <div>. Just replace its <u>contents</u>.

there are no Dumb Questions

Q: So, I know we're going all hardcore simplified for now, but, after changing the `DOCTYPE` to XHTML-Basic, does the mockup we looked at on page 115 still work in Opera Mini 4.2?

A: Yep! You can see this at *http://hf-mw.com/ch3/ex/2a* if you are curious.

Q: Isn't Opera Mini 4.2 pretty archaic? How many people really use that version anymore?

A: Admittedly, it's not a recent browser. But browsers of its vintage absolutely do exist out there in the woolly wilds of Mobile Web Land. It's a good example of the *sort* of browser with the *sort* of constraints one runs into on older feature phones in, especially, emerging markets.

Q: But didn't you just say that smartphones are now outselling these dinosaur feature phones?

A: Outselling doesn't mean outnumbering. There are still vast numbers of existing older smartphones (not really "smart" by our current standards) and feature phones. It will be some time before they disappear.

**Ready Bake
Table Code**

```
<table>
  <thead>
  <tr>
    <th>Type</th>
    <th>Details</th>
  </tr>
  </thead>
  <tbody>
    <tr>
      <td><p>Message<br />Feb 3 8:54PM EST</p></td>
      <td><p><a href="#">Supply Request #493-C4 Approved</a><br />
    Hi, Jess, Good news! I wanted to let you know that we were successful in
tracking down those bottles...</p></td>
    </tr>
    <tr>
      <td><p>Message<br />Feb 3 1:47PM EST</p></td>
      <td><p><a href="#">Supply Request #493-C4 Received</a><br />
      This is an automated message to confirm that your recent Supply Request
has been received and is in process...</p></td>
    </tr>
    <tr>
      <td><p>Event Scheduled<br />Feb 3 8:22AM EST</p></td>
      <td><p><a href="#">Itinerary 39924 Approved LAX -> DAC</a><br />
      Your itinerary for event: "Bangladesh Flood Event" has been approved.
Your calendar has been updated...</p></td>
    </tr>
    <tr>
      <td><p>Personnel Event<br />Feb 2 9:23PM EST</p></td>
      <td><p><a href="#">Re: Personnel Confirmation 03/05 - 03/15</a><br />
        Jessica! Thanks so much for committing to this operation! I think
Dr. Madling is going too and...</p>
      </td>
    </tr>
    <tr>
      <td colspan="2"><div class="morelink"><p><a href="#">More &gt;&gt; </p>
</a></div></td>
    </tr>
  </tbody>
</table>
```

Exercise

Which elements are valid where? Use what we've learned and your own intuitive sense to figure out which tags and attributes are OK in which standards. An element may be OK in more than one standard!

	XHTML-MP 1.2	XHTML-Basic 1.1	HTML5
<font>	☐	☐	☐
<table>	☐	☐	☐
<a target="">	☐	☐	☐
<sup>	☐	☐	☐
<a accesskey="">	☐	☐	☐
<u>	☐	☐	☐
<tbody>	☐	☐	☐
<link>	☐	☐	☐
<strong>	☐	☐	☐
<video>	☐	☐	☐
<iframe>	☐	☐	☐

⟶ Answers on page 126.

> I can't get access keys to work. The Opera Mini simulator doesn't seem to support them, and I don't have a phone with a hard keyboard.

We promise that they do work on a lot of phones, but you don't have to take our word for it.

Access keys are actually supported in most major desktop browsers, too.

Access keys in action

If you want to test out the access keys on the mobile markup, you can view *index.html* in your desktop browser. Test out the access keys by using the following key combinations:

> Chrome or Safari: `CTRL-OPT [accesskey]`
> FireFox: `CRTL-[accesskey]`

Mac

> Chrome or Safari: `ALT-[accesskey]`
> FireFox: `ALT-SHIFT-[accesskey]`
> Internet Explorer: `ALT-[accesskey]`

Windows

> Chrome: `ALT-[accesskey]`
> FireFox: `ALT-SHIFT-[accesskey]`

Linux

Certain operating system shortcut keys or software configurations could take precedence over these, so your mileage may vary.

Get some validation

Remember how we told you that it's important to use valid markup? Let's not just give that lip service—it's time to validate the markup in the mockup and make sure it's up to snuff. Let's head over to the invaluable **W3C Markup Validator** site to check our code.

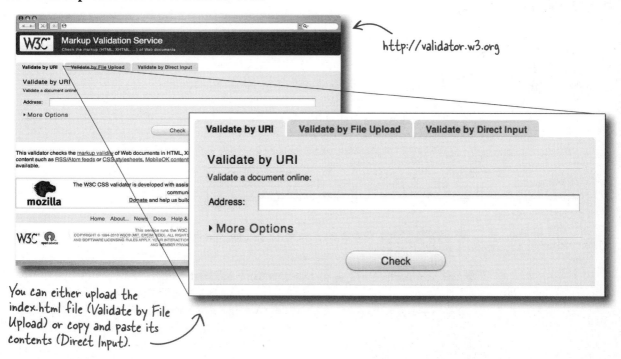

http://validator.w3.org

You can either upload the index.html file (Validate by File Upload) or copy and paste its contents (Direct Input).

So, are we good to go?

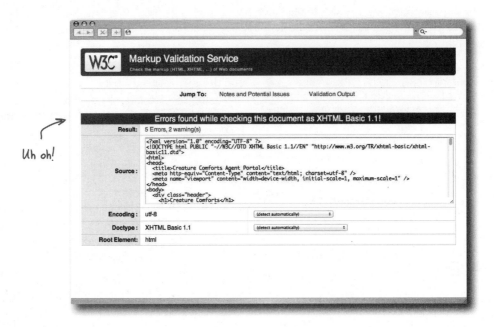

Uh oh!

What went wrong?

Scroll down on the results page to see details about the errors. So, what's the problem here?

1 **`<thead>` and `<tbody>` tags are not supported in XHTML-Basic (or XHTML-MP).**

This is likely the most glaring partially unsupported HTML module in both XHTML-MP and XHTML-Basic. Tables are OK, but you can't use `<thead>`, `<tbody>`, `<tfoot>`, `<col>`, or `<colgroup>`.

These three errors are related to the unsupported `<thead>` and `<tbody>` tags in the mobile mockup HTML.

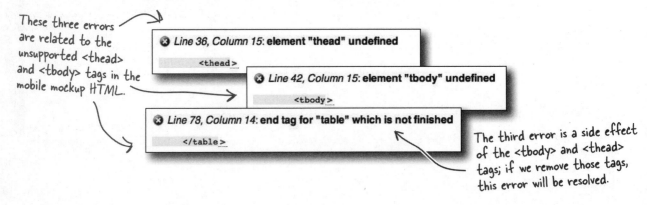

The third error is a side effect of the `<tbody>` and `<thead>` tags; if we remove those tags, this error will be resolved.

Fix the errors

2 **There are some improperly nested tags.**

Even seasoned pros make little typo-esque mistakes like this one. That's one of the reasons to use the validator—even if you're at the top of your game.

From index.html

```
<td colspan="2"><div class="morelink">
<p><a href="#">More &gt;&gt;</p></a></div>
</td>
```

❌ *Line 74, Column 80:* **end tag for "a" omitted, but OMITTAG NO was specified**

...lspan="2"><div class="morelink"><p><a href="#">More >></p></a></div></td>

❌ *Line 74, Column 84:* **end tag for element "a" which is not open**

...lspan="2"><div class="morelink"><p><a href="#">More >></p></a></div></td>

⬥ *Line 74, Column 52:* **start tag was here**

... colspan="2"><div class="morelink"><p><a href="#">More >></p></a></div><...

This isn't actually an error—it's the validator trying to give us hints as to where to find the problem.

Both of these errors were caused by a misplaced </a> tag.

TEST DRIVE

Fix the markup problems in the *index.html* file.

1 Remove the `<thead>`, `</thead>`, `<tbody>`, and `</tbody>` tags from the markup.

2 Fix the improperly nested tags. Put the `</a>` tag within the paragraph in the `.morelink <div>`.

3 Revalidate the updated code with the W3C validator.

Woot! Green means success.

Exercise Solution

How'd you do identifying which tags are valid in which standards?

<font> and <u> are both deprecated— use CSS instead!

	XHTML-MP 1.2	XHTML-Basic 1.1	HTML5
<font>	☐	☐	☐
<table>	☑	☑	☑
<a target="">	☐	☑	☑
<sup>	☐	☑	☑
<a accesskey="">	☑	☑	☑
<u>	☐	☐	☐
<tbody>	☐	☐	☑
<link>	☑	☑	☑
<strong>	☑	☑	☑
<video>	☐	☐	☑
<iframe>	☐	☐	☑

OK. We've got valid code and a basic structure. But it's looking super bland. Can we bring back some CSS?

Mobile-savvy CSS

CSS Mobile Profile 2.0 (CSS-MP) and XHTML-Basic (or XHTML-MP) go together like peas and carrots. The CSS-MP standard was developed with low- to mid-range phones in mind.

What do you get in CSS Mobile Profile? Well, most of what you've come to expect out of CSS2, and even a bit of CSS3. But not everything.

Sounds simple in theory

Browsers that implement CSS Mobile Profile 2.0 are supposed to support the required properties. But the reality is a bit of a downer. CSS support varies quite a bit, and the onus often falls on you, the intrepid developer, to test thoroughly and work around quirks.

In addition, quite a few CSS properties and values are considered *optional* in CSS-MP, meaning browser makers can opt to support them—or not.

Sounds complicated and depressing. How am I going to learn this stuff?

The best way is: less chit-chat, more doing.

Instead of throwing out a tedious list of supported and unsupported CSS properties in CSS Mobile Profile, **let's jump in and figure out how to adapt the existing CSS to be CSS-MP compliant.**

Long Exercise

Buckle up. Roll up your sleeves. Batten down the hatches. We're going to go on a journey here—a journey that, if everything goes right, will end with a loving marriage between XHTML-Basic and CSS Mobile Profile. We'll be editing both *index.html* and *styles.css*.

① Put the `<link>` tag back in index.html.

We're going to want to start using CSS again, so we need that `<link>` tag.

```
<head>
   <title>Creature Comforts Agent Portal</title>
   <meta http-equiv="Content-Type" content="text/html; charset=utf-8" />
   <meta name="viewport" content="width=device-width, initial-scale=1,
maximum-scale=1" />
   <link rel="stylesheet" type="text/css" href="styles.css" />
</head>
```

index.html

② Let's refactor styles.css to be valid CSS Mobile Profile.

The `background-image` and `background-repeat` properties are supported in CSS-MP, but having a big header with a background image wastes a lot of space. Let's just get rid of the background image.

background-position values in percentages and pixels are not supported in CSS-MP, so we'd have to change this if we were keeping the background image.

But we're not. Device support is iffy; heck, even support for background-color isn't assured.

Everything else in this CSS so far is compliant...onward!

```
* {
   padding: 0;
   margin: 0;
}
body {
   font-family: "Helvetica", "Arial", san-serif;
   font-size: 100%;
   width: 100%;
   background-color: #f3ffc2;
   background-image: url('cows.jpg');
   background-repeat: no-repeat;
   background-position: 50% 0px;
}
p {
   font-size: .95em;
   margin: 0.25em 0;
}
h1, h2, h3, h4, h5 {
   font-family: "Times New Roman", serif;
   margin: 0;
   color: #10508c;
   text-align: center;
}
```

styles.css

```css
h3 {
   font-style: italic;
   font-weight: 100;
   font-size: 1.15em;
}
ol {
   width: 100%;
}
a {
   text-decoration: none;
   color: #096c9f;
}
.header {
   height: 150px;
}
#tools ol {
   list-style-type: none;
}
#tools ol li a {
   -webkit-border-radius: 5px;
   -moz-border-radius: 5px;
   border-radius: 5px;
   display: block;
   height: 1.1em;
   width:  94%;
   background-color: #fff;
   margin: 3%;
   border: 1px solid #ccc;
   text-align: center;
   padding: .6em 0;
}
.greeting {
   border: 1px dashed #10508c;
   border-width: 1px 0;
}
#dashboard {
   -webkit-border-radius: 5px;
   -moz-border-radius: 5px;
   border-radius: 5px;
   background-color: #fff;
   border: 1px solid #ccc;
   margin: 1em 3%;
   padding: .5em 0;
   width: 94%;
}
```

styles.css

Since we last used this CSS, we changed our <ul> to an <ol>. These rules will need to be updated to reflect that.

These properties to create rounded corners are invalid in CSS–MP, and most of those older browsers don't support them, anyway. Delete these from the CSS.

Continues over the page.

Long Exercise

③ **Back to index.html: add some classes to the table elements.**

```
<tr class="even">
  <td class="event event_meta"><p><strong>Message</strong><br
/>
  Feb 3 8:54PM EST</p>
  </td>
  <td class="event"><p><a href="#"><strong>Supply Request #493-
C4 Approved</strong></a><br />
  Hi, Jess, Good news! I wanted to let you know that we were
successful in tracking down those bottles...</p></td>
</tr>
```

Hey, hotshot! Apply these classes to the other three rows, too.

But alternate tr.even with tr.odd.

④ **And now back to styles.css: adapt styles to apply to the tabular markup.**

index.html

We switched from <div>s to tables for layout. We'll want to get rid of some properties that no longer make sense, and make a few edits to others.

```
#dashboard td.event {
    border: 1px dashed #ddd;
    border-width: 1px 0 0 0;
    margin: .5em 0;
    padding: 0.5em 0;
    width: 100%;
    clear: both;
    overflow: hidden;
}
#dashboard .odd {
    background-color: #fff;
}
#dashboard .even {
    background-color: #eee;
}
#dashboard td.event_meta {
    width: 30%;
    margin: 0 2%;
    float: left;
}
```

Remove these three properties.

No more float here. And some adjustment to width and margins.

We're not floating content anymore. In addition, browsers that implement CSS-MP are only required to implement the "auto" value of overflow; everything else is optional. You can't rely on overflow in CSS-MP.

styles.css

⑤ Add this CSS rule to styles.css...

Add this new CSS rule (anywhere in the styles.css file).

```
#dashboard table {
  border-collapse: collapse;
  width: 100%;
}
```

styles.css

⑥ ...and remove some unneeded rules.

Find and eliminate the style rules:

Delete all of these!

```
#dashboard div
#dashboard .event_time
#dashboard .event_details
#dashboard .event_subject
#dashboard .event_summary
```

styles.css

⑦ Fix the #status_message <div>.

```
#status_message {
  background-color: #f8f1b2;
  padding: 0.25em;
  line-height: 1.3em;
  border: 1px solid #ccc;
  border-width: 1px 0;
  height: 70px;
  overflow: scroll;
}
```

And, finally, get rid of these.

styles.css

Watch it!

Beware of using the `overflow` property!

`overflow: scroll` is totally taboo in Mobile Land. It's generally not supported on any platform, and is an interactive ickiness.

The behavior of the `overflow` property in browsers that implement CSS-MP is varied—the only value that they are required to support is `auto`. Avoid relying on `overflow` whenever possible.

⑧ Save the files, and you're done!

Hmmm...something is missing

Take a look at this screenshot from the Opera Mini 4.2 simulator of the current mockup. Notice anything? We've lost the list numbering on our `<ol>`—and those numbers indicated the access keys. Uh oh.

Where'd the numbers go?

The numbers are still "there," but we've applied CSS that makes the `<li>` elements look like buttons that span the full width of the window. So the numbers are off to the left of the visible content.

Normally, to "bring them back," we'd use something like:

How the mockup currently looks: no access keys.

```
#tools ol {
    list-style-position: inside;
}
```

`list-style-position: inside` brings the numbers "inside" the `<li>` element and renders them (in this case) next to the contents of the `<li>` (our links). Sounds about right, huh?

Unfortunately, **list-style-position is not supported in CSS-MP**. So we have a problem. Maybe we'll need to convert the links into a simple list of links, instead of the buttony look we have now. Then the numbers will show up again.

Bye bye, buttons

We can regain the numbered list by replacing the CSS rules for `#tools ol` and `#tools ol li` with this:

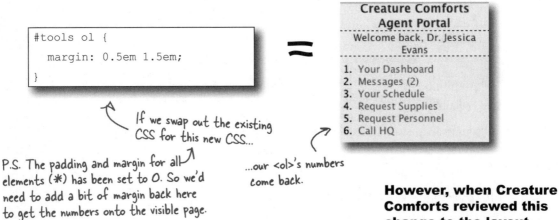

```
#tools ol {
    margin: 0.5em 1.5em;
}
```

=

**Creature Comforts
Agent Portal**

Welcome back, Dr. Jessica Evans

1. Your Dashboard
2. Messages (2)
3. Your Schedule
4. Request Supplies
5. Request Personnel
6. Call HQ

If we swap out the existing CSS for this new CSS...

P.S. The padding and margin for all elements (✳) has been set to 0. So we'd need to add a bit of margin back here to get the numbers onto the visible page.

...our <ol>'s numbers come back.

However, when Creature Comforts reviewed this change to the layout...

The button look is sorely missed!

Hmmm...I'd really prefer it if those utility links looked like buttons and not just links.

Creature Comforts has become attached to the button look and wants it back.

The only way to accomplish this with valid CSS-MP is to convert the list back to a <ul>, add the numbers to the content itself, and update the CSS style rules.

Ahhh, compromises. That's the mobile web way!

TEST DRIVE

Change the CSS selectors in the *styles.css* file and convert the <ol> to a <ul> in *index.html*. Don't forget to add the access key numbers to the text content of the links, too!

styles.css

```
#tools ul {
    ...
}
#tools ul li a {
    ...
}
```

Put the CSS that was used for #tools ol on page 129 here.

And put the CSS previously used for #tools ol li a here.

Change the <ol> back to a <ul> again in index.html.

```
<div id="tools">
  <ul>
    <li><a href="#dashboard" accesskey="1">1. Your Dashboard</a></li>
    <li><a href="#" accesskey="2">2. Messages (2)</a></li>
    <li><a href="#" accesskey="3">3. Your Schedule</a></li>
    <li><a href="#" accesskey="4">4. Request Supplies</a></li>
    <li><a href="#" accesskey="5">5. Request Personnel</a></li>
    <li><a href="#" accesskey="6">6. Call HQ</a></li>
  </ul>
</div>
```

index.html

Great success!

Mockup on a BlackBerry 9330

Looks fine on newer smartphones, like this Android Nexus S.

You can see the final mockup at http://hf-mw.com/ch3/ex/5.

 BULLET POINTS

- It's a big world, and there are billions (yep) of mobile phones. Not all of them are bleeding-edge smartphones, and sometimes you have to make your website or web app work with those phones.

- There are real-life circumstances: older systems, recalcitrant clients, or specific projects that make having a totally **separate mobile website** necessary.

- One of the ways to route mobile traffic to a mobile-specific website is to use **server-side mobile device detection** and redirection.

- **User-agent sniffing** is a popular technique for evaluating whether an incoming request is from a mobile browser.

- User-agent sniffing examines the `User-Agent header` that browsers send as part of each HTTP request. Users can "spoof" their user agent— knowingly or not. This is a weakness of this method.

- Some older mobile browsers (and current, lower-end mobile devices) implement different standards for HTML and CSS.

- **XHTML Mobile Profile** (XHTML-MP) is a mobile-specific standard used by many mobile browsers. It is similar to XHTML, but does not support everything that XHTML does.

- Similarly, **CSS Mobile Profile** (CSS-MP) is a mobile-specific flavor of CSS.

- XHTML-MP was superseded by **XHTML-Basic 1.1,** which is almost the same except for a few new supported elements.

- It's important to choose the **appropriate `DOCTYPE`** for your mobile web project and pay attention to keeping your **markup valid**—bad code can make phones behave very badly.

there are no
Dumb Questions

Q: There's XHTML-Basic/XHTML-MP instead of HTML, and CSS-Mobile Profile instead of full-on CSS2. Is there an equivalent mobile flavor of JavaScript for mobile devices?

A: Yes, there is a mobile-specific JavaScript called ECMAScript Mobile Profile, but you can't rely on it. We've worked with phones where the JavaScript cannot change anything on the page once it is loaded, which means most of the things you use JavaScript for cannot be done. So if you're targeting old phones, you're probably better off not relying on JavaScript.

Q: What about Wireless CSS?

A: Wireless CSS is a standard quite similar to CSS-Mobile Profile, but with support for fewer properties. It's kind of on its way out, and we don't see any reason to use it instead of CSS-MP.

Q: If you use user-agent sniffing to route mobile traffic, and you misidentify a user's browser either because she is spoofing her user agent or because you're just…wrong, couldn't she end up getting redirected and stuck on the mobile version of the site, unable to escape back to the full site?

A: Well spotted! This is important! In a real-life situation, you would want to provide an "escape hatch," often in the form of a link back to the desktop site.

The link on its own isn't enough—you need to let your redirection script know that the user wants the desktop site. You can accomplish this by setting a cookie indicating this preference and not redirecting browsers that have that cookie set.

Q: What happens if I just can't get my site to do what I want in a way that is perfectly valid XHTML-Basic or CSS-MP or whatever? Does the sky fall? Do phones around the world crash?

A: Being successful on the mobile web often means making compromises and trade-offs. While writing valid code is something to shoot for, it's not always 100% feasible. But knowing the rules before you break them is always a good motto to live by.

Q: Do I have to use XHTML-Basic every time I want to support a lot of mobile browsers? It feels constrained.

A: We have to pull out the classic mobile web answer for this: "it depends." In Creature Comforts' case, there were a lot of older, less full-featured phones we needed to support. Our goals were to get a server-side data service to render well on as many feature phones as possible.

Using HTML5 in many cases is a reasonable approach, even on older phones. But we wanted to show you the kinds of things you need to be aware of when targeting older devices.

Q: You neglected to do so on page 127, but I do want to see an exhaustive list of supported and nonsupported properties in CSS-MP.

A: Hey, you're in luck: the CSS Mobile Profile 2.0 spec happens to be a rather quick and easy read. You can find it at *http://www.w3.org/TR/css-mobile*.

BRAIN POWER

Hey, developer types! How could we support users who want the desktop version instead? Can you think of what would be needed to add a link from the mobile to the desktop site, and what modifications you'd need to make to *redirect.php* to write and check for a cookie to store the user's preference?

It's not cool to strand users on a stripped-down mobile site if they'd prefer to escape to the desktop version.

4 deciding whom to support

What devices should we support?

Well, sure your site doesn't work on this phone, but you could have left out the part about "out-of-date technophobe Luddites"...

There aren't enough hours in the day to test on every device.

You have to draw the line somewhere on what you can support. **But how do you decide?** What about people using devices you can't test on—are they left out in the cold? Or is it possible to build your web pages in a way that will reach people on devices you've never heard of? In this chapter, we're going to mix a magic concoction of **project requirements** and **audience usage** to help us figure out **what devices we support** and **what to do about those we don't**.

How do you know where to draw the line?

Every project is a series of compromises. Stakeholder desires. User experience feedback. Search engine optimization. Figuring out what matters for your project can seem like magic to people who aren't in the trenches with you.

Deciding what devices you care about is similar. You take criteria and priorities, apply some brain power, sprinkle in a little magical inspiration, and you come up with a list of devices that are key to your success.

Step away from the keyboard for a second

We've tried to keep everything grounded and hands on so far, but we've reached that point in the movie where the actor stares off into space and contemplates a tough problem. Suddenly, inspiration hits and the actor leaps into action.

The difference here is that you're the actor. You already have all of the tools you need to decide where to draw the line.

But you're not going to find that inspiration at the keyboard, so we'll take a brief interlude from building stuff to talk about the abstract stuff that turns criteria and priorities into a list of devices you support. We're going to help focus your brain a little and then get out of the way.

Don't worry, we'll get back to building stuff soon. The best directors know that all they need to do is give their actors some guidance and let the actors act.

What's this line we need to draw?

Supporting every device ever made is a noble goal. Testing on every device ever made is a sure-fire path to losing your mind. You can hope to support as many people as possible, but to keep your sanity, you're going to have to know the answer to three questions.

1   **What devices do we support?**
Which devices or types of devices are you going to test your pages on to make sure they work as intended?

2   **What happens to devices we DON'T support?**
What can you do to make sure devices that you don't test on are still able to use your site?

2   **What happens to devices we CAN'T support?**
What message do you give people whose devices aren't up to snuff?

> Can you think of some differences between devices you *don't* support and those that you *can't* support?

Things you <u>don't</u> support vs. those you <u>can't</u> support

Once you know what you *are* going to support, everything else is something you don't support. So why make a distinction between what you *don't* support and what you *can't* support?

Although you don't explicitly support a device, that doesn't mean what you've built *won't* work on that device. If you build your web page using well-formed, semantic HTML and progressive enhancement, your page will be accessible by many more browsers and devices than you can guarantee that it will work on.

But sometimes a browser is so old and feeble that you simply *can't* support it.

For example, if you're selling shoes online, you need to use HTTPS to keep credit card information safe. Some old phones don't support HTTPS. When that happens, the best thing you can do is tell the person that she can't buy shoes on her phone.

Don't be a meanie about it

If you can't support someone's browser, be nice about it. He may not have the latest phone in his pocket, but he may have access to a better browser somewhere else.

Besides, no one likes to be told his phone is a jalopy. Be gracious to your guests.

Watch it!

Don't exclude unsupported browsers.

Just because you can't verify that your pages will work in a browser doesn't mean you should exclude people using that browser. If you build the site using semantic markup, it will work in many browsers—including ones you couldn't test on and that were not critical to your project.

I understand not being able to support really old phones that don't have HTTPS, but I thought if you delivered a basic HTML document and then progressively enhanced it with CSS and JavaScript, it would work everywhere.

You're right. In many cases, progressive enhancement means you can support hundreds of different browsers. But your mileage may vary.

Starting with basic HTML and progressively enhancing the document should be the starting point for most web pages. Browsers with advanced features get enhancements like rounded corners and gradients.

However, the minimum requirements for a site or app may be higher than basic HTML can provide. A video game may require WebGL, a graphics library, for game play. There is no content if the browser doesn't support WebGL—that is, until a couple of years from now when you can progressively enhance from WebGL to WebGL 2!

WebGL 2 doesn't exist, but it seems likely, doesn't it?

As they say, you have to know the rules before you know when to break them. You should use progressive enhancement from basic HTML unless you have a really good reason why it won't work.

And even then, a basic HTML document that said, "Sorry, this game requires WebGL support to play" would be a nice starting point upon which to build the game.

Ask questions about your project

It might sound like we're teaching you to suck eggs here, but the first step toward figuring out where to draw the line is to think about your project. **Who** is your audience? **What** functionality is core? **What** features are optional? **What** is the best experience?

Hmm...the travel app I'm working on needs to know where someone is to work. What if that person's phone doesn't have GPS? Would zip code be accurate enough?

The cheapest thing on this site costs $10,000. Might as well call it Filthy Rich 'R' Us. Can we assume most customers will have recent smartphones?

The sales team needs to show the app to potential customers, but standard issue for salespeople is a BlackBerry 4.5 phone. How can we show off the app on such an old device and still make it look good on iPhones?

Our Funny Cat Video site will be great on mobile, but only if the phone supports video. Which phones support video and have good data plans or WiFi ability?

We're getting ready to expand into Japan and South Korea. Do they use the same phones as we do? I heard Japan has a lot of phones not available elsewhere.

Our newest game, Enraged Avians, is graphically intense. We already know the browser will need to support WebGL, but now we're wondering if some phones will be too slow even if they support WebGL.

Ingredients for your magic mobile potion

When you ask questions about your project, you're starting to suss out the factors that can help you figure out which devices matter. Who is your audience and what is it likely to use? What are must-haves versus nice-to-have features?

This is where the magic comes in. Mix these factors together into a magic potion that tells you what devices you need to support.

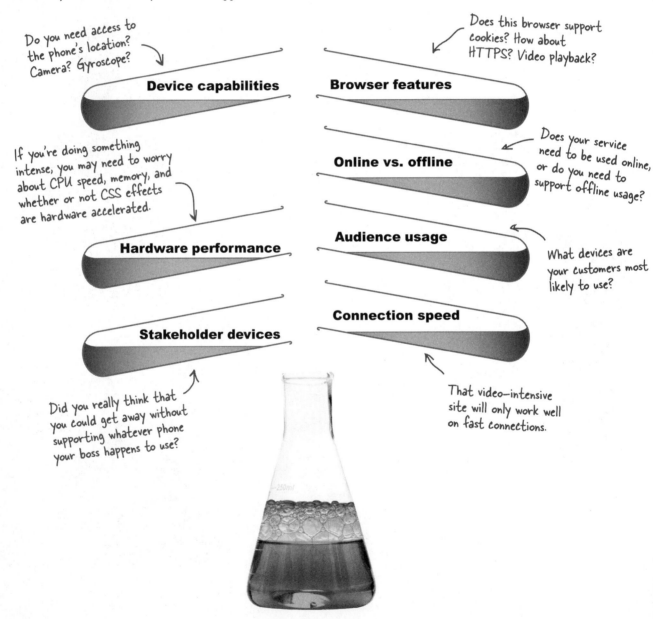

Do you need access to the phone's location? Camera? Gyroscope?

Device capabilities

Does this browser support cookies? How about HTTPS? Video playback?

Browser features

If you're doing something intense, you may need to worry about CPU speed, memory, and whether or not CSS effects are hardware accelerated.

Online vs. offline

Does your service need to be used online, or do you need to support offline usage?

Hardware performance

Audience usage

What devices are your customers most likely to use?

Stakeholder devices

Connection speed

Did you really think that you could get away without supporting whatever phone your boss happens to use?

That video-intensive site will only work well on fast connections.

Draw from your cupboard of tools and data

What goes into audience usage? Dig into your jar of web analytics to see what your current customers are using. Expanding to a new geography? Pull out data on the top phones in those countries to see what the cool phone is in Singapore.

Analytics can be web statistics or other forms of tracking customer usage.

Beware of analytics if your site has a poor mobile experience. Garbage site in: Garbage analytics out.

There are big differences in the phones sold in different parts of the world.

It never hurts to ask!

Income, age, and (to some degree) gender all impact what phone someone is likely to own.

Big collections like the Device Anywhere Data Explorer and Browserscope can help answer questions about which devices support which features.

Is your cupboard bare? You're in luck. Check out this comprehensive guide to mobile statistics at http://bit.ly/m-stats.

Exercise

Time to put your magician's hat on and work some magic. For each case study, build a requirements list based on what the app is trying to accomplish and the target audience.

The list should include must-have requirements and nice-to-have features.

Here's our list of requirements based on the information in this case study.

Example

Case Study

Mo Better Museums is building an app that allows museum visitors to point their phone cameras at a piece of art and see an overlay containing more information about the piece. It can tell which piece of art is being viewed based on the phone's location. Phone reception in museums can be spotty.

Requirements:

- <u>Must have</u>: support JavaScript

- <u>Must have</u>: access to camera

- <u>Must have</u>: access to location

- Nice to have: support offline mode

Requirements:

Case Study

A politician wants an edge in a close election. She would like an app for volunteers to use when they go door-to-door to encourage people to vote. The app will provide the address of people to contact—with a map if possible—and what questions the volunteer should ask. Volunteers are in short supply, so she would like the app to support whatever phone they happen to own.

Case Study

Bowling Boxers is the video-game generation's version of Dogs Playing Poker. You control a boxer, based on a dog in the famous C. M. Coolidge paintings, that is pitted in a fierce back-alley bowling competition. Rendering the characters and all of the insane lane action pushes the limits of many phones.

Requirements:

Case Study

Global Corp has noticed an increase in sales in India. The VP of Sales believes India could be Global's next big market. He would like a localized version of Global's site that will work on the most popular phones in India. He wants it to be as easy as possible for customers to place orders on their phones.

Requirements:

BRAIN POWER

Which requirements are minimum bars, and which can be supported via progressive enhancement?

Exercise Solution

Don't you hate it when someone tells you there is no right answer? Yeah, well, sorry about that. There are no right answers when it comes to requirements.

So don't fret if you have a different answer for these case studies. Your experience may give you a requirement that we've missed. Trust your experience and instincts.

Camera access is a new W3C API. So far, only the latest version of Android partially supports it.

EXAMPLE

Case Study

Mo Better Museums is building an app that allows museum visitors to point their phone cameras at a piece of art and see an overlay containing more information about the piece. It can tell which piece of art is being viewed based on the phone's location. Phone reception in museums can be spotty.

Requirements:

- <u>Must have</u>: support JavaScript

→ • <u>Must have</u>: access to camera

- <u>Must have</u>: access to location

- Nice to have: support offline mode

Case Study

A politician wants an edge in a close election. She would like an app for volunteers to use when they go door-to-door to encourage people to vote. The app will provide the address of people to contact—with a map if possible—and what questions the volunteer should ask. Volunteers are in short supply, so she would like the app to support whatever phone they happen to own.

Requirements:

- <u>Must have</u>: Internet connection

- Nice to have: ability to display images for map

- Nice to have: JavaScript for interactive maps

Nice! Some opportunities for progressive enhancement!

Case Study

Bowling Boxers is the video-game generation's version of Dogs Playing Poker. You control a boxer, based on a dog in the famous C. M. Coolidge paintings, that is pitted in a fierce back-alley bowling competition. Rendering the characters and all of the insane lane action pushes the limits of many phones.

Requirements:

- <u>Must have</u>: support JavaScript
- <u>Must have</u>: support WebGL
- <u>Must have</u>: fast CPU and GPU, or the game performance will suffer

Case Study

Global Corp has noticed an increase in sales in India. The VP of Sales believes India could be Global's next big market. He would like a localized version of Global's site that will work on the most popular phones in India. He wants it to be as easy as possible for customers to place orders on their phones.

Requirements:

- <u>Must have</u>: support basic markup for old phones
- <u>Must have</u>: HTTPS for checkout
- <u>Must have</u>: cookies for login

Iteration helps you uncover extra requirements.

If you were to pull back the curtain on most mobile projects, you'd find that the people who made the site were uncertain about what devices they needed to support. They made the best guess they could and then iterated on it until they perfected the site.

How do I know my customers have the right stuff?

> Now that I have a device requirements list, how do I know if a specific phone fits my criteria?

Great question. There are two main methods: server-side device detection and client-side feature detection. We're going to look at device-detection databases in the next chapter.

We looked at feature detection in Chapter 2 when we talked about progressive enhancement.

It sounds like you're ready for this interlude to end and get back to building things. We told you this wouldn't take long.

Now get ready to roll up your sleeves again and dig into the crazy world of device databases and the bane of web developers everywhere: user-agent strings.

Don't worry. It isn't as bad as it sounds. By the end of the next chapter, you'll be bossing those evil user-agent strings around.

BULLET POINTS

- Every project **draws the line** somewhere on which devices it supports.

- Knowing where to draw the line is a combination of **experience, research, and gut instinct**.

- **There is a difference between devices you *don't* support and those you *can't* support** because they lack critical features that make it impossible to use your site.

- Look at your **project requirements and your target audience** to help decide where to draw the line.

- **Progressive enhancement** should be the **default approach**. This will make your site work on many more devices than you can officially support.

- **Unless you know for certain that you cannot support a device, you shouldn't exclude it**. New browsers show up all the time. Give them a chance to prove they're up to snuff.

- Don't let mobile's complexity overwhelm you. You already have all of the tools you need to know where to draw the line. **Trust your experience and instincts**.

5 device databases and classes

Get with the group

Uh, when you said you were going to take a peek behind the curtain, I didn't think you meant this one... It is possible to know a little *too* much about a user, you know...

Setting the bar for the devices we support doesn't take care of a few nagging issues. How do we find out enough stuff about our users' mobile browsers to know if they measure up before we deliver content to them? How do we avoid only building (lame) content for the lowest common denominator? And how do we organize all of this stuff so that we don't lose our minds? In this chapter, we'll enter the realm of **device capabilities**, learn to access them with a **device database**, and, finally, discover how to group them into **device classes** so that we can keep our sanity.

A panic button for freaked-out students

AcedIt! Test Prep hangs its hat on superior customer service. Its goal is to make each and every one of its students—who are hard at work nerve-rackingly studying for career- or academic-advancing standardized tests and certifications—feel like they have a one-on-one connection with tutors who are experts in their subjects.

Sometimes students panic. That's why AcedIt! wants to create a page on its website specially attuned to its customers who are on the edge. It's called the I'm Freaking Out! page, and its goal is simple: connect the customer with an on-call tutor right away.

Wouldn't it be cool if a freaked-out user on a mobile browser could see a big red panic button that he could press and place a phone call right away?

I'm Freaking Out!

HELP

Pre-test late-night jitters? A math problem that just won't budge? Our expert on-call tutors are standing by to help you through tough moments.

Steve, CEO of AcedIt!

The button is for mobile phones only

Desktop browsers can't make phone calls, so the big, red panic button metaphor is kind of lost there. Steve only wants the button to show up on mobile phones.

We have an IT guy who usually does the website tweaks, but in this case I think we might need help.

But how do we know someone is on a mobile p<u>hone?</u>

Frank: We might be able to do this with CSS media queries based on the window width of the browser.

Jill: Not in this case, I don't think. Just because a window is narrow in width doesn't mean the browser is on an actual mobile phone.

Frank: Right, I guess the panic button would end up showing up on narrow windows and tablets and stuff if we used a width-based media query. Not all mobile devices are phones, either. But what other options do we have?

Jill: Ideally, we'd have some way of getting information about the user's browser and device that is specific enough to give us hints as to whether it's a mobile phone, not just a device with low resolution or a narrow screen.

Narrow window doesn't mean mobile phone!

Mobile device data sources to the rescue

Mobile device databases contain detailed information about the browser, platform, and hardware features of mobile devices and their browsers. By querying the data set with a uniquely identifying key—generally a user-agent string—we can get tons of attributes about that device and its browser.

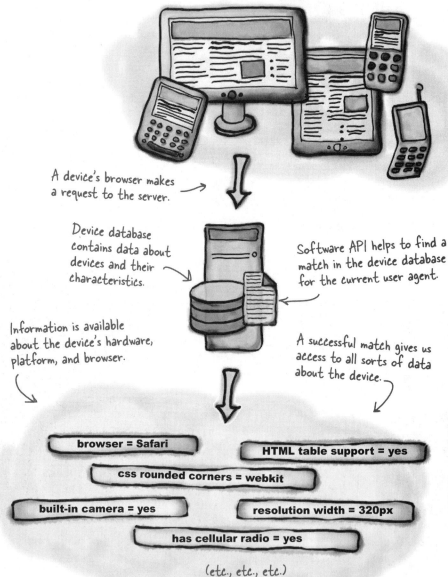

A device's browser makes a request to the server.

Device database contains data about devices and their characteristics.

Software API helps to find a match in the device database for the current user agent.

Information is available about the device's hardware, platform, and browser.

A successful match gives us access to all sorts of data about the device.

browser = Safari

HTML table support = yes

css rounded corners = webkit

built-in camera = yes

resolution width = 320px

has cellular radio = yes

(etc., etc., etc.)

Armed with this data, you can adapt content based on a device's characteristics.

Meet WURFL

WURFL (Wireless Universal Resource FiLe, usually pronounced "wuhr-full") is an open source device database with an enormous amount of information about the specific capabilities of mobile devices and their browsers.

Recently, the longtime maintainers of the WURFL project started a company called ScientiaMobile to provide commercial support for WURFL.

WURFL tracks details about mobile device specifics from ringtone formats to physical screen sizes.

Not all of WURFL's capabilities are of interest to us web developers, but you'll find some real, useful gems in there.

Watch it!

A device is not a platform is not a browser.

*There is no good word meaning "a device's hardware characteristics combined with its platform and OS melded with its browser." There really maybe should be. WURFL's notion of a device is a combination of all three, and contains information about hardware, OS, **and** browser.*

*Terminology makes it difficult to be clear. We're guilty, too, so keep in mind that our use of the shorthand word **device** likely carries some of the connotations of browser, hardware, and OS.*

Exercise

Go out and try it yourself! The ScientiaMobile explorer lets you interact with Tera-WURFL data in a web browser.

1 Go to *http://www.tera-wurfl.com/explore* in a mobile browser.

2 Visit the **See my capabilities** section and browse the capabilities it returns for your mobile device and browser.

The explorer is intended to be used on a mobile browser. If you visit with a desktop browser, a random mobile device will be selected for your capability-viewing pleasure.

You can also visit the explorer in a desktop browser and enter in any user-agent string you'd like to find capabilities for. This can be a quick and handy way to look up device capabilities for a known user agent.

Some of the capabilities listed in the explorer on an iPhone 4.

WURFL and its capabilities

Device who? Capabilities what? What does WURFL actually *do* for me?

WURFL provides information about mobile devices, their platforms, and their browsers as a set of capabilities. You can use this information to adapt your web content accordingly.

There are currently over 500 capabilities that WURFL tracks, grouped into a couple dozen or so categories like *css* (can this browser support rounded corners? What about background images?) and *playback* (what kinds of media can this device play?).

Device data is maintained in a large, single XML file that is regularly updated. The latest version is made available on the project's Sourceforge page. ⟵

Unsurprisingly, the URL is wurfl.sourceforge.net.

There's more than one flavor of WURFL

ScientiaMobile's explorer is based on a particular **implementation** of WURFL (the *Database Edition*, also known as *Tera-WURFL*) that keeps WURFL device data in a database instead in a flat XML file. Tera-WURFL is intended to be set up as a web service or **PHP** library that mobile-oriented websites can query to get device information for user-agent strings.

There are many different APIs and implementations of WURFL, but all have one thing in common: that big ol' WURFL XML file with all of the mobile device data. The full WURFL experience is a combination of the WURFL data file (XML), the way the data is stored, and an API to interact with it.

We'll be using the PHP API

There are WURFL APIs for a number of major programming languages. We'll be using the PHP API and file-based data.

There are thousands and thousands of user agents out there. How could anybody or any organization track all of them and all of the data about each device?!

WURFL works well because of several factors in its favor (one of which is that it doesn't track every single user agent).

WURFL's developer community is constantly contributing to the data source, meaning it isn't left to some poor guy alone in a dim cubicle somewhere trying to track down every new device and browser on the market—not just a thankless task, but likely impossible.

WURFL's various APIs' algorithms are clever when performing matches on user agents. It also doesn't hurt that WURFL has been around a while, has a proven track record, and has been used by (and contributed to) some pretty major web players (ever heard of Facebook?).

And, of course, if WURFL doesn't meet your needs, there are other device databases such as DeviceAtlas, DetectRight, and MobileAware. What makes sense for your project depends on your needs, budget, and licensing requirements.

there are no Dumb Questions

Q: What is ScientiaMobile?

A: ScientiaMobile is a company founded in 2011 by Steve Kamerman, Luca Passani, and Krishna Guda. Luca has been one of the maintainers of the open source WURFL project since he and Andrea Trasatti started WURFL in 2001. Steve created Tera-WURFL, which has become the WURFL Database Edition.

Q: Is WURFL free? Do I have to pay for it?

A: It depends. WURFL is technically open source. The WURFL API is available under the Affero General Public License v3 (AGPL), which is an open source license. The WURFL XML database has a restricted license that only allows it to be used with the WURFL API.

So, if you can comply with the AGPL restrictions, you don't have to pay anything. But AGPL is more aggressive than its GPL cousin. With AGPL, running the software on a server counts as a distribution, which triggers provisions requiring you to open source any derivative work.

If AGPL doesn't work for you (and, in many cases, it probably won't), ScientiaMobile will sell you a commercial license.

Q: If I integrate WURFL with (insert your favorite open source solution here) and build a site on top of it, do I have to open source the whole site?

A: Short answer: buy a commercial license or talk to a lawyer. ScientiaMobile.com also has a licensing FAQ.

Q: Are there other things out there that do what WURFL does?

A: Yes. WURFL is the only device database that offers an open source license, but there are several commercial databases. Device Atlas is probably the best known alternative. Others include Mobile Aware and Detect Right.

Q: What APIs are there for WURFL other than the PHP API?

A: ScientiaMobile provides Java, .NET, and Database APIs in addition to PHP.

Q: How does WURFL data get updated? More to the point, how would I get new data as it's updated?

A: ScientiaMobile keeps an eye out for new devices. Sometimes manufacturers provide information directly. Other times, people using WURFL submit the information. A large part of the work any device database vendor does is related to validating information provided about new devices.

Q: Who decides what capabilities get tracked by WURFL?

A: ScientiaMobile picks capabilities based on suggestions from the community.

Q: Where is this WURFL community of which you speak?

A: The community is a mailing list. WURFL has been around so long that the list is called the WML programming list. There are also conversations happening in the support forums on ScientiaMobile.com.

You can find the wml-programming list at http://tech.groups.yahoo.com/group/wmlprogramming/.

WURFL: Clever API code

When a WURFL API tries to match an incoming user agent to a known device, it doesn't just go belly up if that exact user agent isn't in the data. As it is totally impossible to track every single user agent out there, the API matchers instead perform some clever tricks when the precise user agent is not recognized.

A tree of devices and their families

As the WURFL API analyzes a given user-agent string, a series of increasingly generic fallbacks is evaluated, with the goal of at least slotting the device into the correct family of related devices.

You can think of WURFL's data as a sort of tree of devices, with the trunk being a generic browser and each branch, twig, and leaf a more specific device or group of devices. The API tries to get as far as it can toward the exact leaf, but has the rest of the tree to fall back on if it cannot.

Additionally, the WURFL data for a given device only defines the capabilities for that device (or group of devices) that differ from its parent device or devices. That way, the WURFL XML data file is kept reasonably small (a bit under 10 MB as of mid-2011), despite the amount of information it really contains.

Geek Bits

WURFL APIs use a combination of algorithms to keep from getting tripped up by weird little user-agent quirks.

One way it finds matches is by using **matchers** optimized for a given family of browsers or devices. The most recent PHP API has a few dozen handlers to deal with the analysis of user agents.

The API first determines which handler makes the most sense for the given user agent. User agents with the string "BlackBerry," for example, are handed off to the BlackBerryHandler.

Each handler is savvy about the kinds of differences that matter for user agents in its family, which cuts down on the amount of super-specific user agents that WURFL data maintainers have to track.

The PHP WURFL API combines handlers with **RIS** matching (reduction-in-string—that is, removing pieces of an unrecognized user-agent string until it ends up with one it does recognize) to get to its end result.

It's time to install WURFL on your computer

Check out Appendix iii for installation details.

We can build an explore page, too

Once you have the WURFL PHP API installed, it requires a pretty small amount of code to build a page not unlike the ScientiaMobile explorer page. In fact, we're going to do that right now.

> Wait. If ScientiaMobile's explorer page already lets me get WURFL information about devices, why do I want to go to the trouble of building my own version?

Building the explore page will get your hands dirty with the WURFL API, and it will use data from your own data file.

Learning by doing. That's the ticket. We'll build some underpinnings here that we can reuse for other—more functional—tasks.

> By your data, we mean the current set of data you have in the WURFL XML file you downloaded when installing WURFL.

Also, the ScientiaMobile explorer page is driven by the so-called Database Edition of WURFL. The data is stored and matched slightly differently than the XML file-PHP API combination we'll be using. Bottom line: the **data is a bit different** in little (but sometimes critical) ways.

Plus, by having your own explore page, you know that you're getting data from your version of the data file, not one that is older or newer than the one you have.

Steps for building our explore page

- [ ] Set up our working environment, files, and configuration for WURFL.

- [ ] Write a bit of (boilerplate) PHP code to initialize some WURFL objects so that we can start accessing capability information for the current browser and device.

- [ ] Organize the capability data. Build a page and output the data in an HTML table.

An explore page: Setting up our environment

The first order of business is to get our **directory structure** sorted and a **configuration file** created. You'll find a starting point in the *explore* subfolder of the *chapter5* folder.

By this point, you should have the WURFL PHP API up and running. You'll need to know the location of its installation to create a configuration file (well, one that *works*, anyway).

Directory structure for the explore page

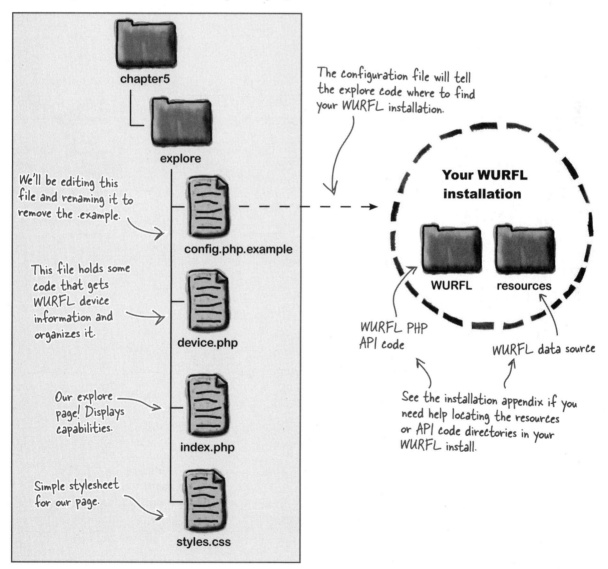

chapter5

explore

We'll be editing this file and renaming it to remove the .example.

config.php.example

The configuration file will tell the explore code where to find your WURFL installation.

Your WURFL installation

WURFL   resources

WURFL PHP API code

WURFL data source

This file holds some code that gets WURFL device information and organizes it.

device.php

Our explore page! Displays capabilities.

index.php

See the installation appendix if you need help locating the resources or API code directories in your WURFL install.

Simple stylesheet for our page.

styles.css

Long Exercise

You've got WURFL installed (we sure hope), but now we need to configure it to work in the web page we're building. To do that, we'll want to create a **configuration file**.

Open *config.php.example* in a text editor. Make edits to the paths below as indicated, and then save the file as **config.php** in the *explore* folder (remove the *.example* extension!).

```
/* WURFL_DIR needs to point to the install directory for WURFL */
define("WURFL_DIR", '/path/to/WURFL/');
/* RESOURCES_DIR needs to point to the resources dir you want to use. */
define("RESOURCES_DIR", '/path/to/WURFL/resources/');
```

Change me, please! You need to edit these paths to point to your own WURFL API code and resources directories.

Write once, reuse indefinitely. We'll be reusing this config file for the rest of the examples in this chapter.

config.php.~~example~~

Don't forget to remove the .example extension.

☑ Set up our working environment, files, and configuration for WURFL.

☐ Write a bit of (boilerplate) PHP code to initialize some WURFL objects so that we can start accessing capability information for the current browser and device.

☐ Organize the capability data. Build a page and output the data in an HTML table.

For help with WURFL installation paths, see Appendix iii.

Now we can write some code to initialize the WURFL objects and start getting at capabilities...

OK! We've got our configuration file. Now we need to create some code that will initialize WURFL stuff and get it all warmed up so that we can plumb its depths for device capabilities. Open *device.php* in your text editor. It's rather empty to start with, so let's plop in some WURFL-y code!

device.php's job is twofold: **initialize WURFL objects** using the `User-Agent` header of the current request (that is, the user's browser) and to **organize the capability data** for the device into something we can display on a page.

This includes our new config file.

```php
<?php
require_once('config.php');
$user_agent = $_SERVER['HTTP_USER_AGENT'];


$wurflConfig = new WURFL_Configuration_XmlConfig($wurflConfigFile);
$wurflManagerFactory = new WURFL_WURFLManagerFactory($wurflConfig);
$wurflManager = $wurflManagerFactory->create();
$device = $wurflManager->getDeviceForUserAgent($user_agent);
```

device.php

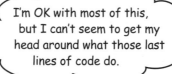

I'm OK with most of this, but I can't seem to get my head around what those last lines of code do.

Those lines instantiate several WURFL objects and populate a device object for us.

Most of this chunk is boilerplate code that we'll cut and paste as needed to get WURFL into shape for our use. If you're a whiz with PHP and this innately makes sense to you, kudos, but if it doesn't, don't sweat it too much.

Continues over the page.

Long Exercise

Let's take a slightly closer look at the last line of the boilerplate code chunk from page 163. It's where we tell WURFL how to build a device object. In our case, we're using `$user_agent`, which currently holds the value of the `User-Agent` header of the requesting client.

That is, we're instructing WURFL to take the user-agent string of the current user's browser and try to find a match in its data file. If it's successful, we'll have a device object containing the capabilities of the browser and device.

```
$device = $wurflManager->getDeviceForUserAgent($user_agent);
```

At this point, if things went right, the device capabilities are ready to use.

The `getDeviceForUserAgent` method in the `WURFL_WURFLManager` class takes a user-agent string and returns the matching device (from WURFL data) as a `WURFL_CustomDevice` object.

Translation: We feed it a user-agent string, and it gives us a device object populated with values for the various capabilities.

☑ Set up our working environment, files, and configuration for WURFL.

☑ Write a bit of (boilerplate) PHP code to initialize some WURFL objects so that we can start accessing capability information for the current browser and device.

☐ Organize the capability data. Build a page and output the data in an HTML table.

Now that we have a populated WURFL device object, let's organize the device's capabilities so that we can display them in an HTML table.

The second job of *device.php* is to organize the capabilities info so that we can display it later. We'll add a chunk of code to the file to organize capabilities by WURFL group.

Drop the following code into *device.php* and save the file. We're done with *device.php* for now.

The getListOfGroups() method simply returns an array of WURFL group names...

...and getCapabilitiesNamesForGroup() gets the names of the capabilities, um, in that group!

```php
$device = $wurflManager->getDeviceForUserAgent($user_agent);
if ($device) {
  $groups = $wurflManager->getListOfGroups();
  $grouped_capabilities = array();
  foreach($groups as $a_group) {
    $grouped_capabilities[$a_group] = array();
    $capabilities = $wurflManager->getCapabilitiesNameForGroup($a_group);
    foreach ($capabilities as $cap) {
      $grouped_capabilities[$a_group][$cap] = $device->getCapability($cap);
    }
  }
}
```

device.php

This code chunk organizes the capabilities of the current device and browser into groups.

This is how we access the values of individual capabilities. We'll look more closely at this in a bit.

It's totally OK if you don't understand everything this PHP is doing; you can just copy this into the device.php file.

→ Still more to do over the page.

LONG EXERCISE

We're done with *device.php* for now. Time to edit *index.php* and add some code.

☑ Set up our working environment, files, and configuration for WURFL.

☑ Write a bit of (boilerplate) PHP code to initialize some WURFL objects so that we can start accessing capability information for the current browser and device.

☐ Organize the capability data. Build a page and output the data in an HTML table.

This part is done!   *Time to do this.*

Ready Bake PHP/HTML

Iterate over the collected WURFL capability data, which is organized by group.

For each group, generate a <dl> with the names and values of the capabilities in that group.

Let's display the user agent and the id attribute of the device (WURFL's ID of what this browser or device is).

```
<div id="devicedata">
  <h2>Device Data</h2>
  <p>Device data for <?php print $user_agent; ?></p>
  <p><strong>WURFL Device ID: <?php print $device->id; ?></strong></p>
  <?php foreach($grouped_capabilities as $group_name => $my_caps): ?>
    <h3 class="group"><?php print $group_name; ?></h3>
    <dl>
      <?php foreach($my_caps as $cap_name => $cap): ?>
      <dt><?php print $cap_name; ?></dt>
      <dd><?php print ($cap) ? $cap : '[no value]'; ?></dd>
      <?php endforeach; ?>
    </dl>
  <?php endforeach; ?>
</div>
```

If there is no value for the current capability, display the string "no value."

Display the capability name in each <dt>, and the value in each <dd>.

OK, let 'er rip! Save index.php and view it in your browser.

index.php

A good start!

You can see all of the capabilities of your desktop browser now, with capabilities organized by group.

- ☑ Set up our working environment, files, and configuration for WURFL.

- ☑ Write a bit of (boilerplate) PHP code to initialize some WURFL objects so that we can start accessing capability information for the current browser and device.

- ☑ Organize the capability data. Build a page and output the data in an HTML table.

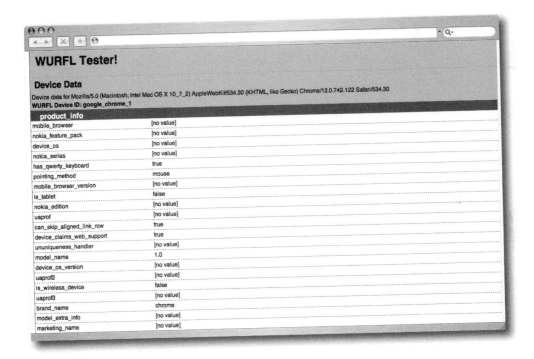

But we can make it better

Instead of just showing the capabilities of the current browser (especially uninteresting if you're in a desktop browser!), let's make the explore page display WURFL data for any user agent. We can do this by dropping a quick HTML form into *index.php* and making a small change to *device.php*.

A quick one-two punch to improve our explore page

A couple of quick changes, and our explore page will be more useful.

$_SERVER['PHP_SELF'] is shorthand for the currently executing script—that is, the form will post to the current page.

```html
<div id="testform">
<form method="post" action="<?php print $_SERVER['PHP_SELF']; ?>"
id="useragentform">
  <p>Test this user agent string:</p>
  <input type="text" name="useragent" id="useragent_field"
    value="<?php print $user_agent; ?>" /><br />
  <input type="submit" name="submit" value="Test User Agent" id="submit" />
</form>
</div>
```

Add a short form that allows the entry of any user-agent string.

index.php

```php
require_once('config.php');
$user_agent = (isset($_POST['useragent'])) ? $_POST['useragent'] :
$_SERVER['HTTP_USER_AGENT'];
$wurflConfig = new WURFL_Configuration_XmlConfig($wurflConfigFile);
```

Edit this line.

In device.php, we now check to see if there is an incoming form value (in $_POST) for the user agent; otherwise, we default to the current browser's user agent.

device.php

Test Drive

1 **Save all of the changes and load up the index.php file in a web browser.**
The first time you load the page, you should see your own browser's WURFL capabilities.

2 **Try a few mobile browser user agents.**
Enter some mobile browser user agents into the form and explore the resulting capabilities.

```
Mozilla/5.0 (Linux; U; Android 2.2.1; en-us; DROIDX Build/
VZW) AppleWebKit/533.1 (KHTML, like Gecko) Version/4.0
Mobile Safari/533.1 480X854 motorola DROIDX
```

Try these.

```
Mozilla/5.0 (webOS/1.4.5; U; en-US)
AppleWebKit/532.2 (KHTML, like Gecko)
Version/1.0 Safari/532.2 Pre/1.0
```

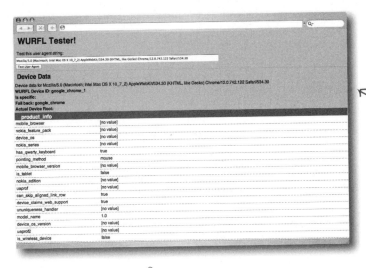

Now you can enter any user-agent string and explore the capabilities of the matched device.

A quick way to find your browser's current UA string:
http://whatsmyuseragent.com

Tired of typing in user-agent strings?

We've got you covered. You'll find a *useful_user_agents.txt* file in the *chapter5* folder. All of the user agents mentioned in this chapter are in it, for easy copying-and-pasting goodness.

Put capabilities to work

I'm up to my ears in capabilities. How can I do something useful with them?

OK, time to get specific.

It's time to figure out how to use WURFL capabilities to determine whether or not we should show that panic button on AcedIt!'s site.

(Oh, yeah, that's what we were up to.)

Use WURFL to help differentiate content

Let's only show the big, red panic button on browsers that WURFL says are **mobile browsers** (not just narrow screens, à la CSS media queries). We'll do this by using WURFL capabilities (bet you didn't see *that* coming)!

Steps to success

☐ Create a configuration file and add some code to initialize some WURFL objects—that is, get information about the current device and make it ready for us to use.

We learned how to do this part in the last exercise!

☐ Ask WURFL about the specfic capability or capabilities we care about.

☐ Add some code to the I'm Freaking Out! page mockup to alter the content delivered to different devices based on the value of capabilities.

Ask WURFL the right questions

Back on page 165, we briefly met the `getCapability` method for the `$device` object.

That's a handy method. Even if this class and instance mumbo-jumbo is generally Greek to you, getting at those capabilities is not too tricky, and we'll show you how.

Do this!

Copy the *config.php* file from the *explore* directory into the *panic_button* directory.

Getting a value for a specific capability looks like this:

$value will either be the value of the device's capability as a string, or NULL if there isn't a value.

Name of the capability we're asking about as a string.

e.g., 'is_tablet' or 'brand_name'

```
$value = $device->getCapability($capability_name);
```

A WURFL CustomDevice object, already initialized and populated.

We'll do this in the device.php file in just a sec.

A couple of examples:

Is this a mobile device?

```
$value = $device->getCapability('is_wireless_device');
```

```
$value = $device->getCapability('cookie_support');
```

Does this browser-device combo support cookies?

Note that when you retrieve capability values, you don't have to worry about what group the capability is in. Groups are a nice organizational concept, but each capability is uniquely named and can be asked for directly. You're not required to use capability groups to interact with WURFL.

Want to see info about all the WURFL capabilities? Check out http://wurfl.sourceforge.net/help_doc.php.

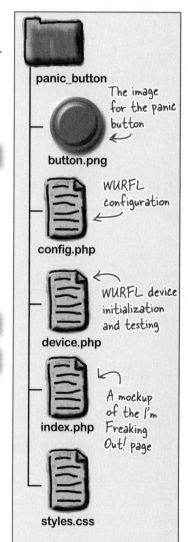

panic_button

The image for the panic button

button.png

WURFL configuration

config.php

WURFL device initialization and testing

device.php

A mockup of the I'm Freaking Out! page

index.php

styles.css

directory and file structure

Initialize the device and get the info ready

You'll see that we've given you a bit of a leg up in the *panic_button* folder. The *device.php* file already contains much of the WURFL boilerplate stuff you need to get your proverbial house in order.

We're going to be using a different method to instantiate the device than we did for the explore page. Instead of using a user-agent string and calling the `getDeviceForUserAgent` method, we'll tell WURFL to use whatever values are in the current server request (contained in PHP's always-available `$_SERVER` variable).

Translation: Give us device data for the device currently accessing the server.

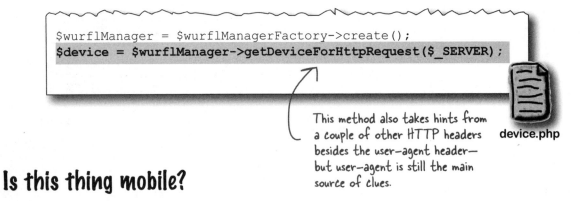

```
$wurflManager = $wurflManagerFactory->create();
$device = $wurflManager->getDeviceForHttpRequest($_SERVER);
```

device.php

This method also takes hints from a couple of other HTTP headers besides the user-agent header—but user-agent is still the main source of clues.

Is this thing mobile?

Now we've got our WURFL device all warmed up. Let's ask it stuff.

WURFL has a nice baseline capability called `is_wireless_device`, which answers the basic question: is this a mobile device? So, it would **seem** we'd want to do something like:

Sounds like a TRUE/FALSE (Boolean) type of question.

```
$device = $wurflManager->getDeviceForHttpRequest($_SERVER);
$is_phone = $device->getCapability('is_wireless_device');
```

device.php

Yeah, right?

Danger, Will Robinson!

In the PHP API, all capability values are returned as strings. That means that the seemingly Boolean capability is_wireless_device has three possible values: 'true', 'false', or NULL (NULL means that WURFL doesn't have a value at all for that capability).

We need to be more explicit, or the value 'false' will evaluate as true, and nonmobile devices will look like mobile ones. So we *must* make this alteration. Replace the last line we wrote with the new version:

In PHP, the string 'false' is truthy. If you have no idea what that means, that's OK. Just use the code below instead of the last code snippet on page 172.

```php
$is_phone = $device->getCapability('is_wireless_device');
$is_phone = ($device->getCapability('is_wireless_device') === 'true') ?
true : false;
```

The triple—equals identity operator here means that the value must be exactly the string of 'true' to pass, not just any truthy value.

device.php

Now, use that value

The *device.php* file gets included in the *index.php* file, so we can access the code we just wrote. We want to add the following PHP conditionals to *index.php*.

```php
<div id="content">
  <h1>I'm Freaking Out!</h1>
  <?php if ($is_phone): ?>
  <div id="panic_button">
    <img src="button.png" alt="HELP!" />
  </div>
  <?php else: ?>
  <h2>Help is only a phone call away.</h2>
  <div id="big_number">
  503-555-2939
  </div>
  <?php endif; ?>
  <p>Pre-test late-night jitters? A math problem that just
won't budge? Our expert on-call tutors are standing by to help
you through tough moments.</p>
</div>
```

For requests that qualify as mobile (per the is_wireless_device_capability), show the panic button...

...otherwise, just show the phone number, real big (via a CSS style).

index.php

TEST DRIVE

Make the changes from pages 171 and 173 to *config.php* and *index.php*, save the files, and then view the resulting I'm Freaking Out! page in a desktop browser and a mobile browser.

The button on a mobile device

The button doesn't show up on desktop browsers, even with a narrow window.

WURFL Exposed

This week's interview:
What's the use of WURFL?

Interviewer: So, WURFL, what exactly did you bring to the table here?

WURFL: Seems pretty clear. You can tell right off if the browser is mobile!

Interviewer: There are other ways to do that, you know. Client-side detection, basic server-side detection—

WURFL: Basic mobile-or-not-mobile is sort of child's play. You're not using me to my full potential.

Interviewer: All right, try me.

WURFL: So, I challenge you to look at the page on an iPod Touch.

Interviewer: OK…[*a long pause while the interviewer digs through a drawer of mobile devices*]…yep, the big red button.

WURFL: Doesn't that seem a bit…well, perhaps not what you intended? When's the last time you were able to make a phone call from an iPod?

Interviewer: Great. The button doesn't make sense on iPod Touches. Now we're back to square one.

WURFL: No, no. Like I said, you're not using me to my full potential. Dig deep and revisit my capabilities. I think you'll make a nice discovery or two.

Interviewer: But you have over 500 capabilities! How will I find the right one?

WURFL: You're complaining because I'm too comprehensive? I can't win! Fine, I'll give you a hint: just because the button is showing up on mobile devices doesn't mean it actually makes a phone call—you haven't linked it yet, so it's a pretty image, but not functional. You might think about that and take another look at my capabilities.

The button shows up on an iPod Touch...where it doesn't make any sense.

Exercise

Go look at our explore page and investigate the capabilities for an iPod Touch (where we don't want the button to show up) versus the capabilities for an Android Nexus S (where we do want the button). You might also look at a desktop browser for comparison.

Can you spot a capability that will help us make the differentiation between a small or mobile device and an actual phone?

```
Mozilla/5.0 (iPod; U; CPU iPhone OS 4_3_2      iPod Touch UA
like Mac OS X; en-us) AppleWebKit/533.17.9
(KHTML, like Gecko) Version/5.0.2 Mobile/8H7
Safari/6533.18.5


Mozilla/5.0 (Linux; U; Android 2.3.3; en-us;   Nexus S UA
Nexus S Build/GRI40) AppleWebKit/533.1 (KHTML,
like Gecko) Version/4.0 Mobile Safari/533.1
```

The WURFL `bearer` capability group has a handsome capability called `has_cellular_radio`. We'll be looking at the value of that capability to evaluate whether the current request is coming from a phone, not just any mobile device.

We're also going to make friends with the `xhtml_make_phone_call_string`, as it will show us how best to create clickable phone number links for this device.

Make the page a bit smarter with WURFL

By testing the value of `has_cellular_radio`, we can get a good idea as to whether the current user is on a phone. We also need to know how we should link the phone number such that when users click on it, it initiates a phone call.

The value in the `xhtml_make_phone_call_string` is a hint to the syntax we should use when linking up phone numbers such that when the link is clicked, the phone knows to instigate a phone call. For the Nexus S, this value is `tel:`.

For the iPod Touch, this value is `none`. The iPod Touch doesn't make phone calls. Desktop browsers will also return a value of `none`.

By combining the value in `xhtml_make_phone_call_string` with the phone number we want to dial, we can create a working link.

> If the has_cellular_radio capability is 'true' and there is a useful value for the xhtml_make_phone_call capability, we'll consider this a phone!

Making phone calls with links

Mobile phone browsers recognize certain URI patterns in links as phone numbers. When a user clicks on this kind of link, an alert box prompts her to confirm that she really wishes to place the call.

`tel:` is the most common URI schema for phone numbers, and works for nigh all modern smartphones. But it doesn't hurt to use WURFL's value in that `xhtml_make_phone_call_string` field. You've got it anyway. Here's what we end up with:

> tel: links work without the country code (+1). But to be correct about things, you should use one. Plus, it makes you seem so worldly.

```
<a href="tel:+15035552939">Make a phone call</a>
```

The panic button: For phones only

We can include additional tests in the *device.php* file to look at the
`has_cellular_radio` and `xhtml_make_phone_call_string` values.

First, let's get the values

We don't need this line anymore.

```
$is_phone     = ($device->getCapability('is_wireless_device') === 'true') ?
true : false;
$has_radio     = $device->getCapability('has_cellular_radio');
$phone_string = $device->getCapability('xhtml_make_phone_call_string');
```

device.php

Now, let's evaluate them

```
$phone_string = $device->getCapability('xhtml_make_phone_call_string');
$is_phone      = false;
if ($has_radio === 'true' && $phone_string && $phone_string !== 'none') {
  $is_phone = true;
}
```

device.php

This is why we have to test both for the existence of $phone_string and that its value is not the string 'none'.

Watch it!

> **'none' is a meaningful value!**
>
> *Recall from page 173 that, in the PHP API,* `CustomDevice->getCapability()` *returns either a string (if a value is present for that capability) or* `NULL` *(only if WURFL does not have a value at all for that capability). The difference is critical.*
>
> *For WURFL-identified devices like the iPod Touch and desktop browsers, the value for* `xhtml_make_phone_call_string` *is the string* `'none'`. *If you treat this as a Boolean value in PHP, it will evaluate as* `TRUE`.

there are no
Dumb Questions

Q: Don't mobile phone browsers automatically recognize phone numbers and link them for you?

A: Most do, yep. But a couple things about that. Most relevant to our present situation: our link was an image, not a phone number. There was no text. A phone likely would not have recognized it.

Also, various phones' abilities to correctly recognize phone numbers is hit or miss. Opera Mini has a tendency to think that zip codes with the plus-4 extension are phone numbers. Trying to place a phone call to a zip code has curious results, as you'd imagine.

Also recall that we are being quite formal with our phone number formatting (+15035552329). One might want to display a slightly different string in the link text itself, yet be confident that the link itself will be formatted correctly.

Q: How come there has to be that pop-up confirmation box after a user clicks on a phone call link? Why can't it just spawn a call directly?

A: This is to protect the user from being tricked. A visible phone number link might have one number, but the link itself another. Some poor suckers might end up calling a scammer when they thought they were cancelling their local newspaper subscription.

In our case, we're not even displaying the phone number, something that is arguably not really a best practice. We could also use a CSS background image instead of an inline image, have the phone number as the text in the link, and use a big negative margin in CSS to hide the text.

Q: In English, please? I didn't major in CSS in college.

A: Using a large negative left margin (e.g., `margin-left:-10000px`) is a way to get text to go way off to the left and be invisible. We like to visualize the text somewhere 10,000 pixels to the left, floating in the air somewhere in our office. But we're weird.

Q: So, we think a browser that has a non-none value for `xhtml_make_phone_call_string` is on a mobile phone that can make phone calls, but do we *know*?

A: WURFL has some intelligent data, but it's not that smart (no one is). There's no clear-cut way to be absolutely certain a user is on a functioning cellular network (versus WiFi or something else) or that there are not other things preventing the actual placement of a phone call. But, really, this gets us more than most of the way there.

Q: Couldn't we just test that the value of `xhtml_make_phone_call_string` isn't 'none' and call it done? Isn't the test for `has_cellular_radio` redundant?

A: You might be on to something, Smartypants.

Q: Speaking of Smartypants, you glossed over it pretty quickly, but I actually do want to know more about the WURFL objects and API....

A: Hey, we heartily encourage you to go look at the PHP classes in the API and see how they work together. If you've installed the API, you've got the files already, so hop to it!

No more button on iPod Touch! But still there on iPhone!

Jim: This could get out of hand! In a more complex project—or even AcedIt!'s site, if it adds more mobile bells and whistles—it seems like using scattered, individual WURFL capabilities all over the code would cause a lot of headache and mess. I mean, if we end up with one capability being tested for in one template, another capability being tested somewhere else… and so on.…

Frank: I agree. It seems like we'd be delivering a slightly different website to every possible combination of capabilities—a nightmare to think through and test.

Jim: A one-way ticket to spaghetti code, yeah.

Frank: But I don't want to throw out the whole concept. Even though I like to try to do feature detection on the client, and we still want to make our stuff as responsive as possible, it does seem like a device database like WURFL can give us insight into some details that we might not be able to get from other sources.

Jim: But how do we corral all of this so it doesn't make us crazy?

Frank: It seems like if we could group devices logically—instead of testing capabilities piecemeal—we might be able to keep our sanity. Remember how we recently spent time thinking through how to evaluate which devices to support by picking and choosing features and drawing the line for phones that don't make the cut?

Jim: Do I ever. I'm still somewhat cross-eyed from those exercises!

Frank: It seems like we could go one step further and create buckets of devices that are within the group of devices we decide to support.

Jim: Interesting…I think you might be on to something.

Exercise

You can find one on page 175.

After updating *device.php* with the changes from page 173 with the stuff on page 177, you might realize that you don't have an iPod Touch on hand to test the changes.

To see what an iPod Touch would see, edit the *device.php* file. Use the `getDeviceForUserAgent()` method instead of the `getDeviceForHTTPRequest()` method and give it an iPod Touch user agent.

Answers on page 180.

Herding devices

A **device class** creates a sort of logical corral into which you can herd devices that have certain things in common.

Just as a rancher might put spotted cattle into one field, giant work horses in another, and little piglets in yet another (can you tell we've never been ranchers?), we can sort our devices into virtual cubby-holes with device classes.

Sort once, then go

Once our rancher identifies an animal as belonging to one of those three groups, he can make further decisions without having to look at the smaller details. He can feed oats to the horses without stopping to reverify that they have legs of a certain length or swishy tails or can support PNG images (everyone knows that horses lack support for transparent PNGs!).

He already knows they're horses because they're in the horse corral. He doesn't have to tailor feeding to each individual animal (that would be a lot of horse meals to keep track of). But, at the same time, he doesn't feed oats to the piglets.

> A **device class** is an abstract collection of common characteristics that define a group of devices (and their browsers).

Exercise Solution

You can test what content gets delivered for a given device or browser by using its user agent when intializing the WURFL device.

```php
$wurflManager = $wurflManagerFactory->create();
$device = $wurflManager->getDeviceForHttpRequest($_SERVER);
$user_agent = "Mozilla/5.0 (iPod; U; CPU iPhone OS 4_3_2 like Mac
OS X; en-us) AppleWebKit/533.17.9 (KHTML, like Gecko) Version/5.0.2
Mobile/8H7 Safari/6533.18.5";
$device = $wurflManager->getDeviceForUserAgent($user_agent);
```

device.php

Device classes

As we learned earlier, we can run incoming requests against
a device database to get device information. By grouping the
capabilities and values that matter for the site at hand, we can
adapt content across an entire device class instead of chasing
down each individual capability's value.

These **device class definitions**, converted into code, sort
devices into one of several groups. Once our devices are
sorted, we can take action without having to keep track of each
individual constituent capability.

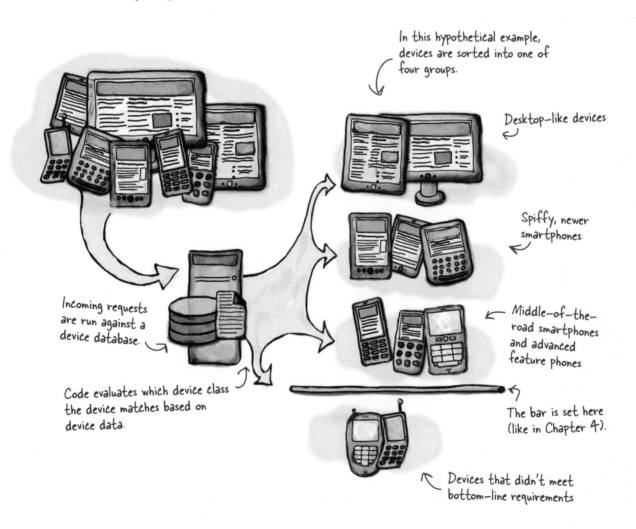

In this hypothetical example,
devices are sorted into one of
four groups.

Desktop-like devices

Spiffy, newer
smartphones

Middle-of-the-
road smartphones
and advanced
feature phones

The bar is set here
(like in Chapter 4).

Devices that didn't meet
bottom-line requirements

Incoming requests
are run against a
device database.

Code evaluates which device class
the device matches based on
device data.

The picture just got a lot bigger

> Hey, you guys. Nice job on that panic button! Do you think you could help us mobile-optimize a big new site we're building?

Expanding a lucrative part of AcedIt!'s business

AcedIt! is building a standalone website for the study aids it sells to its students. It's realized that flashcards, practice test booklets, reference books, and the like are selling like hotcakes, but the only way to purchase things right now is through a printed catalog.

It's time for a change. AcedIt!'s new study-aid-specific site will not only allow users to buy any physical product online, but will also introduce online products like flashcards that can be used interactively, right on the site itself.

AcedIt!'s devs are building these features using JavaScript and other standard web technologies.

An early look at what it has in mind

It's early yet. Logo designs haven't been finalized, content is still being evaluated, and the design is still in simple-mockup phase. But let's see what the company's up to:

AcedIt!'s web folks sent this early mockup of the new site's home page.

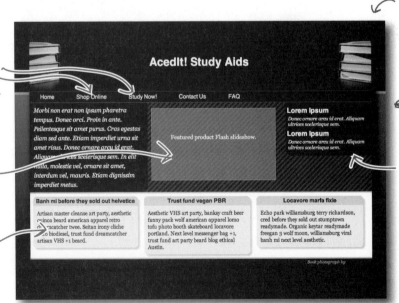

Users can shop online and study now—use interactive products right on the site itself.

AcedIt! will feature products in a snazzy Flash movie.

The home page has excerpts from the company's blog.

These ads are for related services, like paper proofreading and local study groups.

Evaluate the home page wearing mobile-tinted glasses

The scope of the new study aid site is much bigger than the single panic button page. We risk making ourselves crazy if we plan development piecemeal, capability by capability. One way to frame our development approach and make the site work well for different kinds of users is to **group the different experiences using device classes**.

Combining device data with logical grouping

The process of defining device classes is related to the work we did in Chapter 4. We look at the task at hand, figure out what things matter, mumble a few incantations, and come out the other side with some general criteria.

We know. "Group the experiences using device classes" is catastrophically vague. Let's start by reviewing the mockup again and weighing AcedIt!'s priorities against what we know about mobile web characteristics and constraints.

OK, yeah, we know. We only have a rough landing-page mockup for right now. But the scope <u>will</u> be broader on this project...eventually.

AcedIt! has made it very clear that the interactive elements on the site are of mega importance.

We can put the content first and the navigation nearer to the bottom for mobile layouts.

We'll want to adjust the layout by reducing the number of columns and tightening up the header.

We need to keep the JavaScript and AJAX (Asynchronous JavaScript and XML) device capabilities in mind.

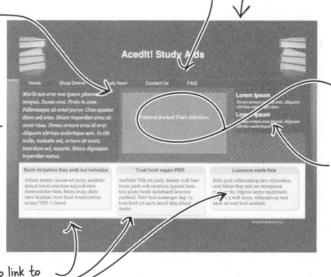

Using Flash content is problematic on mobile devices. We'll need to find an alternate format for mobile.

There's a lot of complex CSS3 styling that won't work on all devices.

AcedIt! has mentioned that it doesn't think the ads need to show up for mobile users.

It seems a bit lukewarm on the whole ad part of the site, anyway.

We might want to link to the blog instead of having the content excerpts right on the page.

Group requirements into multiple mobile flavors

The full-fledged interactive site experience has some high demands. Mobile devices need to have the kind of JavaScript, HTML, and CSS support that is usually found in newer, swankier browsers on smartphones. Specifically, the AcedIt! devs are targeting mobile devices running WebKit-based browsers and designing for screen sizes no narrower than 320 pixels.

But that doesn't mean everyone else should get the cold shoulder. Smaller, slightly less cutting-edge phones are still welcome on the site. They can buy physical products in the online store and visit the other areas of the site. They just aren't cut out for the heavy-duty interactive experience or the hardcore CSS, for example.

Instead of delivering to the lowest common denominator or kicking out devices that don't quite cut it, **let's create two separate flavors** of the site that make sense for each group of devices.

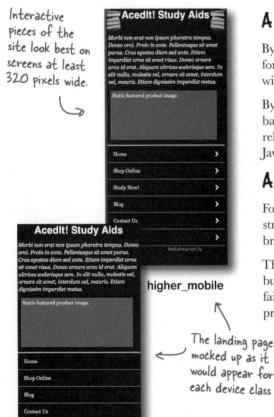

Interactive pieces of the site look best on screens at least 320 pixels wide.

higher_mobile

The landing page mocked up as it would appear for each device class

simpler_mobile

A fuller mobile experience

By creating a device class that encompasses the requirements for the richer mobile experience, we can design something neat without risking poor support on lesser devices.

By specifying that devices in this class must have a WebKit-based browser, we can use CSS goodies like gradients with relative confidence. We can also rely on a certain level of decent JavaScript support.

A simplified experience for simpler phones

For narrower screens and less powerful devices, let's be more streamlined. And let's not assume support for all of the modern browser bells and whistles.

This simpler layout doesn't provide the link to the online products, but users can still shop in the online store. This version works fairly well down to about 176 pixels wide, at which point the product images in the store become difficult to see.

Now we have a rough sense of our two mobile device classes, `higher_mobile` and `simpler_mobile`.

Rounding out our device classes

We now have a rough sense of two mobile device classes we'll want to construct. What else?

Oh, by the way, tablets

AcedIt!'s devs are also working on a tablet-optimized, super-nifty, touch-driven interface for their online products. It's not done yet, but they want to be prepared for its eventual launch by being able to identify **tablets** now.

Where to draw the line

It's important to the AcedIt! folks that their visitors can either shop online or use the online products. If visitors can't do either because of device constraints, the device and browser they are using are considered unsupported.

The company's ecommerce software requires **cookie support** and a bit of **JavaScript support** (not nearly as much as the online interactive products). It is also mandatory that, for security, devices support **SSL**.

Our device class lineup

Totally Required

Based on the priorities and requirements, it seems like the following are the bottom line. Mobile devices must have the following to be considered "supported."

- SSL support
- Cookie support
- At least some JavaScript support
- A resolution of at least 176px

WebKit-based browsers and at least 320px width

higher_mobile

simpler_mobile

Minimal JavaScript support and at least 176px width

Yep, tablets

tablet

Hey, desktop is a device class, too!

desktop

Is delinquent in any of the totally required characteristics

unsupported

Device Classes Exposed

This week's interview:
Abstraction to execution...what exactly is a device class?

Slightly Confused Web Developer: I'm having trouble getting my head around this device class business. A collection of capabilities...tied to an experience?

Device Class: I admit, I am a bit difficult to capture. If I were a painting, I'd be an abstract blur. I'm a concept, a way to think about organizing common things so that we can create just a few flavors of a site, instead of a million billion.

SCWD: So, a device class is a set of WURFL capabilities—

Device Class: Not so fast. Remember that I'm an abstract concept. We'll be using WURFL here, but there's no reason you have to. No reason, in fact, you have to use any device database.

SCWD: This is all starting to feel a bit woo-woo. Can you help me understand where the rubber meets the road here?

Device Class: OK. Let's plan this together. For AcedIt!, we'll have five device classes.

SCWD: Does that mean we'll be making a version of the website for each? That sounds like a big task.

Device Class: No, we only need to focus on the differences. For example, until the new touch-based, tablet-optimized flashcard interface is launched, the tablet-device-class version of the site only differs from the desktop version in that no Flash content will be used.

SCWD: OK, so we have a desktop device class, which is self-evident...and that tablet device class, which has minor differences...let's see. What are the differences between `higher_mobile` and `simpler_mobile`?

Device Class: As we know that `higher_mobile` represents devices with larger screens and capable WebKit-based browsers, we can be more confident that they have the horsepower to handle some of the site's more intensely interactive features.

`simpler_mobile`, by contrast, represents devices with narrower screens and perhaps less cutting-edge browsers. We can give them smaller images (yay! less bandwidth). We know they support a bit of the ol' JavaScript, but can give them a dose of content that is less deluxe.

SCWD: Wait, how do we know that the `simpler_mobile` devices support JavaScript?

Device Class: We will test for at least a modicum of JavaScript support. Devices that don't have the ability to modify the DOM after page load will be shunted off into the `unsupported` device class.

SCWD: So what's up next to keep this ball rolling?

Device Class: We need to map the right WURFL capabilities and their values to the device classes we want to create. After we have a logical representation of the device classes, we'll create code to do some actual testing and slotting.

Pool Puzzle

Time to find the right WURFL capabilities
and values for our device classes.
Your **job** is to take the WURFL
capabilities and values from the
pool and place them into the blank
device classes. You may **not** use
the same item more than once.

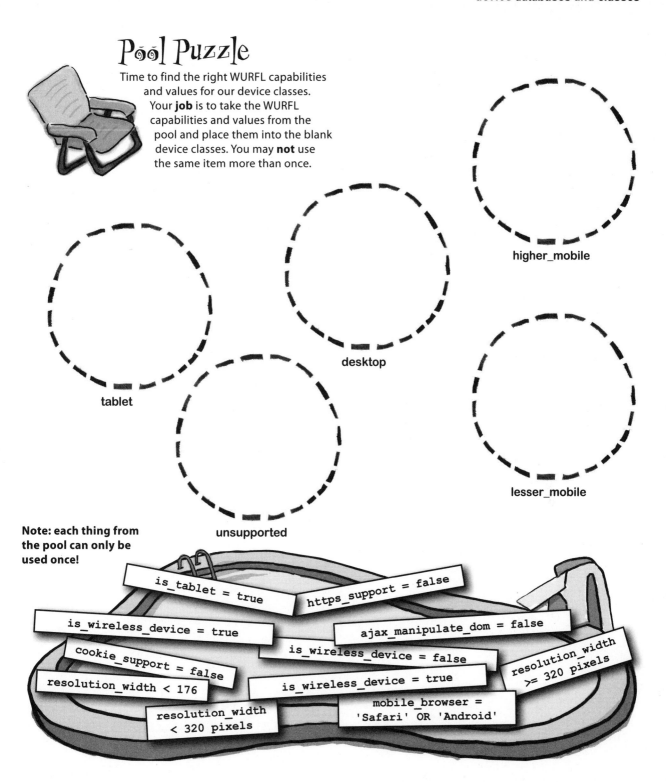

higher_mobile

desktop

tablet

lesser_mobile

unsupported

**Note: each thing from
the pool can only be
used once!**

is_tablet = true

https_support = false

is_wireless_device = true

ajax_manipulate_dom = false

is_wireless_device = false

cookie_support = false

resolution_width >= 320 pixels

resolution_width < 176

is_wireless_device = true

resolution_width < 320 pixels

mobile_browser = 'Safari' OR 'Android'

Pool Puzzle Solution

Now we've collected the right WURFL capabilities and values to build our device classes.

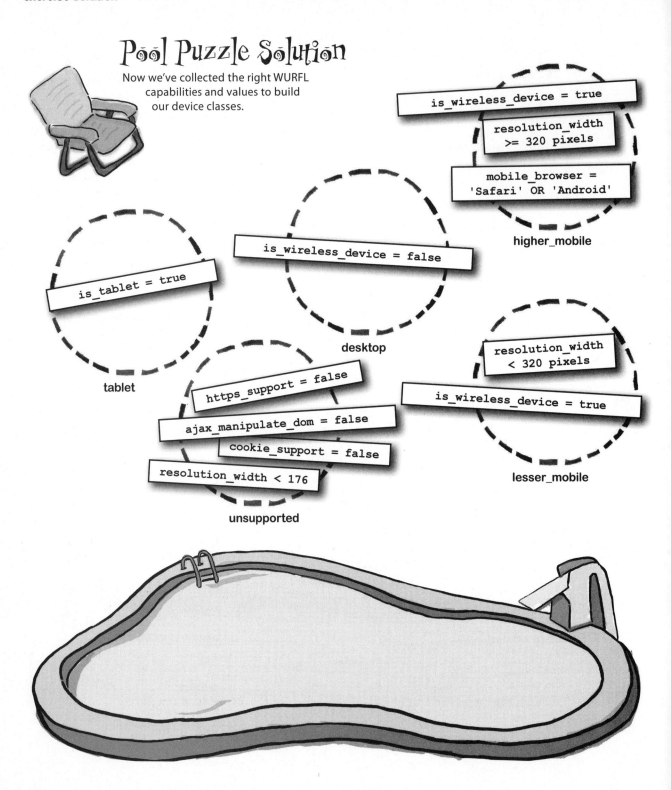

is_wireless_device = true

resolution_width
>= 320 pixels

mobile_browser =
'Safari' OR 'Android'

higher_mobile

is_wireless_device = false

desktop

is_tablet = true

tablet

resolution_width
< 320 pixels

is_wireless_device = true

lesser_mobile

https_support = false

ajax_manipulate_dom = false

cookie_support = false

resolution_width < 176

unsupported

there are no
Dumb Questions

Q: Why the focus on WebKit-based browsers? Are the devs hating on other, totally decent mobile browsers?

A: WebKit-based browsers are seen by many mobile web devs as both fairly advanced and consistent. Browsers with the WebKit rendering engine generally have good support for HTML5, JavaScript, and CSS3.

Note the word *generally* in the previous sentence. The problem is, there is a misconception as to just how consistent browsers based on WebKit are. The sad truth is: there's still a lot of chaos.

Mobile platform strategist Peter-Paul Koch spells out the pitfalls of assuming consistency in mobile WebKit browsers in the thorough post "There is no WebKit on Mobile" on his QuirksBlog (*http://bit.ly/uWnFLa*).

Q: If mobile WebKit isn't really a "thing," why are we basing a device class on it?

A: Consistent and reliable or no, WebKit-based browsers are what the devs have done their development on and testing for. At this point in the project, it is too late to throw the net wider. We're kind of following their lead on this one.

Q: How is testing for the string `'Safari'` or `'Android'` as the mobile browser name equivalent to finding all WebKit browsers?

A: You might recall from Chapter 3 that user-agent strings are wily creatures. Apple's history with respect to WebKit endures in the user-agent string legacy. At time of writing, all known mobile variants of WebKit browsers have either "Safari" or "Android" in their browser name (yes, even WebKit browsers on BlackBerries and Nokia phones and whatnot).

Q: If I use device classes in a project, will I always have five?

A: Nope. You might have 10, 4, or 0. Having fewer means less complexity. Having more means more nuance.

Q: What's with the names `higher_mobile` and `simpler_mobile`? Is there a naming convention I need to know about?

A: Eh, we just pulled those out of a hat. They sounded about right. We used underscores simply so we can translate the names into code more easily. You can call your device classes whatever you'd like. Within reason.

Q: Now that we've got device classes, I can never test an individual device capability?

A: You can totally still test individual capabilities. In fact, the solution for the panic button problem was very appropriate: we were testing for the value of a very specific capability—a value that might differ among devices in the same device class (an iPhone versus an iPod Touch, for example).

Q: Couldn't a device match more than one device class?

A: Yes. We need to arrange our device class testing code in order carefully. The first matched device class will be the device class we assign.

Q: What the heck is the `CustomDevice` object I keep seeing in the code examples?

A: `CustomDevice` is simply the name of the class in the WURFL API that represents a device and its characteristics.

Q: Seems like device classes are not just a mobile web thing.

A: Not at all! Content and layout adaptation is a concern that spans the entire Web. The mobile web doesn't have a monopoly on that.

Q: OK, great. I have some circles with some capabilities and required values in them. Now what?

A: Turn the page, my impatient friend. We're going to start turning these device classes into code.

Let's get this show on the road

Now we need to convert the abstract notion of what we're grouping into real code that will detect and slot devices into the appropriate device class. Here comes the sorting!

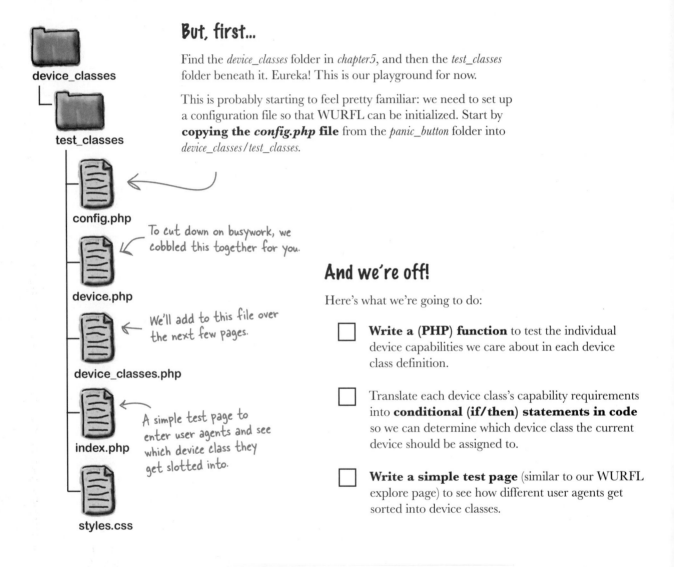

device_classes

test_classes

config.php

To cut down on busywork, we cobbled this together for you.

device.php

We'll add to this file over the next few pages.

device_classes.php

A simple test page to enter user agents and see which device class they get slotted into.

index.php

styles.css

But, first...

Find the *device_classes* folder in *chapter5*, and then the *test_classes* folder beneath it. Eureka! This is our playground for now.

This is probably starting to feel pretty familiar: we need to set up a configuration file so that WURFL can be initialized. Start by **copying the *config.php* file** from the *panic_button* folder into *device_classes / test_classes*.

And we're off!

Here's what we're going to do:

☐ **Write a (PHP) function** to test the individual device capabilities we care about in each device class definition.

☐ Translate each device class's capability requirements into **conditional (if/then) statements in code** so we can determine which device class the current device should be assigned to.

☐ **Write a simple test page** (similar to our WURFL explore page) to see how different user agents get sorted into device classes.

Get acquainted with the matching function

You'll find this matching function already waiting for you inside of
device_classes.php. We'll use it when we create the individual tests for
each device class.

We wanted to tell you a few things about it before we started taking
advantage of it. Stand back; here comes some PHP.

Ready Bake PHP

The name of the
capability to test

A comparison
operator

The value to test
against

Make sure the device
object exists.

Get the value of
the capability
from the device.

We test the
current value from
the device against
the value we are
curious about.

```php
function device_match($capability, $comparison, $value) {
  global $device;
  if (!$device) {
    return FALSE;
  }
  $device_value = $device->getCapability($capability);
  switch ($comparison) {
    case '==':
    case '===':
      return ($device_value === $value);
    case '!=':
    case '!==':
      return ($device_value !== $value);
    case '>=':
      return ($device_value >= $value);
    case '<=':
      return ($device_value <= $value);
    case '>':
      return ($device_value > $value);
    case '<':
      return ($device_value < $value);
    case 'LIKE':
      return (strpos($device_value, $value) !== FALSE);
    case 'NOT LIKE':
      return (strpos($device_value, $value) === FALSE);
    default:
      return FALSE;
  }
}
```

**This function
returns a TRUE or
FALSE (Boolean)
result—whether
or not the given
test passed.**

device_classes.php

What's going on in that switch statement?

$device_value is the value of the capability in question on the current device.

```
switch ($comparison) {
  case '==':
  case '===':
    return ($device_value === $value);
  case '!=':
  case '!==':
    return ($device_value !== $value);
  case '>=':
    return ($device_value >= $value);
  case '<=':
    return ($device_value <= $value);
  case '>':
    return ($device_value > $value);
  case '<':
    return ($device_value < $value);
  case 'LIKE':
    return (strpos($device_value, $value) !== FALSE);
  case 'NOT LIKE':
    return (strpos($device_value, $value) === FALSE);
  default:
    return FALSE;
}
```

$value is the value we'd like to test against.

Depending on the comparison operator supplied, the values are compared in different ways.

LIKE and NOT LIKE allow us to do glob (substring) comparisons.

If $comparison is not one of the recognized comparison operators, we fail.

Some examples

This test passes (returns TRUE) if the device's resolution_width value is 240 pixels or smaller.

```
device_match('resolution_width', '<=', '240');
```

This test passes if the is_wireless_device value for this device is 'false'.

```
device_match('is_wireless_device', '===', 'false');
```

This test passes if the mobile_browser value contains the string 'Safari'.

```
device_match('mobile_browser', 'LIKE', 'Safari');
```

Use the matching function to test capabilities

Now we have a function to test capabilities with. Time to convert our
required capabilities into tests.

☑ **Write a (PHP) function** to test the individual device
capabilities we care about in each device class definition.

☐ Translate each device class's capability requirements into
conditional (if/then) statements in code so we can determine
which device class the current device should be assigned to.

☐ **Write a simple test page** (similar to our WURFL explore page)
to see how different user agents get sorted into device classes.

**Reminder: The device
classes we ended
up with are** desktop,
tablet, higher_mobile,
simpler_mobile, **and**
unsupported. **We figured
out what to test for
each in the pool puzzle
on page 188.**

Exercise

We wrote that matching function for you, but now it's time for you to do a bit of work.
Which tests belong to which device class?

```
........................................  if (device_match('resolution_width', '>=', '320'))

........................................  if (device_match('resolution_width', '<', '176'))

........................................  if (device_match('is_wireless_device', '===', 'false'))

........................................  if (device_match('mobile_browser', 'LIKE', 'Safari') ||
                                              device_match('mobile_browser', 'LIKE', 'Android'))

........................................  if (device_match('cookie_support', '===', 'false'))

........................................  if (device_match('is_tablet', '===', 'true'))

........................................  if (device_match('ajax_manipulate_dom', '===', 'false'))

........................................  if (device_match('https_support', '===', 'false'))

........................................  if (device_match('resolution_width', '<', '320'))
```

Exercise Solution

We've got these tests sorted! Now it's time to convert them into grouped nuggets of real PHP code. Keep truckin'!

This feels like it might be an appropriate test for the desktop device class, but we'll be weeding out desktop browsers immediately by looking at the is_wireless_device capability...

.....**higher_mobile**.....
```php
if (device_match('resolution_width', '>=', '320'))
```

.....**unsupported**.....
```php
if (device_match('resolution_width', '<', '176'))
```

.....**desktop**.....
```php
if (device_match('is_wireless_device', '===', 'false'))
```

.....**higher_mobile**.....
```php
if (device_match('mobile_browser', 'LIKE', 'Safari') ||
    device_match('mobile_browser', 'LIKE', 'Android'))
```

.....**unsupported**.....
```php
if (device_match('cookie_support', '===', 'false'))
```

.....**tablet**.....
```php
if (device_match('is_tablet', '===', 'true'))
```

.....**unsupported**.....
```php
if (device_match('ajax_manipulate_dom', '===', 'false'))
```

.....**unsupported**.....
```php
if (device_match('https_support', '===', 'false'))
```

.....**simpler_mobile**.....
```php
if (device_match('resolution_width', '<', '320'))
```

**Time to put the
code together...**

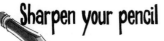

Sharpen your pencil

Comfortable with PHP code? See if you can plunk in the missing
pieces of the code chunk here. These are the device class tests,
grouped and ready to go.

```php
$device_class = NULL;

if (device_match('is_wireless_device', '===', '............')) {
  $device_class = 'desktop';
}
else if (device_match('https_support', '.........', '............') ||
        device_match('........... _support', '.........', '..........') ||
        device_match('ajax_manipulate_dom', '===', 'false') ||
        device_match('............................. ', '.......', '176')) {
  $device_class = '....................................';
}
else if (device_match('is_tablet', '===', '..........')) {
  $device_class = '..................';
}
else if (device_match('is_wireless_device', '===', 'true') &&
        device_match('resolution_width', '>=', '..........') &&
        (device_match('mobile_browser', '..........', 'Safari') ||
          device_match('..........................', 'LIKE', 'Android') ))
{
  $device_class = '..............................................';
}
else if (device_match('is_wireless_device', '===', '.........') &&
        device_match('..................................', '<', '..........')) {
  $device_class = 'simpler_mobile';
}
```

Sharpen your pencil
Solution

All right, now we have our tests!

First and foremost: is this even a mobile browser?

```
$device_class = NULL;

if (device_match('is_wireless_device', '===', ' false ')) {
  $device_class = 'desktop';
}
else if (device_match('https_support', '===', ' false ') ||
         device_match('cookie _support', ' === ', ' false ') ||
         device_match('ajax_manipulate_dom', '===', 'false') ||
         device_match(' resolution_width ', ' < ', '176')) {
  $device_class = ' unsupported ';
}
else if (device_match('is_tablet', '===', 'true ')) {
  $device_class = ' tablet ';
}
else if (device_match('is_wireless_device', '===', 'true') &&
         device_match('resolution_width', '>=', ' 320') &&
         (device_match('mobile_browser', ' LIKE ', 'Safari') ||
          device_match(' mobile_browser ', 'LIKE', 'Android') ))
{
  $device_class = ' higher_mobile ';
}
else if (device_match('is_wireless_device', '===', ' true ') &&
         device_match(' resolution_width ', '<', ' 320 ')) {
  $device_class = 'simpler_mobile';
}
```

Make sure this device doesn't lack our baseline requirements...

Is it perhaps a tablet?

Or are its browser and resolution pretty awesome?

Or maybe it's good enough but not cutting-edge.

All right! Two out of three! We're almost done now!

☑ **Write a (PHP) function** to test the individual device capabilities we care about in each device class definition.

☑ Translate each device class's capability requirements into **conditional (if/then) statements in code** so we can determine which device class the current device should be assigned to.

☐ **Write a simple test page** (similar to our WURFL explore page) to see how different user agents get sorted into device classes.

The home stretch

Time to pound the last few nails into our device class testing project. We want a page with a simple form that will take a user agent and spit out which device class it matches. As this is super similar to what we did for the WURFL explore page, we've done it for you (yippee!).

This simple test form is coded for you in index.php.

The page displays the device ID and the computed device class for the entered user agent.

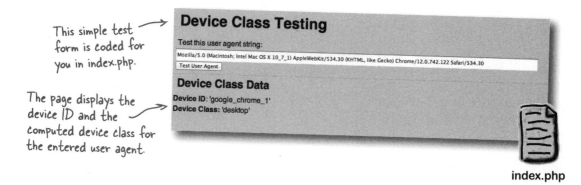

Device Class Testing

Test this user agent string:

Mozilla/5.0 (Macintosh; Intel Mac OS X 10_7_1) AppleWebKit/534.30 (KHTML, like Gecko) Chrome/12.0.742.122 Safari/534.30

Test User Agent

Device Class Data

Device ID: 'google_chrome_1'
Device Class: 'desktop'

index.php

TEST DRIVE

1 **Put code into the device_classes.php file.**
Add the tests from page 196 into the file after the device_match function and save it.

```
Mozilla/5.0 (PlayBook; U;
RIM Tablet OS 1.0.0; en-
US) AppleWebKit/534.8+ (KHTML,
like Gecko) Version/0.0.1
Safari/534.8+
```

2 **View the index.php file in a browser.**
By default, the page will show you the device class assigned to your current browser.

```
PantechP2020/JIUS05172010R;
Mozilla/5.0 (Profile/MIDP-2.0
Configuration/CLDC-1.1; Opera
Mini/att/4.2.19039; U; en-US)
Opera 9.50
```

3 **Test some different user agents.**
Enter the user agents here into the form field to see which device class they get assigned to.

```
BlackBerry8330/4.5.0.77 Profile/
MIDP-2.0 Configuration/CLDC-1.1
VendorID/105
```

```
BlackBerry9300/5.0.0.794
Profile/MIDP-2.1 Configuration/
CLDC-1.1 VendorID/245
```

Well, let's see...how'd it go?

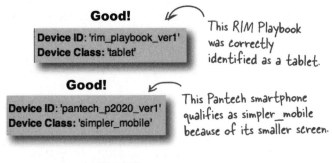

Good!

Device ID: 'rim_playbook_ver1'
Device Class: 'tablet'

This RIM Playbook was correctly identified as a tablet.

Good!

Device ID: 'pantech_p2020_ver1'
Device Class: 'simpler_mobile'

This Pantech smartphone qualifies as simpler_mobile because of its smaller screen.

Good!

Device ID: 'blackberry8330_ver1_sub45077_105'
Device Class: 'unsupported'

This BlackBerry's browser is old enough (version 4.5) that it doesn't allow manipulation of the DOM after the page is loaded.

That is, it doesn't have the kind of JavaScript support required.

Uh oh!

Device Class Data

Device ID: 'blackberry9300_ver1'
Device Class: "

Uh oh! This user agent didn't qualify for any device classes!

Why did the user agent for the BlackBerry 9300 (Curve) fail to match any device classes?

Looks like something went a bit wrong

The problem is that this Curve has a resolution of 320 pixels (meaning it's too wide to qualify for the `simpler_mobile` class), but does not have a WebKit browser (meaning it fails to qualify for `higher_mobile`). This is going to be a problem for other devices that have higher resolution but non-WebKit browsers.

We need to fix this and make sure our device classes don't have any other logical holes that devices can fall through.

Filling in the gaps

We have three options for how to fix the higher-resolution-but-non-WebKit-browser situation:

1. We could create a new device class to handle this combination.

2. We could change the `higher_mobile` device class to allow for other, non-WebKit browsers.

   Grouping by resolution

3. We could edit the `simpler_mobile` device class and remove the 240-pixel resolution maximum.

   Grouping by browser

Each option is totally valid. We have to decide which seems most ideal for the AcedIt! study aid website.

Joe: Do we really need to add yet another device class? Seems like a lot to wrangle.

Frank: I agree. We need to strike a balance between nuance and the number of device classes we have. It feels like we already have about the right number.

Joe: So, what now?

Frank: OK. The problem is that higher-resolution devices that don't have WebKit browsers are falling through and not getting assigned to any device classes—

Joe: Aren't there actually two problems here? One, we're not thinking through what experience those devices should get, like you said. But we also don't have a fallback, default device class overall. Seems possible something could go wrong with device detection or there might be something else we're not thinking of. I think we need a sort of safety net device class.

Frank: Good point. For the first problem, if we're not adding a new device class, we need to fill the gap. The question is: what is more relevant here, device resolution or browser capabilities?

Joe: AcedIt! puts a lot of focus on the interactive elements of the site—that suggests browser capabilities matter more. But at the same time, we were planning on delivering smaller images to those lower-resolution devices.

Frank: I think you're right about AcedIt!'s priorities. How about this for a compromise? We update the device classes such that there isn't a top-end resolution restriction on the `simpler_mobile` class.

That does mean that some higher-resolution devices get a simpler feel, but if I recall correctly, the dev team working on the touch-optimized flashcards is using a framework targeted to WebKit-based browsers. Heh, in fact, I think that's why we were testing for WebKit browsers in our `higher_mobile` class in the first place. Wow, I need to get more sleep; my memory is failing me.

Joe: What about images?

Frank: I think we'd do fairly well if we gave all mobile devices mobile-optimized images that aren't any bigger than 320 pixels in any dimension. Then we can use responsive image techniques to get us through the final mile on the device.

Fill in the gaps in the device class tests

Here are the changes we need to make to our device class tests:

Remove this resolution
restriction for simpler_mobile.

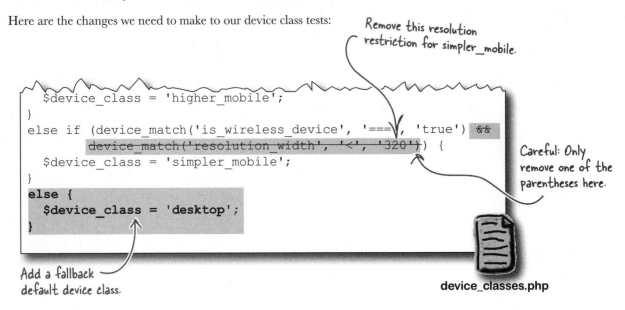

```
    $device_class = 'higher_mobile';
}
else if (device_match('is_wireless_device', '===', 'true') &&
        device_match('resolution_width', '<', '320')) {
    $device_class = 'simpler_mobile';
}
else {
    $device_class = 'desktop';
}
```

Careful: Only
remove one of the
parentheses here.

Add a fallback
default device class.

device_classes.php

TEST DRIVE

Make the changes to the *device_classes.php* file and retry the user-agent strings from page 197 in the test form.

Yay! The problematic
BlackBerry user
agent now matches
the simpler_mobile
device class.

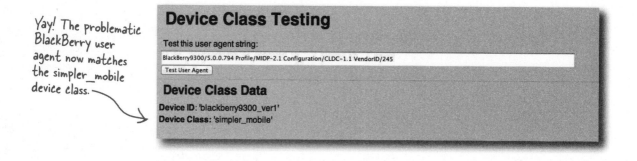

Device Class Testing

Test this user agent string:

BlackBerry9300/5.0.0.794 Profile/MIDP-2.1 Configuration/CLDC-1.1 VendorID/245

[Test User Agent]

Device Class Data

Device ID: 'blackberry9300_ver1'
Device Class: 'simpler_mobile'

Make something actually <u>happen</u> with device classes

Time to take the device classes we've cooked up and get cracking.

The goal: deliver different flavors of the landing page mockup to different users based on device classes.

We'll use our code to sort devices into device classes and deliver different versions of the current AcedIt! study-aid-site mockup to different devices, using the wireframes we whipped up on page 184.

Do this!

Copy the configuration file from the last exercise into the *adapt_content* folder. Yep. Again! This is the last time, we promise.

The HTML and CSS we're dealing with here is pretty basic: AcedIt! is still in the early phases of development on the new site, and so we're working with some pretty barebones mockups.

We'll treat unsupported devices similarly to desktop browsers...for now, at least

We're going to deliver content to the unsupported device class that is basically the same as the desktop content, but we'll explicitly eliminate links to the interactive flashcards section of the site and the online store. We'll also not deliver Flash content to unsupported devices.

> **Relax**
>
> **It's getting a bit late, and we're all tired: to save you some time, we did a lot of this for you.**
>
> We're going to walk through how we did it over the next several pages, but we'll show you where to find the finished code.

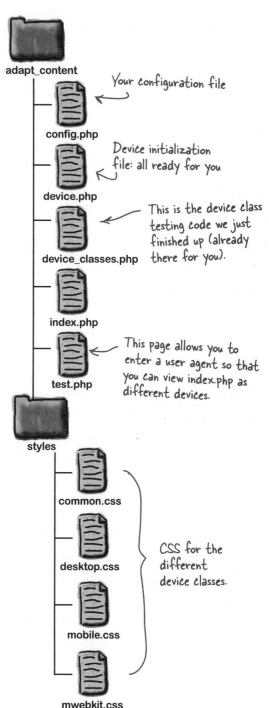

adapt_content

config.php — Your configuration file

device.php — Device initialization file: all ready for you

device_classes.php — This is the device class testing code we just finished up (already there for you).

index.php

test.php — This page allows you to enter a user agent so that you can view index.php as different devices.

styles

common.css
desktop.css — CSS for the different device classes.
mobile.css
mwebkit.css

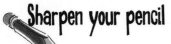

Sharpen your pencil

The starting point of *index.php* has **all** versions of the content (for all device classes) in it. It's time to identify which pieces of content will be delivered (or not delivered) to users who fall into our different device classes. For each number below, find the corresponding markup on the right and fill in the blanks with the appropriate device classe(s).

1 Use this DOCTYPE for the .... device class.

2 Use this stylesheet for the .... , ... , and .... device classes.

3 Use this stylesheet for the .... and .... device classes.

4 Use this stylesheet for the .... device class.

5 Show this version of the navigation for the .... , ... , and .... device classes.

6 Do not show these two links for the .... device class.

Here's the markup from the *index.php* file. Use it to answer the questions on the page at left.

index.php

```
❶  <!DOCTYPE html PUBLIC "-//W3C//DTD XHTML Basic 1.1//EN"
       "http://www.w3.org/TR/xhtml-basic/xhtml-basic11.dtd">
    <!DOCTYPE html>
    <html>
    <head>
      <title>AcedIt! Study Aids</title>
      <meta http-equiv="Content-Type" content="text/html; charset=utf-8" />
      <meta name="viewport" content="width=device-width, initial-scale=1,
    maximum-scale=1" />
      <link rel="stylesheet" type="text/css" href="../assets/common.css" />
❷     <link rel="stylesheet" type="text/css" href="../assets/desktop.css" />
❸     <link rel="stylesheet" type="text/css" href="../assets/mobile.css" />
❹     <link rel="stylesheet" type="text/css" href="../assets/mwebkit.css" />
    </head>
    <body>

    <div id="header">
      <h1>AcedIt! Study Aids</h1>
    </div>
    <div id="navigation">
❺     <ul>
        <li><a href="#">Home</a></li>
        <li><a href="#">Shop Online</a></li>
        <li><a href="#">Study Now!</a></li>    ❻
        <li><a href="#">Contact Us</a></li>
        <li><a href="#">FAQ</a></li>
      </ul>
    </div>
```

Psst...the <u>Study Now</u> section is the interactive JavaScript-based flashcard feature.

→ Continued on next page.

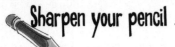

Sharpen your pencil

Oh, you thought you were done? At least you're halfway there!

7 Deliver Flash content to the .... device class.

8 Don't use Flash for the .... , ... ,
.... , or .... device classes.

9 Don't show these sections for the .... or ....
device classes.

10 Show this version of the navigation for the .... and
.... device classes.

11 Hide the link to the interactive flashcards for the .... device class.

index.php

```
<div id="intro">

<p>Morbi non erat non ipsum pharetra tempus. Donec orci. Proin in ante.
Pellentesque sit amet purus. Cras egestas diam sed ante. Etiam imperdiet
urna sit amet risus...</p>

</div>

<div id="feature">

   <div id="featured_product">

      <p>Featured product Flash slideshow.</p>

      <p>Static featured product image.</p>

   </div>

</div>

<div id="ads">

   ...

</div>

<div id="fromtheblog">

   ...

</div>

<div id="navigation">

   <ul>

      <li><a href="#">Home</a></li>

      <li><a href="#">Shop Online</a></li>

      <li><a href="#">Study Now!</a></li>

      <li><a href="#">Blog</a></li>

      <li><a href="#">Contact Us</a></li>

      <li><a href="#">FAQ</a></li>

   </ul>

</div>

<div id="footer">

   <p>Current device class: <?php print $device_class; ?></p>

</div>

</body>

</html>
```

7 **8**

It's probably obvious, but these are just placeholders until the Flash movie and static variant are developed.

We removed a bit of the text content to save space here on this page.

9

10

11

Sharpen your pencil
Solution

Time to look at the markup differences for the different device classes and convert our decisions into code.

1 Use this DOCTYPE for the ....**simpler_mobile**......... device class.

> We'll use XHTML-Basic for the simpler mobile device class. Everyone else gets HTML5.

```php
<?php if($device_class == 'simpler_mobile'): ?>
1 <!DOCTYPE html PUBLIC "-//W3C//DTD XHTML Basic 1.1//EN" "http://
www.w3.org/TR/xhtml-basic/xhtml-basic11.dtd">
<?php else: ?>
  <!DOCTYPE html>
<?php endif; ?>
```

2 Use this stylesheet for the ....**desktop**............. , ...**tablet**........................ , and
.............**unsupported**........... device classes.

> ↖ Recall that we're treating the unsupported device class—mostly—like desktop.

3 Use this stylesheet for the ....**simpler_mobile**............. and ....**higher_mobile**............. device classes.

4 Use this stylesheet for the ....**higher_mobile**............. device class.

> Everyone gets the aptly named common.css.

```php
    <link rel="stylesheet" type="text/css" href="../assets/common.css" />
    <?php if ($device_class == 'desktop'
          || $device_class == 'tablet'
2         || $device_class == 'unsupported'): ?>
      <link rel="stylesheet" type="text/css" href="../assets/desktop.css" />
    <?php endif; ?>
    <?php if ($device_class == 'higher_mobile'
3         || $device_class == 'simpler_mobile'): ?>
      <link rel="stylesheet" type="text/css" href="../assets/mobile.css" />
    <?php endif; ?>
    <?php if ($device_class == 'higher_mobile'): ?>
4     <link rel="stylesheet" type="text/css" href="../assets/mwebkit.css" />
    <?php endif; ?>
```

> There are elements common to both mobile device classes in these styles.

> This stylesheet has gradients and other fancy-pants stuff, specifically formulated for WebKit browsers.

5 Show this version of the navigation for the ....**desktop**............ , ...**tablet**............, and ....**unsupported**............ device classes.

6 Do not show these two links for the ....**unsupported**............ device class.

This is the desktop-style navigation, near the top of the page.

```php
<?php if ($device_class == 'desktop'
     || $device_class == 'tablet'
     || $device_class == 'unsupported'): ?>
  <div id="navigation">
    <ul>
      <li><a href="#">Home</a></li>
      <?php if ($device_class != 'unsupported'): ?>
      <li><a href="#">Shop Online</a></li>
      <li><a href="#">Study Now!</a></li>
      <?php endif; ?>
      <li><a href="#">Contact Us</a></li>
      <li><a href="#">FAQ</a></li>
    </ul>
  </div>
<?php endif; ?>
```

No online shopping or snazzy flashcards for these guys!

7 Deliver Flash content to the ....**desktop**............ device class.

8 Don't use Flash for the ....**tablet**............ , ...**higher_mobile**............, ...**simpler_mobile**............ , or ....**unsupported**............ device classes.

Flash and mobile devices often don't play well together. Ditto for tablets.

```php
<?php if ($device_class == 'desktop'): ?>
  <p>Featured product Flash slideshow.</p>
<?php else: ?>
  <p>Static featured product image.</p>
<?php endif; ?>
```

⟶ Continues over the page.

Sharpen your pencil
    Solution   We're not showing ads on the mobile layouts, and instead of having blog teasers on the page, we'll provide a link to the blog subpage.

9 Don't show these sections on the ....**higher_mobile**........... or ....**simpler_mobile**........... device classes.

```php
<?php if ($device_class == 'desktop'
        || $device_class == 'tablet'): ?>
9 <div id="ads">
    ...
  </div>
  <div id="fromtheblog">
    ...
  </div>
<?php endif; ?>
```

This is the mobile version of the navigation, down at the bottom of the page.

10 Show this version of the navigation for the ....**higher_mobile**........... and
...........**simpler_mobile**........... device classes.

No interactive flashcards for these phones!

11 Hide the link to the interactive flashcards for the ....**simpler_mobile**........... device class.

```php
<?php if ($device_class == 'higher_mobile'
10      || $device_class == 'simpler_mobile'): ?>
  <div id="navigation">
    <ul>
      <li><a href="#">Home</a></li>
      <li><a href="#">Shop Online</a></li>
      <?php if ($device_class == 'higher_mobile'): ?> 11
        <li><a href="#">Study Now!</a></li>
      <?php endif; ?>
      <li><a href="#">Blog</a></li>
      <li><a href="#">Contact Us</a></li>
      <li><a href="#">FAQ</a></li>
    </ul>
  </div>
<?php endif; ?>
```

Only give the link to the flashcards to the higher_mobile class.

Test Drive

Try it out! Find the finished version of *index.php* in *index_solution.php*. Replace the current *index.php* file with *index_solution.php*.

Navigate to *test.php* in your web browser and try some of the user-agent strings from the *useful_user_agents.txt* file to see the different device class versions. Hit *index.php* directly with your desktop browser to see the desktop version of the mockup.

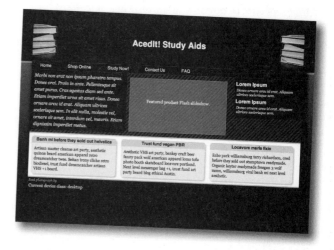

Brain Barbell

We tightened up our device class tests on page 200, but can you think of anything other risks we might not be considering?

Always tread with care and come prepared

Way back in Chapter 3, we highlighted some pitfalls of server-side device detection using user agents. There are some risks that you should keep in mind:

① Browsers don't always send accurate user agents.
Sometimes the user purposely overrides what user agent gets sent, and sometimes browsers just send weird ones. This could cause a device database to return inaccurate data.

② WURFL doesn't always find a (specific) match.
WURFL doesn't always find a successful match, or any valid match whatsoever. You might get a generic device ID, or nothing at all.

Do this! ⟶ Go back to the explore page we created earlier in the chapter and enter the following user agent: `facebookexternalhit/1.1 (+http://www.facebook.com/externalhit_uatext.php)`.

WURFL's "generic" is pretty generic

If you tried out the `facebookexternalhit` user agent in our explore page (and if you didn't, do it now!), you will have noticed that WURFL identifies it as device ID `generic`. This is WURFL's way of shrugging its shoulders and saying, "hey, I tried, but I just don't know what this puppy is."

So what?

The values for capabilities for a generic device aren't meaningful enough to base decisions upon. It's unlikely that the `facebookexternalhit` client has a `resolution_width` of 90 pixels, for example. That just happens to be the value that our WURFL data file has for generic devices.

We need a bigger safety net

When designing a site that uses server-side detection, take some time to think through how the site will behave if a generic ID is returned, or if the device fails to match at all. *Hint: It should still work.*

Accidental success is not good enough

On the AcedIt! study aid mobile test site right now, user agents that result in a generic device match will receive the unsupported device class (try the `facebookexternalhit` user agent to see). This is not an inappropriate device class to assign, but the assignment is kind of happening via dumb luck.

display	
physical_screen_height	27
columns	11
dual_orientation	false
physical_screen_width	27
rows	6
max_image_width	90
resolution_height	40
resolution_width	90
max_image_height	

Detail of our explore page. The generic values for the display group are very generic—we shouldn't rely on them.

WURFL data can vary a bit.

Let's compare the `facebookexternalhit` capability data in our explore page against the data in the ScientiaMobile explorer.

Watch it!

*Visit http://www.tera-wurfl.com/explore and enter the `facebookexternalhit` user agent. The first thing to note is that the Database Edition's variant of the **generic** device ID is called `generic_web_browser`.*

If you explore the capabilities returned for a bit, you'll find more differences. For example, take a look at the display capability group and compare it to the display capability group values for our "generic" device ID above.

Pretty different, huh? It's smart to get familiar with our flavor of WURFL (the PHP API, file-based variant), and it's a good idea that we have our own explore page.

Detail from the ScientiaMobile explorer page capabilities for the facebookexternalhit user agent

display	
physical_screen_height	400
columns	120
dual_orientation	false
physical_screen_width	400
rows	200
max_image_width	600
resolution_height	600
resolution_width	800
max_image_height	

A stitch in time

The PHP API provides a few methods for determining how specific a match was. Let's take a peek.

If there is no device ID at all...

```
if (!$device->id
  || (!$device->isSpecific()
    && $device->fallBack === 'root')) {
  /* FAIL--make sure you have a plan for this situation */

}
```

Or if the match is nonspecific and has fallen back all the way to the root (generic) device

o O

> That seems overcomplicated. Why can't I just test for a specific match and be done with it?

Two reasons: error-checking goodness and the desktop browser patch.

Checking for the lack of a device ID overall feels like good housekeeping. We're being tidy.

The desktop browser patch we're using with WURFL allows us to get basic information about desktop browsers as well as mobile ones.

However, all matches for desktop browsers will return FALSE for isSpecific(), as the data in the patch isn't considered specific. By checking the fallback and making sure it's not root (generic), we can avoid falsely identifying desktop browser matches as failures.

there are no
Dumb Questions

Q: What is this desktop browser patch of which you speak?

A: The default installation of WURFL comes with a patch that will identify, broadly, a set of desktop browsers as well as mobile browsers.

Q: I don't understand what parts of WURFL are the API parts.

A: WURFL itself is just the data. The API is all the code that interacts with it, organizes it, and so on. There are APIs for several major programming languages.

Q: What does the `facebookexternalhit` user agent mean, anyway?

A: When someone shares a link or whatnot on Facebook, Facebook often goes and fetches some content from that page, and/or a representative thumbnail-ish image. This is the user agent it uses when it does so.

Q: Wouldn't the device class testing code be better as a function/object/whatever?

A: It sure would. In real life, for real projects, the code would likely be more elegant, more organized, and more powerful. We're just showing you the basics here.

Q: Excuse me, but if I am not mistaken, the `$device` variable is global. That's stinky.

A: See above.

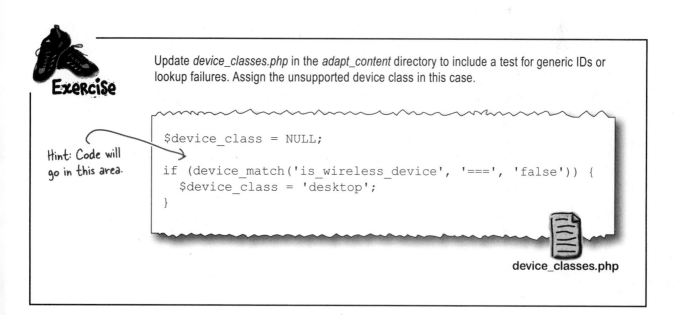

Exercise

Update *device_classes.php* in the *adapt_content* directory to include a test for generic IDs or lookup failures. Assign the unsupported device class in this case.

Hint: Code will go in this area.

```
$device_class = NULL;

if (device_match('is_wireless_device', '===', 'false')) {
    $device_class = 'desktop';
}
```

device_classes.php

Exercise Solution

Now we've battened down the hatches! All done!

```php
$device_class = NULL;
if (!$device->id ||
    (!$device->isSpecific() && $device->fallBack === 'root')) {
  $device_class = 'unsupported';
}
else if (device_match('is_wireless_device', '===', 'false')) {
  $device_class = 'desktop';
}
```

device_classes.php

Congratulations, you've mastered wrangling device capabilities and classes.

It's a complex concept—and you made it! You even have a content-adapted web page to prove it. Good work!

AcedIt! Study Aids

Morbi non erat non ipsum pharetra tempus. Donec orci. Proin in ante. Pellentesque sit amet purus. Cras egestas diam sed ante. Etiam imperdiet urna sit amet risus. Donec ornare arcu id erat. Aliquam ultrices scelerisque sem. In elit nulla, molestie vel, ornare sit amet, interdum vel, mauris. Etiam dignissim imperdiet metus.

Static featured product image.

Home   ›

Shop Online   ›

Study Now!   ›

> How do I make a choice between server-side detection, which can trip up on bad or mysterious user agents, and Responsive Web Design and feature detection, which doesn't have full support in all mobile browsers?

It doesn't have to be one way or the other. You don't have to throw RWD out the window when you use server-side device detection.

Some very handsome things can be accomplished with a combination of the two. Each has its pros and cons. Making the two dance in harmony is part of what we'll look at in Chapter 9, as we look to the future.

BULLET POINTS

- **Device data repositories** like **WURFL** (Wireless Universal Resource FiLe) allow us to get at very detailed information about a whole lot of devices.

- WURFL data contains over 500 capabilities per device, organized into a couple dozen groups.

- We can use a device database to identify a value for a given **capability** and act upon that value.

- **WURFL's PHP API** is one of several APIs for interacting with WURFL data. Different APIs handle and represent the data slightly differently.

- ScientiaMobile was founded in 2011 by some of the original WURFL maintainers. The company provides open source and commercial licenses for WURFL. There are alternatives if WURFL doesn't work for you.

- When working on larger projects, it can be helpful to **group relevant capabilities into device classes**.

- Device classes are abstract groupings of devices based on **common capabilities**.

- By slotting a device into a device class, we can take further action upon it (e.g., delivering adapted content) without having to track individual capabilities constantly.

- It's important to build in **default device classes, error checking, and generic device handling** into any code that uses a device database for identification.

- Like nearly everything on the Web, server-side device detection is not a 100% bulletproof concept.

- **Server-side detection and content adaptation can be married with client-side adaptation**—the two are not mutually exclusive. We'll be looking into this more later.

6 build a mobile web app using a framework

The Tartanator

HTML5, CSS3, JavaScript, mobile frameworks... They sure don't make tartans like they used to.

"We want an app!" Just a year or two ago, that hallmark cry generally meant one thing: native code development and deployment for each platform you wanted to support. But native isn't the only game in town. These days, web-based apps for mobile browsers have some street cred—especially now that hip cat **HTML5** and his sidekicks, **CSS3** and **JavaScript**, are in the house. Let's dip our toes into the mobile web app world by taking a **mobile framework**—code tools designed to help you get your job done quickly—for a spin!

I've heard that you can do all sorts of cool things by using HTML5 on mobile phones, and I've got a *great* idea for an HTML5 mobile web app!

Just like the term *Web 2.0* a few years ago, *HTML5* and *app* are the buzzword darlings of media and Internet folks alike.

The terms mean different things to different people—a free-wheeling semantic party that can be exhilarating or frustrating.

As a web dev, you may already have eager customers beating down your doors asking for HTML5 and web apps specifically. **So, what is it that they're *really* asking for?**

HTML5...app...what do these words even mean?

HTML5 is a specific thing...

HTML5 *is* a specific thing. It's an in-progress standard, an evolution of the HTML we know and love—the language without which there would be no Web. HTML5 clarifies and improves upon the two-decade-old markup language, adding, especially, support for web apps without putting much backward compatibility at risk.

HTML5 introduces new semantic elements like `<section>`, `<article>`, `<nav>`, and `<header>`. It simplifies the syntax for some tags, gives us the power of media with `<audio>` and `<video>` tags, and unleashes interactivity through new JavaScript APIs like geolocation and offline storage.

...but it has come to represent more

When people say HTML5, they often mean the combination of HTML5 itself, super-swanky JavaScript, and CSS3 goodness—in short, the core pieces for building modern, interactive web applications.

And sometimes they just mean "anything cool I've ever seen on the Web."

Which is, well, a bit misleading.

...and what, exactly, is a web app?

What about the *web app* part of an *HTML5 web app*? *HTML5* is a confusing enough term, but with the word ***app***, you're stumbling into even murkier territory, full of dragons and discord.

You can usually look at a website in a browser and have an sense of whether what you're looking at feels applike or not. An emphasis on accomplishing tasks, a layout that fits on a single screen, actions that don't reload the whole page, interactivity—all have been proposed as criteria for what is an app versus what is a regular ol' (content-centric) website.

In short, no one has ever defined the word *app* in a way that makes everyone happy.

Web apps are <u>hard to define</u>, but they share certain <u>interactive characteristics</u> that are well suited for the strengths of HTML5 and its complementary technologies.

How "traditional" websites typically behave

In a traditional website model, a request for an HTML page retrieves all of the components of that page—the HTML itself, JavaScript, CSS, images, etc.

Browsers are often good about caching elements, and web servers can be configured to encourage additional caching. But this model means that each interaction—form submit, link click, whatnot—results in a full-page load.

First page request

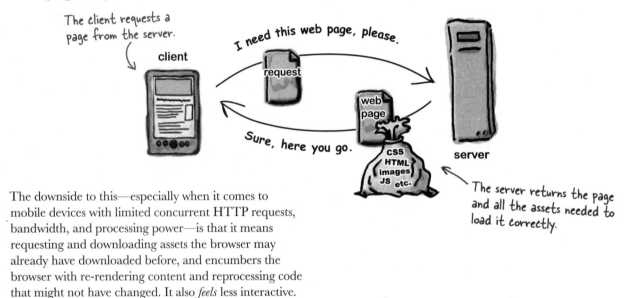

The client requests a page from the server.

client

I need this web page, please.

request

web page

Sure, here you go.

CSS HTML images JS etc.

server

The server returns the page and all the assets needed to load it correctly.

The downside to this—especially when it comes to mobile devices with limited concurrent HTTP requests, bandwidth, and processing power—is that it means requesting and downloading assets the browser may already have downloaded before, and encumbers the browser with re-rendering content and reprocessing code that might not have changed. It also *feels* less interactive.

Subsequent requests

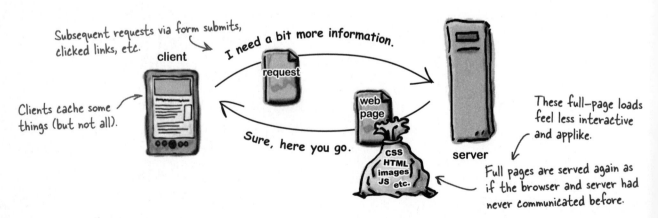

Subsequent requests via form submits, clicked links, etc.

client

I need a bit more information.

request

web page

Sure, here you go.

CSS HTML images JS etc.

Clients cache some things (but not all).

These full-page loads feel less interactive and applike.

server

Full pages are served again as if the browser and server had never communicated before.

How applike websites often behave

In a more applike model, the client tends to play a bigger role, and fewer assets are bandied around in each request. Reusable markup, code, and assets can be stored locally. Requests for changed content or data can be made asynchronously using AJAX. These behind-the-scenes asynchronous requests pull in specific content or assets without causing a full-page reload.

Requesting only relevant pieces of content and not reloading the entire page reduces bandwidth and processing, and improves the sense of interactivity.

A lot of this interactive feeling is accomplished through asynchronous requests.

First page request

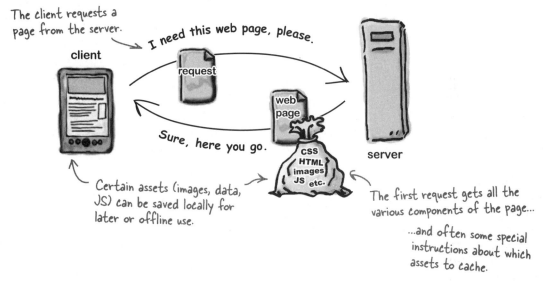

The client requests a page from the server.

client

I need this web page, please.

request

Sure, here you go.

web page

CSS HTML images JS etc.

server

Certain assets (images, data, JS) can be saved locally for later or offline use.

The first request gets all the various components of the page...

...and often some special instructions about which assets to cache.

Subsequent requests

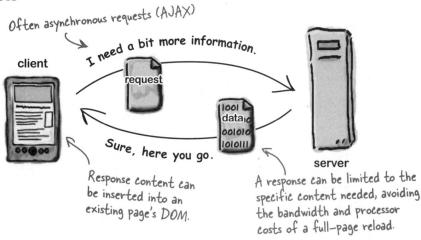

Often asynchronous requests (AJAX)

client

I need a bit more information.

request

Sure, here you go.

1001 data 001010 101011

server

Response content can be inserted into an existing page's DOM.

A response can be limited to the specific content needed, avoiding the bandwidth and processor costs of a full-page reload.

A Tartans Unlimited mobile HTML5 web app

Tartans Unlimited is an international organization that's trying to keep the history and culture surrounding Scottish tartans alive in other parts of the world.

Ewan ⟶

> I have an idea for a web app I want to build. It'll let users find information about us, but—this is more fun—find and share and maybe even create their own tartan patterns.

About Us page

A history of Tartans Unlimited. Links to information about the history of tartans.

↑ This content isn't ready yet. ← Bug Pat about this.

Events page

- It would be nice if the app could somehow "link into" our international events database.

- Could a user's phone help find the nearest events? ??

- Might want to wait until phase 2 or phase 3 of the site for events stuff—complex?

New Website! App?

Welcome message

Keep this simple...link to About Us page for more info...

Tartan events

I have some ideas here...not sure if they are possible!

- Tartans!

This is the main part of the idea...sounds like an *app*?

The Tartanator!

Maybe call the whole app/site "The Tartanator"? Has a nice ring!

- Make it so users can see and explore the tartan patterns right on their phones.
Lots of *images* of tartans!

- Wouldn't it be cool if users could create their own tartans?

!! ✶ ★ Can this be done?

- A collection of tartans: popular "traditional" ones as well as new-world and user-created tartans.

Jill: Hey guys, I know the requirements are pretty vague. When I talked to Ewan, I got the sense that there are two main things he wants to accomplish with the site…or app, or whatever. There's a chunk of **content** pages: info about the organization and education about tartans. Then there's this whole section he's calling the **Tartanator**—

Joe: The Tartanator? Seriously? Heh.

Jill: Yeah. Actually, it seems he wants to call the whole site that, not just one section. Anyway, it seems like it's sort of a combination of a browsable listing of tartan patterns to explore and, he hopes, a way for users to create their own tartan patterns using a form—

Frank: Wow. That sounds simultaneously bizarre and daunting, but possibly fun as an implementation challenge.

Joe: OK, content pages, Tartanator area…what about this note about an Events page?

Jill: Hold your horses! I'm getting there! We've decided to do this project in two rough phases. For the first phase, we'll build basic structure for the content pages and implement the tartan listing. He'd also like us to think about how an interface for users to create their own tartans would look, and maybe prototype the frontend of that.

Joe: So, like, we'd build the form for creating a tartan, but it doesn't need to do anything yet?

Jill: Something like that, yes. In phase 2, we'll make it actually work, and we'll also come back and work on an Events section.

Frank: OK, sounds like we need to go start building a mobile web app.

Some of the tartans that will be in the Tartanator's tartan directory

Tartan for the state of Oregon

MacAlpine clan tartan

Innes clan tartan

Lennox clan tartan

The master plan for phase 1 of the Tartanator

☐ **Build content pages and site structure.**

We need to create basic sections and pages and create an overall structure.

Here's what we need to do!

☐ **Create the tartan listings.**

For the first phase, we'll create a listing of existing popular tartan patterns. The tartans section should be a browsing interface that—of course—looks and feels applike and mobile oriented.

☐ **Build a prototype of the tartan-building form.**

Ultimately, Ewan would like users to be able to construct their own tartans by using an applike mobile interface. He wants to see what that might look like, so we'll whip him up a prototype.

So, we're supposed to build a mobile web app with HTML5 and stuff. I have no idea where to begin. Do I have to build all of this from scratch?

Well, you could build an app from scratch...

If you're up to speed with CSS, HTML, and JavaScript, learn how to put them all together to create awesome web apps with *Head First HTML5 Programming*.

Buy it, it's great! The best HTML5 Programming book on the market. Seriously, you know you want to.

OK, enough plugging now. — Ed.

...or you could use a mobile web framework

To build phase 1 of the Tartanator, we're going to turbo-boost our web aptitude by using a mobile web framework.

We'll still be using our HTML and CSS chops, but a mobile-oriented user interface framework can help us get our job done faster.

Why use mobile web app frameworks?

Let's face it. Building complex, interactive web apps from scratch—especially mobile web apps—can be a daunting proposition. A web development framework—that is, a packaged collection of interactive elements and code tools—can help give us a leg up.

1 **A framework can help us make a website or app <u>look</u> mobile-friendly.**
Mobile-oriented frameworks generally help alter and style HTML elements to look and feel more mobile, often saving us quite a lot of time.

2 **A framework can help us make a website or app <u>feel</u> mobile.**
Frameworks can take the drudgery out of transitions and effects that make a website or app feel more native, or, at least, consistent.

3 **A framework can help us manage cross-platform inconsistencies.**
Framework developers keep on top of obnoxious or curious browser quirks that could really throw a wrench in things, working around them in the framework's codebase so that we don't have to.

> Depending on the project, you might not want to reinvent at least some of the wheels required for an interactive web app. That's where mobile development <u>frameworks</u> come in handy.

Watch it!

Choose and use web frameworks with care.

Frameworks are powerful mojo, but they also have some drawbacks. Many are quite hefty, and can bloat your site's payload by hundreds of kilobytes. Some employ a kitchen-sink approach, including tons of widgets and cutesy animations that not only are large in byte units, but can cause serious performance woes on lesser devices. Finally, make sure you evaluate a framework's device support. Some only support one or a few major, cutting-edge platforms.

Our choice for the Tartanator: jQuery Mobile

To build the Tartanator, we're going to use the **jQuery Mobile** framework.

jQuery Mobile is a user interface framework optimized for mobile devices. It's built atop the immensely popular jQuery JavaScript library.

The reason we chose jQuery Mobile for this project is that it is pretty easy to use and has an architecture that maps well to our HTML5 focus—jQuery Mobile is designed in a way that hooks in easily (sometimes invisibly!) to well-formed HTML5 markup.

Also, if you've ever used jQuery before, you probably know how intuitive and straightforward it feels.

jQuery Mobile, like all of the jQuery projects, is open source.

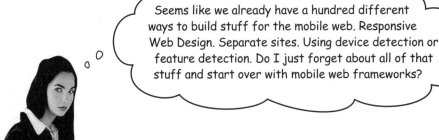

Seems like we already have a hundred different ways to build stuff for the mobile web. Responsive Web Design. Separate sites. Using device detection or feature detection. Do I just forget about all of that stuff and start over with mobile web frameworks?

You're right. It's a complicated landscape.

Here's where we trot out our tired Wild West metaphor about the mobile web. But it's true. There are no simple answers, and pulling off complex feats on the mobile web often involves the cobbling together of several implementation approaches.

So, no, don't throw out everything we've already learned. None of the techniques we've covered so far is mutually exclusive, and each makes more (or less!) sense in different circumstances.

Life is complex. So is the mobile web!

there are no
Dumb Questions

Q: Are there other mobile frameworks out there?

A: And how! There are more every day. Some other mobile web frameworks include Sencha Touch, Wink, iUI, DHTMLX Touch, and JQTouch.

Q: What exactly makes up a mobile web framework?

A: It depends on the framework, but most involve a combination of JavaScript, CSS, and image (or other) assets to aid in the styling of the mobile experience. Some frameworks also include a server-side component to help generate (as opposed to adapt) content.

Q: Wait. What about zepto.js or XUI?

A: Zepto.js (very lightweight JavaScript, with jQuery syntax) and XUI (also very compact JS) both fall more on the library side of the line (versus framework). Frameworks tend to have UI components, while libraries tend to be code—in this case, JavaScript—only. This is a grey area; the division between library and framework isn't easy to define.

Q: So, jQuery Mobile is a mobile version of the original jQuery library?

A: Not so fast, hotshot! jQuery Mobile builds on top of jQuery. It does not replace it. You'll notice that when we start building stuff with jQuery Mobile, the first JavaScript file we include is the core jQuery library.

Q: So, jQuery Mobile is a JavaScript development framework that extends jQuery.

A: Bear with us. Yes, there is JavaScript in the jQuery Mobile framework. But jQuery Mobile is not a *JavaScript* framework. It's bigger than that. It's a user interface framework. That means it also includes stylesheets, icons, and other pieces of the puzzle.

Q: Do we *really* need to use a framework?

A: Do we need to? Technically? No, not at all! In fact, we encourage you to build applike mobile websites from scratch, if that's your bag.

However, the nice thing about frameworks, and jQuery Mobile in particular, is that they take care of a lot of obnoxious, platform-specific quirks and bugs for us. Their team of devs has laserlike focus on the foibles of different mobile browsers.

We have limited time and space here, folks. Trying to pull off what we need to do for the Tartanator without a framework of any sort would be pretty hairy, not to mention the chaos of extra testing that would be required (as we wouldn't have that underpinning of tested cross-platform support).

Q: I still don't get it. How is the Tartanator an app instead of a website?

A: Because Ewan says so. No, really. The subtleties of differentiation between app and site are so vague that the answer sometimes seems almost arbitrary.

Ewan has a vision of the Tartanator as a functional, web-based thing. His focus is on the ability to find and create tartans, and, also, ultimately, to search for relevant events. In his mind, that makes this an app.

Q: But what if it were a site? I couldn't use jQuery Mobile then, right?

A: jQuery Mobile is a user interface framework. It doesn't care whether you call what you're making with it an app or a site. Its job is to make things feel usable and not break across various mobile platforms, using a combination of CSS, JavaScript, and HTML5.

Q: But which mobile browsers support HTML5?

A: No browser supports (all of) HTML5. Don't panic! HTML5 is modular, and mobile browsers are increasingly supporting more and more pieces. Just as no modern desktop browser fully supports every single piece of CSS2.1, it may well be that HTML5 is never fully supported, exactly as it is in the spec, by every browser. Oh, and the spec is still evolving. The website *http://www.caniuse.com* is a good reference if you're looking for info about specific feature support in HTML5 and the other major web technologies.

Build a basic page with jQuery Mobile

chapter6

aboutus.html

findevent.html

We'll be meeting these pages in a few, err, pages.

index.html

extras

You can ignore this folder for now. We'll show you what's in it in a little bit.

tartans

This folder comes a bit later, too.

chapter6 directory structure: your starting point

The first stop on the Tartanator adventure is to learn how to build a simple page with jQuery Mobile so that we can start constructing the pages in the project. You'll be surprised by just how easy this is.

Start basic

By starting with a super-simple HTML page, you can see the basics of jQuery Mobile at work more clearly.

We're using the HTML5 <DOCTYPE> tag.

The entire contents of index.html— seriously, it's this basic!

```
<!DOCTYPE html>
<html>
<head>
    <meta charset="UTF-8" />
    <title>The Tartanator</title>
</head>
<body>

<h1>The Tartanator</h1>

<p>The Tartanator is a community-built
association of groups, businesses, and
individuals bent on keeping the Scottish
heritage alive overseas by promoting
the understanding and enjoyment of
<strong>tartans</strong></p>.

</body>
</html>
```

index.html

Include jQuery mobile code components

Open *index.html* in your text editor and get ready to plop in some jQuery Mobile. First things first: **include** the JavaScript and CSS that will make things go.

The inclusion of jQuery and jQuery Mobile JavaScript will give our web app its mobile—friendly interactions.

Include jQuery Mobile's CSS: this will style our markup in mobile—friendly ways.

Remember that jQuery Mobile is nothing without jQuery (core).

```
<title>The Tartanator</title>
    <meta name="viewport" content="width=device-width, initial-scale=1">
    <link rel="stylesheet" href="http://code.jquery.com/mobile/1.0rc1/
jquery.mobile-1.0rc1.min.css" />
<script src="http://code.jquery.com/jquery-1.6.4.min.js"></script>
<script src="http://code.jquery.com/mobile/1.0rc1/jquery.mobile-1.0rc1
min.js"></script>
</head>
```

index.html

Mark up the rest of the page

We've included the three main jQuery Mobile components from jQuery's CDN (*content delivery network*—that is, the code as hosted on *code.jquery.com*). That's a reliable and fast place to link to the code.

Now that we've included the three core files—theme CSS, jQuery Core, and jQuery Mobile itself—we need to make a few adjustments to the HTML markup within the `<body>`.

By wrapping parts of our content in `<div>` tags with descriptive `data-*` attributes, we tell jQuery Mobile how we want them treated:

We'll explain data-* attributes more in just a moment.

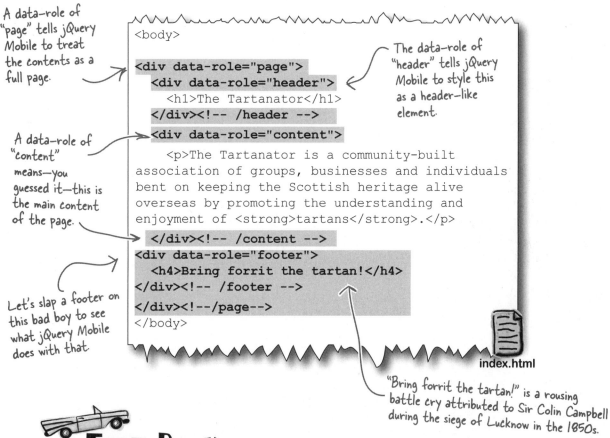

A data-role of "page" tells jQuery Mobile to treat the contents as a full page.

The data-role of "header" tells jQuery Mobile to style this as a header-like element.

A data-role of "content" means—you guessed it—this is the main content of the page.

Let's slap a footer on this bad boy to see what jQuery Mobile does with that.

```
<body>

<div data-role="page">
  <div data-role="header">
    <h1>The Tartanator</h1>
  </div><!-- /header -->
  <div data-role="content">

    <p>The Tartanator is a community-built
association of groups, businesses and individuals
bent on keeping the Scottish heritage alive
overseas by promoting the understanding and
enjoyment of <strong>tartans</strong>.</p>

  </div><!-- /content -->
  <div data-role="footer">
    <h4>Bring forrit the tartan!</h4>
  </div><!-- /footer -->
</div><!--/page-->
</body>
```

index.html

"Bring forrit the tartan!" is a rousing battle cry attributed to Sir Colin Campbell during the siege of Lucknow in the 1850s.

⊸ TEST DRIVE

It really is that easy to make a simple jQuery Mobile page.

Add the items to the head and body of the *index.html* file and save it. View it in a browser (you can view it in a mobile browser if you like!).

And we're off!

We don't have anything too fancy yet (OK, it's actually pretty dull), but the landing page does look somewhat "mobile."

Note how jQuery Mobile adds gradients, sizes, and font treatments, and turns our elements into header- and footer-like chunks.

Our first jQuery Mobile page, as rendered on an iPhone

> **The Tartanator**
>
> The Tartanator is a community-built association of groups, businesses and individuals bent on keeping the Scottish heritage alive overseas by promoting the understanding and enjoyment of **tartans**.
>
> **Bring forrit the t...**

Hmmm...the footer text doesn't quite fit... but let's worry about that a bit later.

What does it even mean to "look mobile"? Doesn't that page mostly look like a native iOS app?

The default jQuery Mobile look definitely smacks of iOS.

For better or worse, the rounded-button, gradient-laden-headers look of the native iOS platform have become a common visual metaphor for web-based mobile apps. And many people now associate that appearance with "looking mobile."

But beyond Apple-esque polish, there are some useful things going on here. Whitespace is increased and font size optimized for small-screen reading. Soon, we'll build forms and be able to see that jQM gives us larger input areas and chunky buttons—big touch targets for our fat fingers.

These are just a couple of examples!

The HTML5 data-* attribute

jQuery Mobile makes heavy use of the `data-*` attribute introduced with HTML5. In our simple page, we used the `data-role` attribute to inform jQuery Mobile of, well, what role the given element has in our page structure. Right now things are pretty simple: we have a header, some content, and a footer.

Build more of the Tartanator

Now that we have a solid foundation, let's start building more of the Tartanator. Right now we have our landing page, but we need to link it to some other basic pages to move forward with the project.

HTML5 data-* Up Close

The `data-*` attribute was introduced with HTML5 as a way to let developers associate lightweight but meaningful data with HTML elements.

In the past, we developers found some ways to do things like this by kind of hijacking other element attributes like `class` or `title`.

But now there is a real, sanctioned way to do this, and jQuery Mobile takes advantage of it.

As we move along, we'll continue to encounter places where jQuery Mobile uses different `data-*` attributes to get its job done.

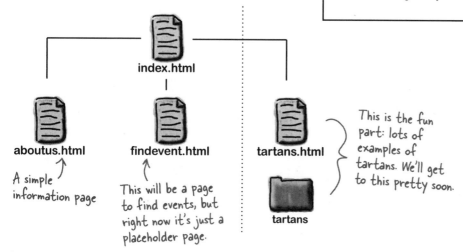

index.html

aboutus.html

A simple information page

findevent.html

This will be a page to find events, but right now it's just a placeholder page.

tartans.html

This is the fun part: lots of examples of tartans. We'll get to this pretty soon.

tartans

Exercise

Time to add a navigation-like list of links to the three subpages. Edit *index.html* and add a very simple `<ul>` after the introductory paragraph inside of the main content `<div>`. The text of the list elements should be the names of the subpages: **About Us**, **Find an Event**, and **Popular Tartans**.

We'll add the actual links in just a bit; for now, just text, OK?

Basic HTML FTW!

```
    <p>The Tartanator is a community-built association
of groups, businesses, and individuals bent on keeping
the Scottish heritage alive overseas by promoting the
understanding and enjoyment of <strong>tartans</strong>.</p>
    <ul>
        <li>About Us</li>
        <li>Find an Event</li>
        <li>Popular Tartans</li>
    </ul>
</div><!-- /content -->
```

index.html

Make it a jQuery Mobile list

If you save your changes and view *index.html* in a browser, you'll likely notice that our little list doesn't look very exciting (or mobile-ish). That's because we haven't informed jQuery Mobile that we want it to take note of its existence. **We need to use the data-role attribute again!**

Hmmm, that's a pretty humdrum list.

> The Tartanator
>
> The Tartanator is a community-built association of groups, businesses and individuals bent on keeping the Scottish heritage alive overseas by promoting the understanding and enjoyment of **tartans**.
>
> - About Us
> - Find an Event
> - Popular Tartans
>
> Bring forrit the t...

```
<ul data-role="listview">
```

We use the data-role attribute to tell jQuery Mobile to treat this as a list view.

That way, jQuery Mobile will style the list nicely and recognize its existence.

jQuery Mobile alters content with the listview data-role to make it look and feel like a more mobile-friendly, interactive list.

Test Drive

Add the data-role attribute to the <ul> in *index.html* and view the page in a browser.

What do you think of the way jQuery Mobile styles the list?

Our list: Better, but not quite there

By default, jQuery Mobile will treat `listviews` like page content, filling the full width of the screen with the `<li>` elements. On our landing page, this looks a bit awkward and cramped.

For our purposes, the navigation list is part of the content, not the entirety of it. jQuery Mobile's list options include *inset* lists—lists that are contained within a page that has other stuff on it. Let's use that.

First try →

The list looks a bit scrunched and odd.

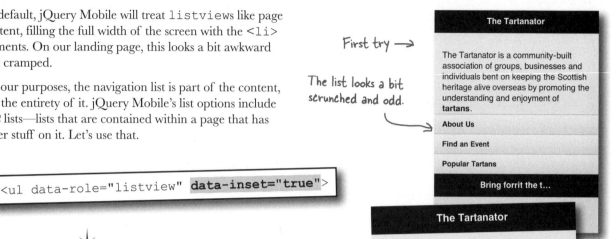

```
<ul data-role="listview" data-inset="true">
```

Do this!

Add the `data-inset` attribute to the list in *index.html* and try viewing the page again.

Second try

The inset list looks much better.

The list looks great and all, but none of its elements are clickable. But, uh, don't we need to make them actually link to something?

You're right. Let's link up the pages!

Time to make the Tartanator more than a one-page show.

Link to multiple pages with jQuery Mobile

Linking to other pages in jQuery Mobile is quite straightforward.
All we have to do is add basic HTML links:

```
<ul data-role="listview" data-inset="true">
  <li><a href="aboutus.html">About Us</a></li>
  <li><a href="findevent.html">Find an Event</a></li>
  <li><a href="tartans.html">Learn about Tartans</a></li>
</ul>
```

index.html

Do this! ➡ Add the links to the list in *index.html* and test them out. What happens?

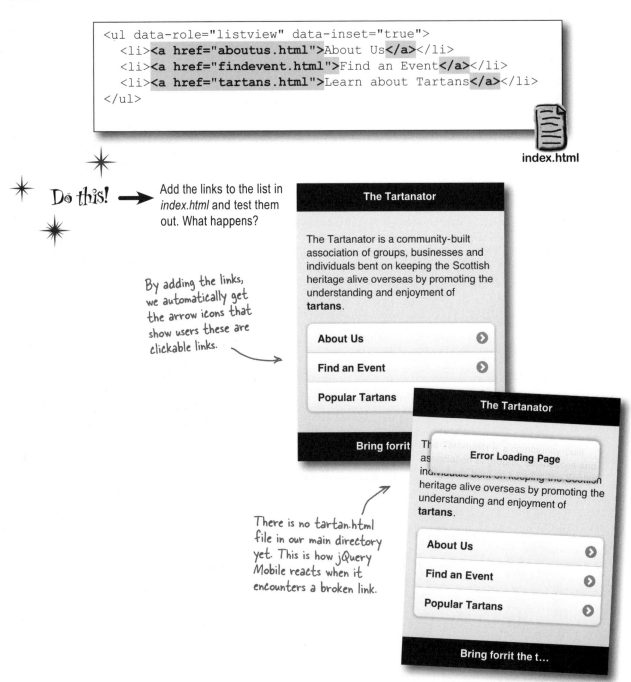

By adding the links, we automatically get the arrow icons that show users these are clickable links.

There is no tartan.html file in our main directory yet. This is how jQuery Mobile reacts when it encounters a broken link.

The Tartanator

The Tartanator is a community-built association of groups, businesses and individuals bent on keeping the Scottish heritage alive overseas by promoting the understanding and enjoyment of **tartans**.

About Us ❯

Find an Event ❯

Popular Tartans

Bring forrit

The Tartanator

Error Loading Page

Th ... as ... individuals bent on keeping the Scottish heritage alive overseas by promoting the understanding and enjoyment of **tartans**.

About Us ❯

Find an Event ❯

Popular Tartans ❯

Bring forrit the t...

jQuery Mobile Exposed

This week's interview:
How does jQuery Mobile handle loading pages?

Head First: I hear you have something to tell us about what a "page" really is, to you.

jQuery Mobile: I do! It's one of my favorite things about myself, so I wanted to explain.

Remember how the structure of one of my pages uses a `<div>` with a `data-role` value of `page`?

Head First: Sure.

jQuery Mobile: The markup contained within that `<div>`—often a header, content area, and footer—is what I consider a page.

Head First: Then what is the point of the rest of the HTML markup? Is it chopped liver?

jQuery Mobile: Definitely not! In a web app designed along my principles, each HTML file is a standalone, autonomous thing that you can visit in your browser.

Head First: I'm lost. If each HTML file is independent, why bother with the `<div>` with the `data-role` of `page`?

jQuery Mobile: Let me back up. When you first navigate to a page in one of my sites or applications, that page is loaded just like any old HTML page on the Web.

But once that first page is loaded, I do something different. When you click on links, I find the page content from the requested HTML document—that is, the stuff in the `<div>` with the `data-role` of `page`—with AJAX and inject it into the current page's DOM—

Head First: But what is the point of that?

jQuery Mobile: There are several points, if you'd let me finish!

Instead of requesting and downloading the whole requested page—scripts, images, styles—and reinitializing and rebuilding the DOM from scratch, I only snag the pieces that matter. That saves on HTTP requests, bandwidth, and processing time and makes the experience feel a bit more natural and native.

Head First: If content pieces are loaded dynamically, how come I see the URL of the link I clicked on in the address bar of my desktop browser?

jQuery Mobile: My modest exterior belies the deep sophistication of my navigation model. I always aim to have real URLs for the pages in my apps, even if the pages are really generated dynamically or there are multiple `<div>` tags with a `data-role` of `page` in a single HTML document.

By having a unique and reusable URL for AJAX-loaded content chunks, I can make them look and act like full-blown web pages. When the browser allows me to (not all browsers do), I even update the displayed URL in the browser's address bar as I load in new content asynchronously.

Head First: If I understand correctly, then, I can access each HTML file in my app or site directly, but the content of those documents can be retrieved independently and dynamically, when linked to, to improve performance and responsiveness?

jQuery Mobile: Exactly!

Head First: Thanks, jQuery Mobile, for a really dynamic chat.

If page content is loaded dynamically with AJAX, what happens to older browsers with limited JavaScript support or browsers with no JavaScript support at all? Do they break?

jQuery Mobile can work even if there is no JavaScript support at all.

Crazy, huh?

Recall that the links in the markup start out as just that: basic HTML links. It's jQuery Mobile's JavaScript that does the magic of converting the links into dynamic AJAX-y goodness for browsers that support it.

For browsers that don't support this, navigation between pages works just like the old-fashioned Web always has.

there are no Dumb Questions

Q: If pages are loaded with AJAX, why do I need to create separate pages at all? Can't I just put all of my app's content into one page and use jQuery Mobile to show and hide it?

A: You could, but you'd be missing out on jQuery Mobile's nice notion of progressive enhancement. You'd be leaving lesser mobile browsers (those that can't do the snazzy JavaScript) out in the cold.

You'd also have a large, complex file that is difficult to maintain and has a heavy DOM that is tough for lesser phones to handle. jQuery Mobile encourages you to author websites and apps like you're used to: with separate HTML files that can stand alone *or* be sucked in with AJAX.

Q: How did jQuery Mobile know which `data-*` attributes to use? Where can I find information about all of the available `data-*` attributes?

A: Developers can cook up any name they'd like for `data-*` attributes (well, they have to start with a letter). There is no prescribed set. The idea is that `data-*` attributes pertain to the functioning of the website that they appear in—that is, they're not intended for communicating data to external applications. Because of that, web developers have relative freedom to generate their own `data-*` naming conventions.

Q: What version of jQuery Mobile are we using?

A: The jQuery Mobile dev team is on a tear! During the time we spent writing this chapter, both 1.0 beta 3 and 1.0 Release Candidate 1 were released, requiring some scrambling on our part.

Oh, wait, we just checked. 1.0RC2 is out now, too! Oh! There's RC3! Oh, no, it's faster than a speeding bullet! jQuery Mobile 1.0 is now released and official!

For the Tartanator, we're using 1.0RC1.

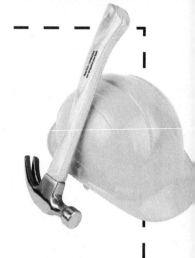

FOOTER (RE-)CONSTRUCTION

As we saw on page 230, the text in the page footer is getting truncated on narrow screens. That's because jQuery Mobile leaves room for button placement around header elements in headers and footers—but we don't have any buttons in our footer. Let's fix it!

Our header, before reconstruction. It's truncated.

Also, it has a bit more visual weight than it needs to. It feels really dark

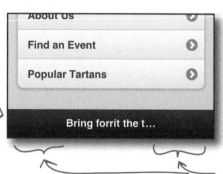

About Us

Find an Event ❯

Popular Tartans ❯

Bring forrit the t...

By default, jQuery Mobile's styling leaves room for buttons around header elements (<h1>, etc.) in headers and footers.

1 Remove the <h4> element surrounding the footer text.

Right now, the footer text is wrapped in an <h4> element. By removing this header element, we'll keep jQuery Mobile from leaving room for buttons and, as a side effect, truncating the text.

```
<div data-role="footer">
  <h4>Bring forrit the tartan!</h4>
</div><!-- /footer -->
```

index.html

2 Add a CSS rule to center the footer text and give it a bit of padding.

Unfortunately, removing the <h4> will also remove the centering and the padding. We need to account for this in our own CSS.

Open *tartans/tartans.css* in your text editor and add this rule at the top of the file (there is already a bunch of CSS in this file).

```
[data-role="footer"] { text-align: center; padding: 5px 0;}
#abercrombie { background-image:url('icons/abercrombie.png'); }
```

tartans.css

This CSS selector applies to elements with a data-role attribute that has the value "footer."

Continues, flip the page.

FOOTER (RE-)CONSTRUCTION

③ Link in the stylesheet.
Edit *index.html* again and add a link to the stylesheet.

```
<link rel="stylesheet" href="http://code.jquery.com/mobile/1.0rc1/
jquery.mobile-1.0rc1.min.css" />
<link rel="stylesheet" href="tartans/tartans.css" />
<script src="http://code.jquery.com/jquery-1.6.4.min.js"></script>
```

index.html

④ Check our progress.
Save the file and view *index.html* in a smartphone browser or simulator.

It's not cut off anymore. But it still feels dark. Also, look, it doesn't always end up at the very bottom of the screen. There's a gap. That makes it feel kind of weird. There must be a way to fix that...

The fix to both of these items involves a couple of small changes to the footer `<div>`.

We want to tell jQuery Mobile to use *fixed positioning* to make the footer stick to the bottom of the page, and we need to change the *theming swatch* to make the footer appear less dominant visually.

The footer isn't always at the bottom of all of the pages; sometimes there is a gap.

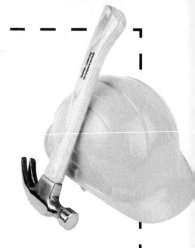

⑤ Use fixed positioning on the footer so that it always shows up in the same place.

By using the `data-position` attribute and setting its value to `fixed`, we tell jQuery Mobile to use fixed positioning on the footer element. That way it will always stick to the bottom of the page.

⑥ Use a different theme swatch to make the footer appear less dominant.

jQuery Mobile's initial stylesheet has five default color groups, called *swatches*. These five swatches are referenced by the letters a through e.

By default, header and footer elements receive swatch a, which has the most dominant contrast.

Our footer isn't a particularly important page element, and right now has too much visual weight. By explictly assigning swatch c, we can make the appearance of the footer much less in-your-face.

You can use the `data-theme` attribute on any element to override jQuery's default swatch for that element.

The default color scheme for swatches a through e is defined in jQuery Mobile's CSS.

```
<div data-role="footer" data-position="fixed" data-theme="c">
  Bring forrit the tartan!
</div><!-- /footer -->
```

index.html

That's it! The footer should look a lot better now. Try saving your changes and reviewing our improved footer in a mobile browser or simulator.

The release of jQuery Mobile 1.0 includes a new Theme Roller tool that makes theming jQM easier. See more at http://jquerymobile.com/themeroller/.

The meat of the Tartanator: The tartans themselves

Let's check in with our status on phase 1 of the Tartanator project:

☑ **Build content pages and site structure.**

We need to create basic sections and pages and create an overall structure.

We've got our basic layout squared away and created the basics of the main pages.

☐ **Create the tartan listings.**

For the first phase, we'll create a list of existing popular tartan patterns. The tartans section should be a browsing interface that—of course—looks and feels applike and mobile oriented.

Next on our list!

☐ **Build a prototype of the tartan-building form.**

We'll get to this in just a bit.

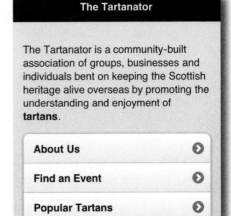

The footer is now positioned correctly and is much less imposing visually. Success!

We've got our core content pages—at least the skeletons of them—in place. Now let's turn our attention to matters that are more interesting: the tartans themselves.

For phase 1, the Tartanator will allow users to **browse a collection of popular and unusual tartans**. Think of it kind of like a quick tartan reference.

 **Do this!** → Copy *tartans.html* from the *extras* folder to the *chapter6* folder (that is, move it up one level).

The tartans directory, which contains the individual tartan HTML pages, should already be in your chapter6 directory.

Get to work on tartans.html

The *tartans.html* file has the beginnings of a list (`<ul>`) for the popular tartans. To get you going, the list contains tartans starting with A and B. Once you've moved the *tartans.html* file into place, load up the Tartanator on a browser (mobile or otherwise) and take a peek. You can click on the tartan names to visit the tartan page for that tartan.

We've given you a head start on the list

The tartan listing section is a combination of a single HTML page with a list of tartans...

...and an individual HTML page for each tartan.

The first swag at the list of tartans—we did this for you already.

tartans.html

tartans/baird.html

Each tartan pattern has its own HTML page. The tartan is a CSS background image.

Take the list from blah to better

The list of tartans is looking a bit lifeless compared to the tartan information pages themselves. Good news! jQuery Mobile makes it easy to drop thumbnails into lists so we can have small icons on the list itself (much snazzier). Here's an example:

Yep. All you need to do is add an image. jQuery Mobile takes care of the rest.

```
<li><a href="tartans/abercrombie.html">
    <img src="tartans/icons/abercrombie.png" alt="Abercrombie" />
    <h3>Abercrombie</h3>
</a></li>
```

Exercise

Add thumbnails to the list items in *tartans.html*. The icons are in the *tartans/icons* directory and have the same name as their HTML counterparts (but with a *.png* extension).

Exercise
Solution

```
<ul data-role="listview">
  <li><a href="tartans/abercrombie.html">
    <img src="tartans/icons/abercrombie.png" alt="Abercrombie" />
    <h3>Abercrombie</h3>
  </a></li>
  <li><a href="tartans/arbuthnot.html">
    <img src="tartans/icons/arbuthnot.png" alt="Arbuthnot" />
    <h3>Arbuthnot</h3>
  </a></li>
  <li><a href="tartans/baird.html">
    <img src="tartans/icons/baird.png" alt="Baird" />
    <h3>Baird</h3>
  </a></li>
  <li><a href="tartans/barclay-dress.html">
    <img src="tartans/icons/barclay-dress.png" alt="Barclay Dress" />
    <h3>Barclay Dress</h3>
  </a></li>
  <li><a href="tartans/barclay.html">
    <img src="tartans/icons/barclay.png" alt="Barclay" />
    <h3>Barclay</h3>
  </a></li>
  <li><a href="tartans/birrell.html">
    <img src="tartans/icons/birrell.png" alt="Birrell" />
    <h3>Birrell</h3>
  </a></li>
  <li><a href="tartans/blair.html">
    <img src="tartans/icons/blair.png" alt="Blair" />
    <h3>Blair</h3>
  </a></li>
  <li><a href="tartans/borthwick-dress.html">
    <img src="tartans/icons/borthwick-dress.png" alt="Borthwick Dress" />
    <h3>Borthwick Dress</h3>
  </a></li>
  <li><a href="tartans/borthwick.html">
    <img src="tartans/icons/borthwick.png" alt="Borthwick" />
    <h3>Borthwick</h3>
  </a></li>
    <li><a href="tartans/bruce.html">
    <img src="tartans/icons/bruce.png" alt="Bruce" />
    <h3>Bruce</h3>
  </a></li>
  <li><a href="tartans/buchanan.html">
    <img src="tartans/icons/buchanan.png" alt="Buchanan" />
    <h3>Buchanan</h3>
  </a></li>
</ul>
```

Drop in the rest of the tartans

There are a whole bunch more tartans that need
to be added to the list (with their nice icons). Don't
worry, we won't make you do that much typing. Go
find *tartan-list.txt* in the *extras* folder. In the file, you'll
find a snippet of HTML that is the full `<ul>` for all of
the tartans. Copy and paste the `<ul>` into *tartans.html*,
replacing the current HTML list.

Now we've got an enhanced
list—hey, nice icons!—and have
included all of the tartans in
the current collection.

Hey, the list's looking pretty nice,
but it seems kind of long. It's hard to
find a specific tartan name without a
whole lot of scrolling.

True. It's a bit unwieldy.

Turns out, jQuery Mobile has more up
its sleeve for us. More easy-to-implement,
good bang-for-the-buck improvements to
our tartan list coming up!

Filter and organize a list

1 **We can add list <u>dividers</u>.**
We can **break up the list** into sections by using list dividers. This will help organize the list by grouping tartans by their first letter.

2 **We can add a list <u>filter</u>.**
With jQuery Mobile, it's eerily easy to drop in a filter for a list. A filter looks like a search field (with a little magnifying glass and everything!) and **filters the list as the user types in it**. No JavaScript coding required!

To add a filter for the list, add a data-filter attribute to the <ul> with a value of "true."

Yep, that's all there is to it!

1
```
<ul data-role="listview" data-filter="true">
```

You can visually separate the list by adding <li>s with a data-role of "list-divider."

2
```
<ul data-role="listview" data-filter="true">
  <li data-role="list-divider">A</li>
  <li><a href="tartans/abercrombie.html">
  <img src="tartans/icons/abercrombie.png" alt="Abercrombie" />
  <h3>Abercrombie</h3>
</a></li>
```

tartans.html

Test Drive

Give the `<ul>` in *tartans.html* a filter field and list dividers. Add list dividers for each letter (except those that don't have any tartans, like Q and X).

Save your work and view the results in a browser. Pretty cool, eh?

Our tartan list is nicer now

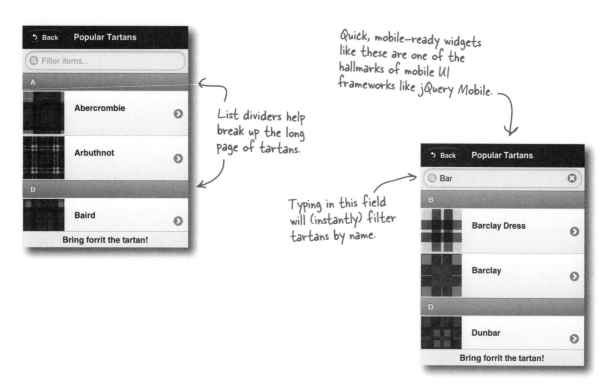

Quick, mobile-ready widgets like these are one of the hallmarks of mobile UI frameworks like jQuery Mobile.

List dividers help break up the long page of tartans.

Typing in this field will (instantly) filter tartans by name.

there are no Dumb Questions

Q: I notice that when you change pages in a jQuery Mobile web app, there is an animation effect. What is that?

A: To make web apps feel more consistent with mobile user interface patterns, jQuery Mobile applies a transition to page changes.

By default, the slide transition will be used, which makes it appear that the new page is sliding in from the right. To change the transition that is used, you can add a `data-transition` attribute to the link in question. Half a dozen or so transitions are supported. See jQuery Mobile documentation (on its website) for details.

Q: Will this stuff work on every phone?

A: No mobile framework can claim that distinction. But jQuery Mobile strives to have as much cross-platform support as possible. You can see a list of the supported devices and browsers and how well they are presently supported at *http://jquerymobile.com/gbs*.

Q: What happens if a device or browser isn't supported? Or if JavaScript is turned off?

A: jQuery Mobile's philosophy is heavily biased toward progressive enhancement. And so is our underlying markup!

Why don't you try it out yourself? Load up the Tartanator in a web browser with disabled JavaScript. Sure, it isn't exactly pretty, but it works.

It's time to show the early Tartanator work to Ewan

How are we doing on the project steps?

☑ **Build content pages and site structure.**

☑ **Create the tartan listings.**

☐ **Build a prototype of the tartan-building form.**

Before we start into the form, let's check with the client to make sure our overall approach so far is OK.

Hmmm...it's...nice, but can you make it feel more...like a native app?

Jim: What does "make it look like a native app" even mean?

Frank: It seems like that's a very subjective thing, doesn't it? I think what Ewan is looking for is something that feels a bit more "app"-y.

Jim: Which means…?

Frank: I guess like tab bars, navigation elements, button-y and icon-y bits. Ewan seemed happy with the transitions, for example. Those, to him, feel native.

Jim: But don't we run the risk of emulating one platform too much at the expense of others?

Frank: Heh, yes. When people say "native," sometimes they are dangerously close to meaning "make it look like iOS, please." Each platform has its own UI metaphors.

Jim: This sounds like a catch-22. To make our customer happy, we need to look native, which might well mean alienating, say, our Android and BlackBerry users.

Frank: I think we need to pick and choose some things we could enhance to make the Tartanator feel more like an app without making it look like an *iPhone* app. To be fair, jQuery Mobile elements in their default skins look kind of iOS style. So we're already partway down this path.

Jim: So the aim is to make the Tartanator feel more like an app without necessarily feeling platform-specific native?

Frank: Exactly. I'll sketch down a few thoughts on some changes we can make to shoot for that goal.

The new goal: make the Tartanator look more applike without necessarily looking platform-specific.

Tricks to make it feel more like an app

Here are some quick things I think we could do to make the Tartanator feel more like an app.

A header that sticks around

Tabs/buttons instead of links

More like an app!

- Replace current <ul> of links with a persistent toolbar/navbar/whatever at the bottom of the screen.

- Buttons with icons for the toolbar will feel more like an app.

- Make the header stick around, too.

What about the About Us page?

- Recent email from Ewan: content isn't panning out as well as he'd hoped.

- Maybe conflate the landing page and the About Us page into one? Use the landing page as the info page?

Make Tartanator feel more applike: to-dos

☐ Convert links on landing page into persistent toolbar with icons.

☐ Do away with the separate About Us page, as content is not forthcoming. Consider the current landing page the *de facto* About page for now.

☐ Make the header bar persistent, too.

Add a footer toolbar

In jQuery Mobile, it's easy to add a fixed-position toolbar to either the header or the footer. To create a more applike feel, let's put a toolbar in the footer instead of having the links to the Tartanator's sections inside a `<ul>` on the landing page.

Construct a navbar

Inside of a header or footer container—so designated by the `data-role` attribute—we can put another `<div>` with a `data-role` of `navbar`. This tells jQuery Mobile to treat the contents as buttons in a toolbar. The basic construction looks like this:

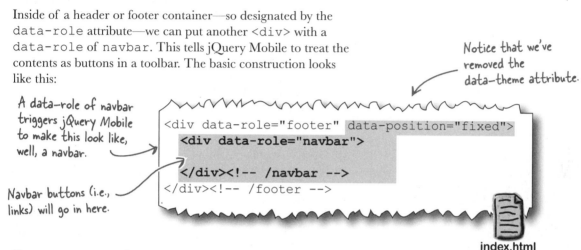

Notice that we've removed the data-theme attribute.

A data-role of navbar triggers jQuery Mobile to make this look like, well, a navbar.

Navbar buttons (i.e., links) will go in here.

```
<div data-role="footer" data-position="fixed">
    <div data-role="navbar">

    </div><!-- /navbar -->
</div><!-- /footer -->
```

index.html

Put buttons in the navbar

Instead of links in a vertically organized list, we're going to make toolbar buttons to access the main sections of the Tartanator. This is a more applike metaphor.

jQuery Mobile will automatically convert linked list elements within a navbar into buttons.

Remember, we're jettisoning the aboutus.html page in favor of using the index.html page as an About page.

jQuery Mobile will automatically make these links look like buttons.

```
<div data-role="footer" data-position="fixed">
    <div data-role="navbar">
        <ul>
        <li><a href="index.html">About</a></li>
        <li><a href="findevent.html">Events</a></li>
        <li><a href="tartans.html">Tartans</a></li>
        </ul>
    </div><!-- /navbar -->
</div><!-- /footer -->
```

index.html

Make the toolbar snazzy

So far, so good, but our toolbar buttons are a bit drab. jQuery Mobile comes with a set of 18 or so default icons that we can use, easily. Let's drop some icons in by using the `data-icon` attribute.

Take 1: Detail of button rendering ↘

They look like buttons, all right, but they could be a bit more fancy.

A list of available default icons can be found in the jQuery Mobile documentation. ↑

```
<div data-role="footer" data-position="fixed">
  <div data-role="navbar">
    <ul>
    <li><a href="index.html" data-icon="info">About</a></li>
    <li><a href="findevent.html" data-icon="star">Events</a></li>
    <li><a href="tartans.html" data-icon="grid">Tartans</a></li>
    </ul>
  </div><!-- /navbar -->
</div><!-- /footer -->
```

The data-icon attribute indicates which icon to use in this button.

index.html

Also, let's denote which section the user is currently viewing by setting a class of `ui-btn-active` on the appropriate link. This will show up with theming that makes it highlighted, thus appearing active.

This code goes in index.html. For the other pages, you'd want to assign this class to the appropriate anchor tag.

```
<ul>
<li><a href="index.html" data-icon="info" class="ui-btn-active">About</a></li>
<li><a href="findevent.html" data-icon="star">Events</a></li>
<li><a href="tartans.html" data-icon="grid">Tartans</a></li>
</ul>
```

index.html

Finalize the structure

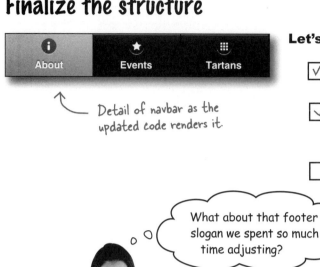

← Detail of navbar as the updated code renders it.

Let's check in on our to-dos:

☑ Convert links on landing page into persistent toolbar with icons.

☑ Do away with the separate About Us page, as content is not forthcoming. Consider the current landing page the *de facto* About page for now.

☐ Make the header bar persistent, too.

↖ We just need to tweak the header a bit now...

What about that footer slogan we spent so much time adjusting?

Ah, yes. Life on the Web! Requirements are always changing.

We've replaced the footer with a navbar, but we don't have to discard the tagline entirely. Let's make it a kind of subheader on the landing page (only).

Make the header sticky, too

While we're in there, let's make the position on the header fixed, too. That will make the header behave in the same way as the footer: always present at the top of the screen, even if the user scrolls.

```
<div data-role="header" data-position="fixed">
  <h1>The Tartanator</h1>
</div><!-- /header -->
<div data-role="header" data-theme="b" class="forrit">Bring forrit
the tartan!</div>
```

index.html

TEST DRIVE

Ah, iterative design. The way of the Web. Let's update the Tartanator.

(1) Implement the new footer navbars.
Edit *index.html, findevent.html*, and *tartans.html*. Replace the footer with the version we cooked up on page 250.

Make sure to assign the `ui-btn-active` class to the correct anchor tag, depending on the page.

(2) Give the header a fixed position.
Add a `data-position` attribute to the header on each page.

(3) Add the tag line to the landing page (index.html).
For *index.html* (only), add the tagline as a subhead.

Both the header and footer are now fixed. They will always show up at the top and the bottom of the page (respectively), even if the user scrolls.

Time to make that tartan-building form

The next step in the project is to create a prototype of a form that will let
users design their own tartans, right from their mobile browsers.

☑ **Build content pages and site structure.**

☑ **Create the tartan listings.**

☐ **Build a prototype of the tartan-building form.**

Ewan would like users to be able to construct their
own tartans by using an applike mobile interface.

Create a tartan design?
What does that even *mean*?

A tartan design is like a recipe.

But instead of a list of food ingredients
and their measurements—ounces, grams,
teaspoons, whatever—it's a list of colors
and their relative sizes in the pattern.
When a tartan is woven, this pattern is
repeated both horizontally and vertically.

**We need to have a rough idea of how
tartans are put together so that we
can build a form to gather the right
kinds of info.**

Tartans: patterns like recipes

Let's look at an example. To create the Carmichael clan tartan, the pattern looks something like:

Each ingredient in the pattern is a pairing of a color and a size.

Color	Size (Stitches)
Black	6
Green	72
Blue	56
Red	4
Blue	4
Yellow	6

The Carmichael clan tartan.

Follow the tartan recipe

To weave the tartan, the pattern is followed in order (in our case, we'll be "weaving" with pixels instead of wool).

For Carmichael, 6 stitches of black are followed by 72 stitches of green, followed by 56 blue, and so on.

When the last color in the pattern is reached (six stitches of yellow, in our example), the pattern is followed in reverse (blue, red, blue, green). When the first color (black) is reached again, the cycle repeats. The pattern is woven both horizontally and vertically (warp and weft) to create the overall tartan pattern.

The first and last colors (black and yellow) don't repeat. In tartan-ese, these are called "pivots" in the pattern.

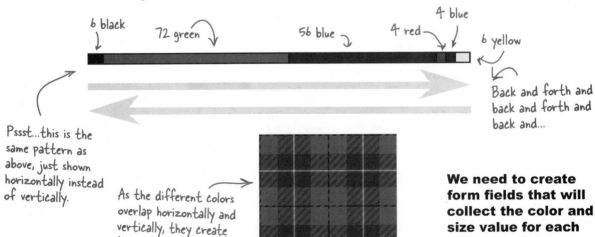

6 black
72 green
56 blue
4 red
4 blue
6 yellow

Back and forth and back and forth and back and...

Pssst...this is the same pattern as above, just shown horizontally instead of vertically.

As the different colors overlap horizontally and vertically, they create the distinctive pattern.

We need to create form fields that will collect the color and size value for each ingredient in a user's tartan design.

Translate tartan patterns to a form

Let's take a look at the form prototype we
want to build. We need fields that allow
users to enter in those color-size pairs
that build a tartan recipe.

*Basic info about the tartan
being created: its name and
an optional description.*

*Color-size field pairs
let users build the
ingredient list for
their tartan recipes...*

**OK, we have a general
idea of the form we
want to build. Let's go
build it!**

*...and so on with the
color-size combo fields.*
  (There are more.)

↺ Back	Tartan Builder

Tell us about your tartan

Tartan Name

> Tartan Name

Tartan Info

> Optional tartan description or info

Build your colors

Color

> Select a Color ⌄

Stitch Count

> 2 ───●────────────

Color

> Select a Color ⌄

Stitch Count

> 2 ───●────────────

Color

> Select a Color ⌄

Stitch Count

ⓘ About	★ Events	⊞ Tartans

Exercise

Create an empty jQuery mobile page to hold the
tartan-building form. Using *tartans.html* as a guide,
create a blank page. Use the same header and footer,
but change the title and header of the page to "Tartan
Builder." Name this file *build.php*.

Build an HTML5 form

The form itself will be a standard HTML5 form: jQuery Mobile will adapt it to make it look and feel more mobile-friendly. In Chapter 7, we'll make the form actually do something, including enhancing its interactivity with JavaScript and spitting out actual tartan images.

For now, we'll lay the groundwork and create a baseline, no-frills form that will work in nearly all mobile browsers.

Tartan recipe

- Tartan name
- Tartan description (optional)
- Series of color-size combinations

These are the things our form needs to collect.

Form structure

We'll want users to name their tartans and, optionally, enter a description. Then, they can define color-size combinations to build the pattern itself. Let's give our form two main sections: a top section for metadata about the tartan and a main section for defining colors and sizes.

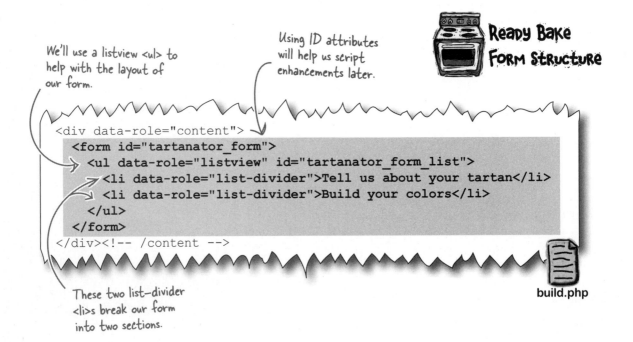

We'll use a listview `<ul>` to help with the layout of our form.

Using ID attributes will help us script enhancements later.

READY BAKE FORM STRUCTURE

```
<div data-role="content">
  <form id="tartanator_form">
    <ul data-role="listview" id="tartanator_form_list">
      <li data-role="list-divider">Tell us about your tartan</li>
      <li data-role="list-divider">Build your colors</li>
    </ul>
  </form>
</div><!-- /content -->
```

build.php

These two list-divider `<li>`s break our form into two sections.

It's time to add some basic fields

The metadata form fields—name and description—are pretty basic. We'll use a text `input` and a `textarea`, respectively. The only difference between the markup we'll use and what you might be accustomed to is that we'll take advantage of the HTML5 `placeholder` attribute. We'll also be careful to use proper, semantic, accessible `label` elements.

The placeholder attribute lets us add initial, placeholding text in a field—it "goes away" when a user clicks into the field and alters its contents.

Ready Bake Form Fields

```
<li data-role="list-divider">Tell us about your tartan</li>
  <li data-role="fieldcontain">
    <label for="tartan_name">Tartan Name</label>
    <input type="text" name="name" id="tartan_name"
placeholder="Tartan Name" />
  </li>
  <li data-role="fieldcontain">
    <label for="tartan_info">Tartan Info</label>
    <textarea cols="40" rows="8" name="tartan_info"
id="tartan_info" placeholder="Optional tartan description
or info"></textarea>
  </li>
  <li data-role="list-divider">Build your colors</li>
```

build.php

Give jQuery Mobile hints about the fields

You may notice above that each field is inside an element with a `data-role` of `fieldcontain`. This `data-role` gives jQuery Mobile a hint that form fields are within this element, ready to be enhanced.

We're using a <ul> to organize our form, so we put the fieldcontain class on each <li> that contains a field.

Lists within lists let the users add colors

Each piece of the tartan pattern is a combination of a color and a size (width). For layout, let's group each of these compound fields into a single `<li>`. For the baseline experience—that is, for browsers without JavaScript support—we'll generate six of these field groups with PHP (saves on typing!).

Here's a starting point:

> So, each color-size ingredient will be contained within a single `<li>`—two actual fields per `<li>`.

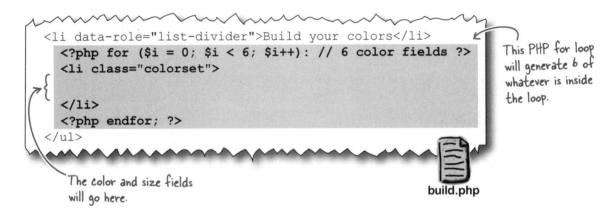

```
<li data-role="list-divider">Build your colors</li>
<?php for ($i = 0; $i < 6; $i++): // 6 color fields ?>
<li class="colorset">

</li>
<?php endfor; ?>
</ul>
```

> This PHP for loop will generate 6 of whatever is inside the loop.

> The color and size fields will go here.

build.php

there are no Dumb Questions

Q: Why are we not assigning the `data-role` of `fieldcontain` class to this `<li>`? It has fields in it.

A: Each of these `<li>`s (li.colorset) will actually contain **two** fields. When we build the fields themselves, we'll place each one of them within its own `<div>`, and we'll assign the `fieldcontain data-role` to that `<div>`.

Q: I'm confused. Which kind of element should I be assigning the `fieldcontain data-role` attribute to?

A: Whichever element contains the field itself—its immediate parent. That could be an `<li>` or a `<div>` or a `<fieldset>` or a `<p>` (or whatnot).

The `fieldcontain data-role` tells jQuery Mobile to group the contained field and its `label` when enhancing the form. So, each containing element with a `data-role` of `fieldcontain` should contain one field (and its `label`).

Q: Do I need PHP for this part of the project?

A: Yep! As we move into the more functional pieces of the Tartanator, we'll be using PHP to do the crunching and thinking.

Color-size ingredient pairs: The color select field

Each set of color fields will have a color (as a `<select>`) and a size input.
The classes of `color-input` and `size-input` are for later, when we
enhance the form with JavaScript.

> It'd be cool if we could use the HTML color input type, but, alas, it's not yet supported in many browsers.

Obviously, we want more than just black and white as color options!
More on that in a moment.

```
<li class="colorset">
  <div data-role="fieldcontain" class="color-input">
  <label class="select" for="color-<?php print $i ?>">
  Color</label>
    <select name="colors[]" id="color-<?php print $i ?>" >
      <option value="">Select a Color</option>
      <option value="#000000">Black</option>
      <option value="#ffffff">White</option>
    </select>
  </div>
</li>
```

> Recall that we're inside a PHP loop; this assigns each field a unique ID.

build.php

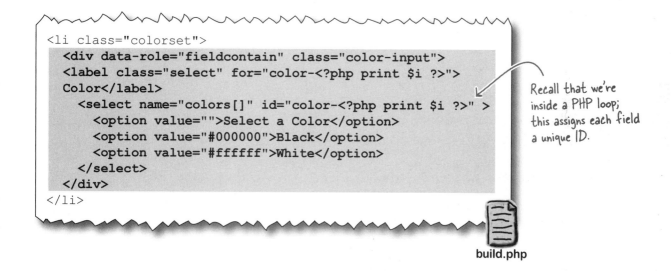

> The field above renders about like this on modern WebKit-based mobile browsers.

Color

Select a Color

Color-size field pairs: The size field

We're using an input type new to HTML5: range. This field type has increasingly good support among modern browsers (though certainly not universally). In supported browsers, it renders as a slider; in unsupported browsers, it degrades to a text field. jQuery Mobile further enhances the slider into something mobile-friendly.

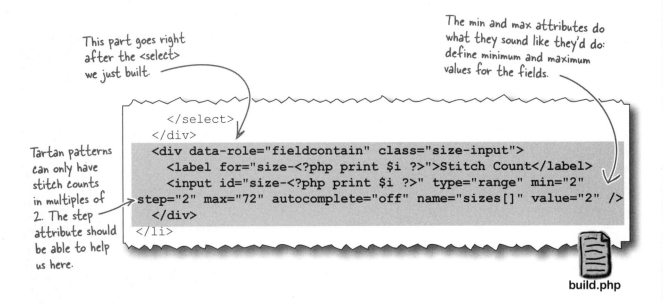

This part goes right after the `<select>` we just built.

The min and max attributes do what they sound like they'd do: define minimum and maximum values for the fields.

Tartan patterns can only have stitch counts in multiples of 2. The step attribute should be able to help us here.

```
      </select>
    </div>
    <div data-role="fieldcontain" class="size-input">
      <label for="size-<?php print $i ?>">Stitch Count</label>
      <input id="size-<?php print $i ?>" type="range" min="2"
step="2" max="72" autocomplete="off" name="sizes[]" value="2" />
    </div>
  </li>
```

build.php

Stitch Count

`2`

The field above renders about like this on modern WebKit-based mobile browsers.

Test Drive

Time to put it all together and build our mobile-looking (if not-yet-functional) form.

① **Put the form fields into build.php.**
Drop in the markup from pages 256 through 260 to create the basic form fields.

Looking (and feeling) more applike.

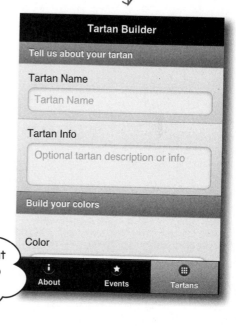

② **Add more color options to the colors field.**
You can use the colors (hex values) from the file in *extras/color-list.txt* and/or add any color you'd like to have available for tartan building.

Save *build.php* and load it up in a mobile browser!

Looks pretty good... but how would users get to the form page?

We need to link to the form and back again in an applike way. Let's do that now!

Link to the form

The build form is considered part of the Tartans section of the Tartanator.
We need to give users a way to get to the form from the Tartans landing
page (the long list of existing tartans). Adding a button in the header
should suffice:

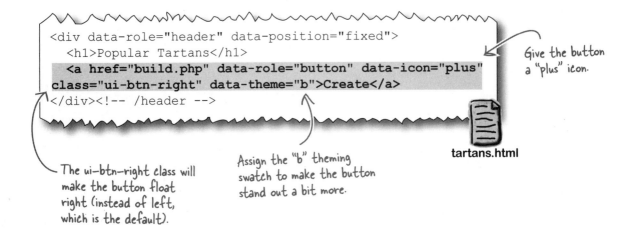

```
<div data-role="header" data-position="fixed">
  <h1>Popular Tartans</h1>
    <a href="build.php" data-role="button" data-icon="plus"
class="ui-btn-right" data-theme="b">Create</a>
</div><!-- /header -->
```

Give the button a "plus" icon.

tartans.html

The ui-btn-right class will make the button float right (instead of left, which is the default).

Assign the "b" theming swatch to make the button stand out a bit more.

...and give users a way back

On the form page (*build.php*), let's add a back button:

```
<div data-role="header" data-position="fixed">
    <a href="tartans.html" data-rel="back" data-icon="back"
data-role="button">Back</a>
  <h1>Tartan Builder</h1>
</div><!-- /header -->
```

build.php

By adding `data-rel="back"` to the anchor tag, we tell jQuery Mobile
to treat this link as a back link. When possible, jQuery Mobile will send
the user to the last location in her history when she clicks this link. For
nonsupporting browsers, we supply a good default `href`, which is, in this
case, *tartans.html*.

TEST DRIVE

① **Link to the form from tartans.html.**
Add the Create button to the header in *tartans.html*.

② **Put a back button on the form page (build.php).**
Add a back link to the header of the Tartan Builder page.

☑ **Build content pages and site structure.**

We need to create basic pages for the site and create an overall structure that looks and feels right on mobile devices.

☑ **Create the tartan listings.**

For the first phase, we'll create a listing of existing popular tartan patterns. The tartans section should be a browsing interface that—of course—looks and feels applike and mobile oriented.

☑ **Build a prototype of the tartan-building form.**

Ultimately, Ewan would like users to be able to construct their own tartans by using an applike mobile interface. He wants to see what that might look like, so we'll whip him up a prototype.

Yay! We're done with phase 1 of the Tartanator. Time for customer review.

Hey, guys. That's looking pretty good. I'm excited about moving on to the next phase of the Tartanator—that's where the fun stuff really happens.

jQuery Mobile Help

We've barely scratched the surface of all of the things you can do with jQuery Mobile in this chapter.

To learn more or find more information about the stuff we've covered, refer to the documentation on www.jquerymobile.com. It's very detailed.

BULLET POINTS

- People want apps! The definition of what, exactly, makes a website a **web app** is fuzzy. Applike websites tend to feel more interactive than content pages. Chunks of content and data are often retrieved asynchronously and inserted into an existing DOM, reducing the frequency of full-page loads.

- HTML5 is a specific, single thing—it's a **spec** representing the evolution of HyperText Markup Language (HTML)—but the term *HTML5* is often used to represent a combination of technologies that create applike web experiences.

- Building mobile web apps from scratch can be very complex. We encourage you to try it! But for our purposes, we used a mobile user interface development **framework** to help us out.

- There are lots of mobile web frameworks out there (more every day!), representing many different approaches and emphases.

- **jQuery Mobile** is a popular mobile web framework. It has a strong relationship with well-formed HTML5 markup, which makes it relatively straightforward to build mobile interfaces from basic code.

- We built the structure for phase 1 of the Tartanator by, among other things, using jQuery Mobile–enhanced listviews, headers, footers, navbars, and form elements.

- Making a web app feel more native is always a balancing act, requiring some careful decisions.

- We used some **HTML5 form element** attributes to build our prototype form. jQuery Mobile helps to adapt these form elements across mobile browsers, including adaptation for those that don't support them yet.

Q: How much of the code in the Tartanator so far is really HTML5? That is, how much of it uses tags or attributes that are new as part of the HTML5 spec?

A: We're using the `data-*` attribute quite a bit. That's new. We are also using the `range` input type and the `placeholder` attribute in our form.

Q: I put the `step` attribute into my `range` input for the size fields of the form, but I can still enter any value between 2 and 72...even and odd numbers both. What gives?

A: Unfortunately, at the time of this writing, jQuery Mobile's `range` slider widget doesn't support the `step` attribute. We'll show you a workaround in Chapter 7.

Q: Colors as a select list—that doesn't seem like the most fantastic user experience.

A: When we enhance the form in Chapter 7, we'll add some JavaScript code that will show the user the color she has selected.

Q: What happens to mobile browsers that don't support `range` inputs yet?

A: As long as the browser supports JavaScript and CSS fairly well, jQuery Mobile will convert the `range` field into a slider widget (actually, it does this for browsers that support `range` inputs also).

If a browser doesn't support `range` inputs and doesn't have JavaScript support (or it's disabled), the range field will most likely appear as a standard text input field.

Q: The header and footer blink sometimes, or are slower to load than the other parts of the page. Sometimes scrolling feels a bit slow. Why is that?

A: One of the ways jQuery Mobile attempts to emulate a native-ish experience is by using fixed-position headers and footers (when you designate them as such, that is). The way this is actually carried out differs on different platforms.

In a nutshell: although the landscape is improving very fast, fixed positioning (in CSS, `position:fixed`) has unpleasantly scattered and weird support in mobile browsers. There are workarounds, but they aren't perfect. The slightly-less-than-totally-snappy performance and occasional peculiarity are often manifestations of the trade-off the framework is making between being applike and adhering carefully to web standards.

Congratulations, you've just built a mobile web app with HTML5 and its friends.

See? It's really not too many steps from the HTML and CSS you already know to a mobile-feeling, applike website!

Super mobile web apps

Pull my pigtails again, and you'll pay! There's nowhere to hide. I can find you *anywhere*...

The mobile web feels like that gifted kid in the class.

You know, kind of fascinating, capable of amazing things, but also a mysterious, unpredictable troublemaker. We've tried to keep its hyperactive genius in check by being mindful of constraints and establishing boundaries, but now it's time to capitalize on some of the mobile web's natural talents. We can use **progressive enhancement** to spruce up the interface in more precocious browsers and transform erratic connectivity from a burden to a feature by crafting a thoughtful **offline mode**. And we can get at the essence of mobility by using **geolocation**. Let's go make this a super mobile web app!

It looks nice...

Now that we're done with phase 1, the Tartanator has that mobile-web-app sheen.

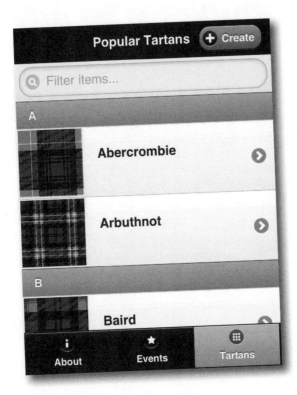

It talks the talk...

There are buttons. And navbars. And cool page transitions. We're loading content selectively with AJAX. We're reducing bandwidth, requests, and JavaScript DOM processing. And jQuery Mobile is helping to make our HTML5 form elements look and feel mobile friendly.

O

o

> Shiny, sure. Mobile-riffic, sure. But it doesn't **do** anything. Doesn't an app need to do something?

Take heart. It may seem like building phase 1 was full of sound and fury, signifying nothing. But we've laid some really good groundwork.

We've got a straightforward structure based on HTML5—now it's time to take it to the next level!

...but it needs to walk the walk

Phase 2 will build on the stuff we've put in place, turning our solid—but admittedly somewhat functionality-free—web app into what we think of as a super mobile app!

Mobile apps in the real world

Mobile web apps that take good advantage of innately mobile characteristics often have certain aspects in common.

What we like to call *super mobile web apps* feel like mobile apps for the real world. They adapt to their users' disparate devices with the robust use of **progressive enhancement**. When the user doesn't have a data connection, these apps can function in an **offline mode**. And they take advantage of browser-accessible **geolocation** to provide location-relevant content.

Super Mobile Web Apps knows all about the three features we'll explore in this chapter to make mobile web apps more "super" and take advantage of its inherent, awesome mobileness.

Geolocation

Progressive enhancement

Offline mode

Sharpen your pencil

What will we do to complete Phase 2 and make the Tartanator a super mobile web app?

Our first task is to get a grip on what it is we'll need to implement to complete the Tartanator as outlined by Ewan in Chapter 6. Highlight the requirements we haven't completed yet. Then we'll boil them down into a few core objectives for this phase.

About Us page

A history of Tartans Unlimited. Links to information about the history of tartans.

This content isn't ready yet. ← *Bug Pat about this.*

• New Website! ~~App?~~

Welcome message
　Keep this simple...link to About Us page for more info...

Tartan events
　I have some ideas here...not sure if they are possible!

• Tartans!

This is the main part of the idea...sounds like an app?

The Tartanator!

　Maybe call the whole app/site "The Tartanator"? Has a nice ring!

- Make it so users can see and explore the tartan patterns right on their phones.
　　Lots of images of tartans!

- Wouldn't it be cool if users could create their own tartans?

!¡★★ *Can this be done?*

- A collection of tartans: popular "traditional" ones as well as new-world and user-created tartans.

Events page

- It would be nice if the app could somehow "link into" our international events database.

- Could a user's phone help find the nearest events? ??

- Might want to wait until phase 2 or phase 3 of the site for events stuff—complex?

Sharpen your pencil
Solution

The major objectives for the second phase of the project really fall into two core goals:

1 **Plug in the pieces that let users generate their own tartans.**
We've got our prototyped form. Now we need to walk the walk and plug in the pieces to make this actually work. We also need to enhance the existing form to make it more usable for fancier smartphones and add a few bells and whistles.

2 **Build a dynamic, searchable, location-aware Events page.**
We'll need to hook into an existing events data source to let users find nearby tartan-related events. That means we'll have to delve into geolocation!

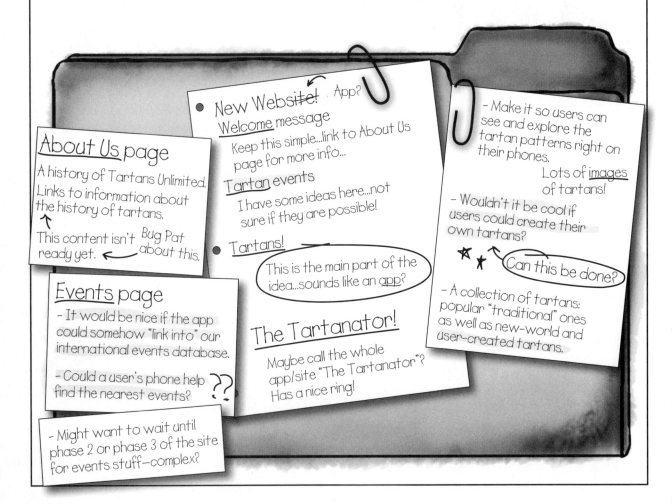

About Us page
A history of Tartans Unlimited.
Links to information about the history of tartans.

This content isn't ready yet. ← Bug Pat about this.

Events page
- It would be nice if the app could somehow "link into" our international events database.

- Could a user's phone help find the nearest events?

- Might want to wait until phase 2 or phase 3 of the site for events stuff—complex?

• New Website! App?
Welcome message
Keep this simple...link to About Us page for more info...

Tartan events
I have some ideas here...not sure if they are possible!

• Tartans!
This is the main part of the idea...sounds like an app?

The Tartanator!
Maybe call the whole app/site "The Tartanator"? Has a nice ring!

- Make it so users can see and explore the tartan patterns right on their phones.
Lots of images of tartans!

- Wouldn't it be cool if users could create their own tartans?

Can this be done?

- A collection of tartans: popular "traditional" ones as well as new-world and user-created tartans.

Frank: That first big requirement is a doozy, isn't it? I think it'll help to break it down into smaller chunks.

Jim: Before we do that—what happened to the outstanding item for the About Us page and historical background?

Frank: Oh, right! The wife of the guy who writes bios and informational copy for Tartans Unlimited just had a baby. The new father has found himself far busier than he expected and isn't going to be able to help out with the project for a while. Big surprise, huh? So we're not on the hook for that one right now.

Jim: Well, that's one less thing, I guess. Let's talk about getting the pieces in place to allow users to create their own tartan patterns. Not to brag, but I've already got a head start on this one. I've been tinkering with a bit of JavaScript to enhance the form.

Joe: Cool. That'll look nice and pretty. But we also need to drop in server-side scripts to do the actual work—

Jim: You server-side guys! Trust me, enhancing the form interface is a really significant improvement.

Joe: Anyway, I've been working on the PHP scripts. What about the events stuff?

Jim: Actually, is it OK if we focus on getting the tartan generation nailed and circle back on the events searching when we're feeling ready to think about it? I only have room in my brain for so much at one time.

Frank: I guess that's fine as long as we get cracking on the custom user tartans stuff right quick. We're on a pretty tight timeline.

To-dos: custom user tartan pattern implementation

Here's our master to-do list for the custom tartans requirement.

We'll start here!

☐ Enhance the form we built to take advantage of capabilities of newer mobile browsers.

☐ Drop in server-side code for processing the form and generating resources (images, HTML, etc.) for user-created tartans.

☐ Make sure the offline experience for this part of the app is acceptable.

Ready, set, enhance!

Strap yourself in. We're about to make a lot of nifty enhancements to the Tartanator's create form—in very short order.

We did the right thing

We designed our form for the baseline experience: we're not leaving anyone out in the cold (well, very few people, anyway). Take a look at what happens if you load up the Tartanator build form with no JavaScript at all.

The form is functional without any JavaScript at all—that's a good thing!

Now let's enhance

It's functional for everyone, but also kind of ugly and unwieldy for everyone. While having six color-size combo fields is OK for a less full-featured browser, it's an encumbrance for more sophisticated ones.

But it's a bit clunky on a newer smartphone browser.

Now that we have our baseline ducks in a row, let's drop in some enhancements that will make the form more of a pleasure to use with smartphones.

First step to a super mobile web app: enhance the UI for the browsers that support it well.

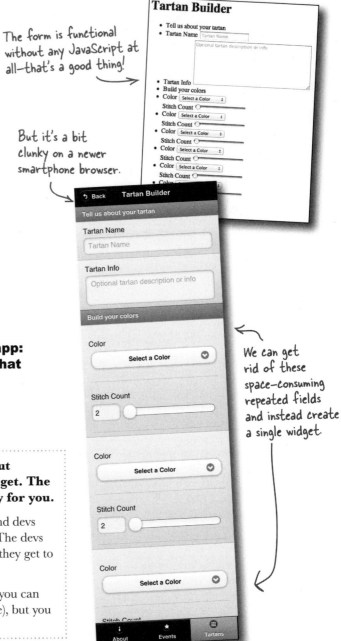

We can get rid of these space-consuming repeated fields and instead create a single widget.

No need to panic about writing your own widget. The JavaScript is all ready for you.

Some crackerjack frontend devs cranked out this enhancement JavaScript. The devs always get so excited and productive when they get to work on mobile web app projects!

We'll walk you through the highlights (and you can always spend some time looking at the code), but you don't have to write it yourself or anything!

Make a better form

Instead of having six fields—both cluttered and limiting—let's use a single widget. This will allow our users to add as many color-size combos as they like! We can do this by using JavaScript to **remove all of the color-size fields except for the first set**.

A custom widget for the color select field

We can override the default select interface in the browser and use one of jQuery Mobile's custom select UI widgets. That way, we can show color swatches for each option.

The custom jQuery Mobile widget we're going to use pops up like a dialog to display the color options.

Only one color-size set, not six

Clicking on "Select a Color" pops up this customized field widget.

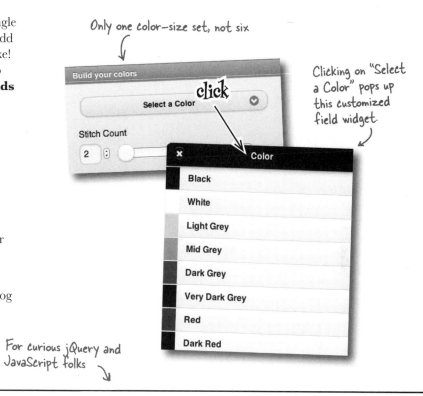

click

For curious jQuery and JavaScript folks

Geek Bits

If you're familiar with jQuery code, the construct `$(document).ready` might be something you see (or use!) a lot. The jQuery `.ready` method is kind of like (though not identical to) the browser's `body.onload` event—when it fires, it indicates that the DOM is loaded and ready. jQuery developers typically wrap their code in this so that it doesn't execute before the page's DOM is ready.

In jQuery Mobile (jQM), you *don't* (usually) want to use `$(document).ready`. Instead, jQM introduces some new page-load-related events, the most important of which are `pageinit` and `pagecreate`. `pagecreate` is fired after jQuery and jQM have completed initializing the DOM of the page, but before widgets are rendered. `pageinit` is fired after widgets are finished, too. And remember that subsequent pages are often inserted into the first page's existing DOM—that means that `pagecreate` and `pageinit` events can fire multiple times in a single full-page load.

Confused a bit? So were we. It takes a few minutes for even seasoned JavaScript and jQuery folks to fully grasp the concept. Read more in the JQM docs (*http://jquerymobile.com/demos*).

jQM also introduces mobile-relevant events for touch, orientation, and transition, among others.

A widget to manage the list of colors and sizes

We've now removed all but one of the color-size field combos. Using that remaining pair of fields, we need to be able to generate an arbitrary number of color-size combos.

To do this, we add a new button: Add This Color. When clicked, the currently selected color and stitch count are added as a list element (`<li>`) to an unordered list (`<ul>`) of current color-size values. We also add hidden form fields to the `<li>` to contain the color and size.

> JavaScript does all of this.

Clicking on an `<li>` in the existing color list will remove it and its contents from the list. Finally, clicking the "Make it!" submit button will generate a tartan pattern with all of the color-sizes currently in the list.

The remaining color-size field pair

When a user clicks the Add This Color button, the color-size combo is added to the list.

Color-size list

ul#colorlist

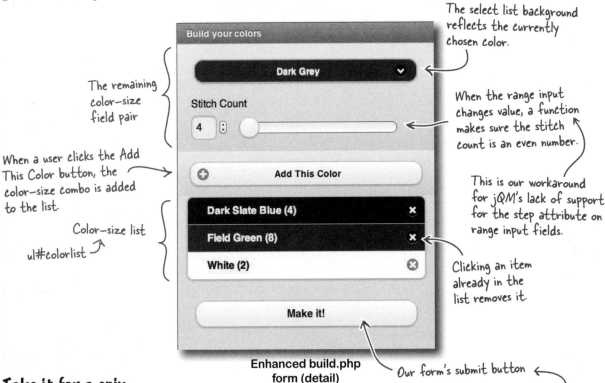

The select list background reflects the currently chosen color.

When the range input changes value, a function makes sure the stitch count is an even number.

This is our workaround for jQM's lack of support for the step attribute on range input fields.

Clicking an item already in the list removes it.

Enhanced build.php form (detail)

Our form's submit button

The button becomes visible once at least one color-size combo has been added to the list.

Take it for a spin

Hey, good news. You don't have to do anything to get the frontend enhancements to work. It's already done for you.

Remember, the form is on the build.php page.

The starting point of the code in the *chapter7* folder already includes the JavaScript enhancements. Go try it out! See how it feels in a mobile browser.

Also, we haven't "hooked up" the backend yet; clicking this won't do anything yet!

A peek under the hood

We promised that you wouldn't have to write the JavaScript, but it might behoove you to get a loose handle on what it's doing.

In a nutshell, there are a bunch of things that happen when the page with the form on it has been fully loaded into the DOM (`pagecreate` event) and also some stuff that happens after the jQuery Mobile widgets are finished enhancing things (`pageinit` event).

In these initialization functions, other functions are attached to various events (form field changes, clicks, form submit, etc.) to enhance user interaction and make our custom widgets functional.

Do this!

Get cozy with the code. Take a few minutes to go hang out with and get to know the updated pieces of the Tartanator app, especially the updated *tartanator.js* script.

WHO DOES WHAT?

Match each function in the JavaScript enhancement code (*tartanator.js*) to what it does, and also to the event(s) that trigger it. Reference the comments in the script and use your noodle to determine what each of these functions does for us.

For an extra challenge!

Function name	What it does	Event that triggers it
onStitchSizeChange()	Refreshes the `<ul>` and `<li>` elements of the current color list.	`pageinit` and `change` (color select field)
styleColorListItem()	Constructs the button to add a color-size combo and inserts it into the DOM.	`click` (on Add This Color button)
buildAddButton()	Sets the background color of the select widget to the currently selected color.	`pageinit`
onColorListChange()	Constructs hidden form fields, puts them in a new `<li>`, and appends the `<li>` to the existing color list.	`click` (on list element in current color list) **and** after new color added to list
addColor()	Adds a colored CSS border (swatch) to the left side of each color select option.	`change` (size input value updated)
setColorSelectStyle()	Makes sure the size value is an even integer.	`pagecreate`

So, that's the frontend enhancement...

☑ Enhance the form we built to take advantage of capabilities of newer   *Done!*
mobile browsers.

☐ Drop in server-side code for processing the form and generating   *Next up!*
resources (images, HTML, etc.) for user-created tartans.

☐ Make sure the offline experience for this part of the app is acceptable.

WHO DOES WHAT?

SOLUTION

Function name	What it does	Event that triggers it
onStitchSizeChange()	Refreshes the `<ul>` and `<li>` elements of the current color list.	`pageinit` and `change` (color select field)
styleColorListItem()	Constructs the button to add a color-size combo and inserts it into the DOM.	`click` (on Add This Color button)
buildAddButton()	Sets the background color of the select widget to the currently selected color.	`pageinit`
onColorListChange()	Constructs hidden form fields, puts them in a new `<li>`, and appends the `<li>` to the existing color list.	`click` (on list element in current color list) **and** after new color added to list
addColor()	Adds a colored CSS border (swatch) to the left side of each color select option.	`change` (size input value updated)
setColorSelectStyle()	Makes sure the size value is an even integer.	`pagecreate`

Interface Enhancement Exposed

This week's interview:
Enhancement: is it all just fluff?

Head First: OK, I gotta ask. We just did a whirlwind tour of a bunch of jQuery Mobile–specific JavaScript interface enhancements. Was it really worth it?

Interface Enhancement: What jQuery Mobile makes possible, quickly, with respect to enhancing the mobile interface is compelling, sure, but I get your drift. Really, I'm trying to illustrate a broader concept here.

Head First: Which is?

Enhancement: Regardless of whether you are using a framework, designing for a baseline and then enhancing is a good philosophy.

Head First: With JavaScript?

Enhancement: Let your mind go a bit here…this is broader than JavaScript, too. We're talking about starting basic, defining the core experience or content, and then making it better—that is, really taking advantage of what more powerful mobile browsers can do.

Head First: By adding bells and whistles.

Enhancement: I like to think that my contributions are bigger than rounded corners and gradients. We've taken a somewhat limited and awkward form and made it better for applicable users.

Head First: You've overridden the rendering of a native form element. The color select field is now using a custom jQuery Mobile widget. Isn't that kind of taboo?

Enhancement: It's true that messing with native form controls is a bit controversial. I don't argue for it as a general rule. However, in our particular case, the styling necessary to give visual clues to the user—color swatches—wasn't possible with traditional select fields.

The underlying markup is still semantically appropriate—a `<select>` element—but we're tweaking it to make it a more usable experience. But yes, you are correct in that we should consider native form control overrides carefully.

The build-a-tartan form in an Android browser

...and now for the backend

The starting point for Chapter 7 code has the structure shown here. Getting the backend pieces plugged in requires a couple of quick steps.

Copy all of the contents of the *extras/scripts* directory into your *chapter7* directory. When you're done, the *chapter7* directory should have three new files—*config.php*, *generate.php*, and *image.php*—as well as an *inc* directory (with two files inside).

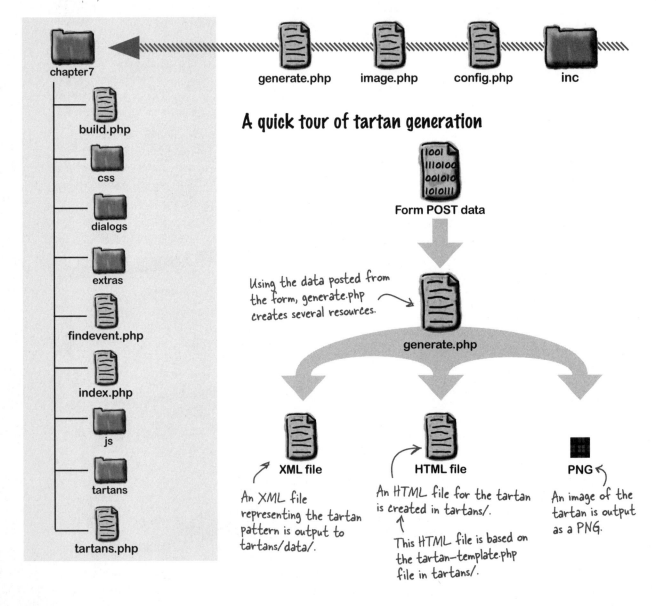

chapter7

build.php

css

dialogs

extras

findevent.php

index.php

js

tartans

tartans.php

generate.php   image.php   config.php   inc

A quick tour of tartan generation

Form POST data

Using the data posted from the form, generate.php creates several resources.

generate.php

XML file

HTML file

PNG

An XML file representing the tartan pattern is output to tartans/data/.

An HTML file for the tartan is created in tartans/.

This HTML file is based on the tartan-template.php file in tartans/.

An image of the tartan is output as a PNG.

The two sides of generate.php

The way that *generate.php* ultimately responds after creating the tartan resources depends on how it was requested.

Requested with AJAX

For browsers that support AJAX appropriately, the JavaScript in *build.php* posts the form data to *generate.php* using XHR (`XMLHttpRequest`). If successful, *generate.php* responds with the URL of the newly created HTML file for the tartan. The content of this new page is then inserted into the current page's DOM.

> We've made sure to support mobile browsers with and without AJAX support.

Asynchronous request with XHR

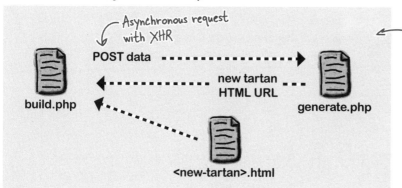

In this method, there's never a full-page reload. The content of the new tartan page is inserted into the DOM of the build page.

Form posted directly

For browsers that don't support JavaScript and XHR, the form is directly posted in a "traditional" way to *generate.php*. After *generate.php* creates the tartan resources, the browser is redirected to the newly minted tartan page.

In both methods, the primary job of generate.php is the same: create the new tartan resources.

"Traditional" method—redirect to the new tartan page

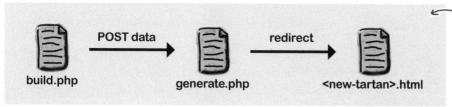

In this method, the client is redirected to the new tartan page (a full-page load).

One last thing!

Now that users can add tartans, the tartan list as shown on *tartans.php* is ever-changing. Drop this line into the *tartans.php* file to include a script that will output `<li>`s for each currently existing tartan.

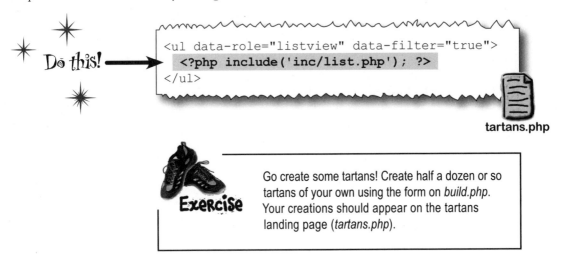

Do this! ➔

```
<ul data-role="listview" data-filter="true">
  <?php include('inc/list.php'); ?>
</ul>
```

tartans.php

Exercise

Go create some tartans! Create half a dozen or so tartans of your own using the form on *build.php*. Your creations should appear on the tartans landing page (*tartans.php*).

there are no Dumb Questions

Q: Help! Something's not working right!

A: If you are having trouble getting your tartan build form to work, or aren't seeing any created tartans, here's a few things to check.

First, make sure that the *tartans/* directory exists and that it and all of its subdirectories can be written to by your web server's user. Also verify that the *tartan-template.php* file is in the *tartans* directory. Finally, double- and triple-check the `<form>` tag in *build.php* for the correct action and method.

Q: How does the tartan list page work?

A: The *list.php* file included in the page looks at the current HTML files in the *tartans/* directory to generate its list. For each, it grabs its associated XML file (in *tartans/data/*) to get further information, like the pretty display name. It then outputs an `<li>` for each tartan, with a link to the tartan's HTML page.

Q: About that XML. What the heck is that?

A: We chose to store the data representation of tartan patterns as XML for a couple of reasons. One, it's a nice, simple, portable data format. Two, it obviates the need to use a database (less work for you!).

Q: By the way, what is this whole super mobile web app thing you're talking about? Some kind of standard or initiative or something?

A: Nah. It's just something we started calling mobile web apps that seem like they take good advantage of the neat things mobile devices and their browsers have to offer.

Two out of three is a great start

We've taken some good steps toward a super mobile web app. We've enhanced the baseline interface to take advantage of savvier browsers. And now the app does something!

☑ Enhance the form we built to take advantage of capabilities of newer mobile browsers.

☑ Drop in server-side code for processing the form and generating resources (images, HTML, etc.) for user-created tartans.

☐ Make sure the offline experience for this part of the app is acceptable.

We need to deal with this requirement.

But we're not done yet

Now we have to deliver on the third piece of the tartan-creation implementation: the tartans need to be available offline.

Frustrating. I want to show a friend the tartan I designed a few minutes ago...but I have dreadful phone service in this building. I can't get a connection...and now my tartan won't show up.

A stable—or even existent— network connection is something we just can't take for granted with mobile devices.

We've got to do something to make tartans available without an Internet connection.

Offline is important

Part of giving a good experience to your users is making your websites and apps behave when there isn't an Internet connection to be had.

For the Tartanator, we need to step back and figure out how we can make things work better for our disconnected users. We need to make certain things available offline.

> How do we control what's available offline? Is that even possible?

We can use something called a *cache manifest* to define which pieces of our app should be available offline.

Make it manifest

Application cache is part of the HTML5 specification. It allows for control over which web resources are cached for offline availability through the use of a *cache manifest*.

A cache manifest is a specific type of file on a web server that gives instructions about how or whether certain web resources should be cached on a user's device. By creating a cache manifest, we can dictate which things are available offline for the Tartanator web app.

Browsers that implement application cache—or *appCache*, as it is almost universally shortened to—also provide the `window.applicationCache` object and its various events, which we can access and manipulate with JavaScript if we like.

Support for appCache is fairly widespread in current browsers, with the notable exceptions of Internet Explorer 9 and Opera Mini. Using a cache manifest won't cause problems for these browsers; they just won't pay attention to it.

BRAIN POWER

Can you think of why it would be difficult for Opera Mini to support application cache?

A basic recipe to create a cache manifest

There are three general steps to creating and using a cache manifest on a website or app.

1 Write a cache manifest file.

2 Add a `manifest` attribute to the `<html>` tag of the applicable pages with a URL (relative is fine) to the manifest file.

The file must have a content-type of text/cache-manifest, or it won't work.

3 Make sure the manifest is served as the correct type of file.

The deceptively simple syntax of a cache manifest

A simple cache manifest file is quite basic in appearance. You list the items you want cached under the (technically not required, but definitely good practice) `CACHE:` heading.

This line, verbatim, is required.

1

```
CACHE MANIFEST
# comments look like this
CACHE:

index.html
foo/bar.html
baz.html
css/styles.css
icons/plus.png
```

URLs can be relative (like here) or absolute (e.g., http://...).

This file doesn't have to be named manifest, but the preferred extension is .appcache.

manifest.appcache

Next, you update your web page(s) by adding a `manifest` attribute pointing to that file. You also need to make sure the file is served as the correct `Content-type` (aka `MIME-type`). You can often do this simply with Apache by adding the following to the Apache configuration file or, more likely, an *.htaccess* file on your website's filesystem.

2
```
<!DOCTYPE html>
<html manifest="manifest.appcache">
<head>
```

3
```
AddType text/cache-manifest .appcache
```

This line tells the web server to serve files ending in .appcache as the text/cache-manifest content type.

The file has to be of this type, or browsers won't recognize it.

.htaccess

Unfortunately, the devil is in the details

In theory, cache management using a cache manifest file is straightforward. List the things you want available offline, add the `manifest` attribute to the `<html>` tag of a page or pages, and let the caching begin!

Don't start panicking quite yet, but creating a cache manifest and getting it to work the way we really want it to can be a bit confusing and sometimes frustrating. There are a fair number of details and gotchas that can trip you up. It helps to have good tools to help you inspect and debug what's going on.

Dev tools to the rescue

WebKit provides a tool called Web Inspector, which is available in both Chrome and Safari (being WebKit-based browsers). You can see great details about appCache information in the Resources tab.

Detail of the Resources tab's info about appCache in Chrome.

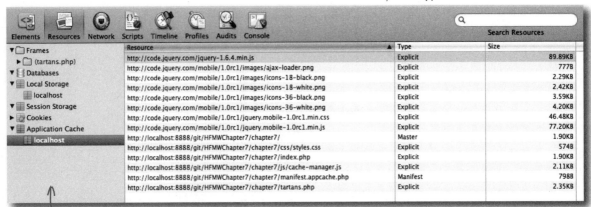

Safari's developer tools look almost exactly the same.

It can be a bit painful to try to excise poorly formed appCaches from mobile devices.

It can be easy to get yourself in a jam working with cache manifests.

Cache manifest behavior can be tough and confusing to debug, and malformed cache manifest files are difficult to find and remove without the right tools. We recommend using either Chrome or Safari for building and testing our Tartanator cache manifest. Also note that appCache isn't supported by Internet Explorer before version 10, which at the time of this writing is still in developer preview.

It will also help you save your sanity to develop and test on a desktop browser first before moving to a mobile device.

Serve the manifest as the correct content-type

> I've never messed around with .htaccess files, and I don't even know if I can do that with my current web hosting service.

It's highly likely that you can use *.htaccess* files on your hosting provider or local web server. But we won't make you.

We do know you can use PHP. So, we'll generate our cache manifest files using PHP and use a snippet of code to set the file's content-type to text/cache-manifest.

Exercise

Implement a basic cache manifest for the Tartanator.

1   Name your file *manifest.appcache.php* and put it in the *chapter7* directory.

The .php extension is needed so that we can execute the PHP code in the file.

2   Add the following line to the top of the file.

```php
<?php header('Content-type: text/cache-manifest'); ?>
```

This sets the content-type of the output of this script to text/cache-manifest.

3   Add a CACHE: section and list the main pages of the site, as well as the JavaScript and CSS files.

Refer to the syntax on page 285.

4   Update the `<html>` tag on *index.php*, *build.php*, *tartans.php*, and *findevent.php* with a `manifest` attribute.

Exercise Solution

The *manifest.appcache.php* file you created should look something like the one below. Note that we're also listing the CSS and JavaScript files from jQuery's content delivery network (CDN).

```php
<?php header('Content-type: text/cache-manifest'); ?>
CACHE MANIFEST

CACHE:
index.php
build.php
tartans.php
findevent.php
css/styles.css
js/tartanator.js
http://code.jquery.com/mobile/1.0rc1/jquery.mobile-1.0rc1.min.css
http://code.jquery.com/jquery-1.6.4.min.js
http://code.jquery.com/mobile/1.0rc1/jquery.mobile-1.0rc1.min.js
```

In addition to relative URLs to resources on your own site...

...you can use absolute URLs to denote resources on other domains that you want to cache.

manifest.appcache.php

The HTML tag on the Tartanator pages should now look like this.

```html
<html manifest="manifest.appcache.php">
```

A trade-off of using PHP to generate our manifest is that we can't use the preferred .appcache extension.

I think I'm doing something wrong. A lot of images and icons aren't showing up, even when I'm online.

Cache Manifest Exposed

This week's interview:
Bending appCache to our will

Frustrated Web Dev: Argh. As I navigate around the Tartanator site, a bunch of images and icons and stuff aren't showing up, even though I'm online.

appCache: Well, that's because you neglected to include some of these resources in the CACHE list. You should go round them up and add them to the cache manifest.

FWD: So, I need to list every resource on the site or they won't show up at all?

appCache: No. You need to add the resources that are needed by the HTML files in the cache.

FWD: I'm totally confused. What does it even mean for an HTML file to be in the cache?

appCache: You already know one way to include an HTML file in the application cache: listing it explicitly in the CACHE section of the manifest file. But it's also worth noting that any HTML file that has a `manifest` attribute on its HTML tag is included in the cache manifest, even if it's not explicitly listed there. Only those pages listed in the manifest or referencing it in a `manifest` attribute—that is, in the cache—need to have all of their resources added to the cache list.

FWD: OK, so for any page in the cache, if I neglect to add each and every resource to the CACHE section, any missed resource won't ever load, even if I'm online.

appCache: Well, that's not exactly true, either. I gather you've learned about the CACHE section, but haven't heard anything yet about the NETWORK section.

FWD: What's it for?

appCache: The NETWORK section lets you define resources that you don't want to cache, and for which the browser should request fresh copies when a connection is available. It has a special handy-dandy wildcard token, `*`, which means that anything not explicitly listed in the CACHE section should be retrieved from the server.

FWD: Eureka! That sounds like the answer I need here.

appCache: Take caution. If something is in the NETWORK section, either explicitly or by dint of the `*` wildcard, it will always be requested afresh. So you need to choose your path carefully.

Decide what things should really be available offline and list them in the CACHE section. It sounds like you do need to track down some icons and images, for example. But for things that really are dynamic—login screens, API calls, etc.—let the NETWORK wildcard do its work.

BRAIN BARBELL

Can you think of some parts of the Tartanator web app that we might not want to make available offline? Why?

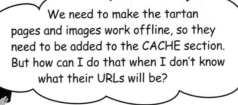

We need to make the tartan pages and images work offline, so they need to be added to the CACHE section. But how can I do that when I don't know what their URLs will be?

Feels like a chicken-and-egg problem, huh?

Fortunately, we're using PHP to generate our manifest file, so we can drop in some code to dynamically output a list of all of the tartan HTML files and images that currently exist.

Find the snippet of PHP code to dynamically generate the list of images and HTML files in the *chapter7/extras* folder. It's in a file called *current_file_list.txt*.

← Do this!

Watch it!

Changes to any of the resources listed in the manifest's CACHE section will not be downloaded by browsers unless the cache manifest file itself changes.

We have css/styles.css in our manifest's CACHE *section. Therefore, we could edit styles.css until the cows come home, but browsers won't see those changes. Once an item is in the cache, it will only be refreshed if the* **cache manifest file itself** *changes.*

A common method for managing this is to use a comment line in the manifest file with a version number. Simply changing this version number will cause browsers to see that the manifest has changed, download it afresh, and check whether any of the resources within it are new or modified.

← Remember that comment lines start with #.

The PHP code we'll use to autogenerate a list of current tartan images and HTML files has the happy side effect of causing the manifest file to be updated when new tartans are added. But, after implementing appCache, we'll need to increment the version number if and when we change other files.

It's easy to create cache manifests that are, shall we say, not quite what we intended.

Remedying a wayward appCache is easiest in the Chrome browser. Type **chrome://appcache-internals** in the URL bar, and you will see information about all current appCache data. Each site cache has a simple Remove link.

In Safari, go into Preferences and select the Privacy tab. You can either Remove All Website Data wholesale, or use the Details button to search for the problematic site and remove its cache.

In Firefox, go to Preferences → Advanced → Network. There is an area in the Offline Storage subsection that lists all sites that have stored data for offline use. You can selectively remove the appCache here.

Exercise

It's time to make our cache manifest behave a bit better. Let's integrate some of the lessons we've learned into the *manifest.appcache.php* file.

1 **Track down the missing static icons and images.**
There are some icons and images, used by jQuery Mobile, that we need to add to the CACHE section.

Kudos if you caught a bunch of these already in the earlier step!

2 **Add the NETWORK: section and the wildcard.**
Put this above the CACHE: section.

```
NETWORK:
*
```

3 **Add the PHP snippet.**
Add the code from *extras/current_file_list.txt* to the end of the cache manifest file.

4 **Remove build.php and findevent.php from the manifest.**
Come to think of it, these are resources that should only be available when the user is online. The Events page doesn't do anything yet, but it will. Soon, even.

Don't forget to remove the manifest attribute from the <html> tag on these pages.

Exercise Solution

manifest.appcache.php should look about like this now.

```php
<?php header('Content-type: text/cache-manifest'); ?>
CACHE MANIFEST

NETWORK:
*

CACHE:
http://code.jquery.com/mobile/1.0rc1/jquery.mobile-1.0rc1.min.css
http://code.jquery.com/jquery-1.6.4.min.js
http://code.jquery.com/mobile/1.0rc1/jquery.mobile-1.0rc1.min.js
http://code.jquery.com/mobile/1.0rc1/images/ajax-loader.png
http://code.jquery.com/mobile/1.0rc1/images/icons-18-white.png
http://code.jquery.com/mobile/1.0rc1/images/icons-18-black.png
http://code.jquery.com/mobile/1.0rc1/images/icons-36-white.png
http://code.jquery.com/mobile/1.0rc1/images/icons-36-black.png
index.php
tartans.php
css/styles.css

<?php // The PHP code snippet from the current_file_list.txt file
        // goes here. We're not showing it to save space.?>
```

Make sure you don't have any blank lines here between the header() line and the CACHE MANIFEST line.

Now, save the file and try it out!

Watch it!

A single problem with a cache manifest can cause the whole thing not to work.

Just what you need, more gotchas. But you should know that if a single resource in the manifest results in a 404 (not found), the entire manifest will be disregarded. Similarly, a single syntax goof can render the whole thing useless.

You can protect yourself. Use the handy-dandy manifest validator at http://manifest-validator.com/ and keep an eye on your developer tools windows to make sure none of the referenced resources is missing.

Confusing. I think it mostly works, but when I add a new tartan, it doesn't show up on the tartans list page right away. I have to reload the page. That's not quite right, is it?

Even though the cache manifest file has been updated, you have to reload the tartans list page (*tartans.php*) before you can see the newest stuff. What gives?

Frank: I went and read up about this. I admit I got a bit sucked in. Here's how it works. Say your browser already has a cache manifest file for the site. Then say you visit the tartans listing page again later after new tartans have been created. Your browser will notice that the cache manifest file has changed—it's different from the one the browser already had because the list of tartan files in it has changed. Your browser will immediately grab the new manifest file and check for updated or new stuff.

Jim: Then why the heck doesn't the updated or new stuff show up right away?

Frank: The browser doesn't wait around for all of the resources that are updated or new to download before rendering the page. Once the browser does finish downloading stuff, the new or updated assets are ready to go, in the browser's cache, but won't show up until the page is refreshed.

Jim: So, the only way for folks to see updated things is to reload.

Frank: Well, I think I might have a workaround for this particular situation. I wrote a tiny little JavaScript tool—

Jim: Always with the JavaScript!

Frank: The part of the page that's dynamic is the stuff that gets output by the PHP file included in it—that is, *list.php*. It outputs one `<li>` per tartan. The rest of the page is static. We really only care about updating the contents of the tartan list `<ul>`.

Jim: True.

Frank: My code uses the `window.applicationCache` object and its methods to see if there has been an update to the cache—which there will be if the manifest file has changed, right? If there has been an update, we want to get the updated output from *list.php*.

Jim: Right. If the cache manifest has updated, we know the tartan list should be updated. Preferably without the user having to reload the entire page.

Frank: Yeah. So, if there has been an update to the cache manifest, my code sends an AJAX request to *list.php*. *list.php* isn't in the manifest and, when requested directly, will always return HTML markup representing the current list of tartans. I then take the markup returned by *list.php* and replace the current—that is, stale—list on the page with it. Voilà!

Test Drive

Let's take Frank's little JavaScript library for a spin and see if it helps us wrap up this complex adventure with appCache.

1 **Go grab the little library.**
Copy *cache-manager.js* from the *extras/js* folder into *chapter7/js*.

2 **Include the script in the Tartanator pages.**
Include the *cache-manager.js* script right after the jQuery Mobile script on *index.php*, *build.php*, *findevent.php*, and *tartans.php*.

```
<script src="js/cache-manager.js" type="text/javascript"></script>
```

3 **Add this JavaScript snippet to tartans.php.**
This code indicates that we want to ensure fresh content for the #tartans-list element inside of the #tartans_page page content <div>, using data returned from *inc/list.php*.

```
<div data-role="page" id="tartans_page">
  <script type="text/javascript" charset="utf-8">
    var tartanPage = $('#tartans_page');
    tartanPage.live('pageinit', function () {
      if (!tartanPage.data.cacheManager) {
        tartanPage.data.cacheManager = new CacheManager('#tartans_page');
        tartanPage.data.cacheManager.ensureFreshContent('#tartans-list',
'inc/list.php');
      }
    });
  </script>
<div data-role="header" data-position="fixed">
```

tartans.php

there are no
Dumb Questions

Q: If you can use a wildcard in the **NETWORK** section of a cache manifest, can't I just use a wildcard in the **CACHE** section to cache everything on my site and leave it at that?

A: For better or worse, you can't use wildcards in the CACHE section. The special wildcard token is only for the NETWORK section, and it's not really a wildcard. You can't combine it with any other text patterns—it is a standalone thing with a specific meaning (which is: unless a given resource on the site is listed in another section explicitly, request it over the network when possible).

Q: What is the point of making it so that pages with a `manifest` attribute in their HTML tags get cached even if they're not listed in the manifest?

A: This can indeed cause confusion and headaches. But the idea is that instead of downloading and caching a bunch or all of the pages on a given site in one go, pages can be added to the cache "lazily"—that is, they get added to the cache when the user visits them first.

Q: What's this about "all in one go"?

A: When a browser gets a new or updated cache manifest file, it immediately starts downloading all of the new resources and/or checking for updates to existing ones. This is something to consider, seriously, when designing your cache manifests.

Q: Our manifest contains all of the tartan images and HTML files. Isn't that an awful lot to download all in one go?

A: We agonized over that a bit. It is a fair number of HTTP requests, yes. But the files are rather minute: most of the images are under 1 KB and the HTML files are even smaller. So, the bandwidth hit is small, and, because the resources are being downloaded asynchronously, the impact on the user should be minimal.

Q: Does the browser redownload everything in the manifest every time it's updated?

A: Thankfully, no. The browser will check to see if the resources it already has cached have changed but will not download them again unless they've been modified.

Q: All of this is well and good, but what happens if the user's browser doesn't support appCache?

A: The site basically behaves like it did before we added a cache manifest. It works fine, but won't have a nice offline experience.

Q: You totally didn't mention the **FALLBACK** section.

A: In addition to the CACHE and NETWORK sections, there is an optional FALLBACK section that allows you to list the offline variants that should be used when an online variant is unavailable—for example, use *offline.html* instead of *login.html*.

Q: appCache is nice, but what about localStorage? It feels like only half of the story here.

A: Hey, smartypants! You're ahead of us. We'll come back to localStorage in Chapter 8 (and if you're new to the term, no worries!).

Watch it!

Watch out for implicit caching via the `manifest` attribute.

We mentioned it already, but we're going to pound it home: any page that has a `manifest` *attribute on its* `<html>` *tag will be cached, whether or not it's listed explicitly in the cache manifest. And, no, you can't get around this by using the* NETWORK *section or any other trickery.*

Victory is (finally) ours

Phew. It was a bit of a battle, but we now have the Tartanator working offline. That means we're done implementing the custom tartans piece of phase 2.

☑ Enhance the form we built to take advantage of capabilities of newer mobile browsers.

☑ Drop in server-side code for processing the form and generating resources (images, HTML, etc.) for user-created tartans.

☑ Make sure the offline experience for this part of the app is acceptable.

Congratulations, you just successfully bent appCache to your will.

Writing cache manifest files that do what you actually want them to do can be tricky—you did it!

It's time for some ~~searchable~~ location-aware searchable events

The other chunk of phase 2 is the building of a page that lets users search for local tartan-related events near them.

The Find Events form that we want to build.

We want to find events that are close to the user's current position. That means we'll need to talk about geolocation.

How geolocation works

Geolocation from a web browser involves using JavaScript to obtain the device's current position. Many modern smartphone browsers implement the World Wide Web Consortium (W3C) Geolocation API, which provides a straightforward interface for getting at geolocation data. There are a few other contenders in the mix, including the now-deprecated Google Gears API and some proprietary APIs. Older phones and even some modern smartphones don't have geolocation support in the browser at all.

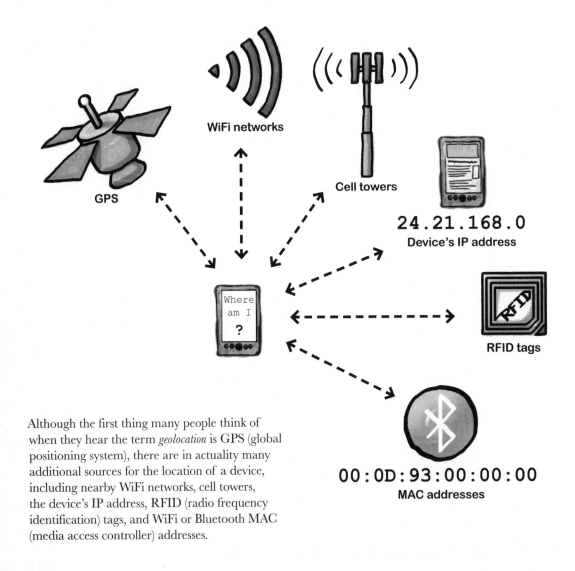

Although the first thing many people think of when they hear the term *geolocation* is GPS (global positioning system), there are in actuality many additional sources for the location of a device, including nearby WiFi networks, cell towers, the device's IP address, RFID (radio frequency identification) tags, and WiFi or Bluetooth MAC (media access controller) addresses.

How to ask W3C-compliant browsers where they are

Browsers that implement the W3C Geolocation API make the feature available via the `navigator.geolocation` object. The most relevant method on that object is `getCurrentPosition`, which attempts to do what it sounds like it would do.

Try to get the current position of the device.

```
navigator.geolocation.getCurrentPosition(successCallback, errorCallback);
```

The name of a JavaScript function to call if a position is obtained.

The name of a JavaScript function to call if an error is encountered.

Handling the info getCurrentPosition gives us

When a location is successfully determined, the function that was given as the name of the success callback will be called and given a `position` object. We get at the info we really care about—latitude and longitude—by looking at the `latitude` and `longitude` of the `coords` attribute of the `position` object.

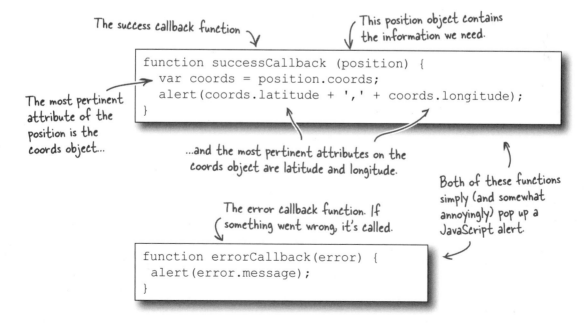

The success callback function

This position object contains the information we need.

```
function successCallback (position) {
    var coords = position.coords;
    alert(coords.latitude + ',' + coords.longitude);
}
```

The most pertinent attribute of the position is the coords object...

...and the most pertinent attributes on the coords object are latitude and longitude.

Both of these functions simply (and somewhat annoyingly) pop up a JavaScript alert.

The error callback function. If something went wrong, it's called.

```
function errorCallback(error) {
  alert(error.message);
}
```

Geolocation JavaScript Magnets

Place the code magnets in the correct positions in the geolocation JavaScript below. You can only use each magnet once, but you may end up with a few that you don't need.

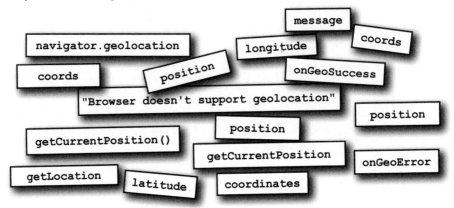

```
function getLocation () {
  // Verify the browser supports W3C geolocation
  if (.....................................) {
    navigator.geolocation............................. (......................., onGeoError);
  } else { // It doesn't
    onGeoError(new Error(.................................................. ));
  }
}


function onGeoSuccess (.......................) {
  var....................... = ......................... .coords;
  alert(coordinates........................ + ',' + coordinates..................... );
}


function ......................... (error) {
  alert(error............................. );
}
......................... ();
```

Answers on page 302.

Start in on the Find Events page: The baseline

The idea of the Find Events page is just that: to find events. We now have a peek into how to find a user's location with JavaScript in applicable browsers. But we've been taking the approach of creating a baseline experience first. What if a user's browser doesn't have JavaScript or geolocation?

Let's start basic and create an events search form that doesn't require either of those things. Providing a simple list of US states in a select list will be our baseline default.

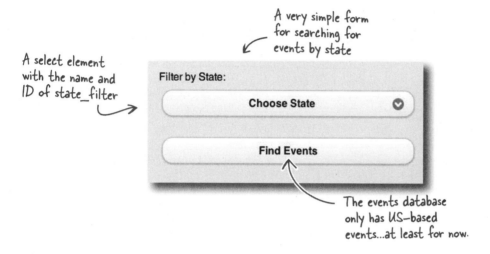

A very simple form for searching for events by state

A select element with the name and ID of state_filter

Filter by State:

Choose State

Find Events

The events database only has US-based events...at least for now.

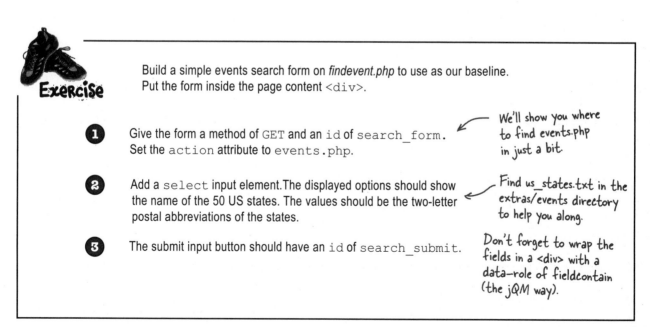

ExeRciSe

Build a simple events search form on *findevent.php* to use as our baseline. Put the form inside the page content `<div>`.

1 Give the form a method of `GET` and an `id` of `search_form`. Set the `action` attribute to `events.php`.

We'll show you where to find events.php in just a bit.

2 Add a `select` input element. The displayed options should show the name of the 50 US states. The values should be the two-letter postal abbreviations of the states.

Find us_states.txt in the extras/events directory to help you along.

3 The submit input button should have an `id` of `search_submit`.

Don't forget to wrap the fields in a `<div>` with a data-role of fieldcontain (the jQM way).

Geolocation JavaScript Magnets Solution

Did you manage to place the magnets in the right position?

```
function getLocation () {
  // Verify the browser supports W3C geolocation
  if ( navigator.geolocation ) {
    navigator.geolocation. getCurrentPosition ( onGeoSuccess , onGeoError);
  } else { // It doesn't
    onGeoError(new Error( "Browser doesn't support geolocation" ));
  }
}


function onGeoSuccess ( position ) {
  var coordinates = position .coords;
  alert(coordinates. latitude + ',' + coordinates. longitude );
}

function onGeoError (error) {
  alert(error. message );
}
  getLocation ();
```

Once you've constructed this code, **put it in a file called** *geolocation.js* in the *chapter7/js/* directory. Then include it in the *findevent.php* page by using a `<script>` tag within the `<div>` with `data-role="page"`.

It should go right above the search form.

You didn't need these magnets.

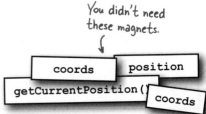

Let's integrate geolocation

We now have a basic form. Oh, and some really annoying
JavaScript alerts.

Let's do the fun part: dropping in geolocation for browsers
that support it. Here's what the form will look like for enabled
browsers after our next set of changes:

*Once we spruce up our form,
users with browsers that
support geolocation will be
able to use their current
location to find events.*

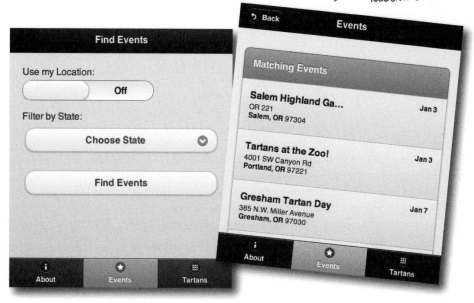

Exercise Solution

Your basic form should look like this.

```html
<div data-role="content">
  <script type="text/javascript" src="js/geolocation.js"></script>
  <form method="get" action="events.php" id="search_form">
    <div data-role="fieldcontain">
      <label for="state_filter">Search by State</label>
      <select id="state_filter" name="state_filter">
        <option value="">Choose State</option>
        <option value="AL">Alabama</option>
        <!-- ETC -->
      </select>
    </div>
    <div data-role="fieldcontain">
      <input type="submit" value="Find Events" id="search_submit" />
    </div>
  </form>
</div><!-- /content -->
```

GEOLOCATION CONSTRUCTION

We're going to fancy up the code in *geolocation.js*. Let's walk through the highlights.

```
(function () {
  var $page, $searchForm, $submitButton, $stateFilter;

  $page = $('#event_page');
  if (!$page.data.initialized) {
    $page.live('pagecreate', initGeo);
    $page.data.initialized = true;
  }
```
When the page initializes, call the initGeo function.

```
  function initGeo() {
    $searchForm = $('#search_form');
    $submitButton = $('#search_submit');
    $stateFilter = $('#state_filter');
    if (navigator.geolocation) {
      initGeoOptions();
    }
  }
```
If the browser supports geolocation, initialize the geolocation-related form elements.

```
  function initGeoOptions() {
    var $latField, $longField, $flipSwitch;
    $flipSwitch = $('<select name="usegeo" id="usegeo"
data-role="slider"><option value="off">Off</
off><option value="on">On</option></select>').
change(toggleLocation);
```
Add a slider-themed on/off switch to let users opt in to using their current location.

```
    $flipSwitch.prependTo($searchForm).wrap('<div data-
role="fieldcontain"></div>');
    $flipSwitch.before('<label for="usegeo">Use my
Location:</label>');
```
```
    $latField = $('<input type="hidden" />').attr({ name
: 'latitude', id : 'latitude'})
    $longField = $('<input type="hidden" />').attr({
name: 'longitude', id : 'longitude' })
```
Add two hidden fields to hold the value of latitude and longitude from the geolocation.

```
    $latField.appendTo($searchForm);
    $longField.appendTo($searchForm);
  }
```

toggleLocation is bound to the change event on the slider switch.

```
    function toggleLocation(event) {
      var geoActivated = ($(event.target).val()
== 'on') ? true : false;
      if (geoActivated) {
        $submitButton.button('disable');
        $stateFilter.selectmenu('disable');
        $.mobile.showPageLoadingMsg();
        navigator.geolocation.getCurrentPosition(
onGeoSuccess, onGeoError);
      } else {
        $stateFilter.selectmenu('enable');
        $submitButton.button('enable');
      }
    }
    function onGeoSuccess(position) {
      var coordinates = position.coords;
      $('#latitude').val(coordinates.latitude);
      $('#longitude').val(coordinates.longitude);
      $.mobile.hidePageLoadingMsg();
      $submitButton.button('enable');
    }
    function onGeoError(error) {
      $('#usegeo').val('off').trigger('change');
      alert(error.message);
    }
  })();
```

If the user just flipped it on, disable the state filter, and disable the submit button (it will be reenabled when the geolocation is complete).

Here's where we trigger the geolocation.

When it's turned off, reenable filter by state.

Here's our success callback. We've altered it to update the latitude and longitude hidden fields with the user's location data.

On error, slide the use geolocation switch back to the off position and fire its change event (which is bound to toggleLocation above).

Try it out! Play with the form to get a feel for what the new JavaScript does for us.

You can find this code in the *chapter7* folder in *extras/js/ enhanced_geo_form.js*.

Update the *geolocation.js* file, save it, and try out the updated Find Events page.

Jim: I was just checking out the geolocation piece on some devices. I know that the BlackBerry OS 5 browser is supposed to have geolocation, but the Use My Location switch isn't showing up.

Frank: Yeah. The BlackBerry OS 5 browser supports geolocation, but it isn't the W3C flavor. I was just looking this up. And older Android browsers don't have W3C-style geolocation, either. They're based on Google Gears.

Jim: This sounds complicated.

Frank: It is. And we're on a tight deadline. I don't think we have time to chase down all of the odds and ends and do exhaustive testing on a whole bunch of obscure devices. What I did find is this open source, drop-in JavaScript library that handles geolocation across a bunch of different platforms, W3C-compliant or no. It's called, simply enough, *geo-location-javascript*.

Jim: But doesn't that mean we'd have to go refactor all of our existing JavaScript?

Frank: Nope. The API for this library emulates that of the W3C spec. All of the major method and attribute names are the same. I think we only need to change a few lines and then we can stop worrying quite so much about cross-platform compatibility.

Jim: Oh, while we're making edits to the JavaScript…the pop-up error for geolocation failures is ugly. And could use some finesse in wording.

Frank: Yep. I think we should use a jQuery Mobile dialog, like the ones I built for form errors on the tartan-creation form.

Jim: Oh, you didn't tell me about that!

Frank: If you try to submit the tartan form without a title, or if you forget a color or size when you add a color-size combo, a dialog will pop up to alert you to the errors of your ways. It's styled in a nice, jQM way.

Jim: How do you make a jQuery Mobile dialog?

Frank: They're standalone jQM pages. Check out the ones in the *dialogs* directory. Then I make them show up from the JavaScript.

Jim: Oh, cool. I can probably figure this out.

Frank: OK. You do that. I'm going to drop in this geolocation library real quick.

Do this!

Copy the *extras/js/geo.js* file into the *chapter7/js* folder. This is the geo-location-javascript library. You can also visit the project's home page, if you're curious about it, at *http://bit.ly/sx7JrH*.

Exercise

Update the Find Events page and the geolocation JavaScript to use the cross-platform geolocation code and show geolocation errors in a pop-up dialog.

1 **Update findevent.php to include the JavaScript for the new geolocation library.**

```
<div data-role="content">
<script src="http://code.google.com/apis/gears/gears_init.js" type="text/
javascript" charset="utf-8"></script>
<script src="js/geo.js" type="text/javascript" charset="utf-8"></script>
<script type="text/javascript" src="js/geolocation.js"></script>
```

2 **Update geolocation.js to use the new library.**
Find and change the following code from:

```
if (navigator.geolocation) {
    initGeoOptions();
}
```

to:

```
if (geo_position_js.init()) {
    initGeoOptions();
}
```

and change this:

```
navigator.geolocation.getCurrentPosition(onGeoSuccess, onGeoError);
```

to:

```
geo_position_js.getCurrentPosition(onGeoSuccess, onGeoError);
```

3 **Create and invoke a dialog for geolocation errors.**
Using the other pages in the *dialogs* directory as a guide, create a nicely worded error dialog for geolocation failures. Name this file *geolocation_error.html*.

Next, replace the `alert` in the `onGeoError` function with a dialog pop up. You can find examples of dialog pop ups in the *js/tartanator.js* file. You should only need to adjust the URL argument.

Exercise Solution

Here's what your `onGeoError` function should look like after you convert the error from a basic JavaScript `alert` to a jQuery Mobile dialog. We trust you also made the HTML page for the dialog itself!

```
function onGeoError(error) {
    $('#usegeo').val('off').trigger('change');
    $.mobile.changePage( "dialogs/geolocation_error.html", {
        transition: "pop",
        reverse: false,
        role: 'dialog'
    });
}
```

Relax

We just blew through some gnarly JavaScript.

We admit, that was pretty intense. And there's some code we didn't explain in depth. But this isn't *Head First JavaScript*, and we didn't want to distract you from the main tasks at hand: winning the battle with appCache and taking advantage of PhoneGap's mediaCapture API (even for browsers that don't support it yet).

Test Drive

Enough, already! Let's see this thing in action. It won't take much to hook this thing up to some search code and sample data.

1 **Copy some needed files from the extras/events directory.**
Copy *event_search.inc* and *event_list.inc* into the *chapter7/inc* directory. Copy *events.php* into the *chapter7* directory.

2 **Try it out!**
Head to the Find Events page in your mobile browser of choice and hit the Use My Location switch.

Nothing found

Ha, ha. Sorry about that. Unless you're lucky enough to be in the Portland, Oregon, metro area, you probably got this result on your first location-based search:

Unless you're near Portland, you'll get this result on your first try.

That's because all of the sample data is local, and the search radius is set to 25 miles. How's about you add some of your own fake events to get this thing to deliver some results?

Exercise

Add a few events in the sample data that are in your neck of the woods. Find the *event_list.inc* file in *chapter7/inc/*. Inside is a big PHP array representing fake data for events. Add a few of your own elements to this array, using an address and lat/long pairs that are within 25 miles of you.

If you feel particularly uncomfortable with PHP, you could try just updating the address and lat/long of a few existing entries. The latitude, longitude, and state are what is used by the search script to find matches.

Use this tool to get a lat/long pair real quick for any address: http://itouchmap.com/latlong.html.

This is looking great, guys! This is what I had in mind when I first envisioned a mobile web app for the Tartanator.

Nice! We've successfully integrated several of the features that make a mobile web app feel super: progressive enhancement, offline mode, and location awareness.

BRAIN POWER

Extra-super extra credit: Can you think of how you would go about adding a `range` input to allow users to determine the search radius? When should it show up? If you can figure out how to add an input with a name of `radius`, the backend search script is already configured to use it!

Looking good in various mobile browsers

This one's an Android.

BULLET POINTS

- Web apps that feel natural and comfortable on mobile devices often share certain characteristics like **well-considered progressive enhancement, a good offline mode, and location-aware features**.

- Starting with a **baseline** is a great way to reach as many users as possible, and thoughtful **progressive enhancement** for more powerful mobile browsers can make things really shine.

- Crafting a relevant **offline experience** is important: mobile devices can't be expected to have an always-available data connection.

- We can take advantage of the **appCache** feature in browsers by creating a **cache manifest** file to instruct the browser which resources to cache and make available offline.

- The construction of cache manifests is straightforward on the surface, but there are a **number of gotchas** that you have to carefully consider.

- In our cache manifest file, we can indicate which resources should be downloaded and cached for offline use (in the **CACHE section**) as well as those that should be requested afresh when an Internet connection is available (in the **NETWORK section**).

- **Geolocation** in the browser is supported widely among modern smartphones. Many implement the **W3C's Geolocation API**, which exposes the `navigator.geolocation` object to JavaScript.

- Similarly to how we enhanced the tartan-creation form for supporting browsers, we also enhanced the Find Events form to integrate geolocation, when it's available.

- Certain mobile browsers, especially on slightly older smartphones, have **implementations of geolocation that are not W3C-compliant**. To manage these idiosyncracies, we used a third-party geolocation library called geo-location-javascript.

- The **geo-location-javascript library** emulates the W3C API, requiring minimal changes to our original, W3C-specific JavaScript code.

Tartan Hunt: Going native

> Ack. Barbed wire.
> Boy, the grouchy old neighbor's really kicked it up a gear this year to stop me from getting the apples in his yard. What I wouldn't do for a bridge right now...

Sometimes you've got to go native. It might be because you need access to something not available in mobile browsers (yet). Or maybe your client simply *must* have an app in the App Store. We look forward to that shiny future when we have access to everything we want in the browser, and mobile web apps share that sparkly allure native apps enjoy. Until then, we have the option of **hybrid development**—we continue writing our **code using web standards**, and use a **library to bridge the gaps** between our code and the device's native capabilities. **Cross-platform native apps built from web technologies**? Not such a bad compromise, eh?

Opportunity knocks again

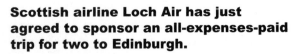

Psst! Hey, guys, check this out. We just landed a new sponsor for the big Scottish convention coming to town. We're going to run a contest, and I want to add it to the Tartanator!

Scottish airline Loch Air has just agreed to sponsor an all-expenses-paid trip for two to Edinburgh.

As part of the upcoming Scottish Celebration Expo in two months, Loch Air wants to run a promotional contest along with Tartans Unlimited, Ewan's organization.

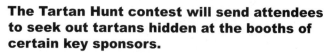

I was thinking we could have a sort of scavenger hunt. Contestants have to take photos of tartan swatches they find at the booths of conference sponsors.

The Tartan Hunt contest will send attendees to seek out tartans hidden at the booths of certain key sponsors.

Players are challenged to find and take a photo of each listed tartan with their devices' cameras; found tartans are then checked off the list of hidden tartans. Once a contestant has found all of the tartans, he or she can show the completed list and be entered to win the trip.

Sounds like a perfect addition to the Tartanator!

Unfortunately, there's a problem.

Access to the camera—and some other device features like audio recording, filesystem operations, network status, and contact data—isn't available for the most part in mobile browsers.

Um. Photos. We don't have access to the device's camera from mobile browsers. What are we going to do? Do we have to go native?

Many device capabilities, like the camera, are not accessible from mobile browsers.

This is slowly changing for the better, but there are still a number of things we can't get at from the browser.

Frank: We obviously don't have the time or budget to rewrite the Tartanator as a native app for a bunch of platforms and also add the new features Ewan wants.

Jim: Does that mean we have to walk away from this work? That would be too bad.

Joe: I wonder if there's a compromise here somewhere. We might consider proposing a *hybrid application*.

Jim: What is that?

Joe: A hybrid application is a native application written with web technologies. Because it's native, we can get at device capabilities like the camera, but the code itself is written with standard web stuff, so we can share the code across several platforms.

Frank: But if it's web-based, and those features aren't available in the browser, how does that work?

Joe: There are several frameworks and platforms that provide bridges between web apps and native code. They take our web app, chew on it a bit, and then spit out packaged apps—native ones—for various platforms. They take care of the various bits and bobs for us so we can just use the web standards we know.

Jim: Should we convert the Tartanator to one of these hybrid apps, then?

Joe: I don't think we have the time to wrap the entire app natively and test it effectively. Given the timeline, what do you think about suggesting that we create a native app just for the contest?

Frank: I kind of like that idea. And we don't have to risk making hurried changes to the Tartanator web app. It has a bit of cachet—attendees show up and can download a special app just for the event and the contest. Joe, if you think we can get the hybrid app thing to work on several platforms, let's float the idea with Ewan.

How do hybrid apps work?

You write your code using standard web technologies like HTML5, CSS, and JavaScript—the same way websites have always been built. A framework or platform then acts as a bridge, providing a common API for you to use to access features natively on the various device platforms. It bridges the gap between your JavaScript and the device's native code (for each platform it supports) and produces apps for various platforms.

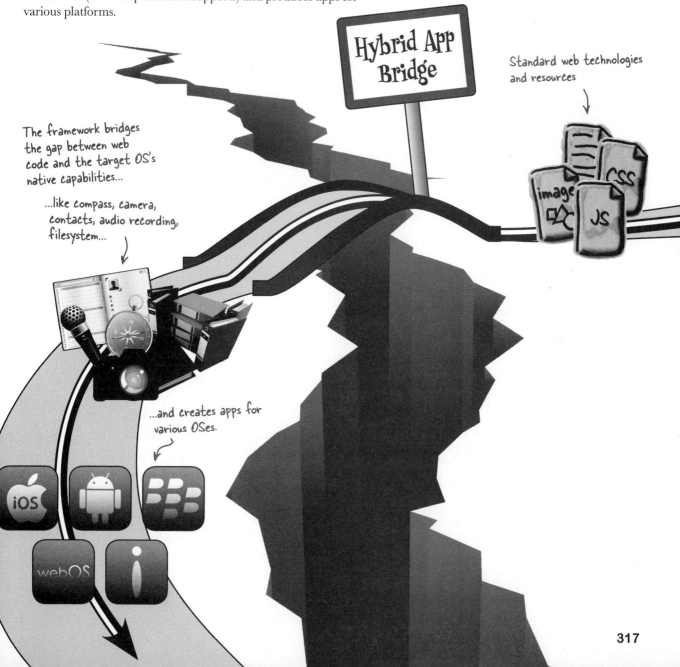

Hybrid App Bridge

Standard web technologies and resources

The framework bridges the gap between web code and the target OS's native capabilities...

...like compass, camera, contacts, audio recording, filesystem...

...and creates apps for various OSes.

Bridge the web-native gap with PhoneGap

PhoneGap is an open source HTML5 platform that allows you to create native apps for several mobile operating systems using the hybrid approach that we've been talking about. You write your code like you're used to, using HTML, CSS, and JavaScript. PhoneGap provides the bridge between that and native code via a consistent, cross-platform JavaScript API.

PhoneGap was developed by Vancouver-based firm Nitobi, which was acquired by Adobe in October 2011. But don't worry: Adobe has already taken steps to make sure PhoneGap remains open source by giving the rights to PhoneGap to the nonprofit Apache Software Foundation. The newly minted Apache Cordova project will make sure that the PhoneGap codebase stays open source going forward.

PhoneGap Build

PhoneGap Build is a web-based service that lets you compile in the cloud for several platforms at once. It takes a bit of the drudgery out of the build process by allowing you to skip installing at least some of the SDKs, plug-ins, IDEs, and whatnot for each platform you want to support.

PhoneGap supports up to seven platforms, but in this chapter we're going to use PhoneGap Build, which supports Apple iOS, Android, BlackBerry, WebOS, and Symbian.

Whereas with standard PhoneGap development, you'd do your own compiling and building, with PhoneGap Build you upload a zip file (or pull from a code repository) and it does the rest.

Ewan has agreed to the Tartan Hunt contest companion app idea. That's cool, but we have an incredibly tight timeline. Where do we start?

We're going to show you how to build a hybrid Android app using PhoneGap Build.

If you don't have an Android device, not to worry. We'll show you how to build and install the app for a real-life device *and* for emulated virtual devices.

How come we're singling out Android for this project? What about iOS and other platforms?

We chose Android as our example platform for a few reasons.

For one thing, it is a popular platform (duh). But, also, building and deploying iOS apps onto devices requires membership in the iOS Developer program ($99/year). We didn't want to assume you'd fork that over.

Android also has a freely available SDK that supports emulating many virtual devices across different versions of the Android OS. And the Android SDK runs on several platforms. With Xcode, the development toolset needed for iOS development, you're out of luck if you don't have a Mac.

Is your development environment ready to go?

If you haven't done it yet, hold everything and visit Appendix iv. You need to have the right stuff installed and an understanding of how to install and uninstall apps on virtual and real devices before moving on to the next parts of the chapter.

Watch it!

JavaScript ahead.

You don't have to be a JavaScript genius to make it through this chapter, but there's no getting around the fact that today's web app development involves JavaScript.

To communicate with native functionality such as the camera APIs using PhoneGap, we need to use a client-side technology—and JavaScript is obviously the right guy for this job.

there are no
Dumb Questions

Q: What other tools, products, or services are there for building hybrid apps?

A: Two of the best-known hybrid development alternatives are Appcelerator Titanium and the forthcoming Sencha Touch 2 product.

Q: What platforms are supported by PhoneGap?

A: PhoneGap presently supports Android, Bada, BlackBerry, iOS, Symbian, WebOS, and Windows Phone 7. See *http://phonegap.com/about/features* for a list of which of its features are supported on which versions of which platforms.

Q: Does PhoneGap Build support the same platforms as PhoneGap?

A: Not quite. At the time of this writing, it does not support Windows Phone 7 or Bada.

Q: Is PhoneGap free?

A: Yes. PhoneGap—or, as it is known going forward, Apache Cordova—is open source and free.

Q: What about PhoneGap Build? Is it free, too?

A: It depends. PhoneGap Build offers tiered levels of service. Its free variant allows developers to have one private app and as many public apps as they'd like. We'll be using this free service to build the Tartan Hunt app. PhoneGap Build's other levels of service increase the number of private apps and project collaborators.

Q: Why did I have to install the Android SDK?

A: We won't be compiling or building the Tartan Hunt App— PhoneGap Build will do that for us—but we still need to be able to install it and test it on an emulator, a device (if you have an Android device), or both. To do that, we need some of the tools provided by the SDK.

We don't, however, need to install the Eclipse IDE, which we'd likely need to do if we were developing and building the code ourselves. So at least we saved that step!

Q: Why is it that some things aren't accessible in the web browser in the first place?

A: There are several reasons that you can't do anything and everything from the browser on mobile devices.

Security is a considerable concern. Giving the browser access to things like the filesystem or the user's contact list is something that has to be done carefully, with a lot of consideration about how to keep things properly sandboxed. Doing these things right takes time.

In addition, some of the proposed standards for these features are new or incomplete, or have multiple variants vying for adoption. As these things get ironed out, expect to see some bumps along the way with conflicting or inconsistent support in browsers.

But here's to a standardized, device-API-rich future! Let's try to enjoy the ride!

BRAIN POWER

If you have a device that is not Android but *is* one of PhoneGap Build's supported platforms, or if you have an Apple Developer Account, we encourage you to try building and testing the examples in this chapter on your platform.

Our test kitchen has run the Tartan Hunt app successfully on various flavors of Android and iOS.

Get acquainted with PhoneGap Build

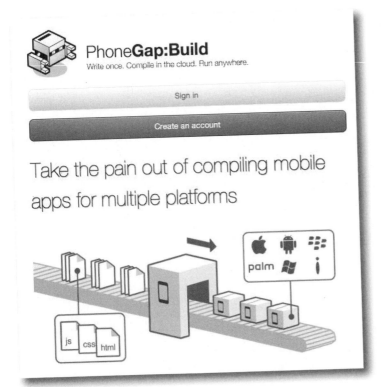

Do this!

Get on over to
https://build.phonegap.com and
create an account. It's free and only
takes a moment.

Roger. PhoneGap Build
account set up, Android SDK
ready. But you know, it'd be great
to know what exactly it is we're
building.

How will the app work?

The landing page of our app will display contest instructions and
a list of tartans to find. Tapping on an item in the list goes to a
display with more information about the vendor at whose booth
the tartan can be found.

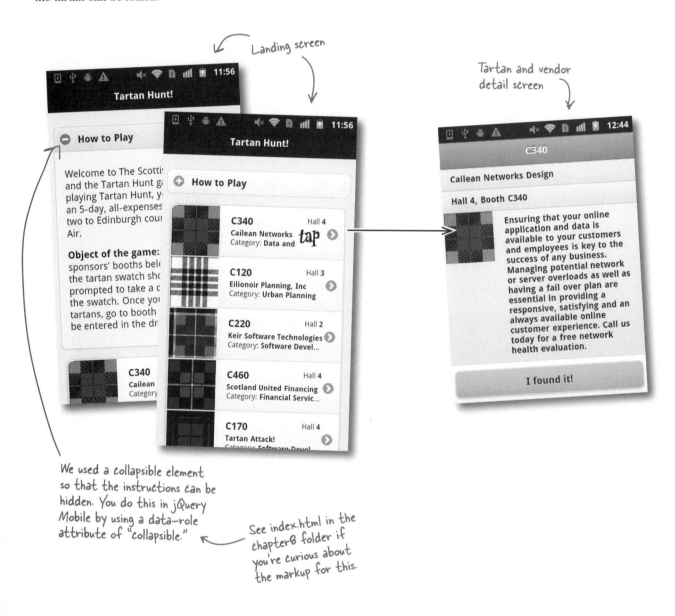

Landing screen

Tartan and vendor
detail screen

We used a collapsible element
so that the instructions can be
hidden. You do this in jQuery
Mobile by using a data-role
attribute of "collapsible."

See index.html in the
chapter8 folder if
you're curious about
the markup for this.

Keep track of discovered tartans

In our completed app, clicking the "I found it!" button will launch the device's camera, and the player can take a snapshot of the discovered tartan. The photo is displayed on the detail page and marked off as "found" in the list on the landing page.

We already have the basic HTML layout, CSS, and images. **Now we need to make them do something and build a native Android app using PhoneGap Build.**

How we'll get from here to there

☐ Set up and configure a PhoneGap Build project. Zip up the current HTML, CSS, and images; build the app; and install it on an Android device or emulator.

☐ Add the ability for players to mark which tartans they've spotted.

☐ Add the ability for players to save photos of the tartans they've spotted.

Anatomy of the Tartan Hunt project

Here's the simplified structure of the content `<div>` in *index.html*.

The structure of our content is a `<ul>` with a bunch of nested `<ul>`s.

Each tartan `<li>` element has a nested list (ul.details) with further info about the vendor and the "I found it!" button.

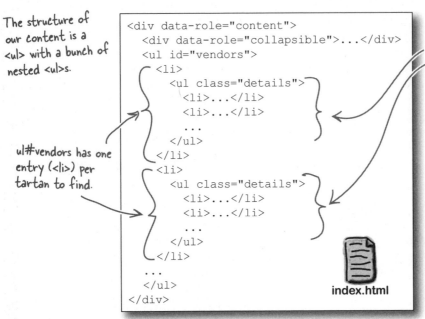

```
<div data-role="content">
   <div data-role="collapsible">...</div>
   <ul id="vendors">
      <li>
         <ul class="details">
            <li>...</li>
            <li>...</li>
            ...
         </ul>
      </li>
      <li>
         <ul class="details">
            <li>...</li>
            <li>...</li>
            ...
         </ul>
      </li>
      ...
   </ul>
</div>
```

index.html

ul#vendors has one entry (`<li>`) per tartan to find.

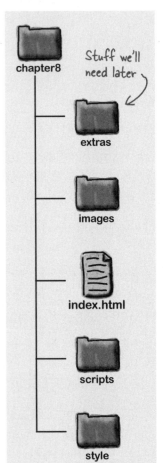

chapter8

Stuff we'll need later

extras

images

index.html

scripts

style

We're using jQuery Mobile again for this project, so the overall look will be generally consistent with the Tartanator.

We're already ~~almost~~ organized for PhoneGap Build

The structure of our starting point is now almost ready to drop into PhoneGap Build.

PhoneGap Build projects have a structure based on the **W3C web widget specification**. Web widgets are encapsulated web apps that are meant as standalone client applications. In their most basic form, they consist of at least one *start file* (in our case, *index.html*) and a *configuration file* (in XML). You can add any number of files that your app will need to the package—things like images and CSS and JavaScript and whatnot.

Wanna read the spec? Here it is: www.w3.org/TR/widgets/.

We're already almost there. But **we need to create a configuration file** to give PhoneGap Build some needed details about our app.

PhoneGap Build will look for a file in our project called *config.xml*. Let's go build that now!

Exercise

Let's make our first PhoneGap Build app. First, we need a configuration file.
Create a file called *config.xml* in the *chapter8* directory. Use the template
below to complete the file's contents.

Give the app a human-readable name and description.

```
<?xml version="1.0" encoding="UTF-8"?>
<widget xmlns       = "http://www.w3.org/ns/widgets"
        xmlns:gap   = "http://phonegap.com/ns/1.0"
        id          = ""
        version     = "1.0.0">
  <name></name>
  <description></description>
  <author href=""
        email="">YOUR NAME HERE
  </author>
  <icon src="images/touch-icon-iphone4.png" height="114" width="114" />
</widget>
```

Let's use com.hfmw.tartanhunt as our app's ID.

Your website and email address. You can use http://hf-mw.com if you don't have your own site.

Let's add icons! These show up on the user's home screen. We've added the first one for you. Find the rest in the images directory and add them as well.

config.xml

Remember that a PhoneGap Build project is either built from a zip file or
pulled from a code repository. We're going to take the zip file route.

Zip up the entire contents of the *chapter8* directory. It doesn't matter what
the resulting file is called, as long as it is a zip archive with a *.zip* extension.

Exercise Solution

Your *config.xml* file should look something like this. But don't lose your identity! We expect you to use your own name and stuff.

```xml
<?xml version="1.0" encoding="UTF-8"?>
<widget xmlns      = "http://www.w3.org/ns/widgets"
        xmlns:gap  = "http://phonegap.com/ns/1.0"
        id         = "com.hfmw.tartanhunt"
        version    = "1.0.0">

  <name>Tartan Hunt</name>

  <description>A companion application for the Scottish Celebration:
win a trip for 2 to Edinburgh from Loch Air!</description>

  <author href="http://www.hf-mw.com"
        email="help@hf-mw.com">
        Lyza Gardner and Jason Grigsby
  </author>

<icon src="images/touch-icon-iphone4.png" height="114" width="114" />
<icon src="images/touch-icon-ipad.png" height="72" width="72" />
<icon src="images/touch-icon-iphone.png" height="57" width="57" />
<icon src="images/icon-48.png" height="48" width="48" />
<icon src="images/icon-36.png" height="36" width="36" />

</widget>
```

PhoneGap Build will give the right icon to the right devices...

config.xml

**Log in to PhoneGap Build to see your dashboard.
It's time to create our app!**

Click the new app
button to get started.

https://build.phonegap.com

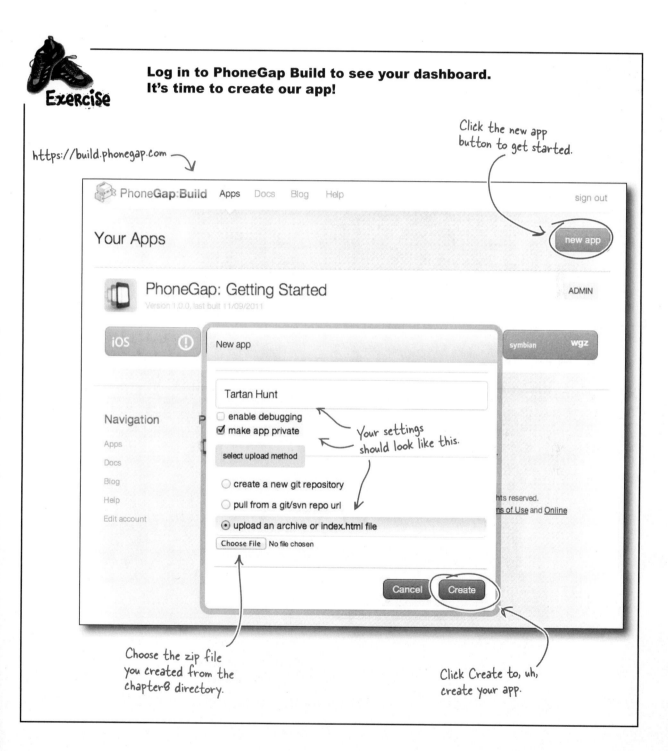

PhoneGap:Build   Apps   Docs   Blog   Help   sign out

Your Apps   new app

PhoneGap: Getting Started   ADMIN
Version 1.0.0, last built 11/09/2011

iOS   New app   symbian   wgz

                       Tartan Hunt

Navigation   ☐ enable debugging
                          ☑ make app private   Your settings
Apps   should look like this.
                          select upload method
Docs
Blog   ○ create a new git repository
Help   ○ pull from a git/svn repo url   ts reserved.
Edit account   ns of Use and Online
                          ⦿ upload an archive or index.html file

                          Choose File   No file chosen

                                              Cancel   Create

Choose the zip file
you created from the
chapter8 directory.   Click Create to, uh,
                                               create your app.

Download your apps

After you upload the zip file, PhoneGap Build will queue
your app for building. Wait a minute or two and refresh the
page. You should see Download buttons for each platform for
which the app was successfully built. We want to download the
Android package (APK) file.

When the build
process is done, you'll
see a Download
button appear, rather
like this.

Download the
Android APK.

APK (Android
Application Package
File) is the packaged
app, ready to install.

**OK, let's get this
thing installed.**

Choose your adventure

Install on an emulator

To prep for installing the app on a virtual device, start the Android SDK. Go to Tools → Manage AVDs to bring up a list of your installed Android virtual devices (AVDs). Launch a device for a recent-ish version of Android. The emulated device needs to be running when you install the app. Don't try to install the app until the emulator is all the way booted up.

OR

Install on a real device

If you have a real-life Android device, woot! Connect your Android device to your computer's USB port. Yep. That's it.

Ready, aim, fire!

The process for installing the app is the same whether you're deploying it virtually or to a real device. Open up a terminal window (Mac or Linux) or type **cmd** in the Start menu's Search box (Windows) to get a command line, and **cd** to the directory where you downloaded the Android APK file.

The command to install the app is:

```
adb install <the name of the package file>
```

We talk about this in more detail in Appendix iv.

Our APK file was named TartanHunt.apk.

Don't forget! Your (real) device must be attached or your emulator fully booted before you run this command.

You should see something similar to this...

```
File  Edit  Window  Help  Tartans
$ adb install TartanHunt.apk
1157 KB/s (683431 bytes in 0.576s)
        pkg: /data/local/tmp/TartanHunt.apk
Success
$
```

We recommend using an AVD for Android 2.3 or 4.0+. Earlier versions have somewhat finicky emulators, especially for the camera stuff we'll do later.

You should now be able to see the Tartan Hunt app in the application screen of your device or emulator. Go ahead and launch the app!

The first time you run the app, it might take a little while—up to about 30 seconds—to launch.

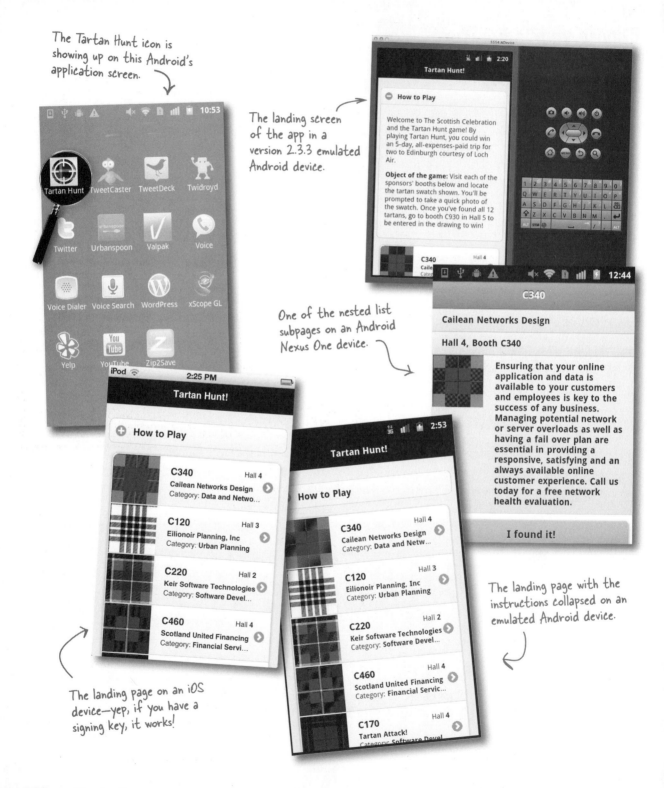

The Tartan Hunt icon is showing up on this Android's application screen.

The landing screen of the app in a version 2.3.3 emulated Android device.

One of the nested list subpages on an Android Nexus One device.

The landing page on an iOS device—yep, if you have a signing key, it works!

The landing page with the instructions collapsed on an emulated Android device.

Interesting. We only have one HTML file. But each tartan I touch seems to take me to a separate page.

jQuery Mobile automatically converts nested <ul>s into separate "pages."

It does this by converting each nested list to a `<div>` with a `data-role` of `page` and using that `<div>` as the active "page" when the list items are clicked. There is still actually only one proper *page*, technically. You'll also note that it uses the title of the parent list element (in our case, the vendor's booth number) as the title of the nested list's page.

Hey, what about BlackBerry?

If you visit your dashboard on PhoneGap Build, you might see something like this:

Our BlackBerry status is FROWNY. :(

We could rectify the iOS situation by providing a signing key (if we had one).

What's with the frowny face for BlackBerry? Well, sadly, there's a problem currently with the combination of PhoneGap Build, BlackBerry, and any filename with a hyphen in it. Several of the jQuery Mobile files we need have hyphens in their filenames.

For purposes of brevity and sanity— and because Ewan has expressed diffidence about supporting the BlackBerry platform, we're not going to address this here...

To make the PhoneGap Build Tartan Hunt app work on BlackBerry OS, you would need to alter jQuery Mobile's icon filenames and update any reference to them in jQM's source code. While this wouldn't take too long, it does mean "hacking" jQuery Mobile's core and introduces a maintenance burden. What do you think? Is it worth it?

Exercise

Let's add a splash screen so that users don't have to look at a boring blank screen while the app loads. Use the PhoneGap Build *config.xml* documentation at *https://build.phonegap.com/docs/config-xml* to figure out how to do this. Find the two splash-screen images in *chapter8/extras/images* and move them to the *chapter8/images* folder.

Update *config.xml*, zip up *chapter8* again, rebuild the app on PhoneGap Build, and reinstall it to see the new splash screen take effect.

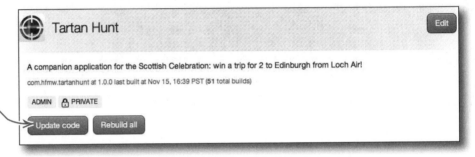

Look for the "Update code" button to upload your updated zip file. The rebuild process starts automatically after upload.

⟶ Answers on page 334.

Watch it!

You need to uninstall the app before you can reinstall it after making changes.

Each time you rebuild the app on PhoneGap Build and need to reinstall it on a device or emulator, you need to uninstall first. Run this command when the device is attached via USB, or when the emulator you want to uninstall it from is running.

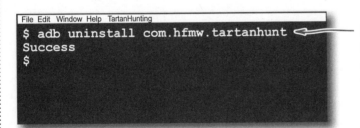

Note that you use the app's package ID with the uninstall command (com.hfmw.tartanhunt or whatever you set the ID to in the config.xml file), not the APK filename like we did with the install command.

Nice work, hotshot!

Rock on. We have an app. Now let's make it do what it's supposed to do. We've broken down the functional pieces into two steps.

First, we want the app to be able to remember which tartans the user has found. When players click the "I found it!" button, we need the app to keep a record of that.

Congratulations, you just built a native mobile app.

Not so tricky, huh? You can use your web dev chops to build native stuff without too much hassle!

Store which tartans users have found

☑ Set up and configure a PhoneGap Build project. Zip up the current HTML, CSS, and images; build the app; and install it on an Android device or emulator.

First, let's build the ability to keep track of which tartans users say they have found.

☐ **Add the ability for players to mark which tartans they've spotted.**

☐ Add the ability for players to save photos of the tartans they've spotted.

Then we'll come back in a bit and enhance the app to prompt users to take a photo.

How am I going to get the app to "remember" which tartans the users claimed they saw? Are we going to have to get down and dirty with native code?

Fortunately, there's a way to do this in JavaScript using an HTML5 web standard called localStorage.

It's already supported in the default mobile browsers of all of the platforms we're targeting with PhoneGap Build.

It's not supported by BlackBerry before OS 6, but we're not supporting BlackBerry currently.

Who's seen what? Store found tartans

We can store simple data on the client—in our case, which tartans have been found—without much fuss using the **localStorage API** in the browser.

What makes localStorage so special?

In the past, developers have often relied on **HTTP cookies** for data that needs to be kept on the client. There are a few downsides to cookies, however.

Every time the client makes a request to a server, the entire contents of all cookies for that domain are transferred. Sometimes, a developer might want to store hefty amounts of data on the client—say, images or considerable amounts of configuration information—which isn't feasible with cookies (or, at least, isn't performance-friendly!).

Also, cookies are notoriously convoluted to work with using JavaScript. They're just kinda clunky. Plus, there is some data we might want to stick on the client that the server just doesn't need to know about (or maybe, as in our case, *there is no server*).

localStorage was designed specifically for the straightforward storage and retrieval of string data in key-value pairs on the client. It gives us methods to set, get, and clear out data—and that's about it. It's not complicated.

Our app has a splash screen now! This is what it looks like on an iPod Touch. ⟶

Exercise Solution

Here's the end of the *config.xml* file, with splash screens added. The two sizes allow us to have a bigger version for devices with higher resolution.

```
<icon src="images/icon-48.png" height="48" width="48" />
<icon src="images/icon-36.png" height="36" width="36" />

<gap:splash src="images/splash2x.png" width="640" height="960" />
<gap:splash src="images/splash.png" width="320" height="480" />
</widget>
```

config.xml

What can localStorage do for us?

When a player clicks the "I found it!" button, we can add an entry to localStorage. And we check for data in localStorage when we want to see which of the tartans the contestant has already found.

Meet the getter and the setter

There are two methods on localStorage that provide most of its utility. First, we set a value:

Both the key and the value must be strings.

A key to name the thing we're storing

The value we want to store

```
localStorage.setItem(key, value);
```

Then, later, we can ask for that value by using its `key`:

The key for which we'd like the stored data, please!

```
var storedValue = localStorage.getItem(key);
```

If a value is found for key, it is assigned to storedValue.

If data for the key is not found, storedValue will be null.

In our case, when a user found, say, the Douglas tartan at a vendor's booth and indicated this by tapping the "I found it!" button, we could do something like:

```
localStorage.setItem('douglas', 'true');
```

Then if we wanted to check if he'd already found the Douglas tartan, we could ask localStorage:

```
var isFound = localStorage.getItem('douglas');
```

localStorage JavaScript Magnets

It's time to update *scripts/app.js* (our app's main JS code) to record found tartans. The updated *app.js* file is on the next page. ⟶ Your job is to add the comment magnets above the lines of code they refer to.

You can only use each magnet once, but you might end up with some left over!

```
// Get the entry from localStorage
```

```
// Click handler for "I found it" button
```

```
// Clear all entries from localStorage
```

```
// Turn off jQM page transitions
```

```
// Create a button-styled <a> element
```

```
// Add a back button to the nested list subpages
```

```
// Check for localStorage support in the browser
```

```
// Insert the reset button into the page
```

```
// Store that this tartan was found
```

```
// Add a click handler for the "I found it!" buttons
```

```
// Call the initDevice function when the DOM is ready
```

```
// Get the ID of the clicked button
```

```
// Add a click handler for the reset button
```

```
// Update the display to show which tartans have been found
```

```
(function() {
  $(document).bind("mobileinit", function() {

    $.extend($.mobile, { defaultPageTransition: 'none' });

    $.mobile.page.prototype.options.addBackBtn = true;
  });

  var initDevice = function() {

    if (typeof(window.localStorage) == 'object') {

      $('.foundTartan').click(tartanFound);

      addResetButton();
    }
  };

  $(document).ready(initDevice);

  var tartanFound = function(event) {

    var tartanKey = $(event.currentTarget).attr('id');

    localStorage.setItem(tartanKey, 'true');
  };


  var addResetButton = function() {

    var $resetButton = $('<a></a>').attr('data-role','button').html('start Over!');

    $resetButton.click(function() {

      localStorage.clear();

    });

    $resetButton.appendTo($('#booths'));
  };
})();
```

app.js

```javascript
(function() {
    $(document).bind("mobileinit", function() {
        // Turn off jQM page transitions
        $.extend($.mobile, { defaultPageTransition: 'none' });
        // Add a back button to the nested list subpages
        $.mobile.page.prototype.options.addBackBtn = true;
    });

    var initDevice = function() {
        // Check for localStorage support in the browser
        if(typeof(window.localStorage) == 'object') {
            // Add a click handler for the "I found it!" buttons
            $('.foundTartan').click(tartanFound);

            addResetButton();
        }
    };
    // Call the initDevice function when the DOM is ready
    $(document).ready(initDevice);
    // Click handler for "I found it" button
    var tartanFound = function(event) {
        // Get the ID of the clicked button
        var tartanKey = $(event.currentTarget).attr('id');
        // Store that this tartan was found
        localStorage.setItem(tartanKey, 'true');
    };


    var addResetButton = function() {
        // Create a button-styled <a> element
        var $resetButton = $('<a></a>').attr('data-role','button').html('start Over!');
        // Add a click handler for the reset button
        $resetButton.click(function() {
            // Clear all entries from localStorage
            localStorage.clear();
        });
        // Insert the reset button into the page
        $resetButton.appendTo($('#booths'));
    };
})();
```

We're turning off the page transitions because they are slow on some Android devices.

We only add the click handler for browsers that support localStorage.

Ditto with the reset button.

The value of 'true' is sort of arbitrary. We just want to store *something*.

You can see that we're adding a button to let the user reset and start the game over.

Hey! We didn't tell you about the clear() method yet—did you figure it out?

It does what it sounds like: clears all keys and their associated values from localStorage.

app.js

Check out what a browser supports

We talked a bit about **client-side feature detection** way back in Chapter 2, and that's what we're doing again here inside of the initDevice function. By checking if window.localStorage is an object, we are detecting if the localStorage feature is supported by the browser.

```
var initDevice = function() {
    if (typeof(window.localStorage) == 'object') {
        $('.foundTartan').click(tartanFound);
        addResetButton();
    }
}
```

We perform some client-side feature detection here to make sure localStorage is supported before adding the click handler and showing the reset button.

initDevice is called on $(document).ready(). Translation: it gets executed when the page's DOM is done being initialized by jQuery.

Client-side feature detection can be quite simple, like this example, but there are also JavaScript libraries that provide detection for all sorts of features. Modernizr (*http://modernizr.com*) is a widely used example of such a tool.

We also did feature detection in Chapter 5 using WURFL device capability data. That's server-side feature detection.

But wait...the story isn't over yet

The leftover comment magnets give us a clue about what else we need to do here. We're storing found tartans, and providing a way to clear them all out, but the interface doesn't change. We need to write some **code that updates the display so players can see which tartans they've found**. Turn the page to get started.

Our leftover magnets. We need to take care of these items!

```
// Get the entry from localStorage
```

```
// Update the display to
// show which tartans
// have been found
```

BRAIN POWER

By only adding click handlers and the reset button if localStorage is supported, we are in effect setting a minimal bar for supported browsers, Chapter 4 style. Can you think of why this might be OK? Can you also think why it might not be in some cases?

Use a function to show which tartans are found

Sounds like we need another function in our JavaScript—one that can update the way the page looks depending on which tartans have been found. Let's dive in again. We're going to call our new function `refreshTartans` because it updates the appearance of the tartan listings and the detail screens depending on which tartans have been found.

Each of the nested lists—`ul.details`—in *index.html* contains information about a single vendor and tartan to be found. We can use the `id` attribute of each of those lists to determine a `key` to look for in localStorage. If there is a value of any sort for that `key`, that tartan has been found and we need to update the interface to reflect that.

Ready Bake JavaScript

So, for each ul.details in the document...

This is jQuery code. It means: iterate (loop) over each element that matches the CSS selector ul.details (<ul>s with a class of "details").

app.js

❶ Figure out the name of the key to look for in localStorage by getting the id attribute of this <ul> and prepending 'found–'

e.g., 'found–douglas'

❷ Check for that key in localStorage.

❸ Toggle the visibility and classes on some elements to reflect whether they've been found or not.

❹ Refresh the jQuery Mobile listviews in the document.

If we don't, any altered content won't be styled correctly.

```javascript
$(document).ready(initDevice);
refreshTartans = function() {
  $('ul.details').each(function() {
    var myID       = $(this).attr('id');
    var tartanKey  = 'found-' + myID;
    var foundValue = localStorage.getItem(tartanKey);
    var isFound    = Boolean (foundValue);
    $('#vendor-'+ myID).toggleClass('found', isFound);
    $('[data-url*="'+myID+'"]').toggleClass('found',isFound);
    $('#'+tartanKey).closest('li').toggle(!isFound);
  });
  $('ul').each(function() {
    if ($(this).data('listview')) {
      $(this).listview('refresh');
    }
  });
};
tartanFound = function (event) {
```

Remember, jQuery Mobile builds on top of jQuery, so we have all of jQuery's methods available to us.

What's all that toggle stuff?

toggle and toggleClass are part of jQuery. Let's take a closer look.

The toggle and toggleClass methods

`toggle` and `toggleClass` are jQuery methods. `toggle` toggles the visibility of an element; `toggleClass` toggles the application of CSS classes to an element.

By selectively applying the 'found' CSS class to certain elements using toggleClass, we can use styling to show which tartans are found...

...and we can hide the "I found it!" button when it's not needed using toggle.

(No button here!)

Let's look at that code chunk again

Remember that `localStorage.getItem(tartanKey)` will either return the value stored for that key (in our case, the string `'true'`) or `null`. We convert that to a Boolean value (`true` or `false`) so we can use it with jQuery's `toggle` and `toggleClass` methods.

We need a real Boolean value (not just the string 'true' or null) to use these methods.

isFound is true if any value exists in localStorage for this tartan; false otherwise.

```
var foundValue    = localStorage.getItem(tartanKey);
var isFound       = Boolean (foundValue);
$('#vendor-'+ myID).toggleClass('found', isFound);
$('[data-url*="'+myID+'"]').toggleClass('found',isFound);
$('#'+tartanKey).closest('li').toggle(!isFound);
```

`toggleClass` will *add* the CSS class indicated (`found`) to the elements that match the selector given if the `isFound` value is `true` (and *remove* the class if it is `false`).

Similarly, `toggle` will show the `<li>` element indicated if it's passed a Boolean with a `true` value. We're doing something a bit clever here and giving it the opposite of the current value of `isFound` (that's what `!isFound` does). Why, you might ask? Well, we want to *hide* that `<li>` if the tartan's been found (that is, `isFound` is `true`). That's the `<li>` that contains the "I found it!" button. We don't need it to show up anymore if the tartan has been found.

Summary: Add the found class to two elements and hide the `<li>` containing the "I found it!" button if the tartan has been found. Remove the class and show the button if not.

Exercise

Add the completed magnets code and the `refreshTartans` function to *scripts/app.js*. `refreshTartans` needs to be called on page initialization and any time localStorage is altered. See if you can figure out where in the code the three calls to `refreshTartans` need to go.

Exercise Solution

Here are the three places `refreshTartans` needs to be called in *app.js*.

When we initialize...

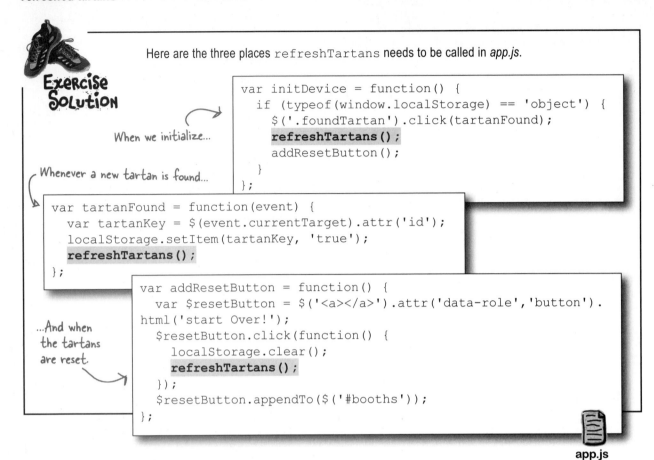

```
var initDevice = function() {
  if (typeof(window.localStorage) == 'object') {
    $('.foundTartan').click(tartanFound);
    refreshTartans();
    addResetButton();
  }
};
```

Whenever a new tartan is found...

```
var tartanFound = function(event) {
  var tartanKey = $(event.currentTarget).attr('id');
  localStorage.setItem(tartanKey, 'true');
  refreshTartans();
};
```

...And when the tartans are reset.

```
var addResetButton = function() {
  var $resetButton = $('<a></a>').attr('data-role','button').
html('start Over!');
  $resetButton.click(function() {
    localStorage.clear();
    refreshTartans();
  });
  $resetButton.appendTo($('#booths'));
};
```

app.js

Test Drive

Edit *app.js* to integrate the changes from the last several pages. Save the file and preview Tartan Hunt's *index.html* in a desktop web browser (this should work just fine). Try clicking on some tartans and their "I found it!" buttons. You should see found tartans and their detail pages receive some CSS style changes (things will turn green).

If you're having trouble, use the Web Inspector tool in Chrome or Safari, or the Error Console in Firefox, to review possible JavaScript errors. If you're really stuck, you can find a finished version of the file in *chapter8/extras/scripts/app.localStorage.js*.

You'll need to replace your app.js with this file if you want to use it.

Do this!

Go ahead and zip up the contents of the *chapter8* directory again and rebuild on PhoneGap Build. Install again on a device or emulator and try it out!

there are no
Dumb Questions

Q: **Which browsers currently support localStorage?**

A: The short answer is: most of them. But not Opera Mini. And if you're still using Internet Explorer version 7, you're out of luck there.

Q: **Do the keys have to have certain names?**

A: Both keys and the values you assign to them have to be strings. Beyond that, the sky's the limit. You can call them whatever pleases you.

Q: **How much data can I store?**

A: The W3C localStorage Specification is sort of adorably vague about this. To quote: "A mostly arbitrary limit of five megabytes per origin is recommended. Implementation feedback is welcome and will be used to update this suggestion in the future."

Most browsers provide between 2 and 5 MB. Some browsers, like Safari, prompt users to allocate more space if the allotment is used up.

Q: **Can other sites or apps access my localStorage data?**

A: No. Part of the spec is concerned with security and mandates certain things that prevent other origins (very rough translation: other sites) from accessing any localStorage data other than their own.

Q: **You said that you can only store strings in localStorage. But earlier you mentioned that you can use localStorage to store images. How could that possibly work?**

A: Strings, yes. But what's to stop us from storing rather large strings? Images can be stored as their BASE64-encoded strings and used directly as the value of `<img>` src attributes or as `url()` values in CSS background images. Browser support for data-URIs (that's what this is called) is pretty decent, with the big exception of Internet Explorer. Read more about it in this article by Nicholas Zakas: *http://bit.ly/sWe7HS*.

Q: **Wait a minute! I was just looking at the code again and noticed we're adding a back button on the nested list pages. That doesn't make sense for Androids—most Android devices have hardware back buttons already.**

A: Well spotted. The back button doesn't just feel awkward for Android, it actually closes the PhoneGap Build–generated app! That *is not good*. We'll come back to this in just a bit and fix it.

Q: **If localStorage is available in the browser to us, why are we using PhoneGap Build at all? Can't we just make this a web app?**

A: Aha! Patience! We're just about there. It's time to integrate the camera into Tartan Hunt.

You found a tartan, eh? Prove it!

☑ Set up and configure a PhoneGap Build project. Zip up the current HTML, CSS, and images; build the app; and install it on an Android device or emulator.

☑ Add the ability for players to mark which tartans they've spotted. ← *We did this with localStorage!*

☐ **Add the ability for players to save photos of the tartans they've spotted.** ↰

Now, how are we going to do this?

There's an API for that

The **W3C mediaCapture API** allows access to the device's audio, video, and camera recording capabilities. It exposes this access via the `navigator.device` and `navigator.device.capture` objects in JavaScript.

Wait a minute. If we can access the camera in the browser through the mediaCapture API, why are we doing this native thing again?

There's a spec, sure, but it's still a spring chicken.

Nobody really supports the mediaCapture API yet. If we want to access the camera with JavaScript, we are still going to need some native support.

Unleash the power of PhoneGap

Until now, we haven't actually used the PhoneGap API! PhoneGap Build has been doing *something*—it's been wrapping and packaging our web code natively. But we're not taking advantage of PhoneGap's access to device features. That's about to change!

One of the things you get as part of the native app packages PhoneGapBuild generates is *phonegap.js*, the cross-platform API that lets you get at those tasty features. To use the API, you simply need to include the script in your HTML.

Rope in PhoneGap to take pictures

PhoneGap's JavaScript API has a good amount of stuff in it, including a bunch of relevant JavaScript events. The one we really care about is one called `deviceready`, which fires when PhoneGap considers the device all suited up and ready to ride. We can look for that event from right within our own *app.js* code.

We want to bind the `deviceready` event to a callback function—and it's in that function that we'll be able to dirty our hands getting at those cameras.

We need to include phonegap.js and listen for the deviceready event. Then we're ready to rock.

By listening for the deviceready event, we can be sure the device is all ready to go!

The deep meaning of this argument is sorta complicated, but it has to do with ignoring the "capture" flow of this event and instead grabbing it as it "bubbles" up the DOM hierarchy.

```
document.addEventListener('deviceready', initPhoneGap, false);
```

Don't sweat it.

In this case, we're saying we want to execute the initPhoneGap function when the deviceready event fires.

Hey, we're going to need to write that initPhoneGap function. We'll do that soon!

Exercise

Take a whack at putting down some stakes for our PhoneGap stuff.

1 **Update index.html to add phonegap.js.**
You'll notice that *phonegap.js* doesn't exist in the *chapter8* folder. PhoneGap Build takes care of adding the correct version of this script to each of the native apps as it generates them. Add the `<script>` tag—it'll work just fine once we build the app.

2 **In app.js, create an empty function called initPhoneGap above initDevice.**
We'll fill it in shortly.

3 **Add the deviceready event listener code snippet (from above) to the very end of the initDevice function.**
That way, `initPhoneGap` will get called when the device has been initialized by PhoneGap.

Exercise Solution

Here's a look at our updated *app.js* and the inclusion of *phonegap.js* into our *index.html* file. We have a couple more things to tuck into place and then it's totally camera time.

```
(function() {
  $(document).bind("mobileinit", function() {
    $.extend($.mobile, { defaultPageTransition: 'none' });
    $.mobile.page.prototype.options.addBackBtn = true;
  });
  var initPhoneGap = function() {
  };
  var initDevice = function() {
    if (typeof(window.localStorage) == 'object') {
      $('.foundTartan').click(tartanFound);
      refreshTartans();
      addResetButton();
    }
    document.addEventListener('deviceready', initPhoneGap, false);
  };
  $(document).ready(initDevice);
```

app.js

```
<link rel="stylesheet" href="style/jquerymobile1_0_min.css" />
<link rel="stylesheet" href="style/app.css" />
<script src="phonegap.js"></script>
<script src="scripts/jquery1_7_min.js"></script>
<script src="scripts/app.js"></script>
<script src="scripts/jquerymobile1_0_min.js"></script>
```

index.html

It can feel a bit confusing because phonegap.js is not in our own codebase, but it will be available once the app is built. This will just...work.

Oh, hey, look, jQuery Mobile released version 1.0 since we last looked!

PhoneGap is almost ready for its close-up

Here we are in the same part of *app.js*, adding a few new tricks. Let's get to filling in that empty `initPhoneGap` function, shall we?

We have this variable out here so that other parts of the JS will be able to access it.

We'll keep track of whether image capture is supported with this variable. Initially: false.

```javascript
(function() {
  var imageCaptureSupported = false;
  $(document).bind("mobileinit", function() {
    $.extend($.mobile, { defaultPageTransition: 'none' });
    $.mobile.page.prototype.options.addBackBtn = true;
  });

  var initPhoneGap = function() {
    if (!navigator.device || !navigator.device.capture) { return; }
    imageCaptureSupported = true;
    if (device.platform && device.platform == 'Android') {
      $('body').addClass('android');
    }
  };

  var initDevice = function() {
```

app.js

OK, if we made it past those tests, we have mediaCapture support.

If something isn't available that we need, we shouldn't go any further here.

Cool! We can check the platform attribute on PhoneGap's device.platform and hide the back button for Androids!

There's a rule in our style/app.css that hides the back button when the <body> element has a class of <u>android</u>.

In our `initPhoneGap` function—that is, the `deviceready` callback—we're double-checking that we have access to `navigator.device.capture` and indicating that we do by setting `imageCaptureSupported` to `true`.

And then—thank goodness—we hide the unnecessary (and actually broken) back button on Android platforms. Most Android devices have hardware back buttons, and duplicating those is confusing and annoying to users. But we do need that button if we want to use the app on an iOS device. Otherwise, users would have no way to get back to the previous screen. This little chunk of code fixes our woes.

Do this!

OK, we're ready to go! Drop that preliminary stuff in to *app.js*, and it's time for lights, camera, action!

<u>Now</u> we're ready for the mediaCapture API

The PhoneGap mediaCapture API, like many of the PhoneGap device APIs, mimics the W3C specification for mediaCapture. There's a lot in that spec, but one particular method is going to help us get our job done. Let's have a meet and greet with the imageCapture method.

A function to call if it worked!

Options! For example, we want the camera to prompt the user to take just one photo, so we'll set that as an option.

```
navigator.device.capture.captureImage(successCallback, errorCallback, options);
```

captureImage launches the device's camera and captures images.

A function to call if it didn't go so well

> OK, but where does this code go? And what needs to be in those success and error functions? I'm going to need a bit of a leg up here.

OK. Let's take a look at what we're trying to accomplish. We want to fire this off when the contestant clicks on the "I found it!" button.

It should open the native camera app on the device and let the user take a single photo. Once the contestant is happy with the photo and OKs it, she's brought back to our Tartan Hunt app and two things happen: the tartan is recorded as found, and the photo just taken appears on the detail page.

The first thing we need to do is update the tartanFound function—that's the click handler for the "I found it!" button—so that it uses captureImage to get a photo from the user's camera. Let's start there!

How will we handle the success?

When a player clicks on the "I found it!" button—assuming she has a device that includes a camera and is supported by PhoneGap Build's mediaCapture—we'll want to kick off `captureImage`.

Remember from our meet and greet that the first argument to `captureImage` is a function that will get called if stuff goes well. In concept, our success callback function will need to look something like this:

Hmmmm...what is this mediaFiles thing?

mediaFiles[0].fullPath gives us the path to the first image in the mediaFiles array.

```
function itWorked(mediaFiles) {
    localStorage.setItem(tartanKey, mediaFiles[0].fullPath);
}
```

Because we'll be setting an option to only take one photo (more on that in a moment), there should only be a single item in that array, anyway.

When `captureImage` is successful, it calls the defined success callback and passes it a list (JavaScript array) of `MediaFile` objects. A `MediaFile` doesn't contain a file; instead, it contains a bunch of metadata about it. Don't despair. It has what we need—the **path to the image file on the device's filesystem**. And instead of our dull old value of `true`, we can save the path to that image in localStorage for later use.

And what if it goes wrong?

If the camera situation doesn't work out so well—say the user cancels out of the camera operation, or something just goes awry—we need to have an error callback function as well. Given that a failure to snap a photo isn't exactly cause for full-scale panic, we're going to keep it simple: we'll just log it to the console should some curious soul be all into debugging it. So, something like this:

This is just an example of an error callback.

```
function ohSad(error) {
    console.log(error);
}
```

It always looks a bit different in real life

Ready to meet the expanded `tartanFound` function? Remember, this
is the function that gets executed when players click on the "I found it!"
button for a given tartan. Well, here it is. We admit, our updates here
look a tiny bit different than the examples we just showed you.

We set imageCaptureSupported in the
initPhoneGap function, remember?

if mediaCapture
is supported and
available, go
off and take
a photo.

For devices
without the
support, just
mark the
tartan as
found by using
our lame old
'true' value.

```javascript
var tartanFound = function(event) {
  var tartanKey = $(event.currentTarget).attr('id');
  if(imageCaptureSupported) {
    navigator.device.capture.captureImage(function(mediaFiles) {
      localStorage.setItem(tartanKey, mediaFiles[0].fullPath);
      refreshTartans();
    }, captureError, {limit:1});
  }
  else {
    localStorage.setItem(tartanKey, 'true');
    refreshTartans();
  }
};
var captureError = function(error) { console.log(error);  }
addResetButton = function() {
```

Here's where we set the option to
limit the # of photos taken to 1.

Our error callback.

app.js

What's going on? That looks
different than the captureImage
method you talked about...

**Because we need the current,
contextual value of `tartanKey`
available to us, we're using
an anonymous function for our
success callback.**

It's just a bit anonymous

Instead of giving `captureImage` the name of a success callback function, we can instead define the whole function right there.

What's the point, you ask? See how we assign the `id` attribute of the element that was clicked on (`event.currentTarget`—that is, the "I found it!" button) to the `tartanKey` variable? By defining the success callback as an ***anonymous function*** here, we have access to the relevant value of `tartanKey` based upon which button was clicked. If we used a function defined outside of the `tartanFound` function, we wouldn't have access to this value in the current context.

tartanKey is the id attribute of the button that was clicked.

The highlighted code is the success callback function.

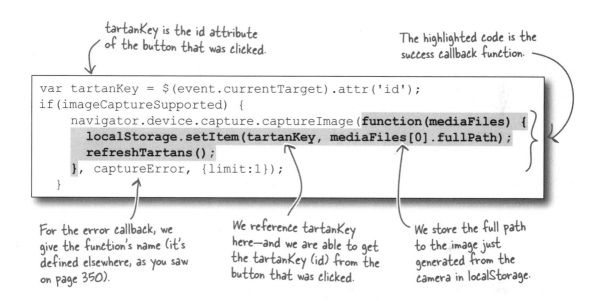

```
var tartanKey = $(event.currentTarget).attr('id');
if(imageCaptureSupported) {
    navigator.device.capture.captureImage(function(mediaFiles) {
        localStorage.setItem(tartanKey, mediaFiles[0].fullPath);
        refreshTartans();
    }, captureError, {limit:1});
}
```

For the error callback, we give the function's name (it's defined elsewhere, as you saw on page 350).

We reference tartanKey here—and we are able to get the tartanKey (id) from the button that was clicked.

We store the full path to the image just generated from the camera in localStorage.

 **BRAIN POWER**

In our code, we update localStorage from within the **imageCapture** success function. If we fail to get a photo for whatever reason, the tartan is not marked as found.

Do you think this is OK? Is there a better way to handle this?

OK, I see that we're storing the path to the image in localStorage. But how do we make use of that?

Glad you asked. We need to update the `refreshTartans` function.

If a user has snapped a photo of a given tartan, let's display that on the detail page for that vendor's booth.

The important thing to know is that we can use the path we stored as the `src` attribute of an `img` element. Not so hard.

Ready Bake JavaScript

When we have a photo path in localStorage, create a jQuery <img> element, use the stored path as the src, and stick it in a new list element on the page.

```
var refreshTartans = function() {
  $('ul.details').each(function() {
    var myID         = $(this).attr('id');
    var tartanKey    = 'found-' + myID;
    var foundValue   = localStorage.getItem(tartanKey);
    var isFound      = Boolean (foundValue);
    $('#vendor-'+ myID).toggleClass('found', isFound);
    $('[data-url*="'+ myID +'"]').toggleClass('found', isFound);
    $('#'+tartanKey).closest('li').toggle(!isFound);
    var hasPhoto     = (isFound && foundValue != 'true');
    if (hasPhoto) {
      if (!$(this).find('.tartanImage').length) {
        var $tartanHolder = $('<p></p>').append($('<img>').attr({
          'src'      : foundValue,
          'class'    : 'tartanImage'
        }));
        $(this).append('<li data-role="list-divider">My Photo of the Tartan!</li>');
        $('<li></li>').append($tartanHolder).appendTo($(this));
      }
    }
  });
  $('ul').each(function() {
    if ($(this).data('listview')) { $(this).listview('refresh'); }
  });
};
```

If there is a stored value for this tartan and it is NOT the string 'true', it must be a photo.

Using the stored path as the src for the img

Test Drive

OK, are you ready? That was a bit of munging around in JavaScript, but the resulting *app.js* is about 75 lines long. We think that's pretty concise for an entire app!

One last thing!

A little tip from us: you'll want to add these two lines to your *config.xml* file. The orientation preference keeps devices—especially emulators—from going into landscape mode when you're launching the camera app. The second line indicates to PhoneGap that we intend to use the camera feature of the API; it will map to the correct Android **permission setting.**

```xml
<preference name="orientation" value="portrait" />
<feature name="http://api.phonegap.com/1.0/camera" />
```

config.xml

OK. Take a deep breath and find a moment of peace after the last several pages' onslaught of code. Make sure you've integrated all of the changes into *app.js* and saved the change to *config.xml*. When you're feeling ready, zip up the *chapter8* folder again, head over to PhoneGap Build, and upload the updated code.

Once the build process is complete, download the APK file and install it on your emulator or device.

← Don't forget to uninstall first!

If you install the app on an emulator and the camera is being kind of cranky, it might not be such a big deal.

We've found that the cameras for the emulators for versions of Android before 2.3 can be pretty flaky. Sometimes they lock up or crash. We recommend using a newer version of Android for your AVD (Android virtual device).

Even on newer emulators, the camera experience isn't exactly a thrill a minute. Some emulators just show a white screen. Others have a retro-corny little animation. But they do successfully generate *some* sort of image. Usually.

Really stuck?

You can find the final version of *app.js* in *extras/scripts/app.final.js*. The final version of the Android app APK file can be found at *http://hf-mw.com/ch8/TartanHunt.apk*.

If you have a friend with an Android, now might be the time to call in a favor. The camera works way better on a real device.

We nailed it!

☑ Set up and configure a PhoneGap Build project. Zip up the current HTML, CSS, and images; build the app; and install it on an Android device or emulator.

☑ Add the ability for players to mark which tartans they've spotted.

☑ Add the ability for players to save photos of the tartans they've spotted.

Who knew? We can turn our HTML5 skills into native apps!

BULLET POINTS

- The mobile web has come a long way, baby. But there are still a **number of things we don't have access to in the browser**.

- A **hybrid application** approach involves **creating native apps from code written with HTML5, CSS, and JavaScript standards**. Hybrid apps can reduce native development costs and complexity because code can be shared across platforms.

- **PhoneGap is an HTML5 platform for building native apps**. It was created by Vancouver-based agency Nitobi. Nitobi was acquired by Adobe in the fall of 2011.

- **PhoneGap Build** is a service that lets you build your PhoneGap projects in a simple web interface.

- PhoneGap Build projects are arranged like **W3C web widgets**. They require, at minimum, a start file (*index.html*) and a configuration file (*config.xml*).

- The **W3C localStorage API** allows for straightforward, **client-side storage of key-value string data**. We used it to denote which tartans the players have found.

- *phonegap.js* is automatically added to PhoneGap Build projects and gives us access to the **PhoneGap JavaScript API**. We saw how to listen for the `deviceready` **event** from PhoneGap so that we know the device features are ready for us to start having fun with them.

- To add camera support to our app, we used PhoneGap's **mediaCapture API**, which is modeled after the W3C mediaCapture API.

- We used the `navigator.device.capture.captureImage` method to spawn the native camera app and take a single picture.

- **We created a cross-platform native app with only about 75 lines of JavaScript and a single HTML page!**

9 how to be future friendly

Make (some) sense of the chaos

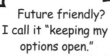

Future friendly? I call it "keeping my options open."

Responsive Web Design. Device detection. Mobile web apps. PhoneGap. Wait…which one should we use?

There are an overwhelming number of ways to develop for the mobile web.

Often, projects will involve **multiple techniques used in combination**. There
is no single right answer. But don't worry. The key is to learn to go with the flow.
Embrace the uncertainty. Adopt a **future-friendly mindset** and ride the wave,
confident that you're flexible and ready to adapt to whatever the future holds.

Now what?

We've covered a lot of ground—from sites to apps, from Responsive Web Design to device detection. There's a ton of different ways to build for mobile. How in the world do you choose?

Mobile Web Strategies

Responsive Web Design

Mobile-First Responsive Web Design

Progressive Enhancement

Separate Mobile Sites

Device Detection

Device Classes

Mobile Web Apps

jQuery Mobile

Offline Support

Super Mobile Web Apps

PhoneGap/Apache Cordova

We'd like to use mobile-first Responsive Web Design, but there's no way we can use a third-party server for every image, and none of the current JavaScript solutions seem reliable. Is it a lost cause?

Every day there are new devices coming out. Device detection seems like an unwinnable arms race.

What about tablets? Do we have to wait for Head First Tablet Web to learn how to build web pages for the iPad?

We need a site and we need apps. This is going to cost a fortune for testing alone.

It's complicated

There's no way around it. Developing for the Web has become a lot more complicated as the number of devices increases. Worse, it's likely to become more difficult before it gets better.

The rate of change is unprecedented. Not only are there new devices introduced regularly, but the technology and software in those devices changes just as fast.

Even the way we interact with computers is being challenged as touch interfaces, camera input, and voice sensors show us new ways to get things done.

So what do we do about it? How can we design compelling experiences in the face of such uncertainty?

Time to dispel our collective illusions of control

We've been fooling ourselves for quite some time into believing we have control over the Web.

These illusions are ingrained in our tools and our processes. Often, we start projects by creating mockups in Photoshop. The first prompt in Photoshop asks us what size canvas we would like to build.

But there is no one-size-fits-all canvas. Not even for the desktop.

And the sooner we come to grips with this reality, the sooner we can start learning how to build websites and apps that adapt to their environment and users.

The very first prompt in Photoshop contributes to the illusion that the Web has a fixed width.

We need a different mindset—
one that accepts diversity
and keeps an eye on adapting
to whatever unknowns the
future may bring.

A future-friendly manifesto

You're not alone in being overwhelmed. A group of mobile developers got together and brainstormed ways to deal with the ever-changing landscape of the Web. The output of the gathering is this future-friendly manifesto.

Find the manifesto at http://futurefriend.ly.

FUTURE ☆ FRIENDLY

In today's incredibly exciting yet overwhelming world of connected digital devices, these are the truths we hold to be self-evident:

Disruption will only accelerate. The quantity and diversity of connected devices—many of which we haven't imagined yet—will explode, as will the quantity and diversity of the people around the world who use them. **Our existing standards, workflows, and infrastructure won't hold up.** Today's onslaught of devices is already pushing them to the breaking point. They can't withstand what's ahead. **Proprietary solutions will dominate at first.** Innovation necessarily precedes standardization. Technologists will scramble to these solutions before realizing (yet again) that a standardized platform is needed to maintain sanity. **The standards process will be painfully slow.** We will struggle with (and eventually agree upon) appropriate standards. During this period, the web will fall even further behind proprietary solutions.

---

* **A NEW HOPE** *

But there's hope. While we can't know exactly what the future will bring, we can:

(1) Acknowledge and embrace unpredictability.

(2) Think and behave in a future-friendly way .

(3) Help others do the same.

The future is ours to make —friendly.

---

* **UNDERSIGNUMS** *

LUKE WROBLEWSKI	SCOTT JENSON
BRAD FROST	JEREMY KEITH
LYZA D. GARDNER	SCOTT JEHL
STEPHANIE RIEGER	JASON GRIGSBY
BRYAN RIEGER	JOSH CLARK

* Home * Thinking * Resources *

We're Creative Commons friendly. Talk to us.

If you can't be future proof, be future friendly

With so much uncertainty about where the Web will go in the future, it's imperative that we build sites and apps that are as flexible as possible. This means ensuring that we keep an eye on the future while we build in the present.

Device proliferation isn't making it easy for us. With the complexity we face, it's more tempting than ever to cut corners and build something that works today, on a handful of devices, and leave worrying about the universal access and future devices for another day.

Web development has always required **compromises**. The trick is to find ways to compromise without locking up your content and data in a way that cannot be retrieved and transformed in the future.

There are no silver bullets

For example, none of the solutions for images in mobile-first Responsive Web Design is ideal. The reason we chose Sencha.io Src—despite the fact that it relies on device detection—was because the HTML markup remained untouched. We can drop Sencha.io Src in now and quickly replace it if a better solution emerges.

Likewise, if on occasion you need to do something that isn't supported in browsers yet, choose technologies like PhoneGap that take their cues from where standards are headed instead of picking proprietary solutions that will have short life spans.

The foundation for future success is semantic markup and progressive enhancement. Keep a focus on those principles, and you'll be in good shape.

Test Drive

Future-friendly thinking has gone into Tartan Hunt from Chapter 8 even though it was built to run as a native app. Grab the Tartan Hunt code and open up *index.html* in a desktop browser.

Does the app work? What, if anything, is missing?

If you need a copy of the final code, you can download it at *http://hf-mw.com/ch9/chapter9.zip*.

App today, web page tomorrow

Even though Tartan Hunt was designed to be a native app, the app works in the browser. Tartans that have been found are recorded and highlighted in green. The only thing missing is the camera.

And because we designed it in a future-friendly manner, using proposed W3C standards, there's a good chance that the pieces of the app that don't work now will start working in the future.

Remove PhoneGap references

Behind the scenes, there are two minor tweaks that would make the app work better in the browser going forward.

1 **Remove the reference to phonegap.js.**
When browser nirvana arrives and the gap between native and web has closed, we won't need the *phonegap.js* library. Nothing breaks by leaving the reference to *phonegap.js*, but the browser gets a file not found (404) error for it. So let's remove it.

> Remove this line from index.html.

```
<script src="phonegap.js"></script>
```

Tactics like these are at the core of future-friendly thinking...

2 **Change the page initialization functions.**
PhoneGap, jQuery, and jQuery Mobile like to arm-wrestle over the ordering of page initialization and creation JavaScript events. In short, you can't rely on them to fire in a particular order, so some of the Tartan Hunt code is written to force them to behave.

But don't worry about the over-the-top tricks we did to get the JavaScript in line. All you need to do is change one line to fix it up.

> Change this...

```
document.addEventListener('deviceready', initPhoneGap, false);
```

> ...to this.

```
initPhoneGap();
```

> BTW, it would be better to give this function a name that doesn't reference PhoneGap. (Oops!)

The Tartan Hunt is ready to go once browsers support the mediaCapture API!

It's a long journey: Here are some guideposts

Looking for ways to translate the future-friendly manifesto into action? Here are some of ideas from *http://futurefriend.ly* to noodle on. These aren't prescriptions, because no one knows what the future will bring, but they are areas to watch for and think about in your work.

★ LASER FOCUS ★

We can't be all things on **all** devices. To manage in a world of ever-increasing device complexity, we need to focus on what matters most to our customers and businesses. Not by building lowest common-denominator solutions but by creating meaningful content and services. People are also increasingly tired of excessive noise and finding ways to simplify things for themselves. Focus your service before your customers and increasing diversity do it for you.

★ ORBIT AROUND DATA ★

An ecosystem of devices demands to be interoperable, and robust data exchange is the easiest way to get going. Be responsive to existing and emerging opportunities by defining your data in a way that:

- Enables multiple (flexible) forms of access and notifications
- Uses standards to be interoperable
- Focuses on long term integrity
- Includes meaningful and permanent references to all content
- Supports both read and write operations

★ UNIVERSAL CONTENT ★

Well-structured content is now an essential part of art direction. Consider how it can flow into a variety of containers by being mindful of their constraints and capabilities. Be bold and explore new possibilities but know the future is likely to head in many directions.

Highly capable smart devices, simple constrained devices, interoperable devices and (a whole lot) more are part of our future. Structure and store your content accordingly.

★ UNKNOWN VESSEL, IDENTIFY ★

Reacting to every device variance makes inclusive design extremely challenging. A high-level, close-enough set of standards for device types can simplify the process of adaptation. Additional, detailed profile information can supplement these standards.

A taxonomy of device types can align manufacturers today while still allowing new devices types to emerge tomorrow.

★ COMMAND YOUR FLEET ★

Having a wide range of devices in our lives enables us to distribute tasks and information between them. When an experience is managed within a device collection, each device can tackle the interactions it does best. This negates the need to tailor all aspects of a service to every device and allows us to work within an ecosystem of device capabilities instead.

This one's a bit out there. Imagine that your watch is a second screen for your phone.

Match each lesson from the book to a future-friendly guidepost.
Multiple lessons may apply to each concept.

Lesson from the book	Future-friendly thinking

Content like water (Chapter 1)   **Laser focus**

Mobile first (Chapter 2)

Client-side detection (Chapter 6)   **Orbit around data**

Where to draw the line (Chapter 4)

Device detection (Chapter 5)   **Universal content**

Semantic markup (Chapters 2 and 6)

Unique URL support (Chapter 6)   **Unknown vessel, identify**

Responsive Web Design (Chapter 1)

Device classes (Chapter 5)   **Command your fleet**

WHO DOES WHAT? SOLUTION

You could make the case that some of these lessons use other future-friendly guideposts as well. Here's what we came up with.

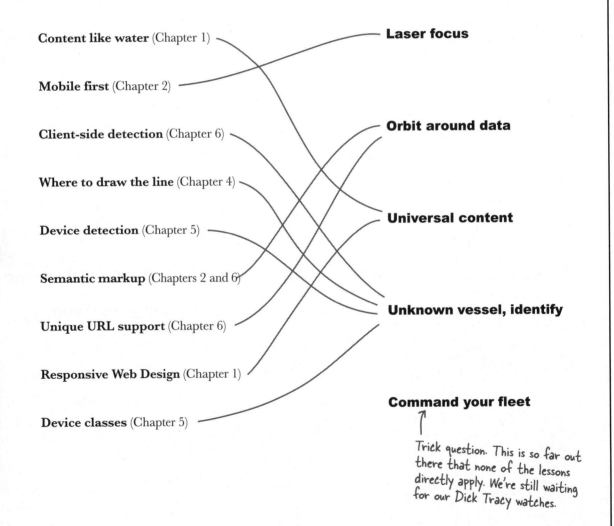

Lesson from the book

Future-friendly thinking

Content like water (Chapter 1)

Mobile first (Chapter 2)

Client-side detection (Chapter 6)

Where to draw the line (Chapter 4)

Device detection (Chapter 5)

Semantic markup (Chapters 2 and 6)

Unique URL support (Chapter 6)

Responsive Web Design (Chapter 1)

Device classes (Chapter 5)

Laser focus

Orbit around data

Universal content

Unknown vessel, identify

Command your fleet

Trick question. This is so far out there that none of the lessons directly apply. We're still waiting for our Dick Tracy watches.

Mix up a batch of mobile goodness

Exercise

Baking a tasty mobile treat means combining ingredients to concoct new deliciousness. What ingredients would take these dishes to the next level and make them more future friendly? Write them down on the recipe cards.

Ingredients

Universal content

Don't try to mimic a native app.

Client-side device detection

Use hCard microformat and address tag.

hCard is a standard set of markup for an address. Learn more at http://microformats.org/wiki/hcard.

HTML5 semantic elements (article, sections, etc.)

Image tags with `alt` attributes for accessibility

Links that set a cookie for user preference

Creature Comforts

Problems

- Needs a way to get from the mobile site to the desktop one.
- Mobile site doesn't have all of the content of the desktop site.

Tartanator

Problems

- Runs slowly on BlackBerry 5.0.
- Scrolling is clumsy and slow.
- There are two back buttons (one from the browser and one that the app created).
- The tartans on the detail page are content, but use CSS background images.

Splendid Walrus

Problems

- All of the content is organized in `<div>`s.
- The address is just text separated by `<br />` tags. The markup doesn't have any semantic meaning.

Exercise Solution

Here's what we came up with. Did you think of other ways to improve these projects and make them more future friendly?

Yes, BB 5.0 supports the needed JavaScript features. It just does it very slowly. Detecting BB 5.0 and giving it the version without jQuery mobile will be a better experience.

Creature Comforts

Problems

- Needs a way to get from the mobile site to the desktop one.
- Mobile site doesn't have all of the content of the desktop site.

If you have to build separate sites, let people pick which site they want to use.

Links that set a cookie for user preference

Universal content

Even with separate sites, people will want to do everything they can on the desktop site.

Tartanator

Problems

- Runs slowly on BlackBerry 5.0.
- Scrolling is clumsy and slow.
- There are two back buttons (one from the browser and one that the app created).
- The tartans on the detail page are content, but use CSS background images.

Client-side device detection

Don't try to mimic a native app.

Image tags with alt attributes for accessibility

Move from CSS images to img tags.

Duplicate back buttons and slow scrolling come from trying to recreate native in the browser. If it isn't in the App Store, why mimic an app?

Our markup would contain more meaning if we used HTML5 elements.

Splendid Walrus

Problems

- All of the content is organized in `<div>`s.
- The address is just text separated by `<br />` tags. The markup doesn't have any semantic meaning.

HTML5 semantic elements (article, sections, etc.)

Use hCard microformats and address tag.

We only mentioned microformats in passing. They add semantic meaning. Some browsers and search engines will recognize microformats in the page and use that information to provide additional features.

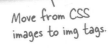

Look toward the future

Don't fret over what devices and browsers the future may throw at you. You've got lots of different tools in your tool belt now. From small to large screens, from mobile phones to Internet-enabled refrigerators, you're ready to handle anything.

With the solid foundation of web standards and progressive enhancement, you can build sites and apps that are accessible to more people than ever.

Embrace the unpredictability of what the Web will become. It is this very unpredictability that makes mobile full of opportunity—not to mention, a lot of fun.

So go forth. Be mobile. Build the future!

The future is ours to make...friendly.

i leftovers

The top six things
(we didn't cover)

Ever feel like something's missing? We know what you mean... Just when you thought you were done, there's more. We couldn't leave you without a few extra details, things we just couldn't fit into the rest of the book. At least, not if you want to be able to carry this book around without a metallic case and caster wheels on the bottom. So take a peek and see what you (still) might be missing out on.

#1. Testing on mobile devices

Mobile testing sucks. There, we said it. There's no way to sugarcoat it. When one phone model behaves quite differently depending on which carrier network it is on, you know you're on the bleeding edge and you can't assume anything.

Here are some of the things we've done to try to keep our sanity.

① Start with valid code in a desktop browser.
If it breaks in the desktop browser, it will also break on mobile. Might as well start where you're more comfortable and the tools are better. Be sure to validate your code to help you find errors early.

② Use mobile emulators and simulators.
Nearly every mobile platform provides an emulator or a simulator. Maximiliano Firtman put together the ultimate list of emulators and simulators for his book ***Programming the Mobile Web***. He updates the list regularly at *http://www.mobilexweb.com/emulators*.

Max's book contains an awesome reference on mobile emulators and simulators.

③ Invest in a small number of devices.
Buying a few phones is unavoidable. Which phones to buy should be guided by the kinds of projects you do and the markets you serve. Find out what key stakeholders will use to review your work and be sure to get those devices as well. Include the cost of buying devices in the budget for every project.

Peter-Paul Koch wrote an A List Apart article with some good tips for selecting phones if you're on a budget: www.alistapart.com/articles/ smartphone-browser-landscape/.

④ Beg, borrow, and steal.
Connect with others doing mobile development and share devices. Consider creating a central wiki of devices in your community so people can easily find and share devices. Better yet, go big and build a community device testing lab like the one we're building in Portland.

Fantastic news! Sue said we can borrow her Samsung Fascinate for testing and wondered if we had a Kindle Fire she could borrow. I'm meeting her tomorrow to swap devices.

> Why yes, I am interested in this phone and the other 20 I loaded web pages on.

⑤ Visit your local mobile testing center.

Nearly every city has a mobile device testing center. You may refer to them by their more common name: carrier stores.

For example, your local Verizon store

Most carrier stores are good about letting people try devices. They're unlikely to let you move your office to their store for the day, but they won't stop you from testing your website on multiple devices.

Be honest about what you're doing and thank them for their help. You'll find that the salespeople will also give you good insight into what devices are selling well and will likely be interested in your work.

⑥ Remote device testing services.

Sometimes you really need to test a specific scenario. For example, you need one particular model of phone that is only available in a certain part of the world and is exclusive to one carrier. In these cases, remote device testing services are the way to go.

Device Anywhere (*http://deviceanywhere.com*) and Perfecto Mobile (*http://perfectomobile.com*) provide remote access to real phones in data centers around the world. Having data centers around the world means that you can test on a specific phone running on the local wireless provider and see the true experience that someone using that phone in that country would see.

Phones are opened up and wired into servers at Device Anywhere's San Mateo, California, data center. You can control these phones from anywhere in the world.

Both services charge an hourly rate, which means you need to be efficient or you can rack up an expensive testing bill.

⑦ Prioritize your testing.

Even if you had access to every device ever made, there would not be enough time to test on all of them. Pick representative devices, and prioritize your testing based on the decisions you made early in the project about the devices your customers are most likely to use.

#2. Remote debugging

We already talked about how difficult it is to see what's going on in a mobile browser. But even if you could see what was happening, it's hard to imagine being able to do much development on tiny screens.

Remote debugging solves this problem by connecting a mobile browser to a desktop debugging tool, which allows you to see what's going on in the mobile browser.

WEb INspector REmote (weinre)

There a few different options for remote debugging, but the one that can be used with the most devices and browsers is weinre (pronounced *winery*). weinre is an open source project started by WebKit contributor Patrick Mueller and later brought under the PhoneGap umbrella.

Download the weinre project at http://phonegap.github.com/weinre/.

How weinre works

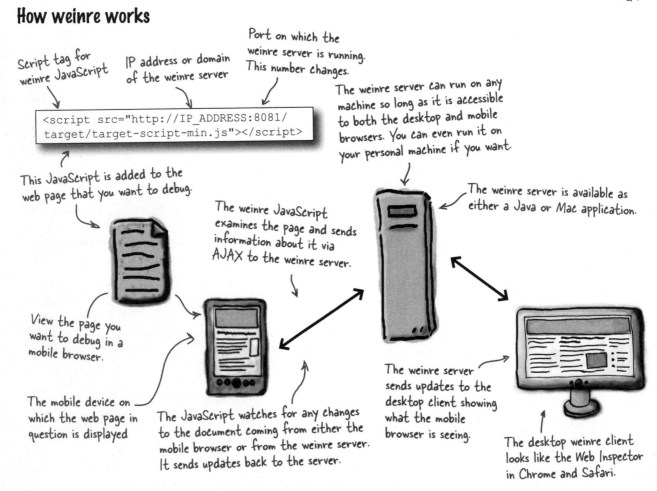

Script tag for weinre JavaScript

IP address or domain of the weinre server

Port on which the weinre server is running. This number changes.

```
<script src="http://IP_ADDRESS:8081/
target/target-script-min.js"></script>
```

This JavaScript is added to the web page that you want to debug.

View the page you want to debug in a mobile browser.

The mobile device on which the web page in question is displayed

The weinre JavaScript examines the page and sends information about it via AJAX to the weinre server.

The JavaScript watches for any changes to the document coming from either the mobile browser or from the weinre server. It sends updates back to the server.

The weinre server can run on any machine so long as it is accessible to both the desktop and mobile browsers. You can even run it on your personal machine if you want.

The weinre server is available as either a Java or Mac application.

The weinre server sends updates to the desktop client showing what the mobile browser is seeing.

The desktop weinre client looks like the Web Inspector in Chrome and Safari.

Running your weinre server

Running a weinre server isn't rocket surgery, but it isn't dead simple either. Fortunately, the kind folks at PhoneGap have set up a public weinre server that is a snap to use. All you need is a desktop and a mobile browser and access to the Web.

> One disadvantage of using the public server is the fact that it's open to anyone. Pick a guid others won't guess easily.

1 **Visit debug.phonegap.com using Chrome or Safari.**
The page is broken down into three easy steps. For Step 1, you need to provide a *guid* (globally unique identifier). Basically, you want to pick a word or phrase that will create your own version of the weinre test service so you don't have another person trying to use the same test instance.

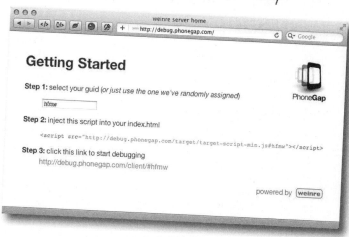

2 **Create an HTML document to test with.**
Create a new HTML document using the markup below and save it as *weinre.html*. Add the `<script>` tag provided by debug.phonegap.com and put the updated file on a public web server.

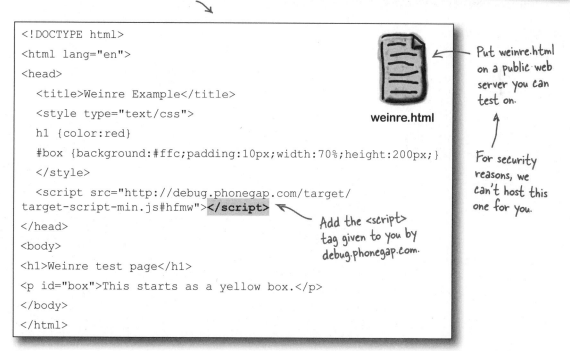

```
<!DOCTYPE html>
<html lang="en">
<head>
  <title>Weinre Example</title>
  <style type="text/css">
  h1 {color:red}
  #box {background:#ffc;padding:10px;width:70%;height:200px;}
  </style>
  <script src="http://debug.phonegap.com/target/
target-script-min.js#hfmw"></script>
</head>
<body>
<h1>Weinre test page</h1>
<p id="box">This starts as a yellow box.</p>
</body>
</html>
```

weinre.html

> Put weinre.html on a public web server you can test on.

> For security reasons, we can't host this one for you.

> Add the `<script>` tag given to you by debug.phonegap.com.

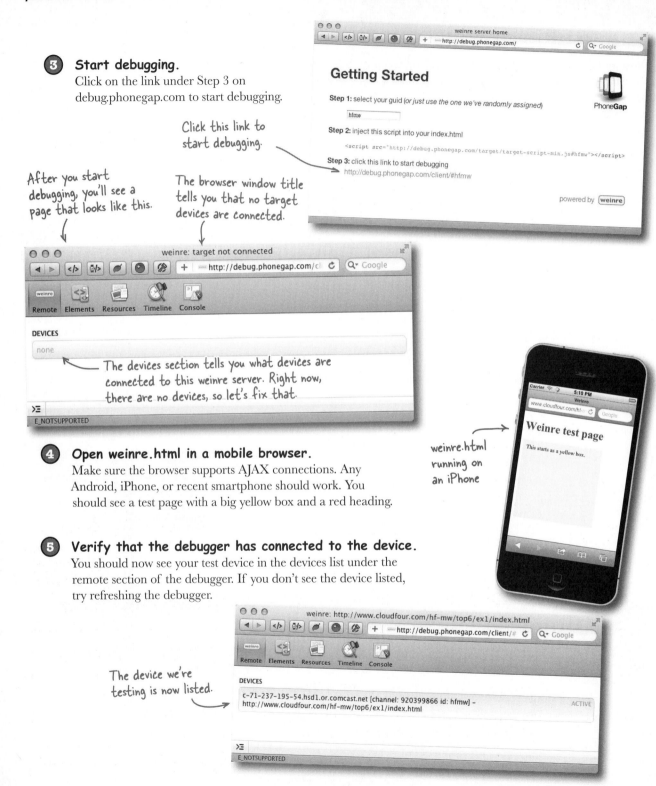

③ **Start debugging.**
Click on the link under Step 3 on debug.phonegap.com to start debugging.

Getting Started

Step 1: select your guid (*or just use the one we've randomly assigned*)

hfmw

Step 2: inject this script into your index.html

```
<script src="http://debug.phonegap.com/target/target-script-min.js#hfmw"></script>
```

Step 3: click this link to start debugging
http://debug.phonegap.com/client/#hfmw

powered by weinre

Click this link to start debugging.

After you start debugging, you'll see a page that looks like this.

The browser window title tells you that no target devices are connected.

weinre: target not connected

http://debug.phonegap.com/cl

Remote Elements Resources Timeline Console

DEVICES

The devices section tells you what devices are connected to this weinre server. Right now, there are no devices, so let's fix that.

E_NOTSUPPORTED

④ **Open weinre.html in a mobile browser.**
Make sure the browser supports AJAX connections. Any Android, iPhone, or recent smartphone should work. You should see a test page with a big yellow box and a red heading.

weinre.html running on an iPhone

Weinre test page

This starts as a yellow box.

⑤ **Verify that the debugger has connected to the device.**
You should now see your test device in the devices list under the remote section of the debugger. If you don't see the device listed, try refreshing the debugger.

weinre: http://www.cloudfour.com/hf-mw/top6/ex1/index.html

http://debug.phonegap.com/client/#

Remote Elements Resources Timeline Console

The device we're testing is now listed.

DEVICES

c-71-237-195-54.hsd1.or.comcast.net [channel: 920399866 id: hfmw] –
http://www.cloudfour.com/hf-mw/top6/ex1/index.html   ACTIVE

E_NOTSUPPORTED

Explore the weinre inspector

Now that the connection has been established, you're looking at a slightly simpler version of the Web Inspector provided by Google Chrome and Safari.

The markup for the page. Click on any element to see styles and properties on the right.

Any resources used for the page, including localStorage and cookies

Timeline shows events that trigger script behavior and how long they take.

The JavaScript console allows you to issue direct JavaScript instructions to the mobile browser.

Shows a list of the connected devices

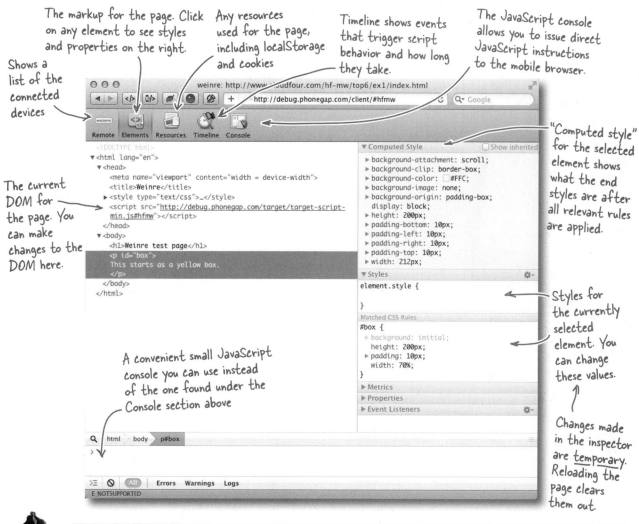

The current DOM for the page. You can make changes to the DOM here.

"Computed style" for the selected element shows what the end styles are after all relevant rules are applied.

Styles for the currently selected element. You can change these values.

A convenient small JavaScript console you can use instead of the one found under the Console section above

Changes made in the inspector are _temporary_. Reloading the page clears them out.

Exercise

You thought you were done with exercises, eh? So did we, but this is a fun one. Make changes to the web page using the inspector and watch them show up on your phone.

1. Hover over the HTML tags on the Elements tab. What happens on the mobile browser?

2. Change the background color from yellow to another color using the inspector.

3. Use the JavaScript console to trigger an alert on the mobile phone.

Exercise Solution

There's something magical about making a change in the weinre inspector and watching the change instantly appear on the mobile browser.

1. Hover over the HTML tags on the Elements tab. What happens on the mobile browser?

The elements are highlighted on the mobile browser as you hover over them on the desktop remote inspector.

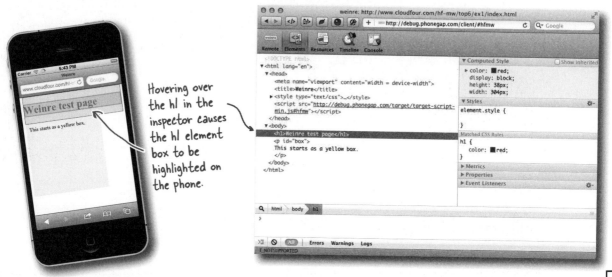

Hovering over the h1 in the inspector causes the h1 element box to be highlighted on the phone.

2. Change the background color from yellow to another color using the inspector.

Click on the <p> tag for the box. Edit the background-color property in the matched CSS rules section.

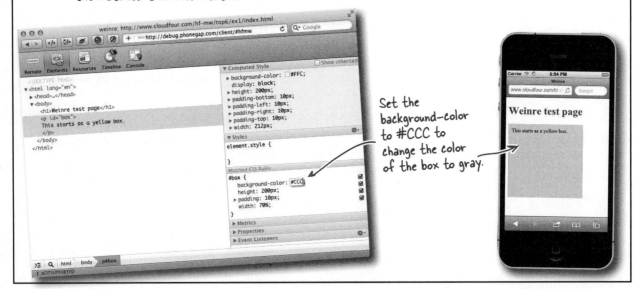

Set the background-color to #CCC to change the color of the box to gray.

3. Use the JavaScript console to trigger an alert on the mobile phone.

Code for a simple Hello World JavaScript alert

```
alert('Hello world!');
```

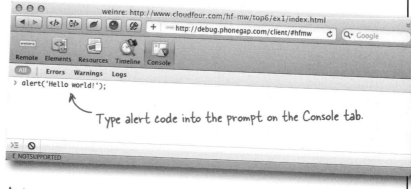

Type alert code into the prompt on the Console tab.

And, sure enough, the alert shows up on the mobile phone.

there are no Dumb Questions

Q: Is debug.phonegap.com secure? Why won't you host a test page?

A: Any security issue would be rare. Someone would need to know the URL of your weinre server and that you were using it at that very moment so he could send nefarious JavaScript to your browser.

As we said, this is pretty unlikely unless you, say, publish the URL for the weinre server in a book, host a test page, and tell everyone to go use the page. Publishing the page would make it a target for naughty people.

Q: You mentioned other debuggers; what are they?

A: Opera Dragonfly (*http://opera.com/dragonfly/*) has a remote debugger that can be used with Opera browsers. The BlackBerry Playbook and BlackBerry OS since version 7 have built-in support for remote debugging. WebKit itself contains the tools to do remote debugging, but it is turned off in most browsers. The day before we finished this section, Maximiliano Firtman created iWebInspector (*http://iwebinspector.com*), a remote debugger for iOS. We haven't tested it yet.

Q: Does Adobe's purchase of Nitobi, the folks behind PhoneGap, mean that debug.phonegap.com will go away?

A: We've been assured that the service isn't going anywhere. If it does, you can still download weinre and run it on your local machine.

#3. Determine which browsers support what

It's all well and good to use progressive enhancement to support more capable browsers, but does it make sense to spend a bunch of time building something to use a browser feature that only a handful of devices can use?

At some point, you just want to know which browsers will be able to take advantage of the fancy gyroscope-based navigation you built.

Don't do this. Navigation controlled by the gyroscope is a terrible idea! 100 times worse than the blink tag. Forget we mentioned it.

Lists of which browsers support what

These sites seek to catalog browsers and what features they support.

Answers the question: "When can I use..."

caniuse.com

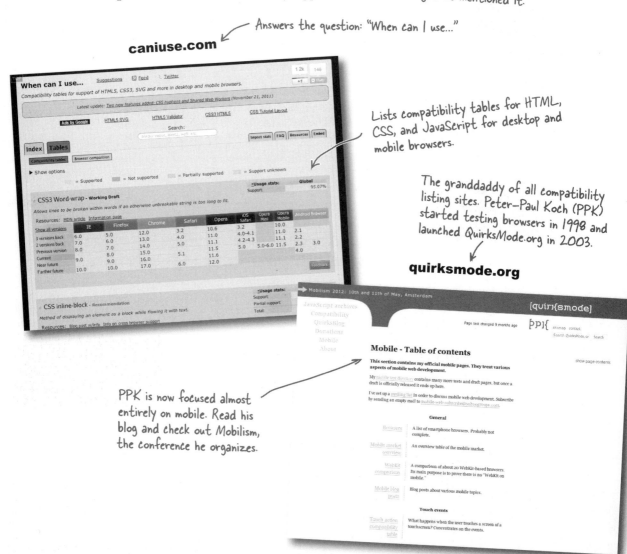

Lists compatibility tables for HTML, CSS, and JavaScript for desktop and mobile browsers.

The granddaddy of all compatibility listing sites. Peter-Paul Koch (PPK) started testing browsers in 1998 and launched QuirksMode.org in 2003.

quirksmode.org

PPK is now focused almost entirely on mobile. Read his blog and check out Mobilism, the conference he organizes.

Test what your browser supports

These sites are more helpful when you have access to a browser and you want to know what it supports. One visit will reveal all.

Uses the Modernizr library (www.modernizr.com) to test how well your browser supports recent features in HTML, CSS, and JavaScript.

haz.io

html5test.com

Checks your browser for support of a bunch of HTML5 features and gives it a top-level score.

Or do both at the same time...

browserscope.org

Browserscope will test your browser's support of features like haz.io, but it also keeps track of what browsers have passed or failed tests in the past.

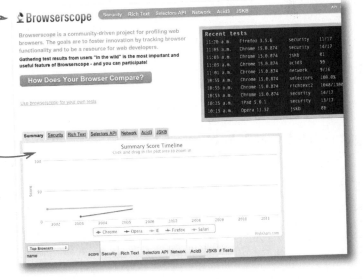

You can create your own tests and store the data on Browserscope. Developers are writing more tests using the Browserscope API all the time, and that makes its data more valuable every day.

#4. Device APIs

Despite their small sizes, mobile phones are powerful devices with capabilities like the address book, calendar, messaging, vibration, sensors, and new technologies like near field communication. We barely scratched the surface of what's possible by using the camera in our PhoneGap app.

Or at least, what's theoretically possible when browsers start supporting device APIs.

What are device APIs?

Originally, the term *device API* referred to a specific set of functionality that was available on mobile devices that traditionally hadn't been available on desktop. The phone camera is the commonly used example.

What started out as a very specific thing that seemed unique to mobile has now become a catchall for everything from adding events to the calendar to accessing system information like CPU usage and network speed.

While scope has become broader, the focus is still the same—give browsers access to the things that make mobile devices so cool.

Standards set by DAP and WAC

The two groups leading the charge to standardize access to device APIs are the W3C's Device APIs Working Group (DAP) and the Wholesale Applications Community (WAC).

The W3C is likely familiar to you, as it sets the standards for HTML and CSS, but you may not have heard of WAC.

WAC was started by network operators and handset makers to create a common platform for app development. They picked HTML5 and consolidated two existing standards into one called WAC 2.0.

There is a lot of overlap between WAC and DAP—both in the specs they are writing and in committee members who participate in both groups. They collaborate more than compete.

These sound great. Why aren't they in the book?

There aren't many browsers that support the device APIs yet. Many of the standards are still in early development.

Let's hope that, by the time we need to write a second edition of this book, these standards will be so common that we'll need multiple chapters dedicated to all the cool things you can do with device APIs.

W3C®

WAC

Track progress of the W3C's Device APIs Working Group on its public roadmap at http://w3.org/2009/dap/.

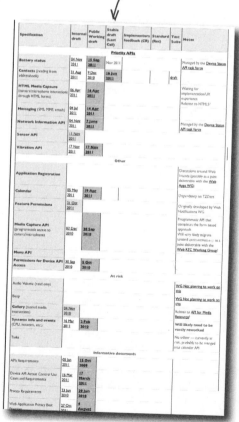

#5. Application stores and distribution

You've built your mind-blowing web app, wrapped it in PhoneGap, and are ready to get in on the app gold rush. How do you make a killing in application stores?

Apple has a trademark on "App Store," so now you can't use that phrase for anything other than its app store. Ergo, it's "application store" from here on out.

Reality check: most apps lose money

That doesn't mean yours won't be one of the exceptions to the rule, but it does mean you should be realistic about the chances of striking it rich.

Still, apps can make a lot of sense in many cases—especially for companies that aren't looking to make a living from selling apps, but instead need apps to augment an existing business.

My app idea is going to make me a millionaire. Sign this NDA before I tell you about it.

Everyone and his brother has a store...

There are too many stores. The Wireless Industry Partnership (WIP) maintains a database of every application store it can find. At last count, there were 120 different application stores.

Find the WIP App(lication) Store database at http://wipconnector.com/appstores.

Each store has different terms and rules, not to mention the various ways that each offers to promote apps. The sheer magnitude of options is daunting.

...and now web apps are joining in as well

The latest trend is so-called HTML5 application stores. Google Chrome, Mozilla, and a bunch of smaller companies have all created new application stores for web-based app sales.

Some nonexpert advice

We're not application store experts. You'll need to look elsewhere to find guidance on that. But we can tell you three things:

1 **Research the market and relevant application stores.**
Know what your competition is doing. Learn more about the application store you will be in and the types of apps it features. Do your homework.

2 **Have a traditional marketing plan in place.**
Don't make your success contingent on being featured by Apple. This isn't the movies. Simply building it isn't enough.

3 **Make your app feel like it belongs on the platform.**
Just because you're building with cross-platform tools doesn't mean an Android user knows how an iPhone app works. Make your app feel right for the user's platform.

#6. RESS: REsponsive design + Server-Side components

In the long run, we don't see either Responsive Web Design or device detection becoming so dominant that the other technique disappears. If anything, we think a combination of those techniques is what will make sense in many cases.

Luke Wroblewski put a name on this combination of responsive design and server-side testing. He calls it RESS.

What Luke calls RESS is not so dissimilar to some of the groundbreaking techniques employed by Yiibu.com's proprietors Bryan and Stephanie Rieger.

Bryan and Stephanie use device detection to make a best guess at a browser's capabilities and then use client-side JavaScript to verify that the device detection was accurate and correct any problems if it wasn't. The JavaScript also sets a cookie that provides information to the server so that it can correct any erroneous assumptions it may have made.

http://www.lukew.com/ff/entry.asp?1392

See Bryan and Stephanie's work in action at http://browser.nokia.com.

Learn more about their approach at http://www.slideshare.net/yiibu and http://yiibuo.com.

Future of RESS

It's hard to say if the name RESS will stick, but the concept of combining Responsive Web Design with server techniques makes a lot of sense to us. Without that combination, it reminds us of an illustration that mobile technologist Jon Arnes Sæterås created recently.

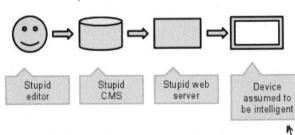

Our goal should be to make sure each piece of the puzzle is acting as intelligently as possible. Solutions like RESS attempt to find a way to make the client and the server share the burden for delivering a great user experience.

http://mPulp.mobi/2011/05/next-steps-of-responsive-web-design/

Gotta start somewhere

You can't spell "mobile web" without the "web." There are no two ways about it. You're going to need a web server if you want to develop for the mobile web. That goes for more than just completing the exercises in this book. You need somewhere to put your web-hosted stuff, whether you use a third-party commercial web hosting service, an enterprise-class data center, or your own computer. In this appendix, we'll walk you through the steps of **setting up a local web server** on your computer and **getting PHP going** using free and open source software.

What we need from you

To complete the exercises in this book, there are some things
you're going to need to do. Don't worry, it's not that bad,
and we'll show you how.

1 **You need to be able to serve web page documents (like HTML pages) and resources (images, CSS, JavaScript, etc.).**
This is the basic idea of a web server, right? So we'll need to get some web server software and configure it.

2 **You need to be able to execute server-side PHP scripts.**
This book's examples use the PHP (PHP: Hypertext Preprocessor) scripting language to generate dynamic content. While you won't have to be proficient at *authoring* PHP, you will need to be able to *run* it.

3 **You need to have at least a certain amount of administrative access to your web server.**
You need to have some control over the permissions of the directories served by your web server and be able to move files around.

> I already have service with a web hosting provider. My web server already has the ability to execute and serve PHP scripts. Do I really need to bother setting up my own, local web server?

We promise it's not that hard (and is really quite useful). However, you don't *have* to set up your own web server.

But you do need to make sure your setup meets a few requirements. Your version of PHP needs to be 5.2 or newer. You need to make sure that your PHP has the GD image library and SimpleXML extension available. Unsure? See page 396 for instructions on how to use the `phpinfo` function to get information about your PHP environment.

Only available locally

Now we'll walk you through setting up a local web server on your own computer.

The web software bundles we're going to install in this appendix are not meant for publicly accessible production environments.

Because these tools are meant to aid in simplified local web development on your own computer, they have some security shortcomings. They are not meant to be used on an externally accessible web server. Please be careful!

Windows and Linux: Install and configure XAMPP

Download the web server package software

We're going to use **XAMPP**, an easy-to-use web stack that contains the **Apache web server** software and **PHP**—both of which we need. It also comes with the MySQL relational database management system (RDBMS) and Perl, which, though we won't use them directly in this book, are also quite lovely.

Point your browser at *www.apachefriends.org/en/xampp.html* and select the appropriate platform link (Windows or Linux). Download the latest version of XAMPP to your computer.

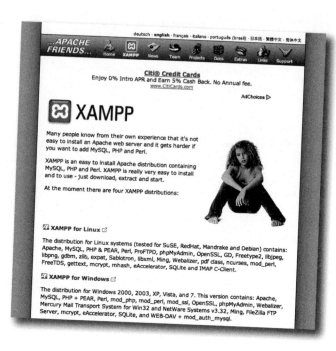

Windows folks, you're up

Launch the downloaded file to run the installer. You'll be prompted to select an installation directory for XAMPP. The default *c:\xampp* folder is fine. Follow the instructions to complete the installation.

You can then launch XAMPP from Start → Programs → XAMPP.

Not there? Check the All Programs section of your Start menu.

The XAMPP control panel

From here, you can start and stop your web server (Apache).

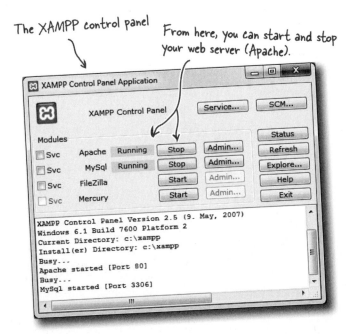

Get going with XAMPP

Linux users, here's your stuff

After downloading the software package, open a terminal window and execute the following commands.

You need superuser (root) access to install XAMPP.

Your filename might be slightly different.

Once XAMPP is installed, use this command to start it.

Use "stop" instead of "start" to stop it. Guess that's kinda obvious, huh?

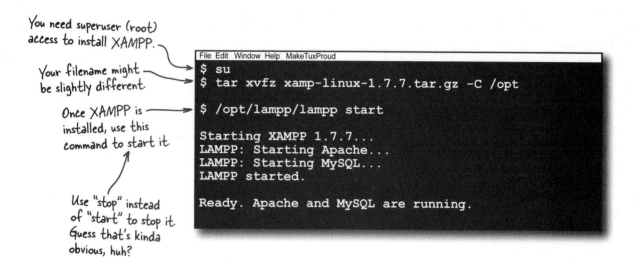

```
File Edit Window Help MakeTuxProud
$ su
$ tar xvfz xamp-linux-1.7.7.tar.gz -C /opt

$ /opt/lampp/lampp start

Starting XAMPP 1.7.7...
LAMPP: Starting Apache...
LAMPP: Starting MySQL...
LAMPP started.

Ready. Apache and MySQL are running.
```

There's a ton more information online

For more commands, configuration options, general info, and troubleshooting, Windows users can find more information at *www.apachefriends.org/en/xampp-windows.html*; if you're running Linux, check out *www.apachefriends.org/en/xampp-linux.html*.

Mac folks: It's MAMP time

For Mac, we recommend the super-simple and fun-to-say web software stack MAMP. Installing MAMP is really easy.

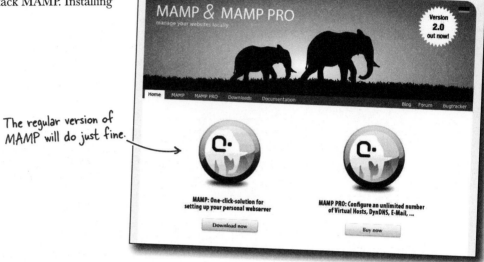

The regular version of MAMP will do just fine.

Kind of like falling off a log

Head on over to *http://mamp.info* and download the software package. Double-click to mount the downloaded disk image and drag the MAMP application into your Applications folder.

When you launch the MAMP application, you'll be able to start and stop your Apache and MySQL services. For our interests, we care about Apache. You'll need this running to complete the exercises in the book.

The MAMP control panel lets you start and stop your web services.

Make sure your Apache server is running.

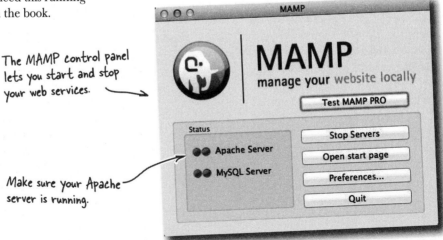

Make sure you dock at the right port

On a Mac...

Recent versions of Mac OS X come prepackaged with
an Apache web server. This runs on port 80, which is the
default HTTP port. You can access your Mac's default web
server (if it's running) by going to *http://localhost* in your
browser. Like we just said, port 80 is the default HTTP port,
so both *http://localhost* and *http://localhost:80* work (that is,
the port number is not required).

> Your Mac's web server
> is controlled by turning
> Web Sharing on or off in
> your System Preferences >
> Sharing panel.

We installed MAMP because we need PHP. Because there's
already a web server on most Macs, MAMP, by default,
runs on port 8888. That means you would access your
MAMP web server at *http://localhost:8888*. It's pretty trivial
to change the port number in the MAMP preferences if
you care to do so.

...and on Windows and Linux

XAMPP runs on port 80 by default. That means that if you
have another web server running on that port, there will be
problems. On Windows, you'll want to check to make sure
you don't have the Windows IIS web server running:

1 Open IIS Manager by going to Start → Control Panel → System and
Security → Administrative Tools → Internet Information Services (IIS)
Manager.

2 In the Actions pane, click Stop. That will stop the IIS web server.

> If you know what you're
> doing, you can configure
> Apache to run on a
> different port instead.

Access your web server

It's probable you'll want to test out some of the examples in the book on a real mobile device, using your computer as the web server. This should work, even if your web server is only available locally. Here's how to make sure you're ready to rock:

① **Figure out your computer's current IP address.**
localhost is all relative. It refers to the computer you're on currently. So if you try to access localhost from another device (mobile or otherwise), you will be referencing the device itself.

To find your computer's current IP address on Mac or Linux, run the command ifconfig from a terminal window. Windows users can run the ipconfig command by typing in **cmd** in the Start menu's search box to get a command-line tool, and then typing **ipconfig**.

ifconfig (or ipconfig) will output information about each of your computer's nework interfaces. Look for an interface that starts with eth or en (Linux or Mac) or IP4 (Windows) to find information about your ethernet interfaces. That's where you should see your current IP address.

↖ *Internal IP addresses usually start with 10, 127, or 192.*

Watch it!

You need to find your *computer's* IP address, not your *external* IP address.

Tools like http://whatismyipaddress.com can be handy ways to find your external IP address quickly. However, this is not the same as your computer's IP address. If you are on a network that uses a modem and/or a router to connect to the Internet, the IP address you'll see on such sites is your modem or router's external IP address. You will (most likely) not be able to access your computer's web server with this IP address.

② **Make sure your device is on the same network.**
Remember that if you have an internal IP address, that IP address is only accessible within the same network. Any device that needs to accesss your web server must be connected to the same network (for mobile devices, that's usually via WiFi). ⟵ *Don't forget to add your port number if it's not 80—e.g., http://10.0.0.2:8888.*

On Windows and still having trouble? Check out this Apache Friends Support Forum post with a workaround for problems accessing your XAMPP server: *http://bit.ly/sG3Qa0.*

OK, I installed the web server software and started it up, but where does my stuff go? Like, where do I put my web pages?

You'll need to put your web pages, resources, and scripts inside your web server's <u>document root</u> to be able to see them.

A server's ***document root*** is the filesystem path representing the top level of your website (e.g., *http://localhost/* or *http://localhost:8888/*). The location of your server's default document root depends on which server software you installed and what platform you use.

Get at the root of it

For Mac users running MAMP, the default document root is */Applications/MAMP/htdocs*. You can keep this as it is, or, if you'd like to change it, edit it in the Apache tab of the Preferences.

For Windows users with XAMPP, the document root is *\xampp\htdocs*. For Linux users with XAMPP, it's at */opt/xampp/htdocs*.

You'll need to put any files or directories you want to access from your web server inside your document root.

phpInfo, please!

To verify the version of PHP you are running and its options, extensions, bells, whistles, and whatnot, create a file called *test.php* inside your document root directory so that it can be accessed at *http://localhost/test.php*.

Inside of that file, add just this one line:

```php
<?php phpinfo(); ?>
```

Don't forget to include your port number if it's not 80 (e.g., http://localhost:8888/test.php).

Save the file and view it in a web browser at *http://localhost/test.php*. This will tell you if PHP is running and all sorts of information about it.

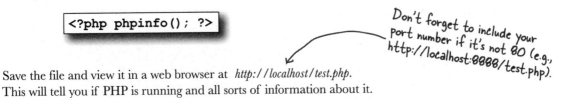

A section at the top of the page indicates which version of PHP you're running.

Check further down the page for the gd and SimpleXML sections. We need these features for some of the examples in the book.

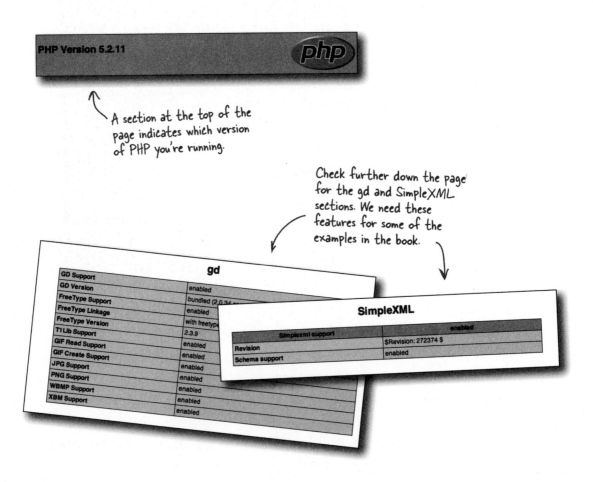

gd	
GD Support	
GD Version	enabled
FreeType Support	bundled (2.0.34
FreeType Linkage	enabled
FreeType Version	with freetype
T1Lib Support	2.3.9
GIF Read Support	enabled
GIF Create Support	enabled
JPG Support	enabled
PNG Support	enabled
WBMP Support	enabled
XBM Support	enabled
	enabled

SimpleXML	
Simplexml support	enabled
Revision	$Revision: 272374 $
Schema support	enabled

iii install WURFL

Sniffing out devices

The first step to solving device detection mysteries is a bit of legwork. Any decent gumshoe knows we've got to gather our clues and interrogate our witnesses. First, we need to seek out the brains of the operation: the **WURFL PHP API**. Then we'll go track down the brawn: capability information for thousands of devices in a single **XML data file**. But it'll take a bit of coaxing to get the two to spill the whole story, so we'll tweak a bit of **configuration** and take some careful notes.

Who's got the brains?

We've got to track down the WURFL API and its data. Here's the plan.

☐ Download and install the brains of WURFL: the PHP API.

☐ Download and install the brawn: the WURFL XML device data.

☐ Make some minor configuration adjustments and take note of some things.

Download the API

Go to WURFL PHP API project page at *http://wurfl.sourceforge.net/nphp/*. Find the link to download the WURFL API package and grab the newest version from the download page.

This is the PHP API. Unzip the downloaded file and put the resulting directory somewhere on your computer. It doesn't matter exactly where you put it, as long as you remember where it is.

WURFL (Wireless Universal Resource FiLe) is an XML data file full of vast amounts of capability and feature support data for mobile devices and their browsers. There is also an API for interacting with the data file. We'll need that, too!

Say it with us: "WURRRR–full."

http://wurfl.sourceforge.net/nphp/

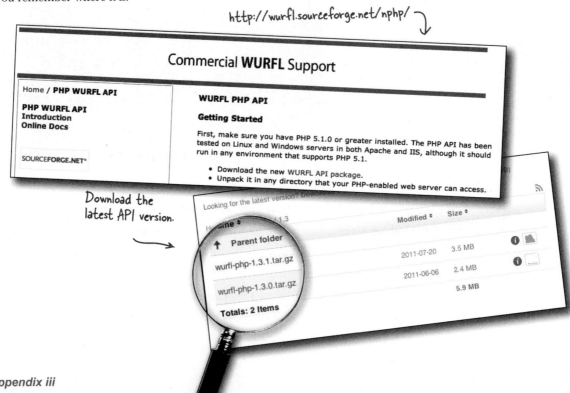

Download the latest API version.

And who's got the brawn?

http://wurfl.sourceforge.net/wurfl_download.php

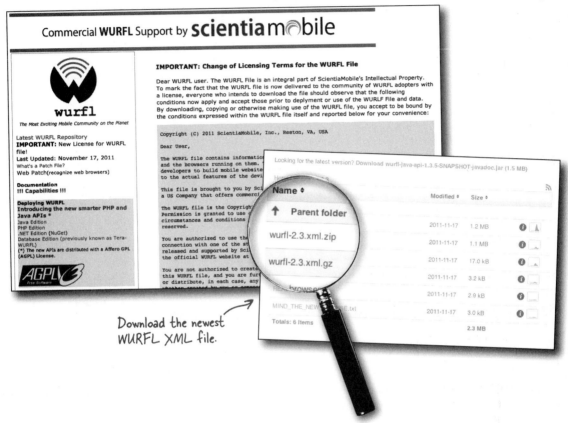

Download the newest WURFL XML file.

The PHP API is clever, but it's nothing without its strongman henchman, the WURFL device <u>data</u> itself.

To get the latest WURFL device data XML file, go to *http://wurfl.sourceforge.net/wurfl_download.php*. You will need to read and agree to the licensing terms before you can download the file.

Once you've downloaded the file, unzip it, rename it *wurfl.xml* and move it into the *examples/resources/* directory in your WURFL PHP API installation (the directory should already exist).

The downloaded file will probably have some version numbers in the filename. Rename it to wurfl.xml.

Getting the two to work together

We're moving along nicely. We need to make a small change to the WURFL configuration file so that our API and data can work together.

Edit the file *examples / resources / wurfl-config.xml* inside your WURFL API installation. You need to make a simple change to one line.

☑ Download and install the brains of WURFL: the PHP API.

☑ Download and install the brawn: the WURFL XML device data.

☐ **Make some minor configuration adjustments and take note of some things.**

Change this...

```
<wurfl-config>
    <wurfl>
        <main-file>wurfl.zip</main-file>
        <patches>
            <patch>web_browsers_patch.xml</patch>
        </patches>
    </wurfl>
```

wurfl-config.xml

...to this.

```
<wurfl-config>
    <wurfl>
        <main-file>wurfl.xml</main-file>
        <patches>
            <patch>web_browsers_patch.xml</patch>
        </patches>
    </wurfl>
```

wurfl-config.xml

Now the WURFL API will know where to find the data.

A bit of filesystem housekeeping

Let's make sure WURFL has access to all of the towels and linens it needs for its stay. The way we have WURFL configured, it will use **filesystem caching**. So we need to be sure that the filesystem is all ready for its arrival.

First, verify that the *examples/resources/storage* directory exists inside your WURFL API directory, and that it has two subdirectories, *cache* and *persistence*.

Create these directories if they're not there.

Your web server will need to be able to write files to these directories for WURFL to work correctly. This tends to work automatically with MAMP (on Mac) because the Apache web server runs as your own user by default. So, if you have write access to these files, so does Apache.

The same is not true on Windows and Linux, however. **On Windows**, right-click the *storage* folder in the Explorer and uncheck Read Only if it is selected. You'll get a confirm dialog similar to the one shown here—and yes, you do want to apply changes to the subfolders and files.

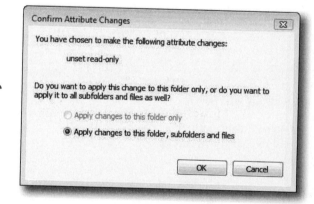

Things should be good to go. But if there are any problems, follow PHP's instructions...

If the filesystem housekeeping didn't quite clear out all of the dust, or something else is a bit off in the WURFL configuration, PHP notices, warnings, and errors will usually tip you off to what's up.

If you get a blank screen any time while working in PHP or WURFL examples, you might not have PHP error display turned on. Create a file called *.htaccess* (if it doesn't exist already) in the same directory as the problematic PHP file and add the following line:

```
php_flag display_errors on
```

(Linux users can chmod and chown until settings are as they see fit!)

Take note!

To get started with Chapter 5's exercises, you'll need to **take note of a couple of paths on your system.**

Mac and Linux paths look like these examples. Windows users should use Windows-compatible paths with backslashes and whatnot.

WURFL PHP API code path

The first is a full path to the location of the WURFL PHP API code. This is located in a subdirectory called *WURFL* inside the WURFL PHP API directory.

For example, if you have version 1.3.1 of the API and you installed it in an (imaginary) directory called */awesome*, your path would look something like:

This part will differ depending on where you installed the API.

You'll use your version of this path for the WURFL_DIR value in Chapter 5.

```
/awesome/wurfl-php-1.3.1/WURFL/
```

This part may differ if you have a newer version of the API.

Don't forget the WURFL directory. That's where the actual <u>code</u> lives (not at the top level of the directory).

Resources path

This is the full path to the *examples/resources/* directory inside the WURFL PHP API directory. For example:

```
/awesome/wurfl-php-1.3.1/examples/resources/
```

You'll use your version of this path for the RESOURCES_DIR value in Chapter 5.

This is where your WURFL <u>data</u> is located.

Case closed!

[✓] Download and install the brains of WURFL: the PHP API.

[✓] Download and install the brawn: the WURFL XML device data.

[✓] Make some minor configuration adjustments and take note of some things.

iv install the Android SDK and tools

*Take care of the environment

OK, that's a neat little ecosystem in place.... Wait. Can it really be? Is that Android sheep I hear? Well, slap my thigh and call me Bo!

To be the master of testing native Android apps, you need to be environmentally aware. You'll need to turn your computer into a nice little ecosystem where you can herd Android apps to and from virtual (emulated) or real devices. To make you the shepherd of your Android sheep, we'll show you how to download the **Android software development kit (SDK)**, how to install some **platform tools**, how to **create some virtual devices,** and how to **install and uninstall apps**.

Let's download the Android SDK

Do this!

Head on down to
http://developer.android.com/sdk
and find the right download link for
your operating system.

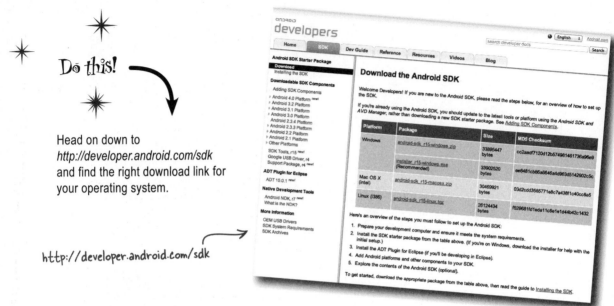

http://developer.android.com/sdk

Download and extract or unzip the SDK software.
Put the resulting Android SDK folder wherever you
keep your applications on your computer.

Good work! You're now done installing the SDK
itself (that was pretty easy, huh?).

Now we need to add some other packages and tools
to the SDK so we can get our work done.

> Windows users get a
> handy-dandy installer
> to simplify this process.

Steps to a happy Android SDK environment

☑ Download and install the correct Android SDK for
  your computer's operating system.   ← Already done.

☐ **Install some needed platform tools and some
  Android platforms (API versions).**

☐ Create some Android virtual devices (AVDs). These
  are the emulators on which you can run Android apps.

☐ Learn how to install and uninstall Android apps on
  emulators and devices.

☐ Configure your PATH settings to make running the
  Android tools more convenient.   ← Optional, but
                                          handy

Get the right tools for the job

Installing the SDK was easy, but we're not ready to ride off into the sunset just yet. We need to add some Android platforms and tools.

Find and launch the *android* executable. It should be within a directory called *tools* in the Android SDK folder (for Windows users, this file is called *Android.bat*).

When you start the SDK, you should see the Android SDK Manager window.

It looks like this on Windows.

It looks like this on a Mac.

We need to install the platform tools.

And some platforms (versions).

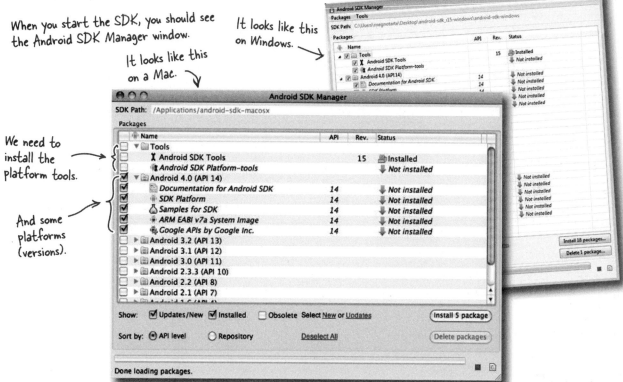

Install platforms and tools

We want to install some platforms (i.e., Android API versions) and tools. To do so, check the boxes next to the items you want to install. Let's go ahead and:

1 **Install two or three recent Android platforms.**
At time of writing, 4.0 is the newest Android version. We also installed 2.2 and 2.3.3 to have a few other versions on which to test. You can install even more than that, if you like.

2 **Install the "Tools" packages.**
We specifically need a tool called adb, which is part of the Android SDK Platform Tools package. Go ahead and select the checkbox next to the Tools folder of packages.

Not all Android versions may be available in all versions of the SDK.

Android 3.0, aka Honeycomb, was a tablet-only Android version. You can install it if you like, but your mileage may vary on its emulators.

Hit the Install button and go make some coffee

Once you've selected several platform versions and the Tools package, click the Install button to start the installation. This will take some time—seriously, upward of 10–20 minutes on some systems—so you might take a break for a bit.

You will probably see an install log that looks something like this.

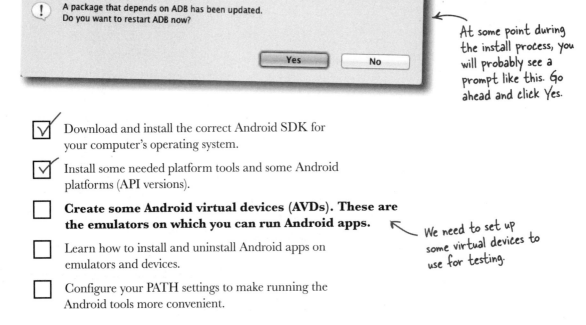

Android SDK Manager Log

```
Parse XML:     http://innovator.samsungmobile.com/android/repository/repository.xml
    Found GALAXY Tab by Samsung Electronics., Android API 8, revision 1
Fetching URL: http://developer.sonyericsson.com/edk/android/repository.xml
Validate XML: http://developer.sonyericsson.com/edk/android/repository.xml
Parse XML:     http://developer.sonyericsson.com/edk/android/repository.xml
    Found EDK 1.1 by Sony Ericsson Mobile Communications AB, Android API 10, revision 1
Done loading packages.
Preparing to install archives
Downloading Android SDK Platform-tools, revision 9
Installing Android SDK Platform-tools, revision 9
'adb kill-server' failed -- run manually if necessary.
Installed Android SDK Platform-tools, revision 9
Downloading Documentation for Android SDK, API 14, revision 1
```

Downloading Documentation for Android SDK, API 14, revision 1 (26%, 1538 KiB/s, 51 seconds left)

[Close]

ADB Restart

⚠ A package that depends on ADB has been updated.
Do you want to restart ADB now?

[Yes]   [No]

At some point during the install process, you will probably see a prompt like this. Go ahead and click Yes.

☑ Download and install the correct Android SDK for your computer's operating system.

☑ Install some needed platform tools and some Android platforms (API versions).

☐ **Create some Android virtual devices (AVDs). These are the emulators on which you can run Android apps.**

We need to set up some virtual devices to use for testing.

☐ Learn how to install and uninstall Android apps on emulators and devices.

☐ Configure your PATH settings to make running the Android tools more convenient.

Do virtual devices dream of electric sheep?

Our underpinnings are there: now we need some emulated devices. In the Android SDK, select the Tools → Manage AVDs menu item.

Android SDK Manager
window on Windows

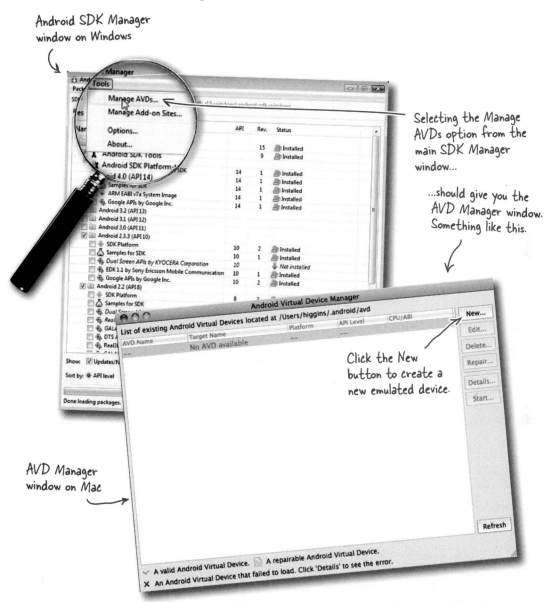

Selecting the Manage AVDs option from the main SDK Manager window...

...should give you the AVD Manager window. Something like this.

Click the New button to create a new emulated device.

AVD Manager window on Mac

We need to add some devices. Click that New button to get started.

Create a new virtual device

Clicking the New button in the AVD manager window should give you a window something like what you see here (this screenshot is from Windows). Edit the settings as shown and click Create AVD.

Name your device something descriptive.

click

New...

Choose your Android version (here called "target").

Don't make the (virtual) SD card too big, or you might end up crashy; 10 MiB is fine.

Go ahead and leave these settings as their defaults.

Do not enable the Snapshot option.

Create new Android Virtual Device (AVD)

Name:	Android2.2_Device
Target:	Android 2.2 - API Level 8
CPU/ABI:	ARM (armeabi)

SD Card:
- ◉ Size: 10 — MiB ▾
- ○ File: [   ] Browse...

Snapshot:
- ☐ Enabled

Skin:
- ◉ Built-in: Default (WVGA800)
- ○ Resolution: [   ] x [   ]

Hardware:

Property	Value	
Abstracted LCD density	240	New...
Max VM application hea...	24	Delete

☐ Override the existing AVD with the same name

Create AVD **Cancel**

Android Virtual Devices Manager

ⓘ Result of creating AVD 'Android2.2_Device':

Created AVD 'Android2.2_Device' based on Android 2.2, ARM (armeabi) processor, with the following hardware config:
hw.lcd.density=240
vm.heapSize=24

OK

Android Virtual Devices Manager

⚠ Result of creating AVD 'android-device-2_3':

Created AVD 'android-device-2_3' based on Android 2.3.3, ARM (armeabi) processor, with the following hardware config:
hw.lcd.density=240
vm.heapSize=24
hw.ramSize=256

OK

You'll see a dialog like this each time you successfully create a new AVD.

Don't forget that 3.0 is a tablet-only version and may not be your cup o' tea.

Do this!

Create three emulated devices on different Android platforms (API versions). We recommend not using a version older than, say, 2.2 or so.

Let 'er rip!

Once you have some AVDs created, you can launch them from the AVD Manager (remember, it's the Tools → Manage AVDs menu item).

To launch a particular emulated device, select it in the list and click the Start button.

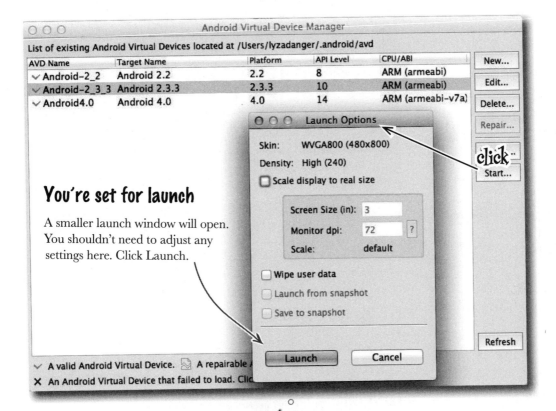

You're set for launch

A smaller launch window will open. You shouldn't need to adjust any settings here. Click Launch.

Launching an emulated Android device can take a while.

Starting up an emulator can be a pretty slow process, especially the first time you launch it. Give it a while, and don't panic if it seems to be taking its sweet time.

If you do find that the emulator won't finish launching or it crashes, double-check to make sure that you haven't made the SD card size enormous and that you haven't turned on the Snapshot option. Finally, sometimes emulators on certain versions just won't work on some systems. If you find that you are fighting really hard with one, consider moving on to a different API version.

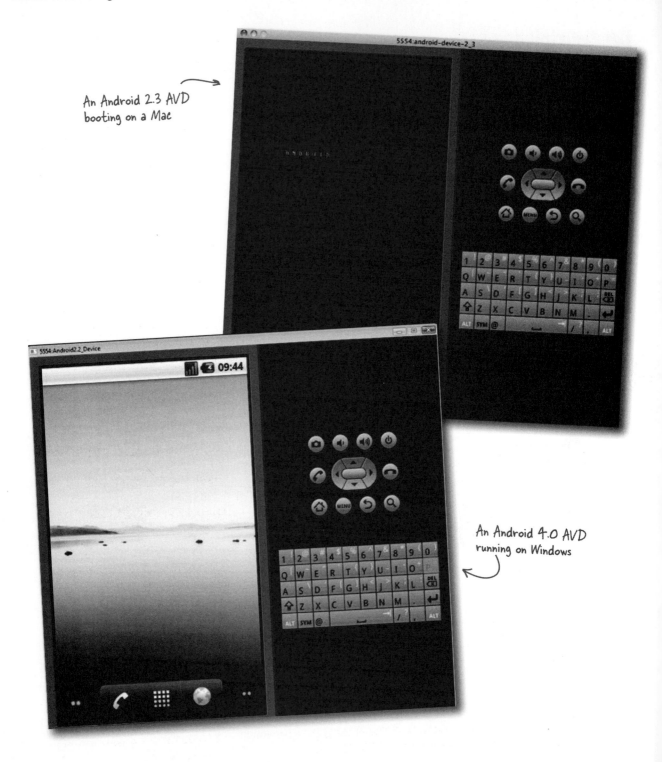

An Android 2.3 AVD booting on a Mac

An Android 4.0 AVD running on Windows

Apps on, apps off

☑ Download and install the correct Android SDK for your computer's operating system.

☑ Install some needed platform tools and some Android platforms (API versions).

☑ Create some Android virtual devices (AVDs). These are the emulators on which you can run Android apps.

☐ **Learn how to install and uninstall Android apps on emulators and devices.**

☐ Configure your PATH settings to make running the Android tools more convenient.

Remember how we installed the Platform Tools package after we downloaded the Android SDK? That package contains a program called **adb**, which is key to installing and uninstalling apps as well as managing virtual and real devices.

The process for installing and uninstalling apps is straightforward:

❶ Make sure the target emulator (AVD) is fully loaded and running **or** your Android device is attached to your computer's USB port.

❷ Use the `adb install` or `adb uninstall` command to install or uninstall the desired app, respectively.

> **adb stands for Android debug bridge. This utility program lets us install, uninstall, and debug Android apps on emulators and devices.**

To install

App package file

```
$ adb install MyApp.APK
```

To uninstall

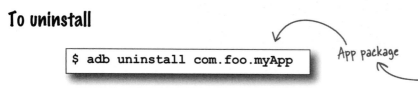

App package

```
$ adb uninstall com.foo.myApp
```

Android apps use Java-style package names, which look like domain names in reverse.

I don't know where to start. Where do I get an APK file that I can install? Where do I go to type the adb install command?

We got a bit ahead of ourselves. Sorry about that!

We'll show you where to find a sample Android app to install. But first, let's show you more about how to run that adb command.

PATH-finding

It's almost certain that the Android SDK tools, including adb, are not in your PATH. So, if you open a terminal window or use Window's command-line tool and try to run adb directly, you will probably get an error message. Your system needs to know where to find adb in order to execute it.

We recommend you update your user's PATH to include the path to the Android SDK tools so that you can run adb from a command line easily.

Semicolon-separated on Windows. →

The $PATH environment variable is a list of colon-separated filesystem paths in which your operating system will look for executable programs when you type a program name at a command prompt.

Usually, this includes a number of directories by default—but not the one where we put the SDK.

If you can't get your PATH sorted out, there are other options.

You can either provide the full path when running adb (e.g., */Applications/android-sdk/platform-tools/adb*) or you can change directories to the *platform-tools* directory and run `./adb` (you need the `./`).

Find the right PATH

Mac people

In a Terminal window, type the following commands. You will then need to **close the Terminal window** and open a new one for the changes to take effect.

This first command takes you to your user's home directory.

Type this exactly as shown. Watch out for the colon (:) and brackets ({}).

Make sure to include the single quotation mark here (and before export).

```
File Edit Window Help 9-9-0-6-9-4-7-X-B-7-1
$ cd ~
$ echo 'export PATH=${PATH}:/Applications/<...>/platform-tools' >> .profile
```

The second command appends the path to the SDK platform tools to the existing ¡PATH variable in your user's .profile file.

.profile gets executed every time you open a new Terminal window.

You need to update this to match the path to the platform-tools directory in the Android SDK.

Windows people

Add the path to the platform-tools folder to the end of the current path value.

❶ In your Start menu, right-click on Computer and then go to Properties. Click Advanced System Settings. In the dialog that appears, the Advanced tab should be selected.

❷ In this Advanced tab, click the Environment Variables button, and then click the Path variable in the System Variables section. Click Edit.

❸ In the Variable value field, put your cursor at the very **end** of the current value, type a semicolon (;), and then enter the path to your Android SDK *platform-tools* folder. You do not need to add a semicolon after the path. Click OK several times to confirm and close the open dialogs.

❹ You will need to log out and log in again for the changes to take effect.

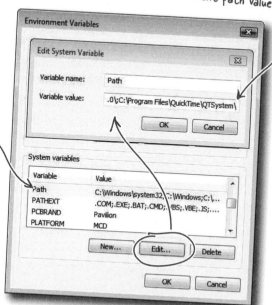

Linux people, we probably don't need to tell you how to do this.

TEST DRIVE

OK, now what we've all been waiting for. Let's try this out and install and uninstall a test app on an emulator.

1 Download the PhoneGap Build demo Android app from *http://hf-mw.com/ch8/PhoneGap.apk.*

2 Launch the Android SDK if it is not already running.

3 Launch an AVD (virtual device in emulation) by going to Tools → Manage AVDs, selecting an AVD from the list, and starting it.

4 Wait for the emulated device to load **fully**.

5 Open a terminal window or command-line tool. Change directories to where you downloaded the APK file.

6 Run the following command:

This assumes you've set up your $PATH to include the platform-tools directory. Otherwise, you may need to provide the full path to adb.

```
$ adb install PhoneGap.apk
```

7 You should now be able to see the PhoneGap example app on your emulated device's app screen. You can launch it and play around with it a bit.

8 From the command line, run the following command to uninstall the application.

```
$ adb uninstall com.phonegap.getting.started
```

This is the package ID of the PhoneGap "getting started" app.

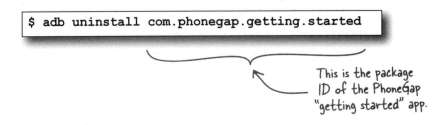

there are no
Dumb Questions

Q: What's a Android package file?

A: An *Android package file* (APK) is a packaged native Android app. It contains the compiled code as well as various resources for the app.

APKs are a kind of Java archive file (JAR). If you're curious about what is inside a particular APK, you can usually trick your computer into showing you its contents by changing the extension to *.zip* and unzipping the resulting file. Voilà!

Q: What's this com.foo.myApp?

A: Android app packages are identified by fully qualified, Java-style package names. These look sort of like reverse domain notation (i.e., like a web domain name backward, sort of).

The adb tool has a number of other nice features for debugging and inspecting apps and devices.

To get more information about what adb does, type <u>adb help</u> from the command line.

Q: How would I know my app's package name?

A: In Chapter 8, we show you how to edit an XML configuration file for the PhoneGap Build service, in which you set your app's package name.

Q: How does adb know which device to install the app onto?

A: adb will install to or uninstall from whatever emulated device is running currently. Or, if you have a real Android device connected to the computer's USB port, it will install to or uninstall from that real device.

Q: Can I uninstall the app from the emulator or device itself?

A: Yep. You can uninstall the app just like you were using it in the real world. Go to the device's menu and find the Manage Apps option. Then you can find and delete the app in question.

Q: I got an error when I tried to install or uninstall the app.

A: Make sure the emulator is fully loaded before trying to install the APK. You can run the command `adb devices` to see a list of any devices or emulators that adb is aware of. You should see one entry if your emulator or device is running properly.

You can't have more than one active device running (real or emulated) when you're installing or uninstalling, or adb will get confused.

Finally, you can't install an app that has already been installed without uninstalling it first.

Q: I have a real Android device. How do I install and uninstall apps?

A: You use the same commands, but instead of firing up an emulator, you simply plug your device into your computer's USB port. Running that `adb devices` command will confirm that adb can see your device.

Whew! You did it!

☑ Download and install the correct Android SDK for your computer's operating system.

☑ Install some needed platform tools and some Android platforms (API versions).

☑ Create some Android virtual devices (AVDs). These are the emulators on which you can run Android apps.

☑ Learn how to install and uninstall Android apps on emulators and devices.

☑ Configure your PATH settings to make running the Android tools more convenient.

Index

C

D

N

names, device classes 189

native applications 246–253, 313

    device capabilities 316

    PhoneGap. *See* PhoneGap

navbars, creating 249–252

networks

    EDGE, 4G phones 65

    WiFi, web requests 45

NETWORK section (cache manifest), wildcards 289, 291, 296

Nitobi 318

O

objects

    CustomDevice 189

    window.applicationCache 294

    WURFL (Wireless Universal Resource FiLe)

        instantiating 163

offline mode 267, 270

    cache manifest 285–296

        browser support 296

        changing resource list 290–296

        content-type 285

        definition 284

        FALLBACK section 296

        .htaccess files 287

        syntax 285

        testing 295

        troubleshooting 292–293

        URLs 285

        WebKit Web Inspector 286

    images 290–296

    Tartanator enhancements 284–296

    web pages 290–296

onColorListChange() function 277

onStitchSizeChange() function 277–278

On Tap Now page

    adding JavaScript 77–78

    hiding map 53

    optimization issues 44–47, 70

    reordering content 59–60

    structure 58–59

    testing with Mobitest 47–53

open source licensing

    AGPL (Affero General Public License v3) 158

    WURFL (Wireless Universal Resource FiLe) 158

Opera Dragonfly 65, 381

Opera Mini 110

    application cache 284

    simulator 111

Opera Mini 4.2 120

Opera Mobile 110

optimization 43, 44–47

    images 67, 69

    On Tap Now page 44–47, 70

ordering content 59–60, 65

overflow: scroll property 131

overlapping content 83–89

P

\<p\> tag, adding links 75–76

pagecreate event 275, 277–278

pageinit event 275, 277–278

panic button. *See* red panic button

Passani, Luca 158

patches, WURFL (Wireless Universal Resource FiLe) 213

Perfecto 375

performance

    4G phones 65

    hardware, device support 144

performance tests, Mobitest 47–53

phone calls, making calls with links 176

U

UAProf (User Agent Profile) 103

<ul> tag 240–243

uninstalling

    Android apps with adb 411–413, 415

    hybrid apps 332

updates, WURFL (Wireless Universal Resource FiLe) 158

URLs, cache manifest 285

User Agent Profile (UAProf) 103

user agents 98–103

    browsers, spoofing 103

    facebookexternalhit 213

    mobile browsers 102–103

    sniffing 97, 101, 135

    strings 97, 98–100

        mobile device detection script 107

        Skyfire 103

V

validating code 374

validation 117

    access keys 123

vertical layouts compared to horizontal 29

videos, YouTube iframe code 35

viewport <meta> tag 22, 72–73, 89

viewports 89

    viewport <meta> tag 72, 89

virtual devices

    installing in Android SDK 407–408

    launching (Android) 409–410

W

W3C device APIs 384

W3C Geolocation API 298

    browsers 299–300

W3C mediaCapture API 344

WAC (Wholesale Applications Community) 384

waterfall charts 48

    analyzing image sizes 54

    HAR (HTTP Archive) 49–50

    reading 51–52

web applications, creating hybrid applications 322–327

web apps 217, 218. *See also* super mobile web apps

    Android 403

        installing 415

        installing with adb 411–413

        testing 414

        uninstalling 415

        uninstalling with adb 411–413

    backend enhancements 280–283

    definition of 219

    form enhancements 274–277

    frameworks (mobile web apps), jQuery Mobile 228–239

    geolocation 267, 270

    HTML5 219

    hybrid applications 313, 317

        creating 322–332

        tools 320

    mobile frameworks 217, 225

        disadvantages 225

    native applications 313

        device capabilities 316

    offline mode 267, 270, 284–296

    progressive enhancement 267, 270